A
writing
STUDIES
Primer

A writing STUDIES Primer

JOYCE KINKEAD

broadview press

BROADVIEW PRESS – www.broadviewpress.com
Peterborough, Ontario, Canada

Founded in 1985, Broadview Press remains a wholly independent publishing house. Broadview's focus is on academic publishing; our titles are accessible to university and college students as well as scholars and general readers. With over 800 titles in print, Broadview has become a leading international publisher in the humanities, with world-wide distribution. Broadview is committed to environmentally responsible publishing and fair business practices.

© 2022 Joyce Kinkead

Library and Archives Canada Cataloguing in Publication

Title: A writing studies primer / Joyce Kinkead.
Names: Kinkead, Joyce A., 1954- author.
Description: Includes bibliographical references and index.
Identifiers: Canadiana (print) 20210370939 | Canadiana (ebook) 20210371145 | ISBN
      9781554815319 (softcover) | ISBN 9781770488151 (PDF) | ISBN 9781460407646 (EPUB)
Subjects: LCSH: Writing—History. | LCSH: Material culture—History. | LCSH: Ethnology—Authorship.
      | LCSH: Autobiography.
Classification: LCC P211 .K56 2022 | DDC 411.09—dc23

Broadview Press handles its own distribution in North America:
PO Box 1243, Peterborough, Ontario K9J 7H5, Canada
555 Riverwalk Parkway, Tonawanda, NY 14150, USA
Tel: (705) 743-8990; Fax: (705) 743-8353
email: customerservice@broadviewpress.com

For all territories outside of North America, distribution is handled by Eurospan Group.

Broadview Press acknowledges the financial support of the Government of Canada for our publishing activities.

Canadä

Edited by Martin R. Boyne

Book design by Chris Rowat Design

PRINTED IN CANADA

For my travel partner and fellow researcher, David F. Lancy

Contents

Acknowledgments 15

Preface: An Introduction to the *Primer* 19

CHAPTER 1 **Writing the Self: Autobiography and Autoethnography** 33

Autobiography and Autoethnography 34

Interrogating Your Writing Life 34

Why Writing Implements Matter 38

Writing and Culture 41

Research Integrity 43

Invitation to Write and Reflect 44

Future Writing 44

CHAPTER 2 **Origins of Writing** 45

Oracle Bones 46

Cuneiform 48

Hieroglyphics 51

Mesoamerican Glyphs 54

Concluding Thoughts 55

Questions to Consider 56

Do-It-Yourself Hands-On Activities 56

For Further Reading 60

Interested in Learning More? 61

CHAPTER 3   **Alphabets, Syllabaries, and Pictography**   63
Pictography   65
Alphabets   67
Syllabaries   68
Some Other Alphabets   70
   Runic   70
   Cyrillic   72
   Arabic   73
   Hebrew   73
   Deseret Alphabet   74
   Braille   74
   Electronic Alphabet   75
   International Phonetic Alphabet   75
Concluding Thoughts   77
Questions to Consider   77
Invitation to Reflect and Write   78
For Further Reading   78
Interested in Learning More?   86

CHAPTER 4   **Pencils, Pens, and Ink**   87
Pencils   87
From Pencils to Pens   92
   Quill Pens   94
   Fountain Pens   98
   Ballpoint Pens   98
Handwriting   99
Ink   101
Erasure   103
Writing Implements, War, and Trade   104
Concluding Thoughts   105
Questions to Consider   105
Do-It-Yourself Hands-On Activities   105
Invitation to Reflect and Write   106
For Further Reading   107
Interested in Learning More?   109

CHAPTER 5   **Paper** 111
The Invention of Paper 112
Life in a Medieval Paper Mill 113
The Demand for Paper 115
Handmade Paper 117
Before Paper 119
Paperless Society? 121
Questions to Consider 122
Do-It-Yourself Hands-On Activity 122
Invitation to Reflect and Write 122
For Further Reading 123
Interested in Learning More? 124

CHAPTER 6   **The Book** 125
Sacred Books 126
Printing and Reproduction of Texts 127
Secular Books 129
The Format of the Book 130
The Book and Mass Production 132
Tiny Books 135
Book Arts 136
Concluding Thoughts 138
Questions to Consider 138
Do-It-Yourself Hands-On Activities 140
Invitation to Reflect and Write 141
For Further Reading 141
Interested in Learning More? 145

CHAPTER 7   **The Printing Press** 147
The History of Printing 148
Gutenberg's Printing Press 151
The Printing Press in England 154
Hawaiian Printing Presses 156
Women and Printing 159

The Edict of Nantes   160
Before Gutenberg   160
Pushback on Industrialized Printing   162
Concluding Thoughts   163
Questions to Consider   165
Do-It-Yourself Hands-On Activity   166
Invitation to Reflect and Write   166
For Further Reading   167
Interested in Learning More?   170

CHAPTER 8   **Punctuation**   171
How Punctuation Developed   172
British and American Punctuation   177
Is Punctuation a Joke?   177
Questions to Consider   179
Do-It-Yourself Hands-On Activities   179
Invitation to Reflect and Write   180
For Further Reading   181
Interested in Learning More?   183

CHAPTER 9   **Gods, Goddesses, Muses, and Patron Saints of Writing**   185
Patron Saints   186
Gods and Goddesses   188
Talismans   195
Inspiration and Intercession   196
Questions to Consider   198
Invitation to Reflect and Write   198
For Further Reading   198

CHAPTER 10   **QWERTY: Typewriters and Computers**   205
The Trendy Typewriter   206
The Origins of Typewriters   208
Social Impact of Typewriters   212
Electric Typewriters   215
International Typewriters   216
Typewriter Nostalgia   217

The Digital Revolution   218
How Computers Changed Writing   221
Voice-to-Text Technology   224
Concluding Thoughts   224
Questions to Consider   224
Do-It-Yourself Hands-On Activities   226
Invitation to Reflect and Write   226
For Further Reading   227
Interested in Learning More?   233

CHAPTER 11   **Writing as Art**   235
Calligraphy   236
Beautiful Books   239
Typography   243
   Typeface Design   245
   Bespoke Typeface   247
Concluding Thoughts   247
Questions to Consider   249
Do-It-Yourself Hands-On Activities   250
Invitation to Reflect and Write   253
For Further Reading   254
Interested in Learning More?   262

CHAPTER 12   **Writing Letters: The Epistolary Tradition**   263
What Is a Letter?   265
Letter-Writing Manuals   267
Letters and War   271
   The Civil War   271
   World War I   279
Posting Letters   280
The Epistolary Novel   282
Electronic Mail   284
PostSecret   285
Dead Letters and the Death of Letters   286
Questions to Consider   287
Do-It-Yourself Hands-On Activities   288
For Further Reading   291
Interested in Learning More?   292

CHAPTER 13   **Writing and School**   295
Ancient Schools of Writing   296
Classical Greek and Roman Schools and Writing   298
Writing and Medieval Schools   300
Twentieth-Century Schools and Writing   303
Ability and Disability   305
Concluding Thoughts   307
Questions to Consider   308
Invitation to Reflect and Write   309
For Further Reading   309
Interested in Learning More?   309

CHAPTER 14   **Writing and Work**   311
What Is Workplace Writing?   312
The Importance of Writing in the Workplace   313
Concluding Thoughts   316
Questions to Consider   317
Invitation to Reflect and Write   317
For Further Reading   318

CHAPTER 15   **Social Media**   331
Is There an App for That?   332
What Does It All Mean?   335
Digital Detox   335
The Dark Side of Social Media   338
Social Media through the Ages   339
Is Graffiti Social Media?   340
Concluding Thoughts   342
Questions to Consider   342
Invitation to Reflect and Write   343
For Further Reading   343
Interested in Learning More?   350

CHAPTER 16   **Writes/Rites of Passage**   351
Writing, Culture, and Preservation   352
School   354
Writing as Therapy   356
Lifespan Writing   357
Questions to Consider   362
Do-It-Yourself Hands-On Activity   362
Invitation to Reflect and Write   363
For Further Reading   364
Interested in Learning More?   367

Glossary   369
Works Cited and Bibliography   379
Permissions Acknowledgments   403
Index   409
Biography   419
Colophon   421

Acknowledgments

This project was supported by grants from Utah Humanities, Utah State University's College of Humanities and Social Sciences, and USU's sabbatical leave program. I am grateful to Dean Joseph Ward and English Department head Jeannie Banks Thomas. The round-the-world trip to investigate the history of writing across time and place led me to many places, several of them one-in-a-lifetime experiences. At the home of the Dresden Codex, we found the exhibition vault closed for a new installation. Disappointed, nevertheless, we entreated everyone we could, even a security guard, who made the crucial call to Katrin Nietzschke, head of the Book Museum. She was a delight and gained our admission into the vault. It was a toss-up who was more impressed—me or my anthropologist husband—by this Codex, the only one of three extant that can be visited by the public. Ancient paper mills in France were, quite simply, amazing. At the out-of-the-way Moulin du Verger near Angoulême, the "master of paper" himself, Jacques Bréjoux, opened the door to us, and even though the mill was not officially open, he spent more than an hour talking to us about paper. These are just two incidences in a long line of helpful and generous people. The museums and people listed here are organized alphabetically by country.

Belgium
Plantin-Moretus Museum, Antwerp
Museum for Industrial Archaeology and Textiles, Ghent

France
Treasury of the Cathedral, Albi
La Médiathèque Pierre-Amalric, Albi
Musée du Papier, Angoulême
Museum of Old Auvillar, Auvillar

Musée Champollion, Figeac
Musée Historique du Papier/Moulin Richard de Bas (Paper Mill Museum),
Ambert
Moulin de Verger, Puymoyen, with special thanks to Jacques Bréjoux, Maî-
tre d'Art (Master of Art: Paper)
Musée de l'Imprimerie, Lyon
Musée de l'Imprimerie, Nantes
The Louvre, Paris

Germany

Katrin Nietzschke, Head of Book Museum of the Saxon State and University
Library (Buchmuseum der SLUB), Dresden
Zwinger Museum, Dresden
Klingspor Museum, Frankfurt
Museum of Communication, Frankfurt
German National Museum, Nuremberg
Museum for Industrial Culture (pencil history), Nuremberg
Deutsche Nationalbibliothek, German Museum of Books and Writing (exhi-
bition on the book), Leipzig
Gutenberg Museum, Mainz
Pharmacy Museum, Heidelberg
Heidelberg University Library: Codex Manesse

India

Kartikeya Singh
Old Delhi Bazaar

Japan

Paper Museum, Tokyo
Printing Museum, Tokyo

Nepal

Tibetan Handicraft & Paper Pvt. Ltd, Nimto Nawang Sherpa, Manager,
Kathmandu
With special thanks to Sangeeta Prasai, tour guide

South Korea

Cheongju Early Printing Museum
    Dr. Tai-Soo Jeong, chairperson of board of directors of the Association
of Daegu-Kyoungbuk Calligraphers (pen name: Sam-Do-Heon)
    Chong Ho Kim, calligrapher

With special thanks to Professor Hye-soon Kim, PhD, Keimyung University

Sweden
Kungliga biblioteket, National Library of Sweden, Stockholm
Världskulturmuseerna Östasiatiska (Museum of Far Eastern Antiquities), Stockholm
With special thanks to Dr. Monica Loeb

Switzerland
Swiss Museum of Paper, Writing, and Printing, Basel

United Kingdom
Cumberland Pencil Museum, Grey Knotts Graphite Mines, Keswick, England
Frogmore Paper Mill, Apsley, Hertfordshire, England
British Library, London
British Museum, London

United States
Asian Art Museum, San Francisco, CA
Hale Pa'i PrintingMuseum, Lahaina, Maui, HI
Robert C. Williams American Museum of Papermaking, *Teachers' Guide: Your Guide to the Science, History, Art and Technology of Papermaking*, Georgia Institute of Technology, Atlanta, GA. With particular thanks to Virginia K. Howell, Education Curator, and other staff members.
The Crandall Historical Printing Museum, Provo, UT
American History Museum, Smithsonian, Washington, DC
Natural History Museum, Smithsonian, Washington, DC
National Postal Museum, Smithsonian, Washington, DC
Folger Shakespeare Library, Washington, DC

And specifically at Utah State University, Logan, UT:
Utah State University Anthropology Museum
Nora Eccles Harrison Museum of Art
Holland Larsen, Printmaker
Jennifer Duncan, Special Collections Librarian
John McLaughlin, Linguistics

I appreciate that Delta Airlines offers a "Round the World" ticket, which assisted my research itinerary, and that David F. Lancy tackled the ticket planner. A second, perhaps unusual, acknowledgement is to my bicycle. In Alan Bradley's wonderful girl detective novels featuring Flavia de Luce, she speaks fondly of her bicycle, Gladys, almost as a friend and confidante. My bike has provided hours of exercise—plus contemplation as I was writing this book.

Dr. Dorys Crow Grover, Professor Emerita of English at Texas A&M Commerce, provided helpful information from her travel and research journals, particularly about the extraordinary letter writer Madame de Sévigné. Alice Schlegel, Professor Emerita of the University of Arizona, thoughtfully sent materials relevant to the book.

Students enrolled in the spring 2020 course on the history of writing who piloted this book provided feedback: Claire Banks, Keenan Bryner, Cameron Cheney, Weston Christensen, Ellen Cluff, Megan Eralie, Dallin Hammond, Lilian Hayes, Sasha Heywood, Kaitlin Johnson, Tristan King, Rob Lehman, Kristi Lusk, Rachel Magnusson, Eliza Nemelka, Ashlee Richards, Adam Robinson, Sophia Sticht, Brady Wallis, McKenna Wilson, and Justin Winsor. Likewise, in the spring 2021 iteration of the class, students—masked-up and socially distanced—were extraordinary. One kicked us off with a book talk on Champollion, another taught us how to seal letters with Elizabethan letterlocking, and yet others led a lesson in cutting quill pens and using homemade ink. Materials had to be sanitized and often handed out in zip-lock bags. One student even provided us GPS directions to social media graffiti chalked on a concrete wall.

The professional staff at Broadview have been wonderful to work with, particularly Brett McLenithan and Marjorie Mather. Martin Boyne provided stellar editorial advice and contributed his expertise. I'm grateful to those who reviewed the manuscript along the way. Although no longer are compositors, engravers, or illuminators needed in the production of a book, I'm aware that even in this digital age, it's all hands on deck to make a book a reality.

This past pandemic year of COVID-19 has emphasized the absolute value of writing and reinforced its significant role in teaching and learning. For several of my college courses, the mode of delivery was entirely online, which meant that all assignments and discussions were *in writing*. Students demonstrate what they are thinking through this literacy activity; they encode their thoughts into script. Likewise, all of my feedback was written. Where would we be without writing?

Finally, I wish to acknowledge my family—my parents, E.B. and Lola, and my sister, Judy Kinkead—who fostered a love of books, reading, and writing when I was growing up on our farm near Warsaw, Missouri. They made a difference.

Preface
An Introduction to the *Primer*

Writing is omnipresent in our lives, yet we rarely stop and consider its history and material culture. By *material culture*, we mean the physical objects that are associated with writing: paper, pencils, pens, digital devices. This volume introduces some of the amazing accounts of writing across time and societies. Although an encyclopedic and global topic, the history of writing is explained by drawing on fascinating chronicles and artifacts like Chinese oracle bones used to divine the future. Too often, we think of writing only in connection with school. The goal is to stop and consider what has been called the most significant development in human history, second only to language itself.

The back-story on the development of writing is truly intriguing. For instance, the term *black market* is derived from smuggling high-quality graphite for pencils. Customs agents would ask smugglers to "Hold up your hands!" Are they smudged? Guilty.

Or how many know that beloved author Henry David Thoreau perfected a formula for graphite and clay for his family's pencil factory when the British and the United States were at odds and imported pure graphite was unavailable? Perhaps the profits from Thoreau's discovery funded his stay at Walden Pond.

Before wood pulp was introduced to papermaking in the late nineteenth century, cotton, linen, and hemp were preferred materials. Colonial children were taught their "rag lessons," and young women were advised to recycle their frayed handkerchiefs, which might return to them as a *billet doux*, a love letter. The need for material for papermaking was worldwide. In 1666, the British government passed a law requiring wool for shrouds for the dead to free up cotton for papermaking.

The "Man of the Millennium," Johannes Gutenberg, has been credited with the development of the printing press in the fifteenth century, a technology not altered until some 400 years later. Although it is a little-known fact, Korea actually enacted moveable metal-type printing 75 years prior to Gutenberg.

These are just a few of the fascinating stories underlying a history of writing.

When I teach a course on the history of writing, I begin with a matching game, asking for dates to be paired with innovations in writing. It's fun, yet most likely challenging, to try.

HISTORY OF WRITING TIMELINE QUIZ

Instructions: Match the Year to the Innovation

Year	Innovation
3200 BCE	Personal Computer
3000 BCE	Felt Tip Pen
1600 BCE	Ballpoint Pens
1300 BCE	Typewriter use widespread
300 BCE	Fountain Pens
100 BCE	Pencils
1455 CE	Printing Press
1790 CE	Paper
1884 CE	Mayan Glyphs
1920s CE	Metal Stylus
1940 CE	Oracle Bones
1960 CE	Hieroglyphics
1975 CE	Cuneiform

Why is this book titled a *primer*? I am turning to the classic primer (pronounced prim•er, rhyming with "trimmer"), a basic introduction, in providing 16 chapters that cover a broad view of a range of topics succinctly, but intriguingly, in semi-chronological order. Chapters include the origins of writing; tools of writing; alphabets; the printing press; the book; letters; social media; and even gods, goddesses, and patron saints of writing. To situate readers' own writing within this 5,000-year span, the first chapter focuses on autobiography or autoethnography to consider writing histories, influences, processes, and material culture—pens, digital devices, or paper—the physical stuff we use to write. The *ethnography* part of autoethnography asks writers to place themselves within their various cultures and question how those markers have influenced their identities and practices. Throughout the volume, readers are asked to reflect on how the particular chapters relate to their own identities as writers. Do they have a muse? What was their schooling in writing? How much writing do they do at work? The final chapter acknowledges how writing is evident in the various rites of passage through the lifespan, literally from cradle to grave. How have documents defined our lives?

THE STORY BEHIND *A WRITING STUDIES PRIMER*

I've been a teacher and scholar of writing for almost 40 years. I entered the profession in Rhetoric and Composition at a really exciting time, as writing classes—from kindergarten through college—shifted from a product to a process approach. I worked in writing programs, writing centers, and writing across the curriculum (WAC). A colleague in anthropology, David Lancy, adopted many of the WAC principles that were being suggested at the time, but he also offered an intriguing course on the "Origins of Writing." It made me consider what I didn't know about writing's history.

Over the years, I became a student of writing history, not really anticipating that it would lead to this very book, but learning about ancient writing during trips to Egypt and Mesopotamia—Syria, Cyprus, Lebanon, Jordan. Even in these early cultures, writing was doing some heavy lifting. As archaeologist Denise Schmandt-Besserat summarizes, "Writing is humankind's principal technology for *collecting, manipulating, storing, retrieving, communicating*, and *disseminating* information [my emphasis]" (1).

The idea for this book began to crystalize when I read Charles Bazerman's challenge in "The Case for Study of Writing as a Major Discipline": we should "begin to put together the large, important, and multi-dimensional story of writing" (33). That story covers thousands of years and almost the entire globe. Where does one begin? The process involved simply looking at my workspace: computers, pencils, pens, paper, printer. As the chapter titles of this volume indicate, the list grew. I was also influenced by the writing about writing (WAW) movement initiated by Elizabeth Wardle and Douglas Downs in a scholarly article (Downs and Wardle) and then embodied in their textbook (Wardle and Downs), which anthologizes important essays that focus largely on academic and personal writing of the college student.

"Writing and School" is addressed in one chapter, but this volume takes up the broader picture of the history of writing across time and place.

How does one study the history of writing? I knew from my travels that being on site was extremely useful. A first step was to begin mapping writing, its history, and sites that address that history. The result was a website entitled *The Geography of Writing*, which can be found here: https://geographyofwriting.wordpress.com/. Developed by undergraduate researcher Morgan Wykstra, the map focused on six themes: Origins of Writing; Writing Systems; Writing Implements; Paper; Printing Presses; and Keyboards. Clicking on the map leads viewers to find museums and other venues they can visit, such as the comprehensive Robert C. Williams Museum of Papermaking on the campus of Georgia Tech in Atlanta, or the Paper Museum in Tokyo, Japan.

Following the map, I began visiting sites such as the Smithsonian collection of museums in Washington, DC to the intimate Hale Pa'I museum at Lahaina on the island of Maui that documents the arrival of the printing press in 1823 and its impact on the Hawaiian nation. Those initial forays were so stimulating that I decided to go all in: a sabbatical year devoted to investigating the history of writing and a round-the-world airline ticket. Thus, in the fall of 2018, beginning in The Netherlands and ending in Japan, I visited more than two dozen sites. I got to dip a screen in a vat of pulp in a fourteenth-century paper mill in France and watch paper being produced in Kathmandu, Nepal, in the same way it's been done for 1,500 years. The results of that journey lie in these pages.

I hasten to add that being on site is truly remarkable; however, I'm also keenly aware that I didn't begin international travel until I was in my 30s. Not everyone can travel. Up until then (and continuing now), I follow poet Emily Dickinson's advice: "There is no Frigate like a Book to take us Lands away." My hope is that this book will take you to places you've not been and inspire you to visit when feasible.

THE BIG TAKE-AWAY MESSAGES

Over my journey, I've learned how paper is made, how to use a penknife to trim a quill, and how books evolved. The experiential invitation to Do It Yourself (DIY) at the end of chapters reflects my belief that we learn by doing. There are some overarching messages about the history of writing that I hope are also transmitted:

- The history of writing is grounded in both the practical and the divine.
- At every stage in the development of writing, change has been difficult.

- Innovation often results in backlash.
- Utility and aesthetics battle one another, as there are trade-offs in efficiencies.
- Access is not always equitable.
- Being crucial consumers and producers of writing means making choices, many of them ethical.
- Writing changed the world, and it is within the individual's power to improve our world through writing.

HOW THIS *PRIMER* ADDRESSES LEARNING OBJECTIVES

This volume is appropriate for a general reader who will find engaging information and compelling stories, and, in fact, I have enjoyed speaking about the topics in this book to wide-ranging audiences beyond my campus. It is also well suited for students in colleges and universities who are studying writing as a discipline. National professional educational organizations have defined learning objectives for the curriculum to ensure that students are achieving the knowledge and skills appropriate for an educated citizen. Three types of learning objectives are included here, beginning with the general objectives of the American Association of Colleges & Universities (AAC&U), moving to the Threshold Concepts suggested by Adler-Kassner and Wardle as "critical for continued learning and participation in an area or within a community of practice," and ending with the Council of Writing Program Administrators' First-Year Composition Outcomes Statement. While this volume does not address each and every objective, its global nature, its invitations to active engagement and reflection, and its rich material and knowledge do tap into many.

1. AMERICAN ASSOCIATION OF COLLEGES & UNIVERSITIES (AAC&U) ESSENTIAL LEARNING OUTCOMES

The Essential Learning Outcomes define the knowledge and skills gained from a liberal education, providing a framework to guide students' cumulative progress.

Beginning in school, and continuing at successively higher levels across their college studies, students should prepare for twenty-first-century challenges by gaining:

Knowledge of Human Cultures and the Physical and Natural World
- Through study in the sciences and mathematics, social sciences, humanities, histories, languages, and the arts

Focused by engagement with big questions, both contemporary and enduring.

Intellectual and Practical Skills, Including
- Inquiry and analysis
- Critical and creative thinking
- Written and oral communication
- Quantitative literacy
- Information literacy
- Teamwork and problem solving

Practiced extensively, across the curriculum, in the context of progressively more challenging problems, projects, and standards for performance

Personal and Social Responsibility, Including
- Civic knowledge and engagement—local and global
- Intercultural knowledge and competence
- Ethical reasoning and action
- Foundations and skills for lifelong learning

Anchored through active involvement with diverse communities and real-world challenges

Integrative and Applied Learning, Including
- Synthesis and advanced accomplishment across general and specialized studies

Demonstrated through the application of knowledge, skills, and responsibilities to new settings and complex problem (AAC&U)

2. THRESHOLD CONCEPTS (ADLER-KASSNER AND WARDLE)

Learning a threshold concept is transformative and entails a conceptual shift in how we understand and see the world. These concepts are integrative, often demonstrating how phenomena are related and helping learners make connections. Threshold concepts from writing studies can be helpful for writers to understand and improve their writing practice.

1. Writing is a social and rhetorical activity.
    a. Writing is a knowledge-making activity.
    b. Writing addresses, invokes, and/or creates audiences.
    c. Writing expresses and shares meaning to be reconstructed by the reader.
    d. Words get their meaning from other words.
    e. Writing is not natural.
    f. Writing mediates activity.
    g. Writing involves making ethical choices that arise from the relationship of the writer and reader.
    h. Writing is a technology through which writers create and recreate meaning.

2. Writing speaks to situations through recognizable forms.
    i. Writing represents the world, events, ideas, and feelings.
    j. Genres are enacted by writers and readers.
    k. All writing is multimodal.
    l. Writing is performative.
    m. Writing is a way of enacting disciplinarity.

3. Writing enacts and creates ideologies.
    n. Writing is linked to identity.
    o. Writers' histories, processes, and identities vary.
    p. Writing is informed by prior experience.
    q. Disciplinary and professional identities are constructed through writing.

4. All writers have more to learn.
    r. Text is an object outside of oneself that can be improved and revised.
    s. Failure can be an important part of writing development.
    t. Learning to write effectively requires different kinds of practice, time, and effort.
    u. Revision is central to developing writing.
    v. Assessment is an essential component of learning to write.
    w. Writing involves the negotiation of language differences.

5. Writing is (also always) a Cognitive Activity
   x. Writing is an expression of embodied cognition.
   y. Metacognition is not cognition.
   z. Habituation can lead to entrenchment.
   aa. Reflection is critical for writers' development.

3. WPA OUTCOMES STATEMENT FOR FIRST-YEAR COMPOSITION (3.0)

As students move beyond first-year composition, their writing abilities do not merely improve. Rather, their abilities will diversify along disciplinary, professional, and civic lines as these writers move into new settings where expected outcomes expand, multiply, and diverge. Therefore, this document advises faculty in all disciplines about how to help students build on what they learn in introductory writing courses.

Rhetorical Knowledge

Rhetorical knowledge is the ability to analyze contexts and audiences and then to act on that analysis in comprehending and creating texts. Rhetorical knowledge is the basis of composing. Writers develop rhetorical knowledge by negotiating purpose, audience, context, and conventions as they compose a variety of texts for different situations.

By the end of first-year composition, students should

- Learn and use key rhetorical concepts through analyzing and composing a variety of texts
- Gain experience reading and composing in several genres to understand how genre conventions shape and are shaped by readers' and writers' practices and purposes
- Develop facility in responding to a variety of situations and contexts calling for purposeful shifts in voice, tone, level of formality, design, medium, and/or structure
- Understand and use a variety of technologies to address a range of audiences
- Match the capacities of different environments (e.g., print and electronic) to varying rhetorical situations

Faculty in all programs and departments can build on this preparation by helping students learn

- The expectations of readers in their fields
- The main features of genres in their fields
- The main purposes of composing in their fields

Critical Thinking, Reading, and Composing

Critical thinking is the ability to analyze, synthesize, interpret, and evaluate ideas, information, situations, and texts. When writers think critically about the materials they use—whether print texts, photographs, data sets, videos, or other materials—they separate assertion from evidence, evaluate sources and evidence, recognize and evaluate underlying assumptions, read across texts for connections and patterns, identify and evaluate chains of reasoning, and compose appropriately qualified and developed claims and generalizations. These practices are foundational for advanced academic writing.

By the end of first-year composition, students should

- Use composing and reading for inquiry, learning, critical thinking, and communicating in various rhetorical contexts
- Read a diverse range of texts, attending especially to relationships between assertion and evidence, to patterns of organization, to the interplay between verbal and nonverbal elements, and to how these features function for different audiences and situations
- Locate and evaluate (for credibility, sufficiency, accuracy, timeliness, bias and so on) primary and secondary research materials, including journal articles and essays, books, scholarly and professionally established and maintained databases or archives, and informal electronic networks and internet sources
- Use strategies—such as interpretation, synthesis, response, critique, and design/redesign—to compose texts that integrate the writer's ideas with those from appropriate sources

Faculty in all programs and departments can build on this preparation by helping students learn

- The kinds of critical thinking important in their disciplines
- The kinds of questions, problems, and evidence that define their disciplines
- Strategies for reading a range of texts in their fields

Processes

Writers use multiple strategies, or composing processes, to conceptualize, develop, and finalize projects. Composing processes are seldom linear: a writer may research a topic before drafting, then conduct additional research while revising or after consulting a colleague. Composing processes are also flexible: successful writers can adapt their composing processes to different contexts and occasions.

By the end of first-year composition, students should

* Develop a writing project through multiple drafts
* Develop flexible strategies for reading, drafting, reviewing, collaborating, revising, rewriting, rereading, and editing
* Use composing processes and tools as a means to discover and reconsider ideas
* Experience the collaborative and social aspects of writing processes
* Learn to give and to act on productive feedback to works in progress
* Adapt composing processes for a variety of technologies and modalities
* Reflect on the development of composing practices and how those practices influence their work

Faculty in all programs and departments can build on this preparation by helping students learn

* To employ the methods and technologies commonly used for research and communication within their fields
* To develop projects using the characteristic processes of their fields
* To review work-in-progress for the purpose of developing ideas before surface-level editing
* To participate effectively in collaborative processes typical of their field

Knowledge of Conventions

Conventions are the formal rules and informal guidelines that define genres, and in so doing, shape readers' and writers' perceptions of correctness or appropriateness. Most obviously, conventions govern such things as mechanics, usage, spelling, and citation practices. But they also influence content, style, organization, graphics, and document design.

Conventions arise from a history of use and facilitate reading by invoking common expectations between writers and readers. These expectations are not universal; they vary by genre (conventions for lab notebooks and discussion-board exchanges differ), by discipline (conventional moves in literature reviews in Psychology differ from those in English), and by occasion (meeting minutes and executive summaries use different registers). A writer's grasp of conventions in one context does not mean a firm grasp in another. Successful writers understand, analyze, and negotiate conventions for purpose, audience, and genre, understanding that genres evolve in response to changes in material conditions and composing technologies and attending carefully to emergent conventions.

By the end of first-year composition, students should

- Develop knowledge of linguistic structures, including grammar, punctuation, and spelling, through practice in composing and revising
- Understand why genre conventions for structure, paragraphing, tone, and mechanics vary
- Gain experience negotiating variations in genre conventions
- Learn common formats and/or design features for different kinds of texts
- Explore the concepts of intellectual property (such as fair use and copyright) that motivate documentation conventions
- Practice applying citation conventions systematically in their own work

Faculty in all programs and departments can build on this preparation by helping students learn

- The reasons behind conventions of usage, specialized vocabulary, format, and citation systems in their fields or disciplines
- Strategies for controlling conventions in their fields or disciplines
- Factors that influence the ways work is designed, documented, and disseminated in their fields
- Ways to make informed decisions about intellectual property issues connected to common genres and modalities in their fields.

READING AND USING THIS BOOK

One aspect of this book that may take readers aback is that on occasion, I use first-person point of view. It's kind of like breaking the fourth wall in theatre—unexpected. Frankly, I debated whether or not to use my personal voice or to adopt a more traditional scholarly voice. In the end, I opted for the first person on a limited basis as I wanted to share the excitement of my lived experience and what I discovered in researching the extraordinary history of writing.

Each chapter offers a broad view of the topic, and most chapters end with questions, do-it-yourself (DIY) hands-on activities, an invitation to write and reflect, additional readings of interest, and a list of books for further investigation. Whenever reading any text, I like to consider this question at the end of a section: What are the big take-away messages for me? Additional questions are specific to the topic.

Readings were selected to offer a deeper look into a particular aspect of the chapter's topic. For instance, in the chapter on "Pencils, Pens, and Ink" (Chapter Four), a Smithsonian intern investigates how NASA derived a safe pen for astronauts to use. The reading at the end of the "Printing Press" chapter (Chapter Seven) delves into 1950s-era toy printers for children. In other cases, the reading is drawn from professional literature, such as Cydney Alexis's investigation of the Moleskine notebook for shaping writer identity (cited for further reading at the end of Chapter Thirteen). Each of these can provide stimulus for research and writing for the reader. The list of books at the end of the chapters serves as resources, particularly for deeper investigation. My students adopted books individually and offered a book talk for the rest of the group, which gave all of us more insight into the topics.

In piloting this book with a class, I asked students to adopt a DIY activity and teach it to the rest of the group. The results were extraordinary. I include the names of these students in full in the Acknowledgements. Here's a brief tour of what they did, which I hope will give ideas about what is feasible.

- Tristan and Kristi taught us how to write on oracle bones, as was done in ancient China; they actually obtained scapula from a cow! (They had something of an advantage as bio-veterinary students.)
- Keenan and Cameron made wax tablets for writing with a stylus.
- Megan led us through digital detox, not an easy task during a pandemic.
- Wes and Will made ink for us to use with the quill pens that Brady and Justin showed us how to trim from feathers.
- Lillian and Rob taught us how to bind a book. (Large-eye needles are helpful!)
- Elizabethan letterlocking was demonstrated by Dallin and McKenna.
- Ellen and Sophia demonstrated how we could recycle calculus homework with a blender and papermaking equipment.
- Sasha and Kaitlin demonstrated calligraphy.
- Rachel and Ashlee modeled how to keep bullet journals.
- Adam led us in a lesson on asemic writing.

Supplies for these activities came from Arnold Grummer's, Blick Art Materials, craft stores, and dollar stores. This is not an endorsement of commercial products but a sharing of the information obtained from experts in the field. We also used resources on our campus: a trip to the Museum of Anthropology, where docents guided us in writing cuneiform and gave us papyrus to write hieroglyphics; the letterpress studio where students printed a poem that had been "locked in" to the frame; a tour of Special Collections, in which students worked with centuries-old manuscripts.

In summarizing working their way through this *Primer*, students talked about the unique nature of the topic. Ironically, writing is not at all unique, but analyzing and looking deeply at an everyday subject resulted in insights and knowledge. They brought new eyes to the materiality of writing. They reflected on big questions about the experience of being human, by connecting ideas from other times and places with their own experiences. They compared and contrasted different ideas both within and across historical periods, cultures, and civilizations. They did this by reading analytically and thinking critically, and to my very great pleasure, they enjoyed the experience. I hope that you will, too.

Joyce Kinkead
Bear Lake, Utah
Ancestral lands of the Shoshone, Bannock, Ute, Sioux,
and Blackfoot Peoples

Chapter One

Writing the Self

AUTOBIOGRAPHY AND AUTOETHNOGRAPHY

> *"I don't know what I think until I write it down."*
> —Joan Didion

> *"I write because I don't know what I think until I read what I say."*
> —Flannery O'Connor

This book is about the history of writing writ large. It explores the origins of writing 5,000 years ago and illustrates how writing developed over millennia across many cultures. It showcases writing implements such as pens, pencils, erasers, typewriters, and computers. It addresses the material culture of writing—the objects that we use to communicate. It looks at the long history and power of letters, the personal correspondence between two people. It explores how innovation and technology have developed to make writing easier and more efficient.

Writing is ubiquitous. It is part of our everyday lives, yet we often taken writing for granted. If language was the most important development for humans, then writing is a close second in its impact. While the rest of this book describes writing on a macro level, this chapter is about the personal, the self, you the writer. It's easy to get lost in a history that crosses so much time and space. To begin, we'll look at your place in a world of writing. The subject is writing, but the subject is also you.

AUTOBIOGRAPHY AND AUTOETHNOGRAPHY

An autobiography is an account of one's life written by the person. A way to explore your own writing self is to engage in *autoethnography*. In contrast to autobiography, it is a type of qualitative inquiry that can help construct and analyze identity through both process and product. The goal is to produce an autoethnography of you as a writer. The parts of the term indicate what it means: first, *auto*, as in *auto*biography or *auto*graph, and certainly there are elements of autobiography in autoethnography. *Graph* is a reference to writing, in this case "I write," as in its Greek origin. It's the *ethno* of the term that gets at how you are placed within a cultural experience. How is your personal experience a reflection of your culture or subculture? You might think of *graph* also as mapping, describing, and analyzing systematically your personal experience.

The process of describing behaviors and actions digs into how you write. You will also look at the artifacts or objects that inhabit your writing world. A systematic analysis should also uncover how you are part of a larger group or culture. There's no need to travel to foreign research sites when the subject is you the writer. You should have at hand a wealth of experience and data to mine. It calls on both subjective and objective ways of looking at the self—*subjective*, to acknowledge that we are emotionally and personally involved in our own lives, and *objective*, to query ourselves from a more neutral or distant stance. A possible pitfall of such self-inquiry is *narcissism*, named after the Greek figure Narcissus, who was entranced with his own image. Let's admit it: People are well defended, often unaware of their own foibles. Autoethnography is sometimes criticized as being too focused or self-absorbed. It is possible to produce meaningful autoethnographies that are more than self-centered reflections and actually provide insight into the experience of writers that can be shared with others. A good autoethnography may even produce empirical data to contribute to the overall picture of the writer. Such autoethnographies inform ourselves but also help us understand what we know about our culture.

INTERROGATING YOUR WRITING LIFE

Carolyn Ellis[1] and her colleagues note that a good autoethnography goes beyond the boundaries of "my story" and engages methodological tools of the researcher and grounds the product within the research literature.

---

1   Ellis is also the author of the intriguing book *The Ethnographic I: A Methodological Novel about Autoethnography* (AltaMira Press, 2003).

What are the tools with which the autoethnographer may engage? A writer may begin with a *data dump*, free writing about "myself as a writer" to uncover the discoverable from memories. These guiding questions may evoke thoughts and recollections. Begin with the earliest memories and work through your lifespan.

- What are your earliest memories of writing?
- Did you have toy writing implements?
- Did you play writing games?
- Did make-believe play a role?
- What writing implements did you use?
- Did you write poetry?
- Did you write stories? What type of stories?
- Did you create theatrical productions?
- Were you a cub reporter, interested in news and journalism?
- Did someone guide you in writing?
- Was your writing saved, displayed, or stored?
- Describe school writing.
- When did you transition from learning to write to writing to learn?
- What are your good memories about writing?
- Do you have not-so-good memories about writing?
- Did you have physical challenges in writing?
- If English is a second language for you, explain how that affected you as a writer.
- Did readers of your writing provide feedback?
- Who were notable teachers in your learning to write?
- Did you author letters or thank-you notes?
- What did you learn about the etiquette of writing?
- How have the objects that you use in writing changed over your lifespan?

As you think about yourself as a writer now, consider these questions:

- What's difficult about writing for you?
- What do you enjoy about writing?
- Do you have role models in writing?
- What do you regard as successes in your writing? Why?
- What are your goals as a writer?
- Did you have any epiphanies as a writer, those moments that had a telling impression on you?

In addition to an historical account as a writer, it is also helpful to analyze current practices. Here are questions about how you write.

- Where do you write?
- Do you have a certain body posture?
- Is there a preferred time of day to write?
- Do you need background noise (e.g., music)?
- Do you prefer a certain type of paper?
- Do you have a favorite writing instrument?
- What kind of technology or digital devices do you use?
- Do you use voice recognition technology?
- Do you ask others for help or response while writing?
- What must happen before you begin to write?
- How do you handle interruptions or breaks?
- Must you be alone as a writer or with others?
- Does correctness—spelling, punctuation—affect how you write?
- Are you concerned about neatness?
- How do you begin a writing task?
- What is your planning process for the product?
- Do you stay on task during writing, or do you daydream or allow your mind to wander?
- How frequently do you stop and reread what you are writing?
- Do you evaluate while you write? Do you rewrite while writing?
- How would you characterize your process?
- How do you go about deleting or erasing writing? Do you save deleted materials?
- What is the storage system for your writing?
- What are your choices in the appearance of your writing? Do you prefer a certain typeface? Consider the aesthetic choices you make in a finished piece of writing.
- When is a piece of writing finished for you?

An autoethnography can be enhanced through quantitative data—the simple act of counting to describe, analyze, and understand patterns of behavior. In this instance, consider tracking the kinds and types of writing you do over the course of a week. Include *everything*, even a browser search on the Internet or a check signature. After a day of logging writing, look at the list and see if classifications appear. Social media? Academic work such as note-taking? Lists? Notes? Letters? How are the tasks being enumerated? By time, number, volume? After seven days, analyze the list and see if you can discern patterns and themes. Following are two graphic depictions of the same data for a group of 20 college students who tracked their writing for a week. The first, a bar graph, gives a sense of the most recurring items—text messages, Snapchat—while the second, a pie chart, gives yet another sense of the distribution. Would these graphs look different depending on the age of the respondents? Quantitative data can contribute to a more *layered account* of a person's writing life.

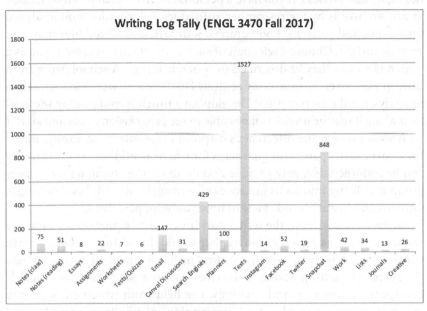

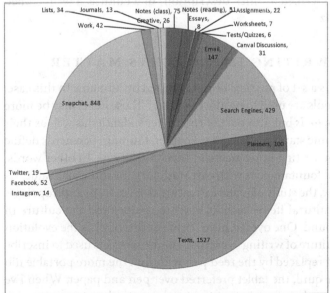

Figure 1.1   Graphs depicting types of writing over the period of a week.

One of the sources of information that arises as a result of these questions is the *artifact*. Is there an archive of your writing through your lifespan? I recall one of my students looking back over her treasure trove of childhood writing and describing her writing like "little sparrows sitting on a telephone wire." That description suggests the literary quality that autoethnography can possess. If you have a personal archive, then it can be treated as any archive is by the researcher, mined for information and analyzed for themes and patterns. Photographs, journals, and stored files may also provide insight. Choose a selection of such artifacts that represent you as a writer. How can they be described in concrete terms? A school paper from third grade? An entry in an essay contest? Do these artifacts yield themselves to analysis and interpretation? Developing a timeline and placing the artifacts along it may be useful. Is it possible to see progression or fits and starts?

Another tool at the researcher's disposal is the *interview*. Family members, particularly parents or guardians for whom a child's entry into literacy can be unforgettable, may provide details about the young writer. A peer group may bring into focus instances of writing from childhood or youth. Others can offer an outside view of how you were perceived.

In the here and now, the writer can function as a *participant-observer* within a group, as a good ethnographer would do, taking *field notes* (with permission, of course) about the cultural milieu. Good field notes illustrate the people, the setting, and the narrative—just as a good story does. Details can speak volumes. In anthropology, the field from which ethnography arises, details are termed a "thick description" of a culture, a term coined by Clifford Geertz.

WHY WRITING IMPLEMENTS MATTER

Material culture is a set of physical objects created by humans. In this case, what objects or tools are used to produce writing? These items may be more than functioning *tools* but also part of the writer's identity as well as their social and economic standing. In a later chapter, fountain pen nerds define themselves by the writing implements in their collections. In other words, they have imbued fountain pens with extraordinary meaning and value. As with ethnography, the study of material culture derives from anthropology, which looks at cultural items such as tools to understand the culture in which they are found. One overarching theme of this book is the evolution of the material culture of writing over time: the metal stylus used to inscribe clay tablets being replaced by the reed pen with ink, the more portable nib pen usurping the quill, the tablet preferred over pen and paper. When I've asked people about their favorite writing implements, they are often quick to respond: "I like a gel pen because of its fluidity although smudges are a problem." Another told me, "I use a pen with four different colors of ink, which helps me categorize notes, particularly in my medical terminology class, where I'm learning vocabulary." Blue, green, black, and red inks delineate terms, definitions, examples, and corrections for this college student. A pen that helps with organizing may appeal to those who keep bullet journals or who just wish to doodle. One of my students, Justin Winsor, who has a "horde of a couple of thousand mechanical pencils," describes his introduction to his revered writing implement this way:

> When it comes to writing implements, I am a fan of the mechanical pencil, not that I refuse to use other forms of writing, but that I like it better than wooden pencils. My experience with them started back in elementary school. I was introduced to writing through the standard #2 wooden writing pencil, and for a long time, I didn't know anything different. Pens were for permanent writing, and pencils were for non-permanent writing. Then, in fourth grade, I found a mechanical pencil. Oh the treasures that the floor provides. I had found something that was truly ingenious. No more sharpening. No more having to get up during class to sharpen my pencil. It was like the world had just invented the greatest thing.

A professional writer on my campus, Mary-Ann Crow Muffoletto, reports that her math anxiety in school caused her to over-click and break pencils, which led her to the Papermate Sharpwriter, which advances the point by twisting the tip, used specifically for math and crossword puzzles. For note-taking, ballpoint pens take too much effort, so for that function she chooses a blue, micropoint felt-tip pen, which is less stressful on the writing hand. Likewise, writers have preferences in their digital devices. Pulitzer Prize–winning author Jhumpa Lahiri prefers writing her books by hand, keeping a notebook nearby for jotting down ideas. When she does turn to the computer, it's one without internet, which helps avoid distractions.

Laura Micciche writes in *The Atlantic* that "Writers Have Always Loved Mobile Devices," but the devices to which she refers are seventeenth- and eighteenth-century writing boxes, which housed writing materials "like paper, inkwells, quills, pens, seals, and wax" and provided a surface on which the writer could compose letters, journals, and documents. The tradition of favoring particular writing implements continues.

A focus on objects in writing brings to the fore how inanimate items may be imbued with meaning. Some writing implements are deemed essential for the writer to be successful. "I have to have my Uni Jetstream," said one writer in my course, as it has "unmatched flow" to help her keep pace with her thoughts. Some writers may even anthropomorphize their writing tools, giving them human traits. The fan of the Uni Jetstream credited it as the "controlling factor" in her success on AP exams. The indefatigable novelist Danielle Steel refers to her 1965 Olympia typewriter as "Ollie."

Writers may also be invested in the ethics of the production of material items that they use. Do they rail against mass-produced paper, use only recycled paper of a certain percent, lean toward handmade paper or notebooks, support the environment through poo-poo paper made from elephant dung? Or the items may carry purely functional importance: "I just need a ream of paper for the printer, and I'm looking for the cheapest package." Micciche says in an essay called "Writing Material" that bringing "notice to production and consumption practices tied to ordinary writing props that have long ceased to be novel... are mostly unrecognizable as technologies" (496). In other words, most of us have forgotten—if we ever knew—how a page of paper is made.

The autoethnography asks for a comprehensive overview of the self as writer; however, some writers have investigated single subjects. Lydia Pyne offers in *Bookshelf,* one in a series of object lessons published by Bloomsbury, to expose "the hidden lives of ordinary things." She traces the storage and display of books from ancient times to the present, including the chained bookshelves of the Middle Ages that kept precious volumes from being stolen. Cydney Alexis explores how the Moleskine notebook contributes to the identity of writers. She describes the "Moleskine phenomenon" (36), which has its own fan blog and Flickr group with "22,000 members and 116,000 uploaded photos." The company has branded the object by associating it with famous writers, with the implication that a person can become a well-known writer by using this product.

If you are curious about the writing implements that writers prefer, then several articles analyze these preferences. Margaret Atwood, author of *The Handmaid's Tale,* leans to "smooth flowing rollerballs" and recalls that she used steel nibs and inkwells in grade school (Filgate). The self-proclaimed Comma Queen of *The New Yorker,* Mary Norris, copy edits with Blackwing pencils, perhaps the Cadillac of pencils. The best biographer of the pencil may be Caroline Weaver, who authored *The Pencil Perfect: The Untold Story of a Cultural Icon* and who owns a pencil shop in New York City that sells hundreds of kinds of pencils that top out at $60.

Pen companies also make much of associations with well-known authors. Conklin Fountain Pens markets the Mark Twain Crescent Filler, based on the fact that the author endorsed the "Self Filling Pen" that put an "end to the days of the eyedropper filling method" ("18 Famous Authors"). On

Ballpoint Pen Day—June 10—"Writers' Favorite Pens" declaims preferred writing implements. Many, such as Emma Thompson, who calls herself a "Luddite," prefer old-fashioned pens, free-flowing ink, and legal pads.

What objects do you turn to for writing? Are they digital? Analog? Try making a list of them and noting the value that you place on each. You may prefer disposable pens, for instance, or free pens collected as part of SWAG or giveaways. On the other hand, you may aspire to the free-flowing prose or poetry engendered by an upscale fountain pen.

WRITING AND CULTURE

What are the cultural implications of the choices made as a writer? Autobiography focuses simply on the story of a person, while autoethnography incorporates autobiography but also looks to the intersection of self and culture. What do we mean by *culture*? The early-twentieth-century anthropologist Bronislaw Malinowski, who is largely responsible for ethnography as an approach to study people and culture, pioneered fieldwork that focused on the anthropologist as participant-observer, immersed in the day-to-day life of a people, in his case, Trobriand Islanders. *Culture* is the social behavior and customs found among people. It is expressed through the arts, religion, rituals, and technologies. Material objects are also indicative of culture.

Culture can thus be a huge topic for any one society. Smaller groups may comprise subcultures of the larger culture. For instance, we are surrounded by various food cultures, which may have roots in ethnic groups or ethical choices such as veganism. Subcultures may be based on religion, occupation, gender, hobbies, or geographic location. Yet defining oneself within a subculture is not always easy. The researcher has to define the *position* within the research study. To be part of a group doesn't necessarily mean that a person has analyzed the language and rituals of the group; it takes mindfulness to do that. A person has to be willing to look at the self in the third person—not taking actions for granted but describing and then pondering the implications. As Socrates is reputed to have said, "The unexamined life is not worth living." It was his belief, shared by his student Plato, that by striving to know and understand ourselves, our lives have meaning and value.

Here are some examples of undergraduates who have investigated their place in culture. Eric Pleasant, who was a student at Texas A&M University-Commerce, chose to conduct an ethnography about punk literacy in mid-1980s Waco, Texas. His essay for class was published in *Young Scholars in Writing*, a professional journal for students who conduct research in writing studies. He describes how his small group of peers adopted the rituals and customs of punk culture, influencing their choices in reading, fashion, and music. Joomi Park, a student at SUNY, investigated National Novel Writing Month (NaNoWriMo), doing field research at write-ins where participants churn out as many words as possible with the support of others in the group. She describes ten-minute sprints, at the end of which writers shout out the number of words they have produced.

Thinking about one's own writing life may also involve describing one's place within a community. In writing his Honors thesis at Wesleyan University, Nicholas Petrie chose to explore the New York City slam poetry community. As a slam poet himself, he is a member of the slam poetry culture but an outsider to this particular site. Petrie employs thick description, historical context, and research literature to begin the thesis:

> I am dripping sweat through the powder blue collar of my day job, rounding the corner of East 3rd Street and Avenue C to reveal the towering projects still casting their unapologetic shadow over The Nuyorican Poets Cafe. This block long ascent, framed by a community garden marked with overgrown rusted bikes turned modern art and the persistent sprawl of upscale bars, does not paint the Nuyorican as intimidatingly as its history would afford.
>
> Founded in 1973 in Miguel Algarin's living room, the Nuyorican originated as a safe space carved out of the chaos of alphabet city for Puerto Ricans living in New York (hence Nuyorican) to make poetry and spoken word and to accidentally innovate an art form. Since its humble beginnings, the Nuyorican has gone through many incarnations (including a long period without budget for a roof or heating bills) until it rose to be the artistic juggernaut it is today. The Nuyo introduced slam poetry to New York City in 1988 under the auspices of Bob Holman's charismatic and charmingly raucous leadership. This first slam was attended by a blindsided audience of 6 people, described by Cristin O'Keeffe Aptowicz as, "totally confused by the numbers being thrown at poems" (Aptowicz 2007, 47). The other two venues in NYC, the Louder Arts Project and the Bowery Poetry Club, originated from the Nuyorican. The Nuyorican was the progenitor of slam in NYC. (17)

Petrie's research interest lies in issues of identity and power within the slam community. He draws on his own immersion into this group, which is new to him, to describe and understand initiation rites. His analysis also leads him to insights into patriarchy, paternalism, and race. His sources are the research site itself as well as published work, interviews, YouTube, and Facebook.

Petrie's thesis focuses primarily on the act of slam poetry. Another group in writing that has set itself apart is the National Novel Writing Month writers, referred to above. This, too, is a group for whom process is foregrounded. The goal is for participants to complete a 50,000-word novel within one month. (A junior version for schools asks for a shorter product.) While process is integral to writing, the tools that writers use can also be studied. Yet another culture study that I found fascinating was done by Cameron Haney, a student in a research methods course, who undertook an autoethnography of his writing life as an NCAA Division I football player. Cameron turned the stereotype that athletes don't write on its head. Through an analysis of his writing and that of his teammates, he found that they wrote almost daily. The textual artifacts of an athlete included plays, reports, film annotations, and writing prior to a game to de-stress. Cameron and his peers showed how writing helps them perform better in games (Kinkead and Haney).

RESEARCH INTEGRITY

A word about the responsible conduct of research (RCR). The autoethnography undertaking suggests that others may be queried for information. Whenever seeking materials from people, it's wise to obtain *informed consent*. In a study involving people, *research* is defined by federal regulations as "a systematic investigation designed to develop or contribute to generalizable knowledge" (US Department of Health and Human Services). Informed consent, even on a project that does not meet this definition, involves informing participants about the project, what you are studying, what the end product will be, and how their information will be used. A form that explains the details and asks for their signature agreeing to have their words used protects everything and everyone involved.

As you consider your own writing life, think about the complexities expressed in the set of questions in this chapter. We take for granted the physical act of writing—although that is not the case for people who cannot physically write due to ability or disability. Writing requires lots of decisions that are not necessarily voiced. This activity asks you to describe and analyze those behaviors and philosophies. Your own autoethnography can reveal the complex person you are as a writer. Once it's finished, keep it to hand and review it in light of the history of writing across time and place that is addressed in the chapters to come. The final chapter, "Writes/Rites of Passages," suggests revisiting this autoethnography, incorporating other writings on which you've reflected in various chapters on "Writing and Work" or "Social Media," for instance, and integrating it into a polished, archival-ready document. The final product may be multimodal and may also cross genres.

INVITATION TO WRITE AND REFLECT

This chapter contains instructions for composing an autoethnography. Consider your history, processes, and identities as a writer. What experiences have informed your development as a writer? To what culture(s) do you belong? Have these been influential to you as a writer? For instance, some cultures recommend keeping a daily journal as a spiritual imperative. How has writing helped you to learn? What artifacts represent your life as a writer? Was work from school kept, displayed, or archived? If you look back at those writings now, what do you learn about your development? What are your preferred implements or material culture for writing? What do you know about those implements? Might you investigate their manufacture and history, incorporating secondary research. Consider inserting illustrations or graphs in your autobiography/autoethnography. If you've kept a tally of a week's worth of writing, then analyze and even depict it graphically.

FUTURE WRITING

Over the chapters in this book, you'll be invited to reflect in short essays on your experiences with writing implements, punctuation, muses, digital devices, letters, writing and school, writing and work, social media, and rites of passage. In the final chapter, an invitation will be extended to revisit the autoethnography developed here and incorporate those further reflections into a longer text that could serve an archival function to chronicle your life as a writer. Over the lifespan, writing is crucial to making knowledge, developing identity, communicating with others, expressing ourselves, and making sense of the world. This autoethnography has the potential to be a lasting legacy to this moment in your development.

Chapter Two

Origins of Writing

Those who write, live on.
—*German adage*

Among the many aspects of writing that we take for granted, perhaps the most overlooked is writing itself. Where did writing come from? How did it begin? What compelled humans to begin to inscribe their thoughts and ideas? Over the course of human history, writing encompasses a fairly short time in that span. Humans actually have *not* been writing longer than they have been speaking.

Humans began writing only about 5,000 years ago. They produced art much earlier than that, about 40,000 years ago, according to the Smithsonian.[1] Making marks to keep track of counts occurred about 77,000 years ago. Around 8,000 years back in time, people were using symbols to represent words and concepts. Writing that could be called *writing* developed over the next few thousand years, notably as cuneiform. Why did it take so long for writing to appear? Physiological developments in humans were important to the creation of spoken language, which preceded writing. The voice box dropped lower in the throat as humans evolved, and the area above the vocal cords lengthened, enabling humans to make a variety of sounds. It is

---

1 Dates for early writing systems around the world are scientifically derived times and can change with new discoveries. In 2018, archaeologists published in *National Geographic* a discovery about a potential drawing that predates by 30,000 years cave paintings in Spain and Indonesia.

not clear when they began talking, but it would have preceded writing by thousands of years.

Ideas and information were transmitted orally prior to the development of writing, but at some point, human societies became sufficiently complex and mobile that a system for storing information across *time* and *place* became necessary. *The Odyssey*, Homer's epic poem, which was performed consistently in the oral tradition, survives to the present day, but how many works were lost? The *Epic of Gilgamesh* (1700 BCE), the oldest long narrative poem in world history, was recorded in cuneiform on clay tablets. It tells of the heroic exploits of Gilgamesh, the first king of the Uruk, and his friend Enkidu. Gilgamesh builds Uruk's first city wall but also journeys into the underworld.

This chapter focuses primarily on three early writing systems: oracle bones from China; cuneiform from Sumer; and hieroglyphics from Egypt. Glyphs from Mesoamerica will also come into the picture. These early writing systems were driven by separate motives: a desire to know the future, a way to record economic transactions, and a method to communicate spiritually.

ORACLE BONES

China is one of the oldest civilizations on the planet and has been the forerunner in many innovations, including paper and movable (non-metal) type. Its entry into writing resulted from wanting to know the future. *Divination* seeks aid or information. Think of it as reading tea leaves, but in this case, it was bones, usually scapula from oxen or the shells of turtles (see Figure 2.1). This is termed *scapulamancy*. The bones were heated in a fire, and as a result, cracks or lines formed, and these were interpreted, providing prediction and answer. What did the priests who performed these divination rites ask? They might make queries about enemies and possible hostile actions, or about the right time to plant crops. The predictions were carved into the bone as a record.

The divination bones were housed in archives, but later, when it was no longer clear what the bones meant, they were often ground into medicines and given the name *dragon bones*. When their purpose was deduced in the nineteenth century, that practice ended, and they became national treasures housed in museums. Bones evolved into bronze, and the lines and cracks gradually changed to *pictographs*, the symbols used in Asian writing systems. Bronze vessels from around the second millennium BCE clearly show inscriptions that anticipate Chinese characters (see Figure 2.2). The advantage of bronze as a medium for communication was that it was more permanent and secure. Still, it did not necessarily travel well due to its weight. It would be hundreds of years more before China found a solution in paper.

Figure 2.1   Oracle bones (scapula and turtle shell). Stockholm Museum of Far Eastern Antiquities (2018).

Figure 2.2   Bronze and Oracle Bones. Stockholm Museum of Far Eastern Antiquities (2018).

CUNEIFORM

In contrast to China, writing began in Mesopotamia to record economic transactions in this important trading region. The emergence of cities and states resulted in more complex societies that needed written records, so memory and oral tradition would no longer suffice. The result was *cuneiform*, the oldest writing system in the world. By 3500 BCE, cylinder seals were being used in the Sumerian civilization to show ownership and legal agreements. Think of cuneiform as a spreadsheet in stone. These seals were rolled over wet clay, leaving an impression—in effect, a contract. By 3000 BCE, clay tablets were being imprinted with marks by a reed stylus, which resulted in wedge-shaped forms (see Figure 2.3). In fact, the word *cuneiform* is derived from the Greek word *cunei*, which means wedge. Originally, these were pictographs, but gradually, they became more stylized. Over a very long time, these wedge marks developed into symbols that might be more recognizable in an alphabet. The two squiggly lines for water ultimately evolved into a letter. The oval with horns for ox may have been the origin of the letter A. The city of Ur was found to have a treasury of these clay tablets, which helped archaeologists and linguists trace the development of cuneiform from pictures to letters of an alphabet.

Cuneiform tablets held in museums today demonstrate the diversity of their uses. One could be a record of a person's land holdings; another could be a recipe for beer. A rich source of cuneiform tablets was found in Ebla, a city in northern Syria. When the city was invaded and burned around 2300 BCE, the clay tablets, which were housed in a library, were, in effect, baked, which preserved them. These tablets helped uncover what ancient civilizations were like, their history and culture being revealed through the stories told in their writing. Cuneiform itself was not deciphered until the nineteenth century, by a variety of scholars and even the self-educated George Smith (1840–76), a printer, who broke the code while studying the *Epic of Gilgamesh* at the British Museum.

Figure 2.3   Cuneiform Tablet.

The Sumerians, who lived in Mesopotamia (modern-day Iraq), are also considered the original farmers. They are credited with writing the first *Farmer's Almanac* about 1500 BCE, found during an archaeological expedition to Iraq in 1949 and housed in the museum at the University of Pennsylvania. Another agricultural-themed text, "The Disputation between the Hoe and the Plow," is an ironic poem dating from the third millennium BCE that involves an argument between two farm implements about which one is better. It ends by invoking the goddess of writing in ancient Sumer, "Praise be to Nisaba."

A true writing system is characterized by signs for vowels and syllables that allow the scribe to express ideas, which did not become consistently apparent in cuneiform texts until after 2600 BCE. This period of growth is characterized by the addition of the rebus principle to cuneiform texts. The rebus isolates the phonetic value of certain signs in order to express grammar and syntax and determine clear meanings. The addition of this principle reduced the number of characters needed from over 1,000 to around 600 and bridged proto-cuneiform with later cuneiform, thus establishing its position as a true written language with word-signs and phonogram signs.

By 700 BCE, the pictographs had involved into representational symbols. Some of these were *syllabic* and some *logographic*. The latter represents a word or phrase while the former represents a syllable—part of a word. Two pictures might be put together to represent a different word entirely. For instance, *cotton* might be formed by two pictures that represent sounds rather than the actual object. Eventually, the marks departed from the originally pictures entirely. This enabled an alphabet that was made of sounds and that could represent concepts that were not concrete: yesterday, joy, heroism. Another development focused on how the letters were named. Acrophony refers to the letter itself being named with a word that begins with that letter. For instance, alpha, beta, delta represent a, b, and d in the Greek alphabet. The acrophonic principle ultimately led to the development of letters from earlier pictograms.

In addition to the literature recorded in cuneiform, such as the *Epic of Gilgamesh*, one of the most important artifacts of this writing system was the *Code of Hammurabi*. Housed in the Louvre in Paris, this basalt *stele*[2] was a monument to demonstrate to anyone who viewed it that Hammurabi I, the sixth King of Babylon (d. 1750 BCE) had enacted a set of laws to guide his empire. It is famous as the world's oldest intact set of laws. Hammurabi had put into writing laws and details of the justice system that had previously been passed on through oral tradition alone. The 282 provisions cover

---

2 A *stele* is a stone or wooden monument that records information and was often used as a funerary decoration to make a statement about the individual. It is usually taller than it is wide. It might be compared to a modern tombstone. The stone *stele* had a greater chance of survival through the ages.

matters ranging from false accusations, personal injury, personal liability, rental and leasehold to debts, assets, and family and inheritance law. Notably, women could, in some cases, inherit. This surviving stele is from the Babylonian city of Sippar, but it is most likely that similar monuments were placed across Hammurabi's territory to ensure that laws were understood and that justice would be meted out consistently, even across vast distances and by individual judges. This system of laws survived Hammurabi and were transferred to other civilizations. In essence, Hammurabi ensured his legacy by turning to writing for a lasting record.

The scribes who recorded these significant stories and documents began as any school child might, practicing writing. The cuneiform tablet held by the Louvre in Paris (Figure 2.4), which acquired it in 1914, tells this tale. It was found in modern-day Iraq, originated in about 1750 BCE during the reign of Samsu-Iluna of Babylon, son and successor to Hammurabi:

> What did you do at school? I recited my tablet, I ate dinner, then I prepared my new tablet, I covered it with writing, I finished it; then I was told my recitation, and in the afternoon I was told my writing exercise. May you reach the heights of the scribe's art... of your brothers, you will be the guide, of your friends, the leader... you have done well your education; you are now a man of knowledge.

For more on this tablet, see Chapter Thirteen.

Figure 2.4
A scribe's essay on learning how to write. The Louvre, Paris (2018).

HIEROGLYPHICS

The third major system of early writing is *hieroglyphics*, which originated in Egypt. Once again, the increasing complexity of a civilization drove the formation of a method for recording information. The oldest Egyptian writing dates from between 5,000 and 5,500 years ago. The term *hieroglyph* itself comes from Greek, meaning sacred writing, which offers a clue to its purpose. Priests and rulers used hieroglyphics to communicate with the all-important gods, who were an essential aspect of Egyptian civilization.

When Napoleon invaded Egypt in the late eighteenth century, his soldiers came across a large chunk of basalt, the same black rock that was used to inscribe Hammurabi's Code. The stone was meant to be used to build fortifications, but the troops noticed that it had writing on it — in fact, three separate scripts. At the top of the stone were inscribed hieroglyphics. Those were followed by demotic, which is a cursive way of writing Egyptian, used to increase the speed for the scribe. Finally, Greek followed. Cracking the code of hieroglyphics was a mystery that had plagued centuries of scholars. Travelers to this "strange and distant land," as Shelley wrote in his poem "Ozymandias" (1818), could not understand this writing system, which they found on almost all monuments such as the Sphinx, the pyramids, and tombs. The Rosetta Stone, so called after the place where it was discovered by Napoleon's soldiers, proved to be the key to unlocking the mystery (see Figure 2.5). Surely it could not be that difficult to divine the meaning of the hieroglyphics from the known Greek letters. But it was. The linguistic detective who eventually succeeded was Jean-François Champollion (1790–1832), a self-educated French man who could speak and write a number of languages, including a number of *dead* languages. Champollion succeeded where others had failed, as he surmised that the symbols inside the oval circles were proper names. These *cartouches*[3] included the names of Cleopatra, Ptolemy, and Ramses (see Figure 2.6). (If you are a tourist in Egypt today, you can have your own name inscribed in a cartouche for a pendant.)

Others assumed that the hieroglyphics were pictures, but Champollion correctly deduced that they represented sounds, a phonetic system for writing. Hieroglyphics include about 750 symbols, but only 150 or so are used with any regularity. He matched these to the known sounds of Greek writing. Because he knew Coptic, the last vestige of spoken Egyptian, he was

---

3 The term *cartouche* comes from the French word for gunpowder cartridges, as Napoleon's soldiers saw a similarity between the two.

Figure 2.5 Rosetta Stone. British Museum, London.

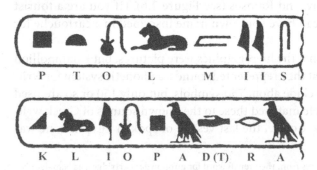

Figure 2.6 Cartouches of Ptolemy and Cleopatra.

able to piece together the ancient language. Egypt, a once-mighty empire, was forgotten in the rise of the Roman Empire and almost invisible for over a thousand years. Champollion—as well as Napoleon—brought it back to the public's attention, which has never waned in the years since.

The glory of the Egyptian Kingdom is evident in its monuments and its writing. Multiple dynasties reigned in the Old, Middle, and New Kingdoms. Hieroglyphics developed about the same time as cuneiform, in the fourth millennium BCE. These sacred signs inscribed in stone served a religious function, imploring the gods and guiding the dead through the underworld. The high-status priests of Egypt dictated what was to be recorded, and scribes did the work. Sculptures of the iconic scribe, who was held in high status, are common in Egyptian collections in museums. Almost always in a block format, the seated cross-legged scribes have a tablet on their laps and hold a writing implement. Their equipment was simple: red and black ink in dry cakes that was moistened to write, and papyrus, an early paper-like material. Unfortunately, papyrus does not weather the ages as stone does. Sheets of papyrus were rolled up and stored in libraries of temples. One of these libraries, a small dark room, is still visible in the temple at Abydos. Hieroglyphics appeared almost everywhere in ancient Egypt. They were on the walls of brightly painted and illustrated tombs, the low relief of temples, and the monuments and *steles* honoring rulers. In Shelley's "Ozymandias," the braggadocious lines are ironic: "My name is Ozymandias, King of Kings; / Look on my Works, ye Mighty, and despair!" (ll. 10–11). The fallen statue of the ruler—assumed to be Ramses II (r. 1279–1213 BCE)—is in pieces on bare and desolate wind-swept sands.

Hieroglyphics themselves are beautiful, even artistic. Indeed, scribes sometimes organized hieroglyphics for their aesthetic appeal rather than for textual logic. But as the demand for more and more writing increased, scribes had to become faster producers of text. They turned to a cursive form of hieroglyphics termed *hieratic*, literally a higher form of script. *Demotic*, which appeared after, was a common or lower form (see Figure 2.7). One of the reasons for speed becoming important was that the variety of texts put into writing diversified. No longer focused just on religion, writing included legal and economic documents, letters, and stories. The sophistication of Egyptian civilization meant a flowering of literary works. Some of these were tales of bravery and may have drawn on stories from the oral tradition. *The Tale of the Shipwrecked Sailor* is similar to *The Odyssey* in that it relates the story of a group of men who travel the Nile River, which has some infamous cataracts, but return home to thank the gods for their lives. Other works include *The Eloquent Peasant* and *The Story of Sinuhe*. Many of the stories provided exemplary instruction in how to live. Egyptian literature spanned diverse genres: poetry, songs, laments, epistles, memoirs, biographies.

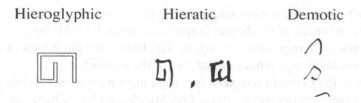

Figure 2.7   How the hieroglyphic was transformed into hieratic and demotic.

Ancient Egypt remains one of the most intriguing civilizations in human history, and the beauty of its writing system, hieroglyphics, is one reason.

MESOAMERICAN GLYPHS

Although not as old as cuneiform or hieroglyphics, Central American glyphs date from several hundred years BCE. Glyphs formed the writing system for the Mayan civilization. These symbols were complex, some pictorial, some with dots and bars or lines. Their purpose was to record history, particularly the chronicles of rulers. They also served for divination, as Mayan priests looked to the gods for answers. The glyphs can be found carved in stone on monuments, inscribed in ceremonial vessels, and written on a codex. They included the sophisticated Mayan calendar cycles as well as astrological information and implorations to the gods.

An early form of a book, a *codex* is one long, continuous document that is folded into leaves rather than rolled, as papyrus scrolls were. The highly painted Mayan codices were considered by the priests who accompanied the Conquistadores to be heathen and the work of the devil. As a result, they burned hundreds of them, a tragedy for world cultures. Three Mayan codices survived the burning of these documents by Spanish priests and conquistadors; they are located in Madrid, Paris, and Dresden, the latter on public display (see Figure 2.8).

As with hieroglyphics, glyphs had to be decoded. While several tried and made some progress, it was Russian linguist Yuri Knorozov (1922–99) who in 1952 said that, like Egyptian hieroglyphics, the Mayans' more than 800 glyphs stood for phonetic sounds—more than a regular alphabet. His work reached Western academic circles through American scholar Michael Coe (1929–2019), who published Knorosov's findings in the late 1950s.

In the twenty-first century, the discovery of a block with a previously unknown system of writing was found in the Olmec territory of Veracruz, Mexico. It appears to have originated early in the first millennium BCE,

Figure 2.8 Detail of the Dresden Codex.

making it the oldest writing in the New World (Martínez). Whether it is a writing system is still under debate. The Cascajal Block includes 62 glyphs with 28 characters. The block appears to be writing, with the symbols arranged horizontally like writing on a tablet. Given their age, they may be the forerunner of later writing systems, but there is no direct connection. The discovery of the Cascajal Block is indicative of how exciting and complex the history of writing can be.

CONCLUDING THOUGHTS

The development of writing was fueled by a need to overcome the limitations of time and distance when memory and oral tradition could no longer suffice. In the beginning, pictures of objects could communicate, but as time went on, that approach became cumbersome and didn't allow for the depiction of intangible concepts such as *hope* or *tomorrow*. The evolution of writing allowed for the phonetic value of the spoken word to be depicted, a more economical way to communicate.

Not every civilization developed its own writing system, however. Some peoples got by (and some still get by) with no writing system at all. Others developed complex systems gradually over time. For instance, the Vai, a small West African group in Liberia, developed their own system of writing early in the nineteenth century. The script continues in everyday use, but no body of written literature exists. In addition to this script, the Vai also use Arabic in Islamic schools and English, which is the official language of the country (Scribner and Cole). The writing systems evident around the globe often took millennia to evolve to their present state. It's an amazing transition for an aspect of our culture that is so often taken for granted yet is so vital.

QUESTIONS TO CONSIDER

1. Decoding ancient writing systems continues to be a challenge. Some stores of cuneiform clay tablets have not yet been transcribed. The Smithsonian article (in For Further Reading below) about unlocking the symbols of oracle bones describes yet another challenge. How could someone become skilled in such work?
2. Humans have been writing for much less time than they have been speaking. Why do you think it took so long for writing to evolve?
3. Some prehistoric and Indigenous peoples painted animals, people, and abstract symbols to make records or tell stories. Caves in France, most famously Lascaux, contain some of these preserved images; likewise, Native American left petroglyphs or rock art. Can these be considered writing systems?
4. Are there societies today where no written language exists? Why?
5. Have you visited the Rosetta Stone at the British Museum in London, the Code of Hammurabi at the Louvre in Paris, sarcophagi from Egypt, or other artifacts that reflect the origins of writing? A local museum may very well have examples of cuneiform clay tablets, and certainly the most famous artifacts are accessible virtually. Why are these prized possessions? (The Rosetta Stone, for instance, changed hands from the French to English.)

DO-IT-YOURSELF HANDS-ON ACTIVITIES

Following are some ancient forms of writing. Writing any of these gives an idea of the skill required to use the particular system. It also demonstrates why faster ways of writing evolved.

1. *Cuneiform*. Try writing cuneiform, using clay and a reed stylus (see Figure 2.9). Actually, a popsicle stick makes a dandy substitute for the stylus, and Play-Doh functions much like clay. Cuneiform features upright, horizontal, and diagonal lines or wedges. Notice that there are no curves. That is because the stylus is pressed into the clay. Immediately it is clear how pen and ink change that writing dynamic. Cuneiform is a syllabary,

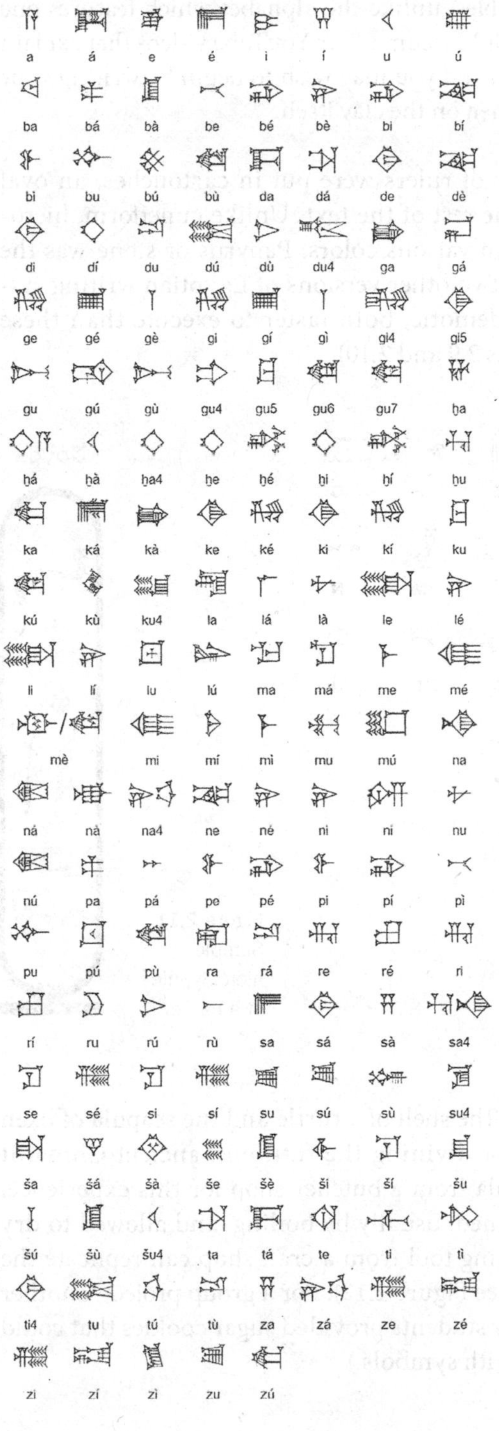

a	á	e	é	i	í	u	ú
ba	bá	bà	be	bé	bè	bi	bí
bi	bu	bú	bù	da	dá	de	dè
di	dí	du	dú	dù	du4	ga	gá
ge	gé	gè	gi	gí	gì	gi4	gi5
gu	gú	gù	gu4	gu5	gu6	gu7	ḫa
ḫá	ḫà	ḫa4	ḫe	ḫé	ḫi	ḫí	ḫu
ka	ká	kà	ke	ké	ki	kí	ku
kú	kù	ku4	la	lá	là	le	lé
li	lí	lu	lú	ma	má	me	mé
	mè	mi	mí	mì	mu	mú	na
ná	nà	na4	ne	né	ni	ni	nu
nú	pa	pá	pe	pé	pi	pí	pì
pu	pú	pù	ra	rá	re	ré	ri
rí	ru	rú	rù	sa	sá	sà	sa4
se	sé	si	sí	su	sú	sù	su4
ša	šá	šà	še	šè	ši	ší	šu
šú	šù	šu4	ta	tá	te	ti	tì
ti4	tu	tú	tù	za	zá	ze	zé
zi	zí	zì	zu	zú			

Figure 2.9
Cuneiform syllabary.

so symbols represent syllables, unlike the alphabet which features one sound per letter. The British Museum offers YouTube videos that explain how to write in cuneiform, and you may wish to begin by writing your name, first on paper and then on the clay itself.

2. *Hieroglyphics.* The names of rulers were put in cartouches, an oval shape, and set off from the rest of the text. Unlike cuneiform, hieroglyphics may be written in various colors. Papyrus or stone was the medium for the writing. Two other versions of Egyptian writing systems exist: hieratic and demotic, both faster to execute than these lovely symbols (see Figures 2.9 and 2.10).

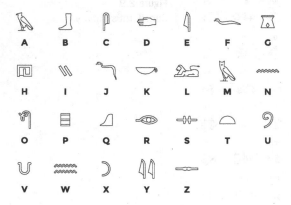

Figure 2.10   Hieroglyphics alphabet.

Joyce

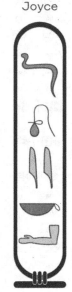

Figure 2.11
Sample
hieroglyphic
of a name.

3. *Writing and oracle bones.* The shell of a turtle and the scapula of oxen were the typical media for divining the future in ancient China. It is feasible to obtain scapula from a butcher shop for this experience. The bones need to be cleaned, usually by boiling, and allowed to dry thoroughly. A wood-burning tool from a craft shop can replicate the symbols of oracle bones (see Figure 2.12). For a group project, another medium may be used. (My students provided sugar cookies that could be impressed/imprinted with symbols.)

人	男	女	子	夫	妻	王	口
rén	nán	nǚ	zi	fu	qī	wáng	kŏu
person	man	woman	child	husband	wife	king	mouth

目	耳	心	日	月	山	雨	田
mù	ěr	xīn	rì	yuè	shān	yŭ	tián
eye	ear	heart	sun	moon	mountain	rain	field

土	水	火	貝	大	小	上	下
tŭ	shuĭ	huŏ	bèi	dà	xiăo	shàng	xià
earth	water	fire	cowrie shell	big	small	above	below

力	中	先	光	肉	出	刀	南
lì	zhōng	xiān	guāng	ròu	chū	dāo	nán
strength	middle	first	bright	meat	to go out	knife	south

北	東	又	好	豕	牛	馬	龜
běi	dōng	yòu	hăo	shĭ	niú	mă	guī
north	east	also	good	pig	cow	horse	turtle

鳥	雞	鳳	魚	兔	象	虎	龍
niăo	jī	fèng	yú	tù	xiàng	hŭ	lóng
bird	chicken	phoenix	fish	rabbit	elephant	tiger	dragon

一	二	三	四	五	六	七	八
yī	èr	sān	sì	wŭ	liù	qī	bā
1	2	3	4	5	6	7	8

九	十	百	千	万	
jiŭ	shí	băi	qiān	wàn	
9	10	100	1,000	10,000	

Figure 2.12
Oracle bone pictography.

4. *Writing Mesoamerican glyphs.* The Mayans developed a beautiful and artistic but highly complex system of writing. It contains both representations of systems and logos (pictures), and a glyph block might combine several of these. The Foundation for the Advancement of Mesoamerican Studies offers helpful guides, "Writing in Maya Glyphs: A Non-Technical Introduction," authored by Mark Pitts, that can be found online: http://www.famsi.org/research/pitts/index.html.

FOR FURTHER READING

Jason Daley, "Museum Offers $15,000 Per Character to Decipher Oracle Bone Script"

In recent years, research into oracles bones, used to divine the future during China's Shang dynasty, has fizzled out. The main reason is that researchers cannot decipher the characters cut into the ox shoulder blades and turtle plastrons used for the soothe-saying, stymieing efforts to understand the writing system. Now, Michael Waters at Atlas Obscura reports, the National Museum of Chinese Writing in Anyang, Henan province, is hoping to revive research into the bones by offering a hefty reward to anyone who can translate the tricky symbols.

Sidney Leng at the *South China Morning Post* reports that the museum is offering 100,000 yuan, roughly $15,000 dollars, for each character researchers are able to translate (with sufficient evidence of course). They are offering 50,000 yuan for anyone with a definitive explanation for some of the many disputed characters. Of the estimated 5,000 symbols found on oracle bones, scholars have only been able to translate about 2,000, meaning there's a lot of room for any brilliant code-breaking scholars out there.

According to Leng, the museum hopes that the cash incentive will draw more researchers into the game and that they will bring new big data and cloud computing applications into the study of oracle bones. Many of the characters on the bones represent the names of people and places, but those references are lost to history.

For over a century, scholars have puzzled over oracle bones, which are also known as dragon's bones. According to Emily Mark at the Ancient History Encyclopedia, a Chinese scholar in the late 19th century named Wang Yirong first recognized that the symbols in oracle bones were a form of writing. As the story goes, Yirong had contracted malaria in 1899. His doctor prescribed dragon bone, a traditional remedy for the disease. When Yirong picked up his bone from the apothecary, it was not ground into powder. Instead, he received a bone with a strange ancient script on it. Yirong, who was interested in ancient writing, bought all the bones he could from apothecaries, who refused to tell him the source of the ancient artifacts. Yirong died (by suicide) before he could crack the case.

In 1908, philologist Luo Zhenyu took up the work, Mark writes, and he was able to discover the source of the apothecaries' bones—there were thousands outside the city of Anyang. Soon, researchers began collecting and translating the bones.

According to the Cambridge University Library, the oracle bones contain the oldest-known Chinese script and have helped researchers confirm the names and succession of Shang dynasty emperors. To interpret the bones, diviners would heat them until cracks formed on the surface. They would then read the cracks answering questions about the future. The answers to those questions were inscribed onto the bones themselves. Mark reports those inscriptions have provided a windfall of information, from the time cities were built to what crops were planted, who married who in the royal household as well as astronomical events and when taxes were raised.

Deciphering even one new symbol could unlock a huge amount of new information from the bones—and, of course, a chunk of change for the person able to crack the code.

INTERESTED IN LEARNING MORE?

Book Recommendations

Michael Coe, *The Art of the Maya Scribe* (Harry N. Abrams, 1998).
Ogden Goelet and Raymond Faulkner, trans., *The Egyptian Book of the Dead: The Book of Going Forth by Day* [the first authentic presentation of the complete papyrus of Ani] (Chronicle Books, 2015).
Andrew Robinson, *Cracking the Egyptian Code: The Revolutionary Life of Jean-François Champollion* (Oxford University Press, 2012).

Film Recommendation

"A to Z: How Writing Changed the World," *Nova*, https://www.pbs.org/wgbh/nova/video/a-to-z-how-writing-changed-the-world/ [53 minutes].

Chapter Three

Alphabets, Syllabaries, and Pictography

"We open our mouths and out flow words whose ancestries
we do not even know. We are walking lexicons. In a single
sentence of idle chatter we preserve Latin, Anglo-Saxon,
Norse: we carry a museum inside our heads, each day we
commemorate peoples of whom we have never heard."
—Penelope Lively, Moon Tiger *(1987)*

The Maldives, located in the Indian Ocean, is a group of islands that appears in the news as the low-lying territory in danger of disappearing as oceans rise due to global warming. The writing system for the main language of this country, Dhivehi, is called Thaana (also Taana or Tāna). Its origins are unique: the first nine letters are derived from Arabic numerals and the next nine from local Indic numerals with the remaining deriving from loanwords. The language has characteristics of a true alphabet but also of an *abugida*, which means that consonants and vowels are paired in what is termed, rather marvelously, *vowel-killer strokes* (see Wikipedia). In the Latin alphabet, consonants and vowels have equal status as separate entities. Linguists note that there is no "apparent logic" to the order of the Thaana alphabet (see Figure 3.1).

Figure 3.1 *Shark* written phonetically in both the Roman alphabet and Thaana. (Some 26 species of shark exist in The Maldives.) Mirihi Resort, 2018.

When I read about logic and alphabet order, I am reminded of the travel guru and self-professed nerd Rick Steves (b. 1955), who believes that travelers look at their own countries differently when they return. G.K. Chesterton (1874–1936) put it this way: "The whole object of travel is not to set foot on foreign land; it is at last to set foot on one's own country as a foreign land." Looking at the writing system of the Maldives made me ask whether there is logic to our ABC alphabet. Why are the letters in this particular order? "Intriguing but unanswerable," according to Oxford Dictionaries. It is basically in the same order as when the Phoenicians—the astounding trading group in the Mediterranean—developed the alphabet around the fourteenth century BCE. The Greeks cleverly added vowels about 400 years later. "Strict alphabetical order did not become established until after the advent of printing" (Oxford Dictionaries).

The order of written words was also in question in ancient writing. Some systems write from right to left—which is true in the Maldives, due to the influence of Arabic—while others write from left to right. What must seem an astonishing order to us is *boustrophedon*. Before the standardization of writing from left to right, ancient Greek inscribers used the *boustrophedon* style, named for a word meaning literally "turning like oxen in plowing." When they came to the end of a line, the ancient Greeks simply started the next line immediately below the last letter, writing the letters and words in the opposite direction, and thus following the analogy of oxen plowing left to right, then right to left. Reverse boustrophedon writing has also been found in which the inscribers turned the document 180 degrees before starting a new line so that the words are always read left to right with every half turn. Not only are the words written in this style, but also some of the letters themselves are "backwards," in what we might recognize today as mirror writing. Take, for instance, looking in a car's rearview mirror at an ambulance. The word is easily recognized in the mirror, but for a person standing in front of the vehicle, it looks like this: ƎϽИA⅃UꟗMA

PICTOGRAPHY

Early writing depicted objects. An ox, for example, was pictured as an ox, a river was symbolized by wavy lines, and a boat by a curved shape. As societies became more complex, systems that could deal with increased information and intangibles had to be developed. Pictures therefore became more stylized. The oval with horns for ox may be the forerunner of the letter A (see Figure 3.2), as we will see in more detail below.

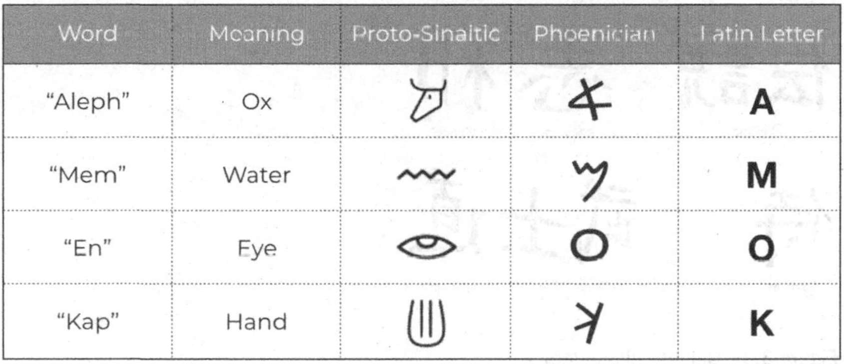

Word	Meaning	Proto-Sinaitic	Phoenician	Latin Letter
"Aleph"	Ox			A
"Mem"	Water			M
"En"	Eye			O
"Kap"	Hand			K

Figure 3.2 How ox horns became the letter A.

Pictographs are the forerunner of true writing. Two other terms come into play here: *ideogram* and *logogram*. The latter stands for a word while the former represents an idea or meaning. Ideograms may also be called ideographs.

A good example of how pictographs developed into a writing system occurs with Chinese writing, developed from pictographic script about 3,000 years ago (see Figure 3.3). Originally, pictograms were actual pictures of the concepts, which later evolved into ideograms, symbols that represent abstract ideas and have symbolic meanings. The number of characters in Chinese is an amazing 80,000, and users must know 3,000–5,000 symbols to communicate adequately in everyday life. In Chinese printing houses, the cases for fonts are huge and surround the compositor. The Chinese typewriter, when finally developed in the early twentieth century, was a large machine to accommodate the number of characters.

Figure 3.3 Chinese characters.

In the previous chapter, we saw that cuneiform, hieroglyphics, oracle bones, and glyphs led the way as the earliest systems of writing. Cuneiform and Egyptian hieroglyphics are examples of logograms—symbols representing words. Of these early systems, none survived as writing evolved, the meaning of these symbols being lost. The library at Ebla held a treasure trove of clay tablets that were not deciphered and whose content remained a mystery until the nineteenth century. Even today, word detectives continue to attempt decoding them. In 2017, The National Museum of Chinese Writing in Anyang, in Henan Province in China, offered 100,000 yuan ($15,000) for each character translated by a researcher. Only 2,000 of the 5,000 symbols found on oracle bones had been translated at the time (Daley). Mayan glyphs have a higher rate of decipherment at 85 percent. Individual cuneiform tablets continue to be translated.

ALPHABETS

What came after these early systems? Alphabets, but also syllabaries. Let's begin with alphabets. These writing systems are phonetic with each letter representing a sound. The alphabet's success has to do with its low number of characters that express the smallest phonemes, or sounds, in language. In Chapter Nine, Cadmus, king of Thebes, is credited with developing a system of letters to represent sounds. Cadmus and his traders needed a method to record and communicate information as they sailed the Mediterranean Sea, moving goods from one area to another. This region, known as the Levant, included early civilizations in what are now known as Syria, Lebanon, Palestine, Israel, Jordan, Cyprus, Iraq, Egypt, and Turkey. These territories encompassed the crossroads of civilization at the time. The Phoenicians did not produce a literature—or at least not one that has been preserved. On the other hand, the Greeks made superb use of language in poetry and prose.

The first alphabet, developed by the Phoenicians, featured 22 consonants. The writing systems for Hebrew and Arabic, which came later, are also based on consonantal script. Around 800 BCE, the Greeks added vowels, a stroke of genius. The first letter in the Phoenician alphabet was aleph, which evolved into the Greek alpha and later to the Roman A. *Aleph* is the Semitic name for oxen, which would have been an important beast. Imagine that the Roman A is the ox head turned upside down. Originally, aleph was a glottal consonant, produced in the throat, but it was later re-interpreted as a vowel. The letter B is rooted in *beth*, meaning house. The Greeks are also responsible for naming their letters: alpha, beta (and it's not difficult to see *alphabet* as one result), gamma,[1] delta, and so on. When speakers say the letter A, it is a direct descendant of *aleph*, the name for ox. It was these origins that led to the first sound of the letters' names, something that we saw in the last chapter is termed the acrophonic principle.

Greek was the leading civilization in this area of Europe, but as Rome and its territories gained power, the Greek alphabet became "Romanized." Greek (see Figure 3.4) was based on the Phoenician alphabet; the Romans created more stylized letters that were easier to produce. As the Roman Empire encompassed much of Europe and even Britain, the alphabet spread widely, so much so that it is the most widely used system in the world today. In its original form, Romans used only capital letters and tended not to insert spaces between words or use punctuation. This allowed for efficiency

---

1 Why does gamma come right after alpha and beta? What happened to "C"? Originally "C" had a "G" sound. According to Robb, it was the Romans who added the crossbar that turned C into G.

Figure 3.4   Early Greek Alphabet on pottery.

for writers and carvers, but eventually, the difficulty in reading led to the insertion of dots between sentences, which evolved into the period. (Punctuation is discussed in more depth in Chapter Eight.)

SYLLABARIES

Not every language, though, features one letter equaling one sound (or phoneme). Syllabaries are systems in which a symbol represents a syllable, that is, a combination of a consonant and a vowel. One of the most famous of these is Cherokee, developed by Sequoyah and representing the written expression of an oral language. This syllabary contains 86 characters and was completed in 1825 (see Figure 3.5). Once developed, the syllabary enhanced Cherokees' fluency in reading and writing. They could write their own stories. On a cave wall in the southeast, the traditional lands of the Cherokee, a mysterious script was discovered in 2006 but not translated until later when Beau Duke Carroll, a Cherokee tribal historian, recognized the writing as Cherokee. The writing described sacred rituals, designed to "leave a record of their practices for future generations" as the tribe was on the cusp of being forced to leave their home due to President Andrew Jackson's Indian Removal Act, which resulted in the Trail of Tears journey to the Oklahoma Territory (Hunt 53).

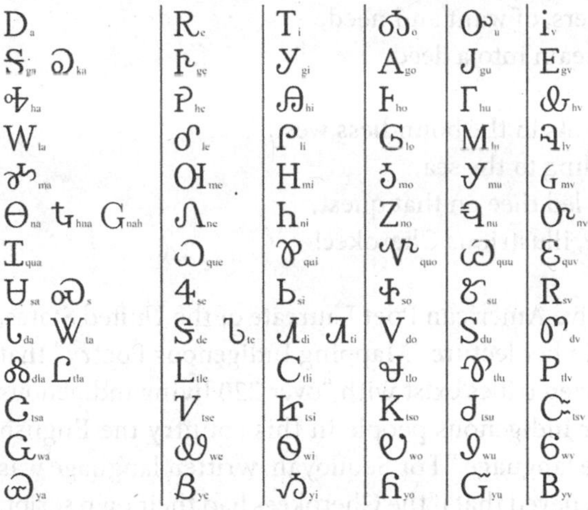

Ꭰ a	Ꭱ e	Ꭲ i	Ꭳ o	Ꭴ u	Ꭵ v
Ꭶ ga Ꭷ ka	Ꭸ ge	Ꭹ gi	Ꭺ go	Ꭻ gu	Ꭼ gv
Ꭽ ha	Ꭾ he	Ꭿ hi	Ꮀ ho	Ꮁ hu	Ꮂ hv
Ꮃ la	Ꮄ le	Ꮅ li	Ꮆ lo	Ꮇ lu	Ꮈ lv
Ꮉ ma	Ꮊ me	Ꮋ mi	Ꮌ mo	Ꮍ mu	Ᏽ mv
Ꮎ na Ꮏ hna Ꮐ nah	Ꮑ ne	Ꮒ ni	Ꮓ no	Ꮔ nu	Ꮕ nv
Ꮖ qua	Ꮗ que	Ꮘ qui	Ꮙ quo	Ꮚ quu	Ꮛ quv
Ꮝ sa Ꮜ s	Ꮞ se	Ꮟ si	Ꮠ so	Ꮡ su	Ꮢ sv
Ꮣ da Ꮤ ta	Ꮥ de Ꮦ te	Ꮧ di Ꮨ ti	Ꮩ do	Ꮪ du	Ꮫ dv
Ꮬ dla Ꮭ tla	Ꮮ tle	Ꮯ tli	Ꮰ tlo	Ꮱ tlu	Ꮲ tlv
Ꮳ tsa	Ꮴ tse	Ꮵ tsi	Ꮶ tso	Ꮷ tsu	Ꮸ tsv
Ꮹ wa	Ꮺ we	Ꮻ wi	Ꮼ wo	Ꮽ wu	Ꮾ wv
Ꮿ ya	Ᏸ ye	Ᏹ yi	Ᏺ yo	Ᏻ yu	Ᏼ yv

Figure 3.5 Cherokee syllabary.

Sequoyah has been memorialized for his contributions in several places, one in the doors to the Library of Congress and another in this poem by Alexander Posey, a Muskogee Creek poet born in 1873.

Ode to Sequoyah

The names of Waitie and Boudinot—
    The valiant warrior and gifted sage—
And other Cherokees, may be forgot,
    But thy name shall descend to every age;
The mysteries enshrouding Cadmus' name
Cannot obscure thy claim to fame.

The people's language cannot perish—nay,
    When from the face of this great continent
Inevitable doom hath swept away
    The last memorial—the last fragment
Of tribes,—some scholar learned shall pore
Upon thy letters, seeking ancient lore.

Some bard shall lift a voice in praise of thee,
    In moving numbers tell the world how men
Scoffed thee, hissed thee, charged with lunacy!
    And who could not give 'nough honor when

At length, in spite of jeers, of want and need,
Thy genius shaped a dream into a deed.

By cloud-capped summits in the boundless west,
    Or mighty river rolling to the sea,
Where'er thy footsteps led thee on that quest,
    Unknown, rest thee, illustrious Cherokee!

Joy Harjo, the first Native American Poet Laureate of the United States, appointed in 2019, noted in her lecture "Mapping Indigenous Poetry" that over 500 federally recognized tribes exist with "over 220 living indigenous languages." She said, "For indigenous people in this country the English language is a kind of trade language." For Sequoyah, written language was the key to power, and he believed that if the Cherokees had their own script, then they could maintain independence and increase knowledge. Unfortunately, although Cherokee was used for newspapers and books, the syllabary didn't prevent the tragic migration of the Trail of Tears.

In yet another language, Japanese, syllabaries play a role. Japanese uses multiple distinct approaches to language: *kanji, katakana,* and *hiragana.* The latter two are syllabaries. Kanji is used for children in particular as it is an easier writing and reading system. Katakana and hiragana have 46 primary characters each, and even more that use diacritical marks. This approach is derived from Chinese. As with that language, literally tens of thousands of characters need to be learned in order to be a literate member of society.

SOME OTHER ALPHABETS

Runic

Before the Roman alphabet was adopted in parts of Europe, some Germanic languages were written in runic alphabets of two dozen characters. The letters are angular, which were easier to carve in stone or wood. The term for this script is *Futhark,* the Viking alphabet. Its name comes from the first six letters in the alphabet. Three versions exist: Elder Futhark, Anglo-Saxon Futhorc, and Younger Futhark. The Elder Futhark was used in the period 100–750 CE. During the seventh and eighth centuries, the symbols changed forms, and the number was reduced from 24 to 16 as the difference between voiced and unvoiced consonants was no longer expressed.

Rune stones were placed beside roads, by bridges, and at places of special significance, where they could be seen and read by many people (see Figure 3.6). They described events, memorialized figures, and described myths or

Figure 3.6   The Vallenberga runestone, Lund.

sagas. The word *rune* means *wise* or *secret* (in Proto-Germanic, the supposed ancestor of the Germanic languages, including English) and may have arisen from writing being a kind of secret communication that only the wise could understand. This was considered the alphabet of the Norsemen by others.

Memorial runes were raised by relatives in memory of someone who had just died, and the inscriptions usually followed a pattern: 1) who has had the stone made, and 2) the phrase "raised this stone after," with the name of the person being honored. Raising a rune stone created an open and public document of great significance. Wealthy widows literally had their power carved in stone, staking a claim to their territory with the aid of runes. Around 800 CE, a Swedish chieftain named Varinn set up an enormous stone weighing five tons and standing eight feet tall in memory of his son

Vamoth. Its surface is covered with the longest runic inscription in existence, some 760 runes in 28 lines. Scholars continue to try and interpret its meaning, but as one archaeologist noted, "It was only meant for the gods" (Weiss). Around 2,500 rune stones have been fully or partially preserved in Sweden, and more across Scandinavia and Great Britain. As with the tablets of Ebla, stone is a great preservative for early writing.

Cyrillic

Another noteworthy script is the Cyrillic alphabet, based on work done by Cyril and Methodoius of the Byzantine era (ninth century CE), two brothers who did missionary work among Slavic peoples in areas such as Russia, Bulgaria, Serbia, and Ukraine. The brothers were canonized as saints for translating the Bible to make it accessible to local peoples. The origin of Cyrillic was the Glagolitic alphabet, which was derived from the Greek alphabet (see Figure 3.7). The result was that Slavic peoples more readily accepted Christianity because they were able to read biblical texts. Later, Peter the Great introduced a script more suitable for civic purposes than religious, a transition that also led to the regularization of the orthography. Several of the letters are like those in the Greek and Roman alphabets; however, many have different phonetic values.

А Б В Г Д Є Ж Ѕ З И І
К Л М Н О П Р С Т Ѹ Ф
Х Ѡ Ц Ч Ш Щ Ъ Ы Ь Ѣ Ꙗ
Ѥ Ю Ѧ Ѩ Ѫ Ѭ Ѯ Ѱ Ѳ Ѵ Ҁ

Figure 3.7   Early Cyrillic Alphabet.

As we've seen across time, alphabets can change. Greeks added vowels, and gamma became the symbol for the letter C. Peter the Great made the Cyrillic alphabet look more Western. As computers took over global writing, typefaces needed to be more regularized, just as the Greek alphabet was "Romanized."

In 2017, Kazakhstan undertook a change in the alphabet of its principal language, Kazakh, from Cyrillic script to the Roman alphabet that is more common in the West. The objectives were both political and cultural. A more westernized approach could improve the economic outlook of the country, while it also signaled distancing itself from "Mother Russia," since Kazakhstan was part of the former Soviet Union. A pilot study of the new alphabet was set to begin in 2019 (Mirovalev). The cost for the change was estimated at nearly $700 million, primarily to support education (Chen). The stages for the change to be enacted over an eight-year period are fascinating: establish a commission to oversee the change; build code to digitally convert Cyrillic to the Roman alphabet; republish textbooks for all subjects; train teachers in the new alphabet; introduce it to the public; update guidelines for teaching texts in the new alphabet; develop programs to translate government documents and news in state-owned media; and, finally, hire influential bloggers for a social media awareness campaign.

Arabic

One of the foremost displays in the British Museum is of the Rosetta Stone; it also has a stunning array of Egyptian artifacts from ancient times. Much less attention is paid to Modern Egypt. When I was at the British Museum in 2019, a special display highlighted an Arabic typewriter from 1922. The first Arabic language typewriter was created in 1914, some time after the typewriter in the United States. Following the Revolution in 1919, which deposed the ruling royal family, an American company created this "Writing Machine Egypt" using gilded letters, appropriate for a country with such a distinguished history. Arabic would not be immediately easy to transpose to keystrokes. It is written in cursive style from right to left and can result in beautiful calligraphy and works of art that embellish mosque and building walls.

Hebrew

The Hebrew alphabet includes 22 letters; vowels are often omitted but can be indicated using diacritics on consonants. Both Arabic and Hebrew are derived from Aramaic script, which is based in the ancient Phoenician alphabet, and both have a system of dots. Likewise, both are written right to left. Hebrew began to emerge around the eighth century BCE. Through the years, it has added a "squared" alphabet to its standard cursive, which is yet another example of Romanizing letters to make them easier to print.

Deseret Alphabet

Early members of the Church of Jesus Christ of Latter-Day Saints, led by Brigham Young (1801–77), developed their own alphabet not only to set themselves apart from others in the United States but also to create a system whereby non–English-speaking immigrants and converts could learn to read and write more easily in their new country. A similar effort was the Shavian alphabet, named after George Bernard Shaw (1856–1950), aiming to provide a simple, phonetic orthography.

Braille

The alphabet of Braille is based on feeling, a tactile script with raised dots. Louis Braille (1809–52), the namesake of this writing system, developed the code in 1824 as he himself had been blinded as a young child. The code is based on a binary system—similar to computer code—that uses cells and dots. Within one cell, six dots are possible to be embossed or raised to be understood through touch. The letter A, for example, is a raised dot in the upper left-hand corner of the cell (see Figure 3.8). B follows with two dots in the upper left and middle register. C features the two dots in the top row.

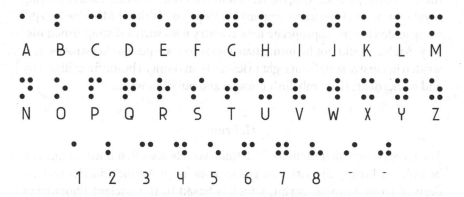

Figure 3.8 Braille Alphabet.

Electronic Alphabet

Efficient and timely long-distance communication was a goal long before telephones, telefaxes, and the Internet. French engineer Claude Chape (1763–1805) developed the semaphore system in 1794, consisting of movable wooden arms that could be read up to 20 miles apart (López 18). It was Samuel Morse (1791–1872), though, who created the electronic alphabet, a system of dots and dashes, that moved messages through wire using the principle of electromagnetism via the telegraph. The dash is three times the length of a dot. The Morse Code applies to the 26 letters of the alphabet, numerals one through zero, and a few punctuation marks. The most used letters are encoded with the shortest code; thus the letter "e" is a single dot while "z" is two dashes followed by two dots. Supported by the US Congress, Morse demonstrated the electric telegraph in 1844, transmitting a message between Washington, DC, and Baltimore. Morse Code enabled messages to be sent and received within minutes and spread quickly as "23,000 miles of telegraph cable crisscrossed the United States" (López 19). The first transatlantic cable was laid in 1858. It could be said that the electronic information age began then.

International Phonetic Alphabet

The International Phonetic Alphabet (IPA) was created in 1888 by a scholarly association to create a standardized representation of the sounds of all languages. It is helpful to those learning a foreign language, but it also is used by special occupations such as opera singers, who must learn lyrics in a foreign language but not necessarily speak the language with fluency and understanding. The chart depicting sounds uttered is complex (see Figure 3.9). The goal of the IPA is to represent the sounds of all languages through a series of symbols and diacritics. The system combines characters from the Roman and Greek alphabets, as well as other symbols.

Imagine how difficult it is to learn English for non-English speaking people. Letters can have multiple signs. A clever party trick is to ask people to pronounce *ghoti*. Theoretically, *ghoti* could spell *fish* when 'gh' is the sound made in enough, 'o' is the sound as pronounced in women, and 'ti' is said as in nation. The IPA provides a useful resource for standard pronunciation.

CONSONANTS (PULMONIC)

© 2018 IPA

	Bilabial	Labiodental	Dental	Alveolar	Postalveolar	Retroflex	Palatal	Velar	Uvular	Pharyngeal	Glottal
Plosive	p b			t d		ʈ ɖ	c ɟ	k g	q ɢ		ʔ
Nasal	m	ɱ		n		ɳ	ɲ	ŋ	ɴ		
Trill	ʙ			r					ʀ		
Tap or Flap		ⱱ		ɾ		ɽ					
Fricative	ɸ β	f v	θ ð	s z	ʃ ʒ	ʂ ʐ	ç ʝ	x ɣ	χ ʁ	ħ ʕ	h ɦ
Lateral fricative				ɬ ɮ							
Approximant		ʋ		ɹ		ɻ	j	ɰ			
Lateral approximant				l		ɭ	ʎ	ʟ			

Symbols to the right in a cell are voiced, to the left are voiceless. Shaded areas denote articulations judged impossible.

CONSONANTS (NON-PULMONIC)

Clicks	Voiced implosives	Ejectives
ʘ Bilabial	ɓ Bilabial	’ Examples:
ǀ Dental	ɗ Dental/alveolar	p’ Bilabial
ǃ (Post)alveolar	ʄ Palatal	t’ Dental/alveolar
ǂ Palatoalveolar	ɠ Velar	k’ Velar
ǁ Alveolar lateral	ʛ Uvular	s’ Alveolar fricative

OTHER SYMBOLS

ʍ Voiceless labial-velar fricative

w Voiced labial-velar approximant

ɥ Voiced labial-palatal approximant

ʜ Voiceless epiglottal fricative

ʢ Voiced epiglottal fricative

ʡ Epiglottal plosive

ɕ ʑ Alveolo-palatal fricatives

ɺ Voiced alveolar lateral flap

ɧ Simultaneous ʃ and x

Affricates and double articulations can be represented by two symbols joined by a tie bar if necessary.   t͡s k͡p

VOWELS

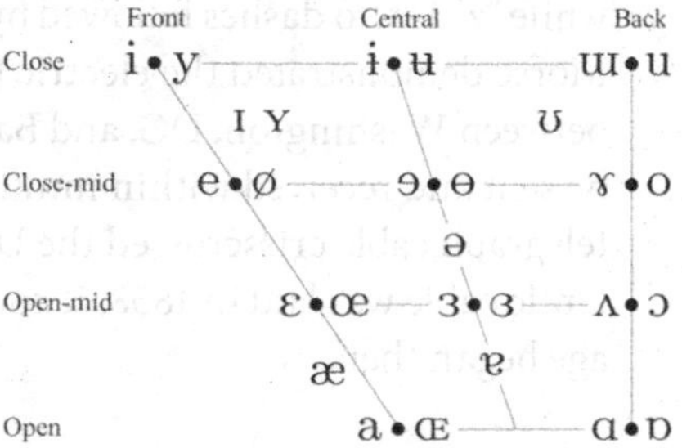

Where symbols appear in pairs, the one to the right represents a rounded vowel.

SUPRASEGMENTALS

ˈ Primary stress   ˌfoʊnəˈtɪʃən

ˌ Secondary stress

ː Long   eː

ˑ Half-long   eˑ

˘ Extra-short   ĕ

| Minor (foot) group

‖ Major (intonation) group

. Syllable break   ɹi.ækt

‿ Linking (absence of a break)

DIACRITICS
Some diacritics may be placed above a symbol with a descender, e.g. ŋ̊

̥ Voiceless	n̥ d̥	̤ Breathy voiced	b̤ a̤	̪ Dental	t̪ d̪
̬ Voiced	s̬ t̬	̰ Creaky voiced	b̰ a̰	̺ Apical	t̺ d̺
ʰ Aspirated	tʰ dʰ	̼ Linguolabial	t̼ d̼	̻ Laminal	t̻ d̻
̹ More rounded	ɔ̹	ʷ Labialized	tʷ dʷ	̃ Nasalized	ẽ
̜ Less rounded	ɔ̜	ʲ Palatalized	tʲ dʲ	ⁿ Nasal release	dⁿ
̟ Advanced	u̟	ˠ Velarized	tˠ dˠ	ˡ Lateral release	dˡ
̠ Retracted	e̠	ˤ Pharyngealized	tˤ dˤ	̚ No audible release	d̚
̈ Centralized	ë	̴ Velarized or pharyngealized	ɫ		
̽ Mid-centralized	e̽	̝ Raised	e̝ (ɹ̝ = voiced alveolar fricative)		
̩ Syllabic	n̩	̞ Lowered	e̞ (β̞ = voiced bilabial approximant)		
̯ Non-syllabic	e̯	̘ Advanced Tongue Root	e̘		
˞ Rhoticity	ɚ a˞	̙ Retracted Tongue Root	e̙		

TONES AND WORD ACCENTS

LEVEL		CONTOUR	
e̋ or ˥ Extra high		ě or ˥˩ Rising	
é ˦ High		ê ˩˥ Falling	
ē ˧ Mid		e᷄ ˧˥ High rising	
è ˨ Low		e᷅ ˩˧ Low rising	
ȅ ˩ Extra low		e᷈ ˥˧˥ Rising-falling	
↓ Downstep		↗ Global rise	
↑ Upstep		↘ Global fall	

Figure 3.9 The International Phonetic Alphabet.

CONCLUDING THOUGHTS

How many writing systems do you understand and use? For the most part, our choice of alphabet is determined by our geographic location and the language(s) we speak. Alphabets, syllabaries, and pictographs are the foundation for literacy, the ability to communicate and understand information; this chapter has introduced some of these, but there are many more. At the simplest level in any language, it's important to be able to name and write the alphabet and identify the sounds made by the letters. More importantly, alphabets carry considerable cultural weight. Being able to read and write is a core skill for success and opens a world of information and literature.

QUESTIONS TO CONSIDER

1. In the United States, many children learn the alphabet by singing the "ABC Song," which was copyrighted by Charles Bradlee in 1834 as "The Schoolmaster." Sung to the tune of "Twinkle Twinkle Little Star," the ABC song originally helped children who may not have had access to schools, but it has been long lasting, as music and rhymes assist in memory. This eighteenth-century tradition of learning ABCs through song is also present in children's programming such as *Sesame Street*. "Who Made the Alphabet Song?" is a question on the children's version of *The Conversation*, a website devoted to providing accurate information on a variety of topics. What questions did you have as a child about writing? If you were to ask children now what questions they have about writing, what would they want to know? Can you answer their questions in a kid-friendly way?

2. Alphabet books for children are perennially popular. The diversity of approaches to illustrating ABCs is extraordinary. *Alphabet City* by Stephen T. Johnson features letters hidden in urban architecture; Mary Azarian's *A Farmer's Alphabet* offers wood-block prints in the tradition of Asia; Patricia Polacco offers a goat-themed approach in *G is for Goat*; Laura Rankin's *The Handmade Alphabet* integrates American Sign Language with each letter; *Into the A, B, Sea* by Deborah Lee Rose features animals who live in the ocean. If you were to design a book of ABCs, what theme would you choose? How would it stand out from the many, many alphabet books already in print?

3. Lexigrams are symbols or figures that represent words, particularly for learning a language. One of the most famous users of lexigrams is Kanzi, a Bonobo (ape) born in 1980, who has demonstrated linguistic ability and communication skills by pointing to a chart (keyboard)

that includes 300 symbols that represent words. Kanzi is able to communicate by pointing to lexigrams such as "chase," "hide," and "carrot," and even evaluative words such as "good" and "bad." How do lexigrams fit in the overall concept of this chapter, which is focused on alphabets, syllabaries, and pictography?

INVITATION TO REFLECT AND WRITE

Adult fiction has an interesting set of titles in which the alphabet is employed. The 2001 novel *Ella Minnow Pea*, by Mark Dunn, is called a novel in letters, but its original subtitle is "a progressively lipogrammatic epistolary fable," lipogrammatic referring to leaving letters out, which happens more and more as the novel goes on. This satire is set on an island off the coast of South Carolina, home to Nevin Nollop, the supposed creator of the pangram "The quick brown fox jumps over the lazy dog." A pangram was used with typewriters to ensure that all keys were striking. Other novels also make use of the alphabet, notably Agatha Christie's *The A.B.C. Murders* (1936) and Sue Grafton's alphabet novels, beginning with *A is for Alibi* (1982). Christian Bök authored *Eunoia* (2001), a *tour de force*, which manages in a five-chapter book to use just one vowel per chapter, which is termed a univocal lipogram.

Consider writing flash fiction (a very short story) that makes use of the alphabet in some way.

FOR FURTHER READING

Rudyard Kipling (1865–1936) was an enormously popular writer and storyteller in the Victorian era. He drew on his own years in India for *The Jungle Book*. The following fanciful origin myth comes from his *Just So Stories* (1902), which includes mainly animal-focused stories such as "How the Elephant Got Its Trunk." The two characters in the alphabet story are Tegumai Bopsulai, a Neolithic man, and his daughter Taffy, who are fishing. The story refers to another tale, "How the First Letter Was Written." The clever daughter suggests using pictograms to represent the sounds of the Tegumai languge, and the two of them create a writing system. It's quite likely that Kipling told this story to his children as a bedtime tale. As he told the story, he also sketched the alphabet.

Rudyard Kipling, "How the Alphabet Was Made"

The week after Taffimai Metallumai (we will still call her Taffy, Best Beloved) made that little mistake about her Daddy's spear and the Stranger-man and the picture-letter and all, she went carp-fishing again with her Daddy. Her Mummy wanted her to stay at home and help hang up hides to dry on the big drying-poles outside their Neolithic Cave, but Taffy slipped away down to her Daddy quite early, and they fished. Presently she began to giggle, and her Daddy said, 'Don't be silly, child.'

'But wasn't it inciting!' said Taffy. 'Don't you remember how the Head Chief puffed out his cheeks, and how funny the nice Stranger-man looked with the mud in his hair?'

'Well do I,' said Tegumai. 'I had to pay two deerskins—soft ones with fringes—to the Stranger-man for the things we did to him.'

'We didn't do anything,' said Taffy. 'It was Mummy and the other Neolithic ladies—and the mud.'

'We won't talk about that,' said her Daddy, 'Let's have lunch.'

Taffy took a marrow-bone and sat mousy-quiet for ten whole minutes, while her Daddy scratched on pieces of birch-bark with a shark's tooth. Then she said, 'Daddy, I've thinked of a secret surprise. You make a noise—any sort of noise.'

'Ah!' said Tegumai. 'Will that do to begin with?'

'Yes,' said Taffy. 'You look just like a carp-fish with its mouth open. Say it again, please.'

'Ah! ah! ah!' said her Daddy. 'Don't be rude, my daughter.'

'I'm not meaning rude, really and truly,' said Taffy. 'It's part of my secret-surprise-think. Do say ah, Daddy, and keep your mouth open at the end, and lend me that tooth. I'm going to draw a carp-fish's mouth wide-open.'

'What for?' said her Daddy.

'Don't you see?' said Taffy, scratching away on the bark. 'That will be our little secret s'prise. When I draw a carp-fish with his mouth open in the smoke at the back of our Cave—if Mummy doesn't mind—it will remind you of that ah-noise. Then we can play that it was me jumped out of the dark and s'prised you with that noise—same as I did in the beaver-swamp last winter.'

'Really?' said her Daddy, in the voice that grown-ups use when they are truly attending. 'Go on, Taffy.'

'Oh bother!' she said. 'I can't draw all of a carp-fish, but I can draw something that means a carp-fish's mouth. Don't you know how they stand on their heads rooting in the mud? Well, here's a pretence carp-fish (we can play that the rest of him is drawn). Here's just his mouth, and that means ah.' And she drew this.

'That's not bad,' said Tegumai, and scratched on his own piece of bark for himself; but you've forgotten the feeler that hangs across his mouth.'

'But I can't draw, Daddy.'

'You needn't draw anything of him except just the opening of his mouth and the feeler across. Then we'll know he's a carp-fish, 'cause the perches and trouts haven't got feelers. Look here, Taffy.' And he drew this.

'Now I'll copy it.' said Taffy. 'Will you understand this when you see it?'

'Perfectly,' said her Daddy.

And she drew this. 'And I'll be quite as s'prised when I see it anywhere, as if you had jumped out from behind a tree and said '"Ah!"'

'Now, make another noise,' said Taffy, very proud.

'Yah!' said her Daddy, very loud.

'H'm,' said Taffy. 'That's a mixy noise. The end part is ah-carp-fish-mouth; but what can we do about the front part? Yer- yer-yer and ah! Ya!'

'It's very like the carp-fish-mouth noise. Let's draw another bit of the carp-fish and join 'em,' said her Daddy. He was quite incited too.

'No. If they're joined, I'll forget. Draw it separate. Draw his tail. If he's standing on his head the tail will come first. 'Sides, I think I can draw tails easiest,' said Taffy.

'A good notion,' said Tegumai. "Here's a carp-fish tail for the yer-noise.' And he drew this.

'I'll try now,' said Taffy. "'Member I can't draw like you, Daddy. Will it do if I just draw the split part of the tail, and the sticky-down line for where it joins?' And she drew this.

Her Daddy nodded, and his eyes were shiny bright with 'citement.

'That's beautiful,' she said. 'Now make another noise, Daddy.'

'Oh!' said her Daddy, very loud.

'That's quite easy,' said Taffy. 'You make your mouth all around like an egg or a stone. So an egg or a stone will do for that.'

'You can't always find eggs or stones. We'll have to scratch a round something like one.' And he drew this.

'My gracious!' said Taffy, 'what a lot of noise-pictures we've made,—carp-mouth, carp-tail, and egg! Now, make another noise, Daddy.'

'Ssh!' said her Daddy, and frowned to himself, but Taffy was too incited to notice.

'That's quite easy,' she said, scratching on the bark.

'Eh, what?' said her Daddy. 'I meant I was thinking, and didn't want to be disturbed.'

'It's a noise just the same. It's the noise a snake makes, Daddy, when it is thinking and doesn't want to be disturbed. Let's make the ssh-noise a snake. Will this do?' And she drew this.

'There,' she said. 'That's another s'prise-secret. When you draw a hissy-snake by the door of your little back-cave where you mend the spears, I'll know you're thinking hard; and I'll come in most mousy-quiet. And if you draw it on a tree by the river when you are fishing, I'll know you want me to walk most most mousy-quiet, so as not to shake the banks.'

'Perfectly true,' said Tegumai. 'And there's more in this game than you think, Taffy, dear, I've a notion that your Daddy's daughter has hit upon the finest thing that there ever was since the Tribe of Tegumai took to using shark's teeth instead of flints for their spear-heads. I believe we've found out the big secret of the world.'

'Why?' said Taffy, and her eyes shone too with incitement.

'I'll show,' said her Daddy. 'What's water in the Tegumai language?'

'Ya, of course, and it means river too—like Wagai-ya—the Wagai river.'

'What is bad water that gives you fever if you drink it—black water—swamp-water?'

'Yo, of course.'

'Now look,' said her Daddy. 'S'pose you saw this scratched by the side of a pool in the beaver-swamp?' And he drew this.

'Carp-tail and round egg. Two noises mixed! Yo, bad water,' said Taffy. "Course I wouldn't drink that water because I'd know you said it was bad.'

'But I needn't be near the water at all. I might be miles away, hunting, and still—'

'And still it would be just the same as if you stood there and said, "G'way, Taffy, or you'll get fever." All that in a carp-fish-tail and a round egg! O Daddy, we must tell Mummy, quick!' and Taffy danced all round him.

'Not yet,' said Tegumai; 'not till we've gone a little further. Let's see. Yo is bad water, but So is food cooked on the fire, isn't it?' And he drew this.

'Yes. Snake and egg,' said Taffy 'So that means dinner's ready. If you saw that scratched on a tree you'd know it was time to come to the Cave. So'd I.'

'My Winkie!' said Tegumai. 'That's true too. But wait a minute. I see a difficulty. SO means "come and have dinner," but sho means the drying-poles where we hang our hides.'

'Horrid old drying-poles!' said Taffy. 'I hate helping to hang heavy, hot, hairy hides on them. If you drew the snake and egg, and I thought it meant dinner, and I came in from the wood and found that it meant I was to help Mummy hang the two hides on the drying-poles, what would I do?'

'You'd be cross. So'd Mummy. We must make a new picture for sho. We must draw a spotty snake that hisses sh-sh, and we'll play that the plain snake only hisses ssss.'

'I couldn't be sure how to put in the spots,' said Taffy. 'And p'raps if you were in a hurry you might leave them out, and I'd think it was so when it was sho, and then Mummy would catch me just the same. No! I think we'd better draw a picture of the horrid high drying-poles their very selves, and make quite sure. I'll put them in just after the hissy-snake. Look!' And she drew this.

'P'raps that's safest. It's very like our drying-poles, anyhow,' said her Daddy, laughing. 'Now I'll make a new noise with a snake and drying-pole sound in it. I'll say shi. That's Tegumai for spear, Taffy.' And he laughed.

'Don't make fun of me,' said Taffy, as she thought of her picture-letter and the mud in the Stranger-man's hair. 'You draw it, Daddy.'

'We won't have beavers or hills this time, eh?' said her Daddy, 'I'll just draw a straight line for my spear.' and he drew this.

'Even Mummy couldn't mistake that for me being killed.'

'Please don't, Daddy. It makes me uncomfy. Do some more noises. We're getting on beautifully.'

'Er-hm!' said Tegumai, looking up. 'We'll say shu. That means sky.'

Taffy drew the snake and the drying-pole. Then she stopped. 'We must make a new picture for that end sound, mustn't we?'

'Shu-shu-u-u-u!' said her Daddy. 'Why, it's just like the round-egg-sound made thin.'

'Then s'pose we draw a thin round egg, and pretend it's a frog that hasn't eaten anything for years.'

'N-no,' said her Daddy. 'If we drew that in a hurry we might mistake it for the round egg itself. Shu-shu-shu! 'I tell you what we'll do. We'll open a little hole at the end of the round egg to show how the O-noise runs out all thin, ooo-oo-oo. Like this.' And he drew this.

'Oh, that's lovely ! Much better than a thin frog. Go on,' said Taffy, using her shark's tooth. Her Daddy went on drawing, and his hand shook with incitement. He went on till he had drawn this.

'Don't look up, Taffy,' he said. 'Try if you can make out what that means in the Tegumai language. If you can, we've found the Secret.'

'Snake—pole—broken—egg—carp—tail and carp-mouth,' said Taffy. 'Shu-ya. Sky-water (rain).' Just then a drop fell on her hand, for the day had clouded over. 'Why, Daddy, it's raining. Was that what you meant to tell me?'

'Of course,' said her Daddy. 'And I told it you without saying a word, didn't I?'

'Well, I think I would have known it in a minute, but that raindrop made me quite sure. I'll always remember now. Shu-ya means rain, or "it is going to rain." Why, Daddy!' She got up and danced round him. 'S'pose you went out before I was awake, and drawed shu-ya in the smoke on the wall, I'd know it was going to rain and I'd take my beaver-skin hood. Wouldn't Mummy be surprised?'

Tegumai got up and danced. (Daddies didn't mind doing those things in those days.) 'More than that! More than that!' he said. 'S'pose I wanted to tell you it wasn't going to rain much and you must come down to the river, what would we draw? Say the words in Tegumai-talk first.'

'Shu-ya-las, ya maru. (Sky-water ending. River come to.) What a lot of new sounds! I don't see how we can draw them.'

'But I do—but I do!' said Tegumai. 'Just attend a minute, Taffy, and we won't do any more to-day. We've got shu-ya all right, haven't we? But this las is a teaser. La-la-la' and he waved his shark-tooth.

'There's the hissy-snake at the end and the carp-mouth before the snake—as-as-as. We only want la-la,' said Taffy.

'I know it, but we have to make la-la. And we're the first people in all the world who've ever tried to do it, Taffimai!'

'Well,' said Taffy, yawning, for she was rather tired. 'Las means breaking or finishing as well as ending, doesn't it?'

'So it does,' said Tegumai. 'To-las means that there's no water in the tank for Mummy to cook with—just when I'm going hunting, too.'

'And shi-las means that your spear is broken. If I'd only thought of that instead of drawing silly beaver pictures for the Stranger!'

'La! La! La!' said Tegumai, waiving his stick and frowning. 'Oh bother!'

'I could have drawn shi quite easily,' Taffy went on. 'Then I'd have drawn your spear all broken—this way!' And she drew.

'The very thing,' said Tegumai. 'That's la all over. It isn't like any of the other marks either.' And he drew this.

'Now for ya. Oh, we've done that before. Now for maru. Mum-mum-mum. Mum shuts one's mouth up, doesn't it? We'll draw a shut mouth like this.' And he drew.

'Then the carp-mouth open. That makes Ma-ma-ma! But what about this rrrrr-thing, Taffy?'

'It sounds all rough and edgy, like your shark-tooth saw when you're cutting out a plank for the canoe,' said Taffy.

'You mean all sharp at the edges, like this?' said Tegumai. And he drew.

"'Xactly,' said Taffy. 'But we don't want all those teeth: only put two.'

'I'll only put in one,' said Tegumai. 'If this game of ours is going to be what I think it will, the easier we make our sound- pictures the better for everybody.' And he drew.

'Now, we've got it,' said Tegumai, standing on one leg. 'I'll draw 'em all in a string like fish.'

'Hadn't we better put a little bit of stick or something between each word, so's they won't rub up against each other and jostle, same as if they were carps?'

'Oh, I'll leave a space for that,' said her Daddy. And very incitedly he drew them all without stopping, on a big new bit of birch-bark.

'Shu-ya-las ya-maru,' said Taffy, reading it out sound by sound.

'That's enough for to-day,' said Tegumai. 'Besides, you're getting tired, Taffy. Never mind, dear. We'll finish it all tomorrow, and then we'll be remembered for years and years after the biggest trees you can see are all chopped up for firewood.'

So they went home, and all that evening Tegumai sat on one side of the fire and Taffy on the other, drawing ya's and yo's and shu's and shi's in the smoke on the wall and giggling together till her Mummy said, 'Really, Tegumai, you're worse than my Taffy.'

'Please don't mind,' said Taffy. 'It's only our secret-s'prise, Mummy dear, and we'll tell you all about it the very minute it's done; but please don't ask me what it is now, or else I'll have to tell.'

So her Mummy most carefully didn't; and bright and early next morning Tegumai went down to the river to think about new sound pictures, and when Taffy got up she saw Ya-las (water is ending or running out) chalked on the side of the big stone water-tank, outside the Cave.

'Um,' said Taffy. 'These picture-sounds are rather a bother! Daddy's just as good as come here himself and told me to get more water for Mummy to cook with.' She went to the spring at the back of the house and filled the tank from a bark bucket, and then she ran down to the river and pulled her Daddy's left ear—the one that belonged to her to pull when she was good.

'Now come along and we'll draw all the left-over sound-pictures,' said her Daddy, and they had a most inciting day of it, and a beautiful lunch in the middle, and two games of romps. When they came to T, Taffy said that as her name, and her Daddy's, and her Mummy's all began with that sound, they should draw a sort of family group of themselves holding hands. That was all very well to draw once or twice; but when it came to drawing it six or seven times, Taffy and Tegumai drew it scratchier and scratchier, till at last the T-sound was only a thin long Tegumai with his arms out to hold Taffy and

Teshumai. You can see from these three pictures partly how it happened.

Many of the other pictures were much too beautiful to begin with, espe cially before lunch, but as they were drawn over and over again on birch-bark, they became plainer and easier, till at last even Tegumai said he could find no fault with them. They turned the hissy-snake the other way round for the Z-sound, to show it was hissing backwards in a soft and gentle way; and they just made a twiddle for E, because it came into the pictures so often; and they drew pictures of the sacred Beaver of the Tegumais for the B-sound; and because it was a nasty, nosy noise, they just drew noses for the N-sound, till they were tired; and they drew a picture of the big lake-pike's mouth for the greedy Ga-sound; and they drew the pike's mouth again with a spear behind it for the scratchy, hurty Ka-sound; and they drew pictures of a little bit of the winding Wagai river for the nice windy-windy Wa-sound; and so on and so forth and so following till they had done and drawn all the sound-pictures that they wanted, and there was the Alphabet, all complete.

And after thousands and thousands and thousands of years, and after Hieroglyphics and Demotics, and Nilotics, and Cryptics, and Cufics, and Runics, and Dorics, and Ionics, and all sorts of other ricks and tricks (because the Woons, and the Neguses, and the Akhoonds, and the Reposi-tories of Tradition would never leave a good thing alone when they saw it), the fine old easy, understandable Alphabet—A, B, C, D, E, and the rest of 'em—got back into its proper shape again for all Best Beloveds to learn when they are old enough.

But I remember Tegumai Bopsulai, and Taffimai Metallumai and Tes-humai Tewindrow, her dear Mummy, and all the days gone by. And it was so—just so—a little time ago—on the banks of the big Wagai!

Of all the Tribe of Tegumai
Who cut that figure, none remain,—
On Merrow Down the cuckoos cry
The silence and the sun remain.
But as the faithful years return
And hearts unwounded sing again,
Comes Taffy dancing through the fern
To lead the Surrey spring again.
Her brows are bound with bracken-fronds,
And golden elf-locks fly above;
Her eyes are bright as diamonds
And bluer than the skies above.
In mocassins and deer-skin cloak,

> Unfearing, free and fair she flits,
> And lights her little damp-wood smoke
> To show her Daddy where she flits.
> For far—oh, very far behind,
> So far she cannot call to him,
> Comes Tegumai alone to find
> The daughter that was all to him.

Questions

1. The late Stone Age, when this story is set, occurred in 15,000–10,000 BCE. When did writing systems originate?
2. What do you think of this origin tale of alphabets?
3. Kipling lived in the age of the British Empire. What aspects of that time and culture do you notice in this story? Are there hints of imperialism or colonialism?
4. The myth of the creation of the alphabet by Kipling privileges these letters over ideograms, depictions rather than phonemes. This might be said to be an ethnocentric view of "progress." What is lost in the evolution from ideograms or pictography to alphabets?

INTERESTED IN LEARNING MORE?

Book Recommendations

Lyn Davies, *A Is for Ox: A Short History of the Alphabet* (The Folio Society, 2006).

Akira Nakanishi, *Writing Systems of the World* (Charles E. Tuttle, 1994).

Don Robb, *Ox, House, Stick: The History of Our Alphabet* (Charlesbridge, 2007).

Andrew Robinson, *The Story of Writing: Alphabets, Hieroglyphs, and Pictograms*, 2nd ed. (Thames and Hudson, 2007).

David Sacks, *Letter Perfect: The Marvelous History of Our Alphabet from A to Z* (Broadway Books, 2004).

Film Recommendation

"A to Z: The First Alphabet," *Nova*, https://www.pbs.org/wgbh/nova/video/a-to-z-the-first-alphabet/ [54 minutes].

Chapter Four

Pencils, Pens, and Ink

> *"Every pencil has a story."*
> —Caroline Weaver, Pencil Connoisseur

PENCILS

Nuremberg, Germany, is infamous for its role in Nazism. The site of fanatical public gatherings orchestrated to support Adolf Hitler, it was also the place where notorious war criminals were tried following World War II. Yet Nuremberg also holds a less horrific title: "Pencil Capital of the World."[1] It is home to three family-owned and -operated pencil factories: Faber-Castell, Staedtler, and Stablio. The latter is fewer than 200 years old, but the others trace their origins to the seventeenth and eighteenth centuries (see Figure 4.1).

The pencil that we know today—at least in the United States—is a shaft of graphite encased in wood to which an eraser *plug* is often attached by a metal *ferrule*. In other parts of the world, rarely is an eraser integrated in the design. Although erroneously referred to as *lead*, a holdover from Roman pens, the pencil's core of graphite is a marvel that came about by accident. A storm near Borrowdale in Cumbria, England, toppled a tree, revealing a large deposit of graphite, notable for its "pure" state that could be sliced. Shepherds used it to mark their sheep, but people began seeing other uses for

---

1 The fictitious town of Stanleyville is termed the "pencil capital of the world" in the film *The Odd Life of Timothy Green* (2012). Shelbyville, Tennessee, terms itself "Pencil City," but only one of several pencil manufacturers survives: Musgrave Pencil Company.

this marvel. Wrapped in string, the graphite sticks made quite good writing instruments. In fact, this high-quality graphite became an exceedingly valued commodity. Smugglers traded it, but the graphite left incriminating marks on their hands, leading to the term *black market*.

German engineers were invited to help find further deposits but returned home to suggest that their own country might enter the burgeoning pencil market. Friedrich Staedtler applied to the Nuremberg Council in 1662 for permission to manufacture pencils using an innovative process: encasing the graphite in a wooden core. The council rejected his proposal, noting that the production would cross guilds, which owned exclusive rights to professions like carpentry. Undeterred, Staedtler proceeded anyway. Each pencil was constructed of a square-shaped graphite core, two wooden slats, and glue. The pencil maker inserted the graphite between the two grooved wooden parts, glued it, and then tied it with string and wax until the pencil dried. The end result looked something like the square carpenter's pencil of today. Without the pure graphite of England, Ger-

Figure 4.1
Pencil-making
workshop.

man production innovated, crushing the inferior but available graphite and mixing it with clay.

The Nuremberg Council realized its error when the lucrative pencil business started to gain traction. In 1675, Staedtler was granted citizen rights for his accomplishments. Staedtler was joined by Faber-Castell, which terms itself the "world's oldest pencil manufacturer." Kaspar Faber (1730–84) was a cabinetmaker (i.e., a member of the carpenter guild), who produced pencils on the side, but the enterprise proved so successful that he established a company that took off in the late eighteenth century and continues to be successful today.

The quest for good-quality graphite for the core of the pencil continued. The French, specifically Nicholas-Jacques Conté (1755–1805), refined the formula for graphite mixed with clay in 1795, although it would never come up to the standard of the "rare English pencils." Faber pencils acquired mineral rights to Siberian graphite in 1856. Transported by reindeer from the mountains, the graphite made a long journey via the Pacific, Indian, and Atlantic Oceans before arriving in Hamburg. The wooden shafts came

Figure 4.2
Pencil seller,
1810.

Fliegender Händler um 1810

from Florida trees—truly an international product. The fourth generation of Fabers not only outsourced materials but also instituted the modernization of production and developed a marketing scheme with an iconic illustration of two knights jousting—one with a Castell pencil and one with a broken inferior brand (see Figure 4.3).

Figure 4.3   Jousting Knights Logo of Faber-Castell.

The company was modern in its thinking for the mid-nineteenth century. Working conditions included light and airy buildings for healthier employees. Male employees focused on more strenuous duties, while women oversaw end processes of engraving and packaging. Children attended a kindergarten; a company health insurance program was established, as was a pension program; comfortable housing, a library, and a grocery store provided a standard of living unusual for the time.

Faber's international reach extended to the United States. Although theirs was not the first pencil factory in the country when it was established during the Civil War in Brooklyn, Faber had a significant global reputation. The pencil industry in the United States was centered in New England, where in 1812, William Munroe (1778–1861) invented a machine to cut and groove wooden slats. A graphite paste filled the wooden hollow. Unfortunately, the quality of these pencils was below standard. That changed when, a few years later, the J. Thoreau Company (see Figure 4.4) produced "Best Quality Pencils, for drawing or writing, and all the purposes required of a good pencil." The son of the Thoreau Company family, Henry David Thoreau (1817–62), researched possible formulas for better pencils in the Harvard Library. The inferior mix of graphite with wax and other components was replaced by the formula of graphite and clay—the recipe that Conté had discovered. The Thoreau pencil became the standard, with a harder, darker core than others. He also designed a graphite grinding machine and a boring machine to drill the core in the wooden casing so that the lead slipped inside. The success of the Thoreau Pencil reaped financial awards for the family—and allowed Henry David to take time off and live at Walden Pond.

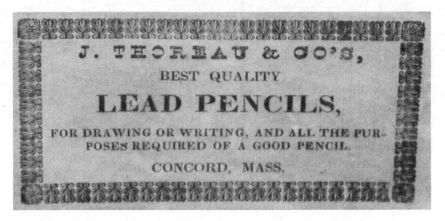

Figure 4.4   Thoreau Pencil Company packaging.

Colored pencils were pioneered by Faber-Castell (a Castell having married into the founding pencil family). Even when the pencil industry suffered losses, as when the ballpoint pen rage took hold after World War II, the line of colored pencils has held up its end. The popularity of adult coloring books in the twenty-first century, for instance, has revived an interest in the pencil. Another innovation was the mechanical pencil, which offered the possibility of replacing the graphite when it ran out and did not require sharpening. Its point could be extended with just a click.

In Europe, Faber-Castell and Staedtler shops cleverly market their products, particularly for gifts, using packaging that appeals to children or that celebrates birthdays, holidays, and other events.

In the days of electric pencil sharpeners, perhaps the notion of artisanal-crafted pencil sharpening seems outlandish (see Figure 4.5). But no: David Rees practices manual pencil sharpening. A former cartoonist, Rees approaches the task of American-made pencil sharpening with deadpan humor with his manual on pencil sharpening, which includes a chapter on—for experts only—a behind-the-head technique. If pencil satire is appealing, then Rees's book is a must-buy.

Figure 4.5   How to Sharpen Pencils (2012) by David Rees.

FROM PENCILS TO PENS

People often refer to the *lead* in pencils; however, as mentioned above, the core is graphite, not lead. Why, then, do people continue to call it lead? It's a holdover from ancient Rome, where the stylus used for writing was made of lead. The Romans used lead for several products, including cooking vessels and water pipes. The lead stylus may have left marks on parchment or be used to record on wax tablets. The wax tablet was generally made of two pieces bound together with rope or string so that it closed like a book, the wooden frame being filled with wax. Perhaps the most famous depiction of the wax tablet and stylus is the fresco housed in the National Archeological Museum of Naples, "Woman with wax tablets and stylus" from Pompeii, Italy (50–79 CE), which was unearthed in 1760 when the buried city had been discovered and was being excavated (see Figure 4.6).

Figure 4.6
"Woman with wax tablets and stylus" from Pompeii, Italy (50-79 CE).

In *Empire of Letters: Writing in Roman Literature and Thought from Lucretius to Ovid*, author Stephanie Frampton puts forward the idea that writing technologies influenced how Romans "thought about thought." Students practiced writing the alphabet and syllables using wax tablets. Unlike paper, the information on wax tablets had to be erased each time to make way for the next lesson. This drove an emphasis on memory. In classifying the aspects of writing, Aristotle (fourth century BCE) included invention (what is often termed *prewriting* by contemporary rhetoricians), style, arrangement, audience, memory, and delivery. It should be noted that rhetoric originally focused almost exclusively on oratory. These were the times of great speeches and speech-makers. Much later, even as late as the twentieth century, rhetoric began to shift to a focus on writing rather than oratory. The contemporary technique of memory palaces that help people through mnemonic[2] devices draws on the relationship between concepts and locations. Cicero (first century BCE), one of the greatest orators and writers of all time, used the memory palace technique to commit his speeches to memory. Frampton writes that tablets became a metaphor for how our minds work: "The mind is like a wax tablet where you can write and erase and rewrite."

The stylus used in Rome was a descendent of the earlier Mesopotamian version, which depended on reeds that grew alongside rivers. They were

---

2 Mnemonic (the "m" is silent) is derived from Mnemosyne, the Greek goddess of memory. A mnemonic device helps remember a concept or fact. For instance, in grade school, I learned to spell *arithmetic* by this mnemonic device: **a rat in the house may eat the ice cream.**

sliced, and the ends were made into sharp points. The cut end made a wedge-shaped mark on the clay tablets used to record cuneiform. In fact, the name cuneiform is derived from the word *wedge*. The instructions for making a pen out of a reed—such as a cattail—are fairly simple. Once the reed is cut, remove any detritus and cut to about an eight-inch length. The end that will function as the *nib*—the writing end—is soaked in water. The goal is to have a square end. This requires slicing the reed to a tapered end. The interior of the reed is scraped so that only the tube is left. The tricky part is getting the nib shape by cutting at an angle while still leaving a flat end. This flat, square end is trimmed across its width with a sharp knife (like a box cutter). Finally, the tip is split, again with a very sharp knife. The purpose is to allow ink to flow from the hollow part of the reed. Shaving the tip smoothly ensures a finer line of writing. Once the pen is dry, it can be refined further with scraping. Then ink is put in the reed channel carefully. This is not a large reservoir, so the reed pen needs to be re-inked often. The actual writing requires a light touch, not the hard pressure that writers tend to use with ballpoint pens.

The Roman lead stylus did not use ink at all. This made it more attractive to some writers, as a secondary source was not needed. Instead, its sharp point was used to write on wax tablets, or the lead itself could leave a mark on papyrus, particularly useful for drawing lines for the text. Because of its design, the stylus drew straight lines, not the curves typical of cursive. The look of the Roman alphabet was thus influenced by the writing tool. The top of the stylus was usually blunted so that it could be used to "erase" the writing on tablets by rubbing across the text, creating friction, which literally melted the wax.

Note that in digital writing, the electronic writing instrument is named a *stylus*, developed for touch-screen *tablets*. This kind of stylus looks familiar, as it is typically shaped like a very small ink pen, but no ink flows from it. It is a throwback to the Roman lead stylus. Instead, the pressure of touching the stylus to a flat surface such as a monitor, mobile device, or tablet allows the person to write or draw. No longer a wax tablet, the digital tablet provides a more mobile tool than a desktop or laptop computer, and, frankly, the stylus may not be needed at all, as a person's finger can swipe right or left, or can write or sign.

Quill Pens

The rise of the quill pen was due to its ability to hold more ink so that writers had to "dip" less. The hollow of the feather held the ink. Whether the writer was left-handed or right-handed determined the side of the goose, swan, turkey, or even peacock from which feathers were drawn for pens. Quill pens were used for a very long time. Egyptian scribes are shown with these instruments, and Romans used quill pens to write on vellum around 200 BCE. In fact, the word *pen* itself comes from a Latin word meaning feather. These writing implements and an accompanying vial of ink were commonplace until the nineteenth century, when steel nibs replaced them. Until that time, the feather pen had outperformed other metal nibs, even though that latter had been used as early as the days of Pompeii.

Producing quill pens became an important industry. One successful site was Auvillar, France, a quaint medieval town in the southwest region of the country that produced hundreds of thousands of *plumes d'oie* (goose feathers) at its height. The village had an accessible port on the Garonne River, crucial to exporting its products. It also sits on the pilgrimage route, known as the *Chemin de Saint Jacques Compostelle*. The region is also famous for its *foie gras*, goose liver, a delicacy that dates back to ancient Egyptians and Romans. In addition to harvested birds, feathers were often obtained when the birds molted. The supply of feathers provided the stuff needed for the village to become famous for its writing implements.

The complex process of transitioning from the feather or quill to a writing instrument changed over the centuries but had the goal of creating a more rigid shaft, which would last longer. The primary feathers made the best pens, and goose feathers were preferred, although crow feathers were used at times for the more delicate handwriting of ladies. In the thirteenth century, according to the Auvillar museum, quills were *clarified*. They were bound together in a bundle and placed in a stew pot to steam for one hour. Then the feathers were dried by a fire. The second day, the quill was scraped with the back of a knife and smoothed with a woolen cloth. After several days, these feathers hardened for cutting the ends to form the nib. The Dutch apparently preferred dipping quills into hot sand to harden the barrel and dry the inner membrane so it could be extracted (see Figure 4.7).

In the seventeenth-century version of clarification, the craftsperson started by removing the outer skin of the feather by scratching and then cutting off its end. Then it was immersed in boiling water containing alum and salt. After 15 minutes, it was dried in a pan of hot sand and then in an oven. In the eighteenth century, the preferred process was called *quenching*, that is, moistening the feathers for some hours or days prior to heating the feather or a flame, which helped in removing the membrane covering what would become the reservoir. The feather was rubbed, polished, and filed. Pens were bundled and shipped to stationers' stores, where finishers might complete the work on the tip so that they were ready to use and sell.

If a person found an appropriate feather and wanted to make a quill pen

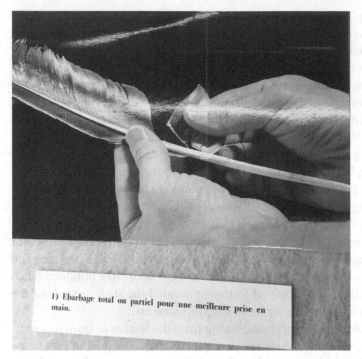

1) Ebarbage total ou partiel pour une meilleure prise en main.

Figure 4.7 Explanatory illustration on quill making, Pencil Museum, Auvillar, France. [Translation: For better handling, remove all or some of the feathers.]

today, the steps are fairly straightforward. (Craft shops often carry such feathers.) The pen maker begins by *dressing* the quill, which means removing the lower feathers for an easier handhold (see Figure 4.7). Then a *pen knife* (or a box cutter) is used to scrape off the membrane covering this surface. The first cut slices the tip at an acute angle, opening up the shaft so that the interior *quick* can be extracted. A second cut is made similar to the first but shorter and at a blunter angle. Just as with a reed pen, a slit must be cut into the center of the tip to allow ink to flow. Depending on the desired width of line to be written, the pen is trimmed to a fine point or a broader one for calligraphy. Over the life of the quill pen—which is admittedly limited—the tip can be trimmed and sharpened.

Many paintings of the era depict writers using the quill pen, and some show a scholar sharpening one, a particularly popular subject with seventeenth-century painter Gerrit Dou (see Figure 4.8). The act of sharpening the pen could be a metaphor for sharpening the intellect, preparing to move thoughts to words. For well-off writers, a boy assistant most likely kept the supply of pens sharpened for consistent writing.

Figure 4.8   "The Scholar Sharpening a Quill Pen" by Gerrit Dou (1633).

The material on which the writing implement is employed determines in part what tool is used. The quill pen had a natural affinity for vellum and parchment. As wood-based paper came into mass production in the late nineteenth century, the quill did not perform nearly as well on this surface, but the metal nib did. The fineness of the line also determined the writing tool. Asian characters and calligraphy called for a brush or a broad-tipped pen, while other scripts required a finer point.

The quill pen had a long period of use from approximately 600 to 1900 CE. A real drawback of the feathered writing tool and the metal nib that followed, however, was its lack of portability and efficiency: It had to be accompanied by a bottle of ink. The *dip pen*, as its name implies, had to be dipped into ink, as it typically did not have an ink reservoir. How could the two components become one in a more effectual package? The fountain pen was the answer.

Fountain Pens

Although Leonardo da Vinci's (1452–1519) drawings include a pen with a reservoir and various instances followed that Renaissance invention, the fountain pen did not become mass produced until the mid-nineteenth century. Designers had to overcome issues with the corrosive nature of iron gall ink and understand the physics of air and gravity for an even flow. Fountain pens rely upon the same capillary action that made reed and quill pens function.

The people who can be credited for the development of the fountain pen resided in various places around the world. Petrache Poenaru (1799–1875), a Romanian, received a patent in 1827 for a pen that used the barrel of a large swan quill. In North America, Azel Storrs Lyman (1815–85) got a patent in 1848 for a pen with an ink reservoir. The Waterman Company of New York City, which still exists, began to dominate the field with its refined pen in the 1880s. Even with the combined pen and ink, filling the reservoir could be messy, so an eyedropper was used to make the transfer. Clearly, a pen that could be self-filling was needed. These began around the turn of the twentieth century, with the Sheaffer and Parker models out in front. Eventually, no-mess ink cartridges that could be easily inserted into the pen's core were developed.

The fountain pen—even with leakage issues—dominated until the 1960s and is still used by many. By that point, though, the ballpoint pen had cornered the market as the preferred everyday writing instrument.

Ballpoint Pens

Elizabeth Wein's popular novel *Code Name Verity* (2012) integrates the story of how the ballpoint pen achieved success. The book focuses on two young British women in World War II, one—Queenie—a spy who is captured in France by the Gestapo, interrogated, and tortured. She is given a pencil as well as an inkwell and dip pen to write her story, spinning out tales like Scheherazade to delay her execution. Her friend Maddie, a civilian pilot who transports planes for the Royal Air Force, desperately tries to rescue Queenie. She is also behind enemy lines but hidden in a barn, where she, too, is writing—but with a ballpoint pen. She says of the writing instrument: "It's called an Eterpen, a truly wonderful thing, no messy ink to refill and it dries instantly. He said they have ordered 30,000 of them for the RAF to use in the air.... Maddie was ridiculously pleased with her pen" (49–50).

The story behind the ballpoint pen almost sounds like fiction, but it's true. Who would imagine that the invention of the ballpoint pen features the Nazis, the Royal Air Force, and Argentina? László Bíró (1899–1985) was a Hungarian journalist who invented the ballpoint pen out of frustration from having to refill his fountain pen so often. Because he worked at a newspaper, he noticed that the ink used on newsprint dried quickly with no smudges. He enlisted the help of his brother, Georg, a chemist, to create a pen that used this same ink in a cartridge feeding it to a rotating ball (bearing) on its tip, replacing the traditional nib. The invention was patented on June 15, 1938. But the brothers were Jewish. They escaped Hitler and fled to South America in 1941, where they set up their company Bíró Pens of Argentina, marketing the pens under the brand name *Birome* (a term still used in Argentina for pens).

The British Air Command had difficulty with fountain pens at high altitudes and was searching for a better tool. They invested in the upstart company, which made the Bíró Company's future. The Bíró pens were immediately popular and gained appeal beyond the flying squads. Not surprisingly, other companies wanted in on this attractive tool; some paid for rights while others simply copied the design. Notably, Frenchman Michel Bich (1914–94) paid a royalty to the Bíró company in 1950 and brought out his own pens in 1952, shortening the name of the brand to Bic, which continues to dominate the market. The era of the disposable ink pen had arrived.

Two other innovations in pens are felt-tip and gel pens. The former traded the metal ball for felt, which is porous. Marker pens, so-called "magic markers," which had thicker tips for wider marks, came out on the market in 1953. These evolved into specific uses for highlighting, writing on whiteboards, and creating permanent labels. The fine-tip felt pen was developed in 1962 by Yukio Horie of the Tokyo Stationery Company, and the *Pentel* (a pen to tell a story) became the standard. The *Fude Pen* is an example of how the type of writing determines the instrument. A brush or fiber tip makes the Fude appropriate for calligraphy, but it looks much like a regular pen. The *Sign Pen* has a cult following in Japan, as that felt-tipped pen is designed more for writing, particularly Japanese characters, but offers more flair, like an artist's pen. The pen uses ink that is gel-based, offering permanence yet smoothness.

HANDWRITING

When I was asked during the writing of this book what the subject was and answered, "It's about the history of writing," almost every person assumed it was about *handwriting*. The intensity of learning to write by hand is still uppermost in some people's minds. Handwriting continues to be under scrutiny even in a digital world. Admittedly having a vested interest in handwriting, the Bic pen company launched a campaign to promote handwriting.

Studies have shown that handwriting does promote cognitive development, motor skills, writing skills, and comprehension. Researchers Mueller and Oppenheimer found that students taking notes by hand as opposed to typing had to process the information and condense it, and that thinking was useful to learning the material. Note-taking involves "summarizing, paraphrasing, and concept mapping" as opposed to transcribing.

Another debated topic is whether cursive handwriting should be taught to schoolchildren, or if print is sufficient. Although not being able to decode cursive script seems a liability, others may be happy to do away with the Palmer Method, the laborious drills to master letters.[3] Likewise, *penmanship* is no longer in a golden age. When I was in grade school, the students in my class competed to see whose thank you notes were the most elegant— to send to the parents (read: mothers) who brought treats to the class for their child's birthday. It was a rite of passage to move from print to cursive. Florey writes a history of the rise and fall of handwriting in her *Script and Scribble*. She argues that handwriting is "beautiful, useful, and historically important." Truly beautiful handwriting was the art of the engraver, such as George Bickham (1684–1758), renowned "penman," whose book *The Universal Penman* popularized the English Round Hand, full of flourishes and panache. This kind of penmanship was featured on official documents, and a twentieth-century college in Zanesville, Ohio taught its students—primarily male—how to achieve these beautiful results until the widespread use of typewriters and then computers.

The removal of cursive from the school curriculum is sometimes blamed on the need to have time for keyboarding skills or the national core curriculum, which does not include handwriting in its standards. Some schools and even lawmakers have reacted negatively to the loss. One outgrowth of the lack of training in cursive in schools is the rise in private instruction—often by teachers—for those students who, by their own choice or that of their parents, want to continue the script tradition. Handwriting without Tears, which is part of a larger curriculum termed "Learning without Tears" (see www. lwtears.com/), offers instructional materials for both print and cursive. This may be the ticket for those who find learning to write script a bit masochistic.

Josh Giesbrecht, a teacher, believes he knows what killed cursive, and it wasn't standards but the ballpoint pen itself. In an article in *The Atlantic*, he cites the less fluid ink of the ballpoint pen—in contrast to the fountain

---

3   Named for the famous American "penman" Austin Palmer (1860–1927), who authored a guide on writing for business (1894), the Palmer Method sought to replace the more elaborate Spencerian Method of writing, particularly for business letters. Palmer's approach was plainer and thus more efficient. By this time, handwriting was beginning to compete with typewriting. The Palmer Method was very popular and remained in vogue until the 1950s.

pen—and the grip needed to move the pen across the page. He recommends revisiting the "historical use of ordinary technologies as a way to understand contemporary ones."

INK

When my husband, David, was in fourth grade in a small-town school in Pennsylvania, he had a reputation as a mischievous lad. The old-fashioned desks were bolted to the floor in straight lines, pupils sitting in a row. Attached to the front of the desk was the folding seat for the next pupil. Each wooden desk could be lifted for storage, and the surface featured a shallow depression for pencil and pen as well as a place for the inkwell. These young scholars had to dip their pens in the ink to practice forming the alphabet, as illustrated in a border above the blackboard. Almost every school and classroom featured the ABC's posted in this manner, and students learned to write in cursive through the Palmer Method.

The girl seated in front of David had long blond braids that dangled enticingly on his desktop. The temptation was too great: He uncapped the inkwell and dipped each of the braids into the black India ink. The punishment was swift; the teacher taking her paddle and giving him a wallop on the backside. The days of corporal punishment, cursive handwriting instruction, and young scholars seated in fixed desks may be gone, but India ink perseveres.

Although used primarily by artists and the medical profession at this time, India ink at one time ruled the writing world. Ironically, its source was not India but China, notable for so many of the innovations in early writing. Ink has been in use for over forty centuries, which is also the title of an important scholarly volume on the history of the substance (Carvalho). Two theories exist as to how India got credit for this important component of writing. One is that China obtained some of the ingredients for the manufacture of ink from India. A second is that the British interpreted ink as coming from India. Sometimes India or Indian ink is referred to as *Chinese ink*, but graphic artist David Lance Goines's poster of the iconic India ink bottle confirms that most give credit to India (see Figure 4.9).

Figure 4.9 David Lance Goines, "India Ink" (1974).

In fact, both China and Egypt were using ink by 2000 BCE or even earlier. These leading civilizations had a demand for both writing and drawing. The recipe for making ink included carbon black and a glue to bind; the carbon may have been lampblack or soot, while the glue was most likely from animal hides. In China, solid ink sticks were preferred; a wet brush rubbed against the stick liquefied it for use. Recall that the Chinese alphabet featured logographs, so a brush was the chosen instrument. In other words, the alphabet determined the form of the ink. It is important to note that the development of paper or paper-like material had to go hand-in-hand with the invention of ink. The type of ink had to be matched to the writing material, whether that was papyrus, bark, or rag-based paper.

Egyptian scribes used reeds to write, so fluid ink was essential. A scribe's writing tools are depicted in ancient sculptures, one way in which their craft was understood. The posture for scribes is famously depicted in museum pieces, sitting cross-legged with their linen skirt pulled tight across their lap. They might be said to be the first version of a "laptop" for composing. The motivation for developing this medium—as opposed to carving in stone or making marks in wet clay as in cuneiform—was an easier way to document government, legal, economic, and religious information. It was thought in countries that practiced Buddhism that producing these religious texts in itself was a form of worship. That philosophy is also true of medieval monks who were copying scriptures and other religious texts.

Eventually, two approaches to making ink evolved. One involved carbon, glue, and water, as developed by the Chinese. The second drew on tannin from gallnuts as an essential ingredient, along with iron sulfate, gum, and water. The latter became the standard for ink; however, the problem with this type was its interaction with paper. Its corrosiveness can actually damage paper over time. As a result, some medieval manuscripts that used the older recipe are still readable, while more recent texts may have faded.

As technologies for printing developed, new formulas for ink had to be developed. The standard ink of Gutenberg's time was inappropriate to his printing press. He continued to use soot or lampblack but added oil, varnish, and egg whites. Later, printer's ink evolved to include soot, turpentine, and walnut oil.

In his *Forty Centuries of Ink*, Carvalho includes numerous recipes, or "receipts" as he terms them, for ink. One of his favorites is made from pomegranates and comes from Persia:

Of the dried Pommegranite (apple) rind take an ounce, boil it in a pint of water until 3/4 be gone; add 1/2 pint of small beer wort and once more boil it away so that only a 1/4 pint remain. After you shall have strained it, boiling hot through a linnen cloth and it comes cold, being then of a glutinous consistence, drop in a 'bit' of Sal Alkali and add as much warm water as will bring it to a due fluidity and a gold brown color for writing with a pen. (57)

A "green" approach to ink is made from soybeans, which are more environmentally friendly than petroleum-based ink. Soy ink came to the fore in the 1970s during the early days of the environmental movement, but it was also driven by high petroleum prices from oil-producing companies. Soy ink is said to produce brighter colors for advertisements and is especially useful in newspaper production, where its slower-drying properties are not a disadvantage due to the nature of the paper.

Although it might seem that ink has gone out of style, the US Secret Service doesn't think so. Its International Ink Laboratory, named in honor of Dr. Antonio A. Cantu—who would be to ink what Dard Hunter is to paper—has more than 15,000 samples dating back 85 years, used to help solve crimes. (Hunter makes a more extended appearance in Chapter Five.) The lab can date ink, even from the nineteenth century, and also determine authors of threatening letters (Voice of America).

One last note about ink: the pocket protector. Known as a nerd fashion accessory, pocket protectors to hold pens that have the potential to leak were invented during World War II by Hurley Smith. They became popular with college students, particularly engineers, as well as those in industries that needed quick access to pens. With the rise of computers, they became less necessary.

ERASURE

The father of author Saul Bellow (1915–2005) disapproved of Bellow's writerly aspirations, telling him, "It's just writing, then erasing. What kind of profession is that?"[4] Bellow won the Nobel Prize for Literature, the Pulitzer Prize, and the National Book Award—the latter an unprecedented three times.

How does a writer get rid of unwanted writing? Sure, now, we can hit the delete button, but what happened before computers? In early days, an *erasing knife* or sandstone scraped away unwanted text. Or it might have been washed off. This was not only to correct errors but also sometimes to re-use the parchment or vellum, given that these materials were costly. Paper on which the original writing shows through barely is termed a *palimpsest.*

---

4 Quoted in *The Writer's Almanac*, 10 June 2019. http://www.garrisonkeillor.com/radio/twa-the-writers-almanac-for-june-10-2019/.

Sometimes the original is more valuable than the new text, which has led modern scholars to seek ways to discover what was effaced, aided by modern technology such as digitized images.

Another erasure method used bread. Yes, bread was moistened and wadded to remove writing. In 1770, Joseph Priestley (1733–1804) discovered a better eraser when he reached for a ball of moist bread and instead grabbed a ball of India gum. He found that it "rubbed" the text away much better than the bread. And, thus, the "rubber" was born, a term still preferred in the United Kingdom to the American term, eraser. While Priestley[5] made the discovery, British engineer Edward Nairne (1726–1806) is generally credited with developing and marketing the first rubber eraser in Europe. It took Charles Goodyear (1800–60)—think tires—to invent a method of curing the rubber, in a process termed vulcanization, to make it less crumbly and more sturdy. Meanwhile in America, why not be efficient and package the writing and erasing elements together? In 1858, Hymen Lipman (1817–93) patented the eraser *plug* that is attached to the wooden shaft with a *ferrule*.

The typewriter eraser wheel with an attached brush tried to do the same for the keyboard.[6] It was an awkward process to make corrections. In my day, when we used manual or electric typewriters, we turned to other erasure methods. In 1956, Bette Nesmith Graham (1924–80), a single mother who worked as a typist, sought a way to cover up her poor typing skills. She invented the first correction fluid (Liquid Paper) in her kitchen. Her fortune funded the music lessons and guitar for son Michael Nesmith (b. 1942)—a founding member of The Monkees, a popular 1960s band.

WRITING IMPLEMENTS, WAR, AND TRADE

Nuremberg's role as the "pencil capital of the world" was pushed aside during World War II, but throughout history, wars have had a deleterious effect on the production of writing implements. Napoleon's reign resulted in 20 years of war and political instability in Europe. At the same time, the stellar graphite deposits in England were being depleted. Coupled with reduced trade due to warring factions, the quality of German pencils suffered. The same result was felt in the young United States. The new technology of a graphite–clay mix invented near the end of the eighteenth century offered

---

5   Priestley may also have been the recipient of the first steel pen. Samuel Harrison, a manufacturer in Birmingham, England, made a pen for the chemist in 1780 (Daniels 313).

6   Claes Oldenburg (b. 1929) and Coosje van Bruggen (1942–2009), sculptors famous for large-scale versions of common objects, created a marvelous *Typewriter Eraser, Scale X* (1999), which is included in the National Gallery of Art Sculpture Garden. Ironically, its purpose may not be recognized by those who never had to roll the platen of a typewriter to make corrections.

gradations in hardness and softness for pencils, customizing the result. Think #2 pencil.

Likewise, the Civil War, with its Atlantic Ocean blockades, wreaked havoc on markets. German manufacturer Faber dispatched one brother, Eberhard (1822–79), to establish a pencil industry in New York. The trademark rights were lost to the Faber family as a result of World War I due to anti-German sentiment and not regained until 1994. Ironically, it was the same branch of this German family that brought the Bíró pen to the United States.

CONCLUDING THOUGHTS

Writing implements are tools that we take for granted. These inventions and innovations are not generally celebrated, but for millennia they have advanced communication and occupy an important place in our history, not only for their work but also for the documents produced as a result. Some contemporary authors continue to prefer analog to digital. Actress and writer Emma Thompson, responding to an interview question in *Parade* (July 2008), jested, "I'm a Luddite, and I write longhand with an old fountain pen" (qtd. in Reynolds). Stephen King concludes his novel *Dreamcatcher* (2001) with this author's note: "This book was written with the world's finest word processor, a Waterman cartridge fountain pen." The horror writer claims that a traditional pen and ink put him "in touch with language" (692).

QUESTIONS TO CONSIDER

1. The pencil is derived from the Latin *pencillum* for a fine brush. The word *crayon* is derived from the French term for pencil. What other word origins have surprised you as you have been reading this history of writing?
2. This chapter addresses several implements used to produce writing but not all. What is the history of blackboard chalk? When did it make an appearance? Are there other writing tools not mentioned?

DO-IT-YOURSELF HANDS-ON ACTIVITIES

Detailed directions and videos on these processes are readily accessible online.

1. Make a reed pen using a cattail or another appropriate plant.
2. Make a quill pen. While goose feathers can be rather pricey, turkey feathers are reasonably priced and often available at craft stores.
3. Follow one of the recipes and make ink, preferably to use with a quill pen.

INVITATION TO REFLECT AND WRITE

This is the first of several short essays inviting you to explore a topic about writing in more depth. This essay may be integrated into the writing auto-ethnography from Chapter One.

1. Writing implements—pencils, pens—are considered part of the *material culture* of writing. Material culture can be described as objects that humans use to survive, define social relationships, represent facets of identity, or benefit social or economic standing. For instance, some writers spend large amounts of money on fountain pens.

    Choose your favorite writing implement among pencils and pens for the focus of this essay. Why do you like it? What are the characteristics that make it valuable to you? If you are noncommittal on a favorite writing implement, then explain why that is. What do your choices say about you and your values? If you admire a certain writing implement, what is its history, its corporate identity? What is your history with this writing implement? When did you settle on a preferred writing implement?

    Research through primary and secondary sources can strengthen the narrative, for instance, information about the company that produces a particular writing instrument. It is possible, for instance, to locate the patent application for a particular pen and include its drawings in the essay.

2. The material culture of writing can inspire responses in a number of genres. Read the following ode to a pencil by Kimiko Hahn, which appeared in the Academy of American Poets' "Shelter in Place" program during the coronavirus pandemic and then later in the weekly "Teach This Poem" initiative.

    To a No. 2 Yellow Pencil on May 1, 2020
    —Kimiko Hahn

    To see you is to smell
    your wood and lead shavings
    that spill from the gray
    metal pencil sharpener
    nailed to the window sill
    in Mrs. Rote's classroom—
    all these decades ago. Today,
    my mechanical one, empty,

with no shopping in sight,
I declare I hold you dear.

The Teach This Poem instructions suggest that students take a closer look at their school supplies. What do you "hold dear" among those supplies or the objects that you use to write? Consider writing your own ode, a formal address to a thing, place, or person, such as Keats's famous poem "Ode on a Grecian Urn" or work by Sappho. What other genres might be useful in celebrating (or even lambasting in an ironic tone) an item of writing's material culture?

FOR FURTHER READING

The British Royal Air Force found a solution in the Bíró pens produced during World War II. Another challenge for air travel was the one faced by astronauts. In addition to needing a writing tool that could work in weightless conditions, it had to be safe—unable to contribute to a fire in an oxygen-rich environment. This essay was authored by an intern at the Smithsonian and uncovers the process by which NASA found a solution. If you were to write an explanatory essay similar to this one that would shine a light on a piece of history, or on a Smithsonian or other museum artifact, what would it be?

Caleb Wong, "The Saga of Writing in Space"

Deconstructing a Myth

From dashing off a quick note to creating painstaking calligraphy, we often take writing for granted. But in space, where the stakes are high, how does one write? After all, the ink in pens isn't held down by gravity, so how do you write upside down?

This is a question that some have pondered since the United States and the Russians sought to reach space first. There's a rumor that the United States spent $12 billion developing a pen that would function in space because normal ballpoint pens were not reliable in zero gravity, while the Soviets used a pencil.

While it might make for a good parable—after all, simple solutions often work better than costly, high-tech ones—the story is false.

In fact, both the Soviets and the Americans used pencils on space-flights. Starting with Project Gemini, NASA's second human spaceflight program, pencils were attached via retractable strings to the walls of the

---

command module. The astronauts used these writing utensils in space to write mission reports, conduct post-mission analysis, or record anomalies on fireproof paper. The pencils were generally safe to use, but they came at a huge cost: NASA paid $4,382.50 for 34 mechanical pencils from Tycam Engineering Manufacturing in Houston, or $128.89 per pencil.

Inventing a Zero Gravity Pen

Inventor Paul Fisher would provide more options with standardized, innovative pens. Unsatisfied with the state of ballpoint pens in the 1950s, which all took different cartridges and often leaked, he decided to invent a universal refill that would fit in most pens. Then he took it a step further and created a refill using semisolid thixotropic ink to create a pen in which the ink would turn from a gel into a liquid when the writer applied pressure. The nitrogen in the pen pressurized the ink cartridge, enabling writing in any direction. It seemed like a perfect fit for astronauts who needed to write notes on flight logs while weightless in space, so Fisher offered to supply these pens to NASA in 1965.

Pens and Safety

When testing the pens, NASA had to keep in the mind the tragic Apollo 1 test mission in 1967, which killed three astronauts when a fire blazed through the command module. The space agency learned that even a single spark could cause a fire in a 100 percent oxygen environment. Every material object on a spacecraft, including seemingly mundane writing instruments, had to be retooled for travel into space.

"NASA made sure everything on board was not dangerous," said curator Jennifer Levasseur, who curates small astronaut equipment. "In that kind of atmosphere, anytime there's a spark, anything that could serve as a fuel would catch really quickly."

After rigorous tests, NASA decided to purchase 400 pens at a cost of $6 each (a 40 percent discount) for the 1967 Apollo 7 mission, fulfilling both cost and safety requirements. Modifying them for space, NASA wrapped them in Velcro so they could stick to the astronaut's suits or the walls for easy access. The Soviet Union also decided to upgrade their writing utensils. They purchased 100 Fisher pens and 1,000 ink cartridges for use on its Soyuz spaceflights; beforehand, the Soviet astronauts used grease pencils.

Possibly wanting even more variety, astronauts also brought felt-tip pens—they work much like Sharpies—from the Duro Space Company of Brooklyn, New York, on the Apollo missions.

How a Pen Saved the Apollo 11 Mission

Pens In space not only recorded information, they even helped astro nauts get off the Moon. In his book *Magnificent Desolation,* Buzz Aldrin recounted that he couldn't turn on the ascent module to get off the Moon on the 1969 Apollo 11 mission. The circuit breaker that turned the engine on had broken. He had no idea what to do. Houston's mission control didn't either. But he had a felt tip pen made by the Duro Pen Company attached with a small piece of Velcro to the shoulder pocket in his coveralls. After a sleepless night, Aldrin had a eureka moment: he realized he could insert the pen where the small circuit breaker should have been. "We were going to get off the Moon, after all," wrote Aldrin. Even mundane objects can be used for extraordinary things.

The Future of Pens in Space

If you want a piece of history, mere earthbound mortals can buy an "Original Astronaut Space Pen" for $59 today. But in the future, will these pens become artifacts or will they remain vital tools in space? It's unclear. "They do use laptops extensively, so it's entirely possible that they are generating most their documentation electronically and sending them via email," Levesseur said of astronauts working at the International Space Station. Some are probably old fashioned, however, and still like to keep handwritten notes, or draw or sketch up there, she added.

Even if pens no longer go up in space, they will still have a special place in the heart of at least one astronaut. After all, you might say that the Buzz Aldrin's felt-tip pen may have saved the Apollo 11 mission.

INTERESTED IN LEARNING MORE?

Book Recommendations

Pencils

Allan Ahlberg, *The Pencil* (Candlewick, 2012). [Children's book.]

Adam Braun, *The Promise of a Pencil* (Scribner, 2015).

Henry Petroski, *The Pencil: A History of Design and Circumstance* (Knopf, 1992).

Caroline Weaver, *Pencils You Should Know: A History of the Ultimate Writing Utensil in 75 Anecdotes* (Chronicle Books, 2020).

————, *The Pencil Perfect: The Untold Story of a Cultural Icon* (Gestalten, 2017).

Writing Accessories

Ian Spellerberg, *Reading and Writing Accessories: A Study of Paper-Knives, Paper Folders, Letter Openers and Mythical Page Turners* (Oak Knoll, Press, 2016).

Ink

David Nunes Carvalho, *Forty Centuries of Ink* (1904).

Handwriting

George Bickham, *The Universal Penman* (1941). [A book about the beautiful handwriting done in business and government prior to typewriters; official documents had the "engraved" look of this eighteenth-century master of the art.]

Chapter Five

Paper

> *Rags are as beauties which concealed lie,*
> *But when in paper, how it charms the eye!*
> *Pray save your rags, new beauties to discover,*
> *For of paper, truly, every one's a lover;*
> *By the pen and press such knowledge is displayed*
> *As wouldn't exist if paper was not made.*
> *Wisdom of things, mysterious, divine,*
> *Illustriously doth on paper shine.*
> *—Dard Hunter,* Papermaking *310*

In eighteenth-century America, a child's education included a "rag lesson," an exhortation to save rags in order to have supplies for the manufacture of paper. Newspapers recommended that husbands encourage wives to make a rag bag and "hang it under the shelf where the big Bible lies" or use the bag as part of interior decorating, displaying an "elegant work-bag as part of the furniture of their parlours in which each scrap of rag is carefully preserved for the papermakers." Young women were advised to submit worn handkerchiefs to the papermakers as they might be returned as a love letter, a *billet doux.*

Poems even implored readers to save their rags. Benjamin Franklin, for instance, offered his own poem, "A Conversational Pleasantry," about the qualities of paper and how different types suited different personalities: *foolscap,* a term for large-sized paper, is used by politicians, the Founding

Father opines. As a printer, he was deeply invested in the production of information, particularly as communication was key to the colonial cause. Cutting ties with Great Britain also meant that the new country must be self-sufficient. Franklin is reported to have helped start eighteen paper mills, and he delivered a paper in 1788 to the American Philosophical Society on "Description of the Process to be Observed in Making Large Sheets of Paper in the Chinese Manner, with One Smooth Surface" (Weeks 93–94).

In short, rags were crucial to the production of paper, a situation that continued until wood pulp was introduced as an alternative, first in Germany in the mid-1800s and then after the Civil War in the United States. The rag shortage crisis was averted only when the alternative became feasible. Even today, though, high-rag-content paper is preferred for important documents such as diplomas, licenses, and certificates, as it is more durable. Environmentally conscious users of paper may be more likely to ask what percentage is recycled rather than what proportion comes from rags; in fact, recycling has been part of paper production from the very beginning.

THE INVENTION OF PAPER

When Benjamin Franklin addressed the learned group in 1788, he referred to the "Chinese manner" of papermaking. He was going to the source, as China was the birthplace of the invention. Around 105 CE, Tsai (also spelled Cai) Lun is credited with inventing this essential material for writing. How did he do it?

To be clear, *paper* has a specialized meaning. It is traditionally plant-based, and source materials were soaked in water and pulverized. Paper-like materials that preceded this innovation included papyrus, parchment, hammered bark, and palm leaf. Tsai Lun prepared a pulp using old fishing nets, hemp waste, rags, and the inner bark of the mulberry tree. His recipe for making paper includes putting the materials in water and then stamping or beating them to pulverize the fibers. In the seventeenth century, the Dutch created the "Holland beater," which pounded the raw materials much more quickly, but until that time, much of the hard labor was done by hand.

When the material, which has been cleaned and boiled, is sufficiently macerated, then a screen—much like a window screen—is placed in the vat of water. As it is lifted, the water drains, and the pulp adheres to the screen forming a thin layer. The wet paper is placed on a flat surface to be pressed and dried. The screen is returned the vat to collect another "page" of pulp. In a less efficient system, the form for the page could be set out to dry, but this meant that a papermaker could make only as many pages per day as molds available.

Naturally, China was reluctant to share this technology, but it spread eventually to other parts of Asia, first to Korea and then to Japan. It wasn't until 500 years after the invention that paper spread beyond Asia. In 751, during a Sino-Arab war, some papermakers were taken prisoner in Samarkand, in what is now Uzbekistan.[1] They earned their release by revealing the secret of papermaking. The Arabs improved upon the system with mechanical beating mills (Tschudin 14) and also by trading wood pulp for cloth rags.

In the early twelfth century, papermaking appeared in Moorish Spain.[2] Another important center for paper sprung up in Fabriano, Italy, most probably with the knowledge gained also from Arabic influence. A paper and watermark museum on the site tells the story of paper in medieval Italy. In France, paper mills populated the central region around Ambert, with its lush forests and rivers.

LIFE IN A MEDIEVAL PAPER MILL

After Gutenberg's invention of the printing press in the fifteenth century, the demand for books—and therefore for paper—increased. Some medieval towns were better positioned than others, particularly those where colleges and universities were located. Basel, Switzerland, was one of those places. Berthold Ruppel (d. 1495), an apprentice of Gutenberg, relocated to Basel in 1468. The city was located strategically on the Rhine River, enabling a lively trade. Its university, collegiate churches, and monasteries housed a good supply of ancient manuscripts, ready to be printed and distributed more widely. It was a hotbed of humanism, known for an open-minded atmosphere that tolerated differing points of view. This was one of the reasons that noted philosopher Erasmus (1466–1536) and painter Hans Holbein (c. 1497–1543) moved there. The latter designed the colophon for Johann Froben. By 1500, 580 books had already been published by some 70 different printers.

What was life like in a paper mill? The Swiss Museum for Paper, Writing, and Printing, located in a historic paper mill, offers insight. Typically, a family would own and operate the mill, where a dozen or so people would have worked—hard work and unhealthy work. Craftsmen and apprentices spent 12 or more hours each day in the damp, cold mill. Water was ever present on the flooring as the fiber pulp was churned and screened. At the

---

1 The world's oldest paper was discovered by Swedish explorer Sven Hedin (1865–1952) during an expedition to Central Asia at the turn of the twentieth century. He found writing materials in Loulan, a Chinese garrison; these are housed in the Ethnographic Museum in Stockholm.

2 An important museum on the history of paper is located in Capellades, Spain, in an old paper mill.

vat where fibers disintegrated, three craftsmen worked together as a team: the vatman, the couchman, and the layman. It took three strong men to operate the machinery, but each had a specific job. The vatman dipped the screen or mold into the tub of water, lifting it out until the fibers had lined up in a nicely covered sheet. The couchman pressed the sheet between felt. Then all layers were pressed, squeezing out any remaining water. The individual papers were then hung to dry. Apprentices, laborers, and temporary itinerant journeymen assisted.[3]

Women and children were employed in the rag cellar and on the drying floor. The rag cellar, also termed the "rotting cellar," was a particularly unhealthy place. The source of the rags could have been from those lately deceased. The rag workers were responsible for removing all buttons and any other extraneous materials from the cloth, including ripping out seams. It was cut into smaller pieces and sorted by quality. Then it was washed, usually in boiling water. Then one of two methods was used so that it would deteriorate. Either it would be left to rot on the floor for up to eight weeks, or it would be placed in barrels or vats to decompose faster. The fibers had to be broken down before they could be added to the water for maceration. The master papermaker organized the work and also the sale of paper. His wife would tend to the care and feeding of the workers.

Papermakers eventually wanted to brand their work, and as a result, watermarks were developed. The screen that took the wet pulp included additional brass wires sewn onto the wiring of the mold. The watermark might be functional—about the size or quality of the paper—or it might label the maker of the paper. Later, around 1800, decorative intaglio watermarks appeared. Paper might need to be held up to the light to see these distinctive marks.

Paper was packaged for sale in regularized quantities, just as a dozen eggs is the standard for a carton. Even now, when we refill a photocopy machine, we insert a *ream* of paper, 500 sheets of paper—a term derived from Arabic word *rizma*, meaning a bundle or pack. Other fascinating units of measure include a *quire* of 25 sheets; 20 quires equal 1 ream, and 10 reams make up 1 *bale*.

---

3 The authoritative text for papermaking was *L'Art de faire le papier* (*The Art of Papermaking*) (1761), by Joseph Jérôme de Lalande, published in the fourth volume of the *Description des arts et métiers* (*Description of skills and professions*) of the Royal Academy of Sciences in Paris. This was the most detailed description of papermaking of its time. It describes all the steps, from the preparation of raw materials through to the finished sheet of paper. It claimed to be the most complete and scientific description of papermaking available in order that methods could be understood and in the future more rapidly be improved.

THE DEMAND FOR PAPER

The need for paper was intense. A black-market trade in rags arose to supply the paper mills. As with most countries, in England, demand far outstripped supply. Legislation was therefore enacted to make it easier for paper mills to obtain cotton and linen. The Burying in Woollen Act, passed in 1666, made it illegal to construct shrouds of anything but wool. Dard Hunter, paper researcher extraordinaire,[4] reported that this saved 200,000 pounds of cotton and linen that could be put toward the production of paper or other items. The act remained in effect for almost 150 years (11).

As Kittler notes, the supply of old rags became the "unlikely object of attention" on which the information revolution depended (14). Rag smuggling was a problem that required laws and enforcement. Those successful in obtaining this material could literally go from rags to riches. The stakes were high. Italy, one of the earliest sites of papermaking, notably in Fabriano, engaged in the nineteenth century with England and France in what Kittler terms an "international war over rags" (18). The latter countries, though, won as their technological innovations led to new sources for papermaking, particularly wood pulp.

The first industrialized manufacture of paper occurred at Frogmore Mill in 1803, which in its long lifetime had formerly been a corn mill. Its success as the first mechanized paper producer occurred when the mill was acquired by the Foudrinier brothers from France, who designed the machine that transferred water and pulp into paper. Unfortunately, as is often the case, the original designers went bankrupt. Their design was refined by others, and sources for paper moved gradually from traditional materials to wood pulp. I visited the Frogmore Mill in December 2019, and the elongated machine used in the early twentieth century was truly amazing (see Figure 5.1). A watery substance came up onto the long bed of the machine, and before it had traveled very far, the water was eliminated through a screen, and, quite suddenly, there was paper moving down the track and onto a system of rollers.

---

4 Dard Hunter (1883–1966) was a leading authority on paper, learning how to make paper, and how paper was made around the globe. He was the author of 18 books on paper, and his collection is housed at the excellent Robert C. Williams American Museum of Papermaking at Georgia Tech University. The *Saturday Evening Post* profiled the "Paper Detective" (Clark), called the Sherlock Holmes of paper detection for solving mysteries such as Japanese explosive balloons and Nazi counterfeit British pounds in World War II.

Figure 5.1   Foudrinier brothers' papermaking machine. Model at Frogmore Mill (2019).

Supply and demand for paper became a vicious cycle with ever more uses for paper. Increased supplies finally became available in the 1850s and 1860s. Dard Hunter catalogued its uses in clothing, churches, watches, tires, and many other items (Clark). Paper collars became particularly popular, as they were disposable and accessible to lower socio-economic classes. They allowed men to assume "white collar" jobs. In 1862, a popular music hall tune was "The Age of Paper." The sheet music, written by Howard Walker, included a drawing of the singer dressed entirely in paper (Grom). Today, paper clothing is making a reappearance, particularly in Asia.

The use of wood pulp for paper revolutionized the manufacture of paper. In 1844 in Germany, Friedrich Gottlob Keller (1816–95) invented a wood grinder. Because of the Civil War, the United States did not move to wood as a source for paper until 1866, when the Keller grinder was imported (Robert C. Williams American Museum of Papermaking). Although newspaper publishers were initially skeptical about the quality of paper made from wood, gradually they were won over. The forests of the country were subsequently attacked for source material. Their value became immediately apparent; unfortunately, their future was grim. Late in the nineteenth century, it became clear that education and research needed to lend a hand, as acres of forest were being denuded without thought for future supplies or the environment. The first forestry school in the United States was established at the Biltmore Estate in Asheville, North Carolina, home to the Vanderbilt family. It was modeled on European schools of forestry, and its head was imported from Germany—Dr. Carl Alwin Schenck (1868–1955)—who established practices used by other colleges and universities. Schenck also conducted the first census of trees in the United States. It was not until the 1970s, with the rise of Earth Day and the environmental movement, that concern about felling forests and polluting streams to produce paper that yet another recycling paper initiative became popular. Just as rags saw new life as paper, waste paper that would normally have populated a landfill returned as new paper products.

HANDMADE PAPER

The mass production of paper was one result of the Industrial Revolution of the late nineteenth century. Craftsmen such as William Morris (1834–96) of England and Dard Hunter of the United States railed against the loss of good-quality paper. In Asia, handmade paper continued—and continues—to be highly valued. Indeed, China celebrated its role as the inventor of papermaking at the Beijing Olympics in 2008.[5] In Japan, the term for handmade paper is *washi*. The Buddhist monk Doncho is believed to have brought the art of papermaking from Korea to Japan in the 600s. The fibers came from the bark of cultivated or wild plants such as the paper mulberry tree (*kozo*), the Thymelaeaceae species known as *mitsumata*, and certain species of the genus Wikstroemia (*gampi*). Kozo, mitsumata, and gampi all have fine strong, shiny fibers. Entire villages were devoted to papermaking. Early photographs show houses surrounded by drying screens. Villagers in the town of Shiqiao in China's Guizhou province continue to produce highly valued masterpieces of handmade paper (Knorovsky).

Likewise, Nepal, drawing on its artisan tradition as well as inexpensive labor, continues to make paper using the Lotka bush, a source material that has been used since the twelfth century (see Figure 5.2). The Lotka is noteworthy for being sustainable, and its product could be termed "planet-friendly" paper. The Forest Stewardship Council (FSC) offers certification of products from responsibly managed forests. An alternative is the Sustainable

---

5 The Beijing Olympics Opening Ceremonies included four of China's inventions: gunpowder, the compass, paper, and movable type. Movable type printing began with the engraving printing of the Sui Dynasty (581–618 CE). Bi Sheng of the Song Dynasty (960–1276) improved the movable type printing by using baked clay movable characters for typesetting printing. Gutenberg's later invention used metal for the movable type.

Figure 5.2
Lotka tree bark,
Kathmandu,
Nepal. Tibetan
Handicraft &
Paper Factory
(2019).

Forestry Initiative (SFI), which also offers certification but is said to be less rigorous. Leading stationers, such as Paperchase in the United Kingdom, advertise that its products are FSC-certified.

Source materials for handmade paper vary widely. One unique approach is dung. Thailand has solved some resource problems for papermaking by turning to elephant "poop," popularized by the environmentally sensitive and socially responsible PooPooPaper Company (see Figure 5.3). Using traditional processes of papermaking, the group draws primarily upon elephants, which produce quantities of excrement that can otherwise be problematic. The fiber-filled waste serves as the base of the pulp mixture. It's an up-cycled product that is very popular with zoo gift shops but also available online at the company's "Pootique" (see www.poopoopaper.com/).

Figure 5.3
Poo Poo Paper.

Although expensive, handmade paper sends a signal that the message itself is of as much value as the recipient. Buyers of handmade paper honor the artisan and/or company that produced the item and may also be making a declaration against mass production. The quality of handmade paper makes it less likely that it will be thrown away or recycled but rather kept in an archive of keepsakes. Eco-friendly materials also indicate a preference for reducing the carbon footprint by making "green" purchases.

BEFORE PAPER

What did writers use before the development of paper? In Sumer, the preferred writing material was the clay tablet. The word *paper*, however, derives from Greek *papuros* and Latin *papyrus*. But papyrus does not qualify as paper because it is a laminate, produced by first cutting or slicing stalks of the plant from end to end and then gluing them together in thin sheets. To truly be *paper*, the product must be made of dissolved or macerated fibers. Used since the third or fourth millennia BCE, papyrus was written on and then stored in rolls. Extant temples in Egypt (e.g., Abydos) may have a rather tiny room with shelves that is termed the "library." This is where papyrus scrolls would have been stored. There was even a goddess to watch over writers: Seshat, "she who is foremost in the house of books." Papyrus had a tendency to deteriorate or split, however, as its materials had not been processed to the same extent that paper was.

Scribes, who are depicted in Egyptian sculpture seated cross-legged, had the important job of recording religious and government documents. For a right-handed scribe, the unwritten section of a papyrus roll lies inconveniently under the right wrist. In order to avoid blotting the ink, the scribe wrote from right to left. As a result, books in the Arab world begin on what most westerners would consider the last page. This includes any language group that originated in the Nile region, such as the Semitic languages Arabic and Hebrew, whose scripts are written in that direction.

In Europe, the skin of calves—*vellum*—was used before paper was invented in China. *Parchment* was also made from animal skins but was not of as fine a quality as vellum. The shape of pages and books was determined by this rectangular output of animal skins. Parchment could be rolled for scrolls or folded for books or codices. The two sides of a sheet of parchment differed, as one was from the animal's exterior and the opposite from the interior, which is lighter. Pages were organized so that two light sides would face each other, and likewise with the darker sides. Even though paper was expensive when it was introduced to Europe, it was still cheaper than animal skins.

In the pre-Columbian Americas, codices were recorded on *bark paper* known as *amate* around the fifth century CE. Not truly "paper" in the sense that we know it, bark paper is created by boiling and pounding the inner bark of trees. Only a few rare Mayan codices exist, such as the one on public display in Dresden, Germany (see Figure 2.7). *Bark cloth*, also known as *tapa*, was used by Pacific Islanders, and its origin is the mulberry tree. Although used for writing, it is better known as art or clothing.

Before paper was invented in China early in the second century, silk, bamboo, and wooden slats were used for writing. In New Caledonia, sections of bamboo were inscribed and carried as "magic plants" to protect them when they traveled (Musée Hèbre de St Clément). Paper is cheaper than silk and more portable than bamboo and wood. As the technology and the quality of the material improved, paper became a practical item that ordinary people might afford. Early on, paper from East Asia was incorrectly called *rice paper*, but rice paper is a paper-like painters' material from the nineteenth century that is neither paper nor made of rice. The smooth, white material is shaved off in spirals from the pith of the stems of *Tetrapanax papyrifer*. Like papyrus, it is not made of dissolved fibers and thus cannot be classified as real paper.

In ancient Rome, wooden boards and then wooden tablets covered in wax were employed by writers and even schoolchildren. According to Frampton in her book on Romans and writing, Quintilian cautioned against giving children wax tablets too early until they had practiced their "ABCs" sufficiently and would "not err in free-form composition" (67). Wax tablets could be "erased" through the heat generated by the friction of rubbing the blunt end across the inscriptions. A similar write-and-erase material is the school slate. Unlike the gray slate used for roofing, the quarried slate for schools is fine-grained, soft, and dark. Enclosed in a wooden frame, the school slate was written on with chalk, and then students used a cloth to erase. They were particularly popular in the mid- to late- nineteenth century but still in evidence until almost the mid-twentieth century in the United States, manufactured generally by one of two companies located in Slatington, Pennsylvania (Rinker). My father used the slate pictured in Figure 5.4 in the 1920s at the Limestone School, a one-room schoolhouse a horse-ride away from the farm where he grew up near Warsaw, Missouri. Slates were also used to teach freed enslaved peoples to read and write. I learned at the North Carolina Museum of History in Raleigh that Black refugees from the South, where teaching enslaved peoples to read or write had been a crime, attended pop-up schools in Union-controlled camps. In contemporary schools, child-sized whiteboards offer the same flexibility as ancient tablets or slates. They provided writing materials when paper was non-existent, too expensive, or environmentally wasteful.

Figure 5.4
1920s-era writing
slate of E.B. Kinkead,
Limestone School,
Warsaw, Missouri.

PAPERLESS SOCIETY?

When computers became commonplace, it seemed that paper might become unnecessary. Offices and schools talked about becoming "paperless"; ironically, the use of paper increased with the Digital Revolution. Information is still communicated through paper, although some businesses have turned to paperless processes to save money and to be environmentally sensitive. Paperchase, a UK-based stationery company, advertises that it has "saved 200,000 sheets of paper and 40,000 till [cash register] rolls" annually (Paperchase, "It's Good"). Research studies suggest that in many instances, paper is the preferred mode of communication and that writing by hand is a better way to learn. On the other hand, newsprint and newspapers are declining as people get their news online or through other sources. While the uses of paper may branch out to fashion or innovative technologies, paper continues to be a major way of storing information and culture.

QUESTIONS TO CONSIDER

1. The lore of the Rag Man being a creepy monster who abducts or harms children apparently dates back to the Brothers Grimm. How did someone who holds an important role in the social and economic framework devolve into a dark creature?
2. Paper sizes are standardized internationally, except for North America. How did conventions of paper sizes come about, and why did the United States diverge from that standard?
3. The frontispiece of Richard Powers's Pulitzer Prize–winning novel, *The Overstory* (2018), which focuses on nine separate life stories and the trees that influence them, begins with this statement:

> *The Overstory* is printed on 100 percent recycled paper. By using recycled paper in place of paper made with 100 percent virgin fiber, the paperback first printing has saved:

> 637 trees
> 614,962 gallons of water
> 206,700 pounds of greenhouse gas emissions
> 62,925 pounds of solid waste.

> Totals quantified using the Eco-Calculator at https://rollandline.com/.

How does this information influence your choices on book purchases? Can you calculate your own paper use over a certain period of time?

DO-IT-YOURSELF HANDS-ON ACTIVITY

Interested in making your own paper? Recipes for papermaking are available online. The process requires some source material—like mass-produced paper—as well as water, a tub, a screen, felt sheets, a sponge, and a blender. (Papermaking equipment is also available through such sources as the Arnold Grummer company, which also hosts an annual paperfest.)

INVITATION TO REFLECT AND WRITE

1. In France, Jacques Bréjoux was designated in 2015 a *Maître d'art* (Master of Art) for his work with heritage paper. I visited him at the Moulin du Verger at Puymogen in 2018, where he continues with a small group

of dedicated artisans to produce handmade paper, particularly useful for restoring old or damaged books. Do you have a master of paper locally? Consider interviewing someone who is an artisan in handmade paper or plan a field trip to watch paper being made. There may even be a historic site or museum focused on paper (or another aspect of writing such as printing) that could be visited.

2. Create a 2–4-minute radio script, modeled on John Christensen's "The Rag Man," below, that focuses on an important aspect of paper (or other topic in the material culture of writing).

FOR FURTHER READING

John Christensen, "The Rag Man"

Rightly or wrongly, others often see our work as defining who we are, and prize some occupations over others. Meet George Goddard, who spent three years traveling Utah and collecting waste.

Today, most Americans make recycling a regular part of their lives. But, in the nineteenth century, the collection of waste was considered unhygienic and was a job left—if at all possible—to the immigrant poor. Utahns were no different in having an uneasy view of the waste trades. In 1861, however, LDS Church leaders were in desperate need of pulp to supply the *Deseret News's* paper mill, in which they'd made a substantial investment. Brigham Young asked women to save old clothing, sheets, wallpaper, wagon covers—any fabric that could be mulched into pulp and turned into paper. But Young needed someone to travel the territory collecting the waste, and so, he called English immigrant George Goddard on a "rag mission."

When Goddard heard the news, he felt it was a "severe blow to [his] native pride." A well-respected merchant and auctioneer, Goddard was now the "rag man." He recalled that, "The humiliating prospect almost stunned me...To be seen on the streets going from door to door with a basket on one arm and an empty sack on the other, enquiring for rags at every house. Oh, what a change in the aspect of affairs..."

For three years, Goddard swallowed his pride and travelled Utah collecting discarded rags for the mill. He performed this task despite the fact that mothers began using him to frighten their children. "You better behave," they disciplined, "or we'll give you to the ragman."

Goddard collected more than 100,000 pounds of rags for the paper project. He later reflected that he never regretted it, believing it was God's

> work and in service of his community. He counseled young Mormons to accept their mission calls without complaint. Things could be worse, he implied, you could always get called to collect waste. In 1867, church leaders turned rag collection over to the women's organization known as the "Relief Society."

INTERESTED IN LEARNING MORE?

Book Recommendations

Nicholas A. Basbanes, *On Paper: The Everything of Its Two-Thousand-Year History* (Vintage, 2014).

Dard Hunter, *Papermaking: The History and Technique of an Ancient Craft* (Alfred A. Knopf, 1947; repr. Dover, 1978).

Mark Kurlansky, *Paper: Paging through History* (Norton, 2017).

Chapter Six

The Book

> *What an astonishing thing a book is. It is a flat object made from*
> *a tree with flexible parts, on which are imprinted lots of*
> *funny dark squiggles. But one glance at it and you're inside the*
> *mind of another person.... Writing is perhaps the greatest of*
> *human inventions, binding together people who never knew each*
> *other, citizens of distant epochs. Books break the shackles of time.*
> *Books are proof that humans are capable of working magic.*
>
> *—Carl Sagan*

What do books mean to you? For Carl Sagan (1934–96), noted astronomer and science communicator, books were magical. When I was growing up, I felt that same wonder about the enormous potential and power of books. A treat was the weekly trip from our farm to town, where my mother left me at the Boonslick Regional Library to peruse the shelves and check out books. It was a small-town library that did not even require library cards, but it was the world to me. I concur with Emily Dickinson: "There is no frigate like a book to take us lands away." Through the pages of each volume, I explored the Civil War in *Across Five Aprils*, learned about the childhoods of famous Americans like Annie Oakley and John Deere, and thrilled to the adventures of *The Boxcar Children*. Our family owned few books, and I looked forward to an annual gift of a Nancy Drew mystery. I knew when I was having my tonsils removed and received two volumes of the girl sleuth's adventures that it meant my parents were indulging me—and were also fearful about the surgery. My ideal as an adult was to have a home library that requires a rolling ladder to gain access to a tall wall of books. Although the bookcases are not that tall, they contain hundreds of titles, a testament to my own love of books and reading. And I supply a Little Free Library installed across the street in a neighborhood park.

The book itself is a remarkable invention. Its function is to warehouse knowledge. Prior to the Internet, this was the primary storage system for data, information, and stories. Sagan gives a definition of the book above, but its form evolved slowly over time. As with writing, the origin of the book was to convey information and stories in one place that required more space than a letter or a tablet. The first "books" weren't actually in the form that we see today. They were clay tablets,[1] scrolls, slabs of bamboo, or codices. Wax tablets, which came after the codex, proved a cumbersome medium for book-length materials. How different our reading today would be if the scroll had won out over the codex as the format for our books. But we should remember that when reading an e-book, we still "scroll" through the text. Even when Gutenberg revolutionized printing in the fifteenth century, the book was still developing. As late as the seventeenth century, books were often sold as a stack of pages. The buyer took these pages to a bookbinder to be sewn together and bound with a cover of the owner's choosing. The cover might be richly decorated or plain, depending on how much the person wished to invest in the book (*Form & Function*). Notably, books were often accessible only to the wealthy.

SACRED BOOKS

Writing and the ability to write were held in high esteem in the ancient world. People believed that writing originated from God, which led to books and writing being venerated. This was true in cultures with a pantheon of gods or for those that believed in monotheism. Sacred books are important to the three major world religions—Judaism, Christianity, and Islam. The Torah, the Bible, and the Quran contain texts that have been handed down over the millennia. The appearance of these books is affected by the rules that govern each religion. The Torah is plain while the Christian Bible may be richly decorated—or illuminated as during the Middle Ages. Islam prohibits images; as a result, the Quran may have luxurious ornamentation and beautiful writing or calligraphy.

Producing sacred texts was important in other religions, too. Buddhist texts, termed *Jikji*, drove the earlier-than-Gutenberg production of movable metal type in Korea. Before movable type, texts and images were produced and reproduced using woodblock printing. China and Japan accomplished

---

1   The *Epic of Gilgamesh*, for example, was written on clay tablets in densely inscribed cuneiform.

this as early as the eighth century; the former made advances in movable type made from clay or wood by the eleventh century. This technology was slow to be exported though (Newman). It was actually sluggish to catch on in the East, too, due in part to the vast number of characters—in contrast to the Latin alphabet with which Gutenberg worked. China can claim the oldest printed book in the world to be dated. The *Diamond Sutra*, a Chinese translation of a Sanskrit holy text—*The Diamond That Cuts through Illusion*—was published in 868. It was printed using wood blocks, and only seven of them as its length is a mere 6,000 words.

Palm trees provided materials for another form of book, one in which the leaves were cut in narrow oblong strips and then strung together on cords threaded through them. This approach is akin to the Venetian blinds that cover windows. Wooden boards provided ends that protected the leaves, which were fragile. Each leaf was flipped to move through the reading. Because of the delicate nature of the palm leaves, they might be replaced by bamboo or even metal.

Prior to the printing press developed by Gutenberg in the fifteenth century, books were written primarily by hand. The writing implements themselves were not always pens but also styluses or even chisels, depending on the writing material: leaves, bark, papyrus, clay, bronze, vellum, parchment, paper. Evidence of early books is usually sparse due to the ravages of time; however, Egyptian books were often placed in tombs where they were protected, or the material, such as clay, endured to be discovered through excavations in the great archaeological searches of the nineteenth century.

PRINTING AND REPRODUCTION OF TEXTS

The desire for exact copies or reproduction of texts drove inventions. Imagine that a scribe took three years to copy one Bible, and, still, it could be filled with errors. Thomas Jefferson employed a clever machine for almost exact copies of his letters, a Hawkins & Peale[2] polygraph that was marketed in the early 1800s. For this machine, two pens were connected through levers so that when one pen wrote or was dipped in ink, the second did the same. The result? A copy for the writer's files. But it was only a single copy, not the multiple copies that some may want. For contemporary writers, it's so much easier to hit the "Copy" button on a photocopy machine or print multiple copies from personal printers.

---

2 Hawkins invented the polygraph but assigned the patent to his partner, Peale, who further developed and marketed the instrument. Charles Willson Peale (1741–1827) was a noted painter, particularly for portraits of Colonial leaders, but he was also a Renaissance person—inventor and scientist.

The contrast to the fifteenth century is stark. Chapter Seven reports the media revolution that occurred when Gutenberg's typesetting and printing technology became widely accessible. The culture of handwriting was replaced. Scribes became irrelevant. The mass production of identical books became a reality. While printers initially were publishers, too, eventually the role assignments split into printer and publisher and, later, into booksellers. The book became an important commodity in the marketplace, and literacy levels improved dramatically. Increased access to reading also drove technology such as the refinement of spectacles—reading glasses.

A steady customer for printed books in the Western world was the Catholic Church, which desired authoritative editions of the Bible. These sacred books printed by hand frequently contained errors and featured a notation system for the omission of letters, words, or whole lines—if they were caught.[3] Scholars of the day debated various editions or versions of the Bible, arguing about the choice of a single word. Could the inspired word of God contain errors? Although it was practically heresy, yes, acknowledging human error did happen. The stakes were high, though.

The practice of Catholicism involved a substantial amount of printing. In addition to sacred texts, indulgences—designed to be sold to individuals seeking remission from sins—were printed as single sheets in the thousands. This practice, among others, spurred the Protestant Reformation. Ironically, the leader of the Reformation, Martin Luther, born in 1483 after the spread of the press, made excellent use of the new technology by having his own treatises printed and made available cheaply to a growing number of followers. Karant-Nunn and Lotz-Heumann note, "His rebellion against the Catholic Church made him a celebrity, and it stimulated the publishing industry." It also kindled increased interest in literacy, as people wanted to read this information, and Luther's approach was to distribute in the people's language so that it would be accessible, rather than in the language of the Church: Latin.

In England, Julian of Norwich (1342–1416?) is credited with writing one of the first books in English by a woman. Although not published until 1670, *Revelations of Divine Love* grew out of the visions she had of God. She wrote about these mystical experiences in a series of chapters that she revised over two decades. These writings are in keeping with the focus on religious texts of the time, her interpretations of God and nature: "God is never out of the soul, in which he will dwell blessedly without end."

---

3   The contemporary St. John's Bible, the first handwritten and illuminated Bible to be created in several hundred years (2000–11) by professional calligraphers in the United States and Wales, acknowledged that human error in copying would occur and created a system for noting errors in the margins. This stunningly beautiful work, which measures 24 by 36 inches when open and crosses seven volumes, is discussed further in Chapter Eleven.

SECULAR BOOKS

In the Middle Ages, schools served primarily to educate males to become priests. The curriculum was based on three parts, known as the *trivium*: grammar, rhetoric, and logic. The focus of grammar was to train students to read, write, and speak Latin, which was the universal language across geographic boundaries in the Western world. Rhetoric focused on the art of public speaking. Aristotle had defined five areas of rhetoric: invention, arrangement, style, memory, and delivery. These five canons originally focused on oratory; however, in contemporary Writing Studies, they became associated with writing, except for memory and delivery, which applied directly to public speaking. Logic was taught to ensure that arguments were valid. Speakers could draw on *logos*, *ethos*, and *pathos* to convince audiences of the soundness of their opinions (see Chapter Nine, particularly Figure 9.5).

The trivium was later joined by four additional curricular areas, known as the *quadrivium*: arithmetic, geometry, astronomy, and music. These were essential skills for the clergy in overseeing and managing church affairs. The trivium and quadrivium combined to form the seven liberal arts. The term *liberal* does not represent a political position but rather refers to the fact that it is a "liberated" education, that which a free man should enjoy. Aristotle is typically depicted in medieval images as representing logic, while Cicero, perhaps the most noted orator of all time but particularly of the ancient world, represents rhetoric.

With the rise of universities in the twelfth century, subjects beyond the spiritual infiltrated the curriculum. Classical texts, including those from Aristotle, Plato, and Cicero, were housed in university libraries and continued to be influential. They were joined by philosophical, legal, and scientific texts as well as by literature. Cities that were also important spiritual centers became sites for the first universities: Paris, Bologna, Salamanca, Padua, Oxford, and Cambridge. Paris's Latin Quarter grew out of the fact that students attended lectures and tutorials in this sector—delivered in Latin. The universities gave rise to humanism—a belief that humans and knowledge about human activities are valuable—and an emphasis on critical thinking and evidence. In contrast, religion might be based on faith, acceptance, and doctrine.

It should be noted that in the Arabic world, a university was established in Fes, Morocco, even earlier, in 859. Born out of the *madrassa*, which educated clergy, Arabic universities included Islamic studies, the law, medicine, and sciences. During the Moorish rule of the Iberian Peninsula, education and books were highly valued (eighth to fifteenth centuries); during the final years of the Reconquest, led by Queen Isabella of Castile (r. 1474–1504), Arabic books of learning were torched. In 1492, with the last stronghold of Granada fallen, Muslims and Jews were expelled, their libraries raided, and non-Christian books burned. This was particularly devastating for the knowledge of medicine, science, and mathematics that was lost. Books have continued to be objects of contention over the centuries. The fifteenth-century burning of books was unfortunately not the last.

Figure 6.1 Conrad von Soest, "Brillenapostel" ["The Glasses Apostle"] (1403).

Printed books allowed a larger readership to learn and also provided a forum to expand topics behind religion, law, and the Classics. Social and political topics were given book-length treatment. Chronicles, memoirs, travelogues, and sciences were devoured by an expanding public. Advances in the sciences, particularly in botany, zoology, geography, and medicine, were unveiled in books. The sixteenth century was a time of exploration at home and abroad. The advance in eyeglasses (see Figure 6.1) was paralleled by the development of the microscope, which led to a host of scientific discoveries. Botanical information was paired with vivid illustrations made from wood (xylography) or copper engravings that aided scientists and pharmacists.

THE FORMAT OF THE BOOK

Book printing originally resulted in pages that could be bound together and then protected with a cover. The parts of the book that readers rely on for user-friendliness—title page, table of contents, chapter headings, and page numbers—came about in the early sixteenth century. As the publishing industry evolved and moved from the single source of the printer, what had been obvious about the structure of the book to the printer was not necessarily transparent to the publisher. How did the pages fit together? Numbering pages in sequence helped demystify the manuscript and made the work of the bookbinder easier.

The process of assembling the book was complex and designed to protect its pages, and it was still done by hand and required several different types of equipment. A technical vocabulary defines the various parts of the book. The top edge of the book is the *head*, while the bottom is called the *tail*. The non-bound side of the book is the *foredge*. Pages are referred to as *leaves*, and a *gathering* of leaves forms the *textblock*, the manuscript. *Endleaves* form the front and back, which serve to protect the text. At each end is the *pastedown* that covers the edges of the book cover that have been turned in, while *flyleaves* are not glued. *Boards* are covered with cloth or leather to wrap the text and extend slightly beyond the actual pages as *squares*. The gathering of leaves is sewn together to assemble the text. The stitches can add structural weight to the book and result in *shoulders* that flare out on the *spine* of the book. Bumps or humps on the spine where the sewing supports are concealed are known as *bands*. *Kettle stitch* is used to link the various sections. The stitches visible at the top and bottom of the spine, often decorative as well as structural, are known as the *endband*. The exterior of the book may feature gilding, either on the cover or the edges of the leaves. Metal closures, *clasps*, keep the book shut tightly.

Originally, the cover of the book did not necessarily include its title. Instead, it might have been the name of the patron of the book, scholars, nobility, or even the bookbinder or perhaps a portrait. Before the beginning of the nineteenth century, therefore, it may have been difficult to "know a book by its cover." By the end of the nineteenth century, the book may even have taken on the shape of its subject. A die-cut book is one in which the book is shaped not in traditional rectangle form. The 1863 publication of *Little Red Riding Hood*, for instance, shows the girl carrying her basket with a wolf near her feet. The cut-out outlined her head and the showy scarlet cape. Louis Prang publishers brought out several die-cut volumes in its "Doll Series" ("First Shape Book").

The standard book format was played with in various ways over its history. One medieval book opened in six different ways so that the reader had access to six books in one package. A sixteenth-century German book contained six devotional texts, including Martin Luther's work. Each section was secured by a clasp (Marshall).

The typeface of books also evolved. In the beginning of printing, fonts were designed to look like handwriting or calligraphy. Gutenberg's assistant, former scribe Peter Schoeffer, designed the Gothic typeface that was used in producing the 42-line Bible. This rather heavy black-letter font gave way to antiqua forms that echoed classic Roman script. These fonts included *serifs*, a small line or stroke attached to the letter. Fonts that do not include these are known as *sans serif* (without serif) and are more contemporary. (Further information on typography is included in Chapter Eleven.) The turn to the Roman style of font was driven in part by the emphasis on classical studies favored by humanists in university settings. Because university libraries were repositories of manuscripts, printers often settled nearby to make use of these texts as the drive to produce books swelled.

THE BOOK AND MASS PRODUCTION

As one of the leading cities in education, Paris saw the rise of booksellers as early as 1530. The first *bouquinistes*, as they were termed, carried their merchandise in a pannier suspended from around their neck. Their beat was along the Seine River from the bridge at Saint-Michel to Notre Dame (see Figure 6.2). Only a dozen booksellers were authorized in 1578; however, others operated illegally. Today, the green stalls along the banks of the Seine

Figure 6.2   History of Paris sign for the first booksellers (2019). [Translation: From 1530, the rise of the book contributed to the influence of the capital. Alongside the large booksellers and printers established in the Latin Quarter, hawkers of gazettes and lampoons appeared very early on they were entitled to shops and set up their goods on trestles, or even pieces of canvas placed on the ground, when they were not carrying their merchandise in a wicker basket hanging from their necks. A sentence of the bailiff of the Courthouse, dated 1578, authorizes 12 booksellers, forced to settle two by two on authorized sites, around the Saint-Michel de Notre-Dame bridge. The others remained illegal until 1618, when they were required to wear a copper mark or badge on their doublet.]

that offer books, typically second hand or antiquarian, have been designated a UNESCO World Heritage site.

The popularity of books was not limited to Western Europe; it was a global phenomenon. In Japan, several factors led to an extraordinary explosion of bookstores by 1700. According to Asian Studies scholar Mary Elizabeth Berry, "Since 1640 or so, remarkable numbers of commercially published texts [had been] converting private knowledge into public information" (1). Increasing emphasis on literacy and education meant that Japanese children were using primers to learn history, geography, and cultural standards. Government leaders promoted "state-making," centralizing power in urban environments and requiring samurai and nobles to live in the city for at least part of any year. Japan had also invaded Korea and returned with fonts from its movable type printing press, a technological innovation that the invaders didn't have previously. Likewise, Jesuit missionaries brought Roman-based alphabet type to Japan and established presses. The increase in the number of books was also due to support for entrepreneurship, which resulted in a robust publishing industry. Readers could then purchase fiction, maps, travel guides, and much more. In short, books were much more accessible.

In Jane Austen's day (1775–1817), a novel cost about $100; however, subscription-based libraries provided a source for fiction readers. According to scholar Lee Erickson, author of *The Economy of Novel Reading*, circulating libraries began as another source of income for booksellers, who charged members a fee for access to books (qtd. in Blakemore, "How Lizzie"). These libraries were set up in destinations for leisure classes that had the time to read and the finances to do so. Notably, it provided women with greater access to books.

Some books, such as the Bible, could be produced more cheaply through a process called stereotyping. A mold was made of the typeset page, cast onto a plate of type metal, and reused for printing. This saved typesetting the page again when more copies were needed; however, a publisher had to be quite sure that the book would go into multiple printings in order for this to be financially feasible. Predicting bestsellers could be a risky undertaking ("How Books Became Cheap").

The nineteenth century saw the rise of industrialization and advances in printing, automatic typesetting, paper manufacturing, and illustration that made books more affordable. Typography diversified. Bodoni and Garamond were joined by Times New Roman, Helvetica, and Optima—among others. While the era of pulp fiction—books printed on cheap pulp paper for readership—did not occur until the first half of the twentieth century, already in the latter part of the nineteenth century, some like the writer William Morris

(1834–96) decried the lack of quality in book printing. Co-founder of the Arts and Crafts Movement in England, Morris was an outstanding printer and pioneered book arts. An admirer of medieval manuscripts, he started his own printing business, Kelmscott Press, in order to create the "ideal book" that was in complete harmony from cover to typeface. He aimed for the noble book, carefully crafted to be treasured by its owner.

Such ideal books were not necessarily accessible to the general public, however. At the lower end of the price scale, dime novels—so named for their cost—featured thrilling stories of the Wild West. Harold Hill sings in *The Music Man* a litany of telltale signs of "Trouble in River City"—the corruption of youth—which includes finding a "dime novel hidden in the corn crib." The paperback, the inexpensive relative of hardback books, typically held together by glue rather than stitches, was originally viewed as slightly immoral. In contemporary terms, these are sometimes referred to as massmarket paperbacks, and they no longer have the bad reputation they once did. Travelers often picked up such books to pass the time at railway stations or airports. In Great Britain, perhaps dime novels were cheaper as they were termed "penny dreadfuls."

British-based Penguin Books made inroads in turning around the skewed perception of paperbacks by bringing out reprints of high-quality literature in the 1930s. These bright orange and white books were popular with readers, and the high quantity of sales guaranteed profit even when the individual unit price was low. Pocket Books—branded with Gertrude the Kangaroo—debuted in the United States just prior to World War II. The war itself was a golden opportunity for publishers of paperbacks, as the US soldiers received novels when stationed overseas; it's said that Fitzgerald's *The Great Gatsby* was revived and survived as a result of so many service people reading it. The paperback eventually became an accepted medium for books. Indeed, so-called trade paperbacks denote high-quality paperback books today.

Holding a book and leafing through its physical pages is regarded by some as a more genuine way to read in contrast to electronic books or e-books. Still, when digital books came into vogue at the beginning of the twenty-first century, they provided, yet again, more access to books. A primary benefit is mobility, as multiple books can be stored at one time on a slim device. E-books also are searchable, and devices typically have features that allow for notations and links to definitions and explanations. Ironically because of its name, Project Gutenberg,[4] created in the 1970s, aims to digitize publicly available books, particularly books that are out of print.

---

4   Project Gutenberg's extensive digital library of almost 60,000 free eBooks can be found at this site: https://www.gutenberg.org/. I have found it particularly useful for classical works of literature.

TINY BOOKS

In the Netherlands, *dwarsliggers*, tiny books, take pocket-sized books to new levels—diminished levels (see Figure 6.3). These quirky books, the size of a cellphone, have onionskin thin pages and a horizontal orientation as well as a hinged spine so that they lie flat. Extremely popular in Europe, these mini-books are being produced in the United States by Penguin Random House, which is appropriate given Penguin's history with cutting-edge paperbacks in the 1930s. Popular young-adult novelist John Green signed on to have four of his books receive the mini-book treatment. Reviews on Amazon have been very positive. Users comment that they are not just "adorable," but "easy to hold and read," whether on a treadmill or an airplane. Their convenience makes them very attractive for packing or for gift giving (see Alter; Charles).

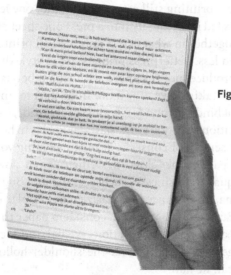

Figure 6.3   Dwarsligger.

While tiny books seem a recent innovation, in fact, miniature books have been popular throughout the centuries. In the Middle Ages, women in particular carried small prayer books in bags attached at the waist. The *psalter*, a volume containing the Book of Psalms, often also included a calendar of holy days, red-letter days as they were printed in red, in contrast to regular days of the week, as well as prayers designated for specific hours of the day. Art historian Alexa Sand suggests that in these miniature books, "Word becomes flesh and flesh becomes book" (181), the objects serving almost as "amulets" to protect the wearer against disease or evil.

Bromer and Edison surveyed several thousand years of the history of tiny books, including the prayer book that Anne Boleyn (c. 1501–36) carried to her execution and Shakespeare's *Complete Works*. Napoleon Bonaparte (1769–1821) assembled a library of tiny books for his campaigns. Nutshell Library brought out tiny versions of children's author Maurice Sendak's (1928–2012) work. The Miniature Book Society was established in the United States in 1983 and focuses on books that are no more than three inches in height, width, or thickness.[5] The Grolier Club in Manhattan, the oldest society of book lovers in the country, exhibited 950 books from Patricia J. Pistner's collection. Pistner originally began collecting miniature books for her doll houses, so that their libraries would contain real books, not just decorative covers (Lyall).

BOOK ARTS

William Morris's ideals live on in courses, workshops, and individual efforts in the book arts. Letterpress printing still sets type by hand, one letter at a time. High-quality paper is fed individually into a press one sheet at a time. Then the pages are sewn together in what is typically a small print run of a few hundred copies or even less. Letterpress printers are in style due to the quality of the work they produce, not the speed with which books appear, with the process sometimes taking a year or more from start to finish. The American Academy of Bookbinding, founded in 1993 in Telluride, Colorado, offers training and certification to "book enthusiasts." Experts in bookmaking may make books from scratch or conserve or repair existing volumes.

Letterpress printing is part of the "slow" movement (as in slow foods) that emphasizes care and quality. Businesses such as Horse and Buggy Press in Durham, North Carolina, for instance, emphasize old-school traditions. The owner of Horse and Buggy, Dave Wofford, considers paper thickness, illustrations, end papers, and book construction—visual and tactile elements. Fine press books generally feature over-the-shoulder-hollow hand binding so that the book can lie flat.

In Santa Fe, New Mexico, the oldest town in the western United States, the Palace Print Shop & Bindery continues to publish books on its historic presses. One publication, *Broncho vs Bicycle*, is a recovered cowboy poem of the nineteenth century that details the race between a big-wheel bicycle and a bronco. The decisions inherent in slow publishing are evident in a project called *Dr. Franklin and Spain*, an account of Benjamin Franklin's correspondence with Spain during the American Revolution. Spain was a quiet supporter of the colonies, funneling its funds through France to the revolutionaries. Over the course of three years, the printers worked to

---

5 The Miniature Book Society information can be found at https://www.mbs.org/.

produce just the right book to tell the story of rediscovered letters between Franklin and the Spanish Crown. The paper, of course, came from Spain. The typeface, Bodoni Old Face, is one that Franklin himself admired. The endpaper maps are taken from Richard W. Seale's 1744 atlas, show Spanish interests in the New World, and are maps that Franklin himself would have known. The binding is brown morocco with deep-blue leather lettering, gilt. The cover itself is hand-marbled paper. A custom box houses the volume. Only 100 copies were produced.

Works produced by book artists may be single copies. These artifacts tend to be produced in an artistic or craftsperson approach. They may look like books, or their format may diverge significantly from the tradition of the codex. It may be formed in conventional ways using binding, stitching, glue, text, illustrations, and metalwork. Book artist Keith A. Smith has created more than 200 one-of-a-kind books and also published multiple guides to bookmaking—*Bookbinding for Book Artists*; *Quick Leather Bindings*; *Non-Adhesive Binding: Books without Paste or Glue*, and *Structure of the Visual Book*; *Non-Adhesive Binding: Exposed Spine Sewings*—which offer some insight into the variety of approaches in book arts. His approach is for readers to have a "book experience" in which words, pictures, and form blend in complementary ways.

Exhibitions of artists' books typically include a range of styles: accordion books, scrolls, boxes, pop-ups, and forms that definitely don't seem book-like. They may be jeweled or beaded or feature fabric. They may be in the shape of their subject, not just die-cut, but in a three-dimensional format such as a text within the shell of a nut or a cage. The images may pop up from the page. The book may be tied with string or ribbon or have a clasp or be encased in a box or package—even a candy box. The artist may have taken an existing book and folded the pages in interesting ways or cut through the pages to make letters from the negative space that results. The illustration in Figure 6.4 is from the Klingspor Museum in Offenbach, Germany, which specializes in the art of modern book production, typography, and type. Its fine art books were collected by Karl Klingspor, an owner of a foundry.

Figure 6.4   Book art.

CONCLUDING THOUGHTS

The immensity of the history of the book makes a single chapter almost ludicrous. Keith Houston calls the book "the most powerful object of our time." Actually, that is too limited in scope. The book, no doubt, has been an important object for more than a thousand years. Houston emphasizes the tactile experience of the physical book—the paper, ink, thread, glue, and board—and the actual heft of a book. He finds e-books a threat to the book tradition. What I hope is clear from this chapter is that books take many forms and have many lives. An e-reader may be the most convenient medium for the traveler who is away from home for several months, while the physical contact with a riveting beach read may be just the ticket for a vacationer. Audio books may accompany people while they take a walk. Artists' books can delight the eye of the beholder in museums and galleries. Books are just one more aspect of writing that we tend to take for granted. Take some time and truly look at books. Are they the magical objects that Carl Sagan suggests?

QUESTIONS TO CONSIDER

1. In a *New Yorker* article from December 1, 2018, Katy Waldman asks, "Are Tiny Books a Sign of the Twee-Identification of Literary Culture?" "Twee" is attractive to young people and is defined as being affectedly dainty, delicate, cute, or quaint. *Dwarsliggers*, as discussed in this chapter, are very small versions of books, made tiny through the use of onion-skin paper, a trend that started in The Netherlands. The young-adult literature author John Green, who is known as the "teen whisperer," is a proponent of the trend toward tiny books in the United States. Waldman says, "A *dwarsligger*'s teeniness is inseparable from its tweeness." Consider reading the article and determine if you agree or not; alternatively, look at examples of *dwarsliggers* online or physically and argue whether or not they fit the definition of *twee*.

2. In book arts, single-copy books may "straddle the art-craft divide," according to Audrey Niffenegger in her introduction, "What Does It Mean to Make a Book?," in Wasserman's *The Book as Art*. Is such a book the work of an artist or a craftsperson? What might the differences in approach be?

3. It's said that there's a book inside everyone. What does the book inside you look like? Is it a novel? An information book? A one-of-a-kind artist's book?

4. Many libraries hold special collections of books, including books produced prior to printing. Rare books are treated with special care, being

placed on support structures and handled with white gloves. Libraries may also have facsimiles of rare books—like a tiny medieval psalter. Investigate your local or campus library for its holdings of rare books.

5. Handwritten books were very valuable, and this is evident in books that were "chained" to prevent theft. Scribes, who would have worked for several years most likely on a single book, sometimes inscribed the book with warnings about theft of the text: "If anyone take away this book, let him die the death; let him be fried in a pan; let the falling sickness and fever seize him; let him be broken on the wheel, and hanged. Amen" (Laskow). To see more such warnings, look at Marc Drogin's investigative book, *Anathema! Medieval Scribes and the History of Book Curses* (1983). What book curse would you inscribe in your favorite titles?

6. Atlas Obscura is a fascinating website devoted to finding quirky stories. One asks, "What would a book look like if it were a work of art?" It then describes the artists' books collection at the University of Michigan, which includes "eight wedge-shaped booklets printed to look like cherry pie and stored together in a clear plastic takeout container," as well as a book called *20 Slices* by Ben Denzer, which is truly a book with 20 slices of American cheese bound between the covers (Cain, "Every Page"). Is this a travesty against "the book" in all its glory, or is it a funky way of rethinking what books might be?

7. The book has been called one of the world's greatest technologies. Book and technology may not be words that you thought about together. What are the technologies that make up a book?

8. At Hull House, the innovative settlement residence to provide for the poor on the west side of Chicago, established by Jane Addams (1860–1935), the first American woman to win the Nobel Peace Prize, contemporary workshops on bookbinding are inspired by the work of Hull House co-founder Ellen Gates Starr (1859–1940), who established the original Hull House Bookbindery (c. 1899). In these workshops, participants collaborate to create hand-bound books from simple and recycled materials. Their function is for "slowing down, sharing stories, and connecting with one another and highlight community voices." The workshops help social change. How do you think bookbinding and book arts can accomplish this?

9. Western culture tends to think ethnocentrically. When asked about the first novel ever written, we might tend to credit Daniel Defoe's *Robinson Crusoe* (1719) or Samuel Richardson's *Pamela* (1740). A more inclusive answer might be Cervantes' *Don Quixote* (1605). In Japan, Murasaki Shikibu's *The Tale of Genji* (1030) is credited as the first

Figure 6.5
Murasaki Shikibu statue
by Sugimura Hisashi.
Kyoto, Japan.

novel, some several centuries before the British or Spanish volumes. She was recognized by UNESCO in 1965 as "one of the world's great people," the first Japanese to be so honored (see Figure 6.5). Have you read this story by a noble lady-in-waiting? Why is *The Tale of Genji* not as well known in Western culture?

DO-IT-YOURSELF HANDS-ON ACTIVITIES

1. *Bookbinding.* Commercial bookbinding kits are available, or instructions can be found online. I've used the Pocket Bookbinding Kit for sale from the source Cleverhands (https://www.etsy.com/listing/545424975/pocket-bookbinding-kit-learn-to-make-two?ref=shop_home_active_10&crt=1) for class demonstration. Side-sewn and pamphlet stitch are illustrated, and materials call for the paper and cover to be bound, a pushpin to make the holes for the stitches, a heavy-duty needle with a large eye, and waxed thread for sewing. Binder clips are useful to hold the material together while sewing.

Approaches to bookbinding include Coptic, Japanese Stab, and Long Stitch. Book boxes to store books are also possible, particularly appropriate for books to be archived and treasured.

The Center for the Book is a US Library of Congress initiative that promotes literacy and books and has sites throughout the nation and territories (http://www.read.gov/cfb/). Book arts programs often offer workshops for such activities as bookbinding, and the Internet also offers resources in videos.

2. *Creating Your Own Bookplate.* Books can be highly valued possessions, and owners from the Middle Ages on have marked them with bookplates, noted with the *Ex Libris* Latin phrase, which means "from the library of." Bookplates might include the owner's crest or motto and could be decorated. It is then pasted to the front endpaper to announce ownership. Commercially-designed bookplates are available for purchase and typically include a phrase such as "From the Library of," "This book belongs to," or the classic "*Ex Libris.*" Design your own bookplate.

3. *Building a Bookwheel.* Although not exactly a DIY activity, a sixteenth-century bookwheel designed for engineers to read multiple volumes at once by rotating a geared wheel was actually constructed by contemporary engineering students at the Rochester Institute of Technology. The project is described in an article, which includes the actual plans (Voon). The wheel allowed for an early version of hypertext, the ability to consult multiple texts simultaneously.

INVITATION TO REFLECT AND WRITE

1. What are the most influential books in your reading life?
2. Carl Sagan said, "Books are proof that humans are capable of working magic." What is your interpretation of that statement? Has a book worked magic on you?

FOR FURTHER READING

Reading 1

This blog post from the British Library Medieval Manuscripts division offers a whimsical journey through the process of creating a book. Source: https://blogs.bl.uk/digitisedmanuscripts/2017/09/a-rough-guide-to-making-a-medieval-manuscript.html. Visit this site to see the illustrations that are described in captions within this blog.

A Rough Guide to Making a Manuscript
September 6, 2017

Tonight, when you pick up your book, observe the legacy of sewn gatherings in the fixings of the pages. Discern, in your fountain pen, the memory of the hollow feather.

What follows is a general, Wiki-How-style overview of how a medieval manuscript would have been fashioned. The craft flourished for over 1,000 years and dominates the material foundation of Western literary culture.

[Illustration]
A page which bears the scars of vigorous scraping, which have become ingrained with dirt over the years: from a Bible, Central France (Tours), 1st half of the 9th century, Harley MS 2805, f. 149r

1. Make your parchment
You may choose to outsource parchment but, just for the sake of it, here's the process:

- Source an animal, such as a cow, sheep or goat.
- For high-quality pages, select an unblemished skin (skins are a consequence of meat production, as much in the Middle Ages as today).
- Remove hair by soaking the skin in lime for a few days and rubbing over a wooden stump.
- Stretch skin on a frame and scrape with a curved blade to get rid of all the flesh.
- Stitch fly-bites or tears with strips of parchment.
- Dry the stretched skin in a warm place.

[Illustration]
Fly-bites received while the animal lived grow when the skin is stretched and dried. Larger flaws can be stitched: examples from the Sherborne Cartulary, 2nd quarter of the 12th century, Add MS 46487, f. 48r (left) and a 12th-century Gospel-book from St Augustine's, Canterbury, Royal MS 1 B XI, f. 53r (right).

2. Prepare your gatherings (or quires)
- Cut sheets from your parchment. You may need more than one skin for each gathering of sheets. If you're making a deluxe Bible, you may need thousands.

- Fold your sheets into *bifolia* (Latin for two leaves, or pages).
- Prick your sheets as a guide for ruling, using a knife or other metal point.

Pricking marks on folio 38v of Add MS 46487.

- Rule your sheets in dry-point (using a sharp-ish stylus) or lead-point. Ruling defines the position, number and spacing of the lines of text per *folio* (page or leaf). If you (and your patron) are feeling flush, leave nice big margins and lots of space between lines.

Illustration, f. 45*r, how pages might have looked prior to writing.

- Assemble your bifolia into a gathering or quire. It is quite common for quires to consist of four bifolia (called quaternians), which will give you eight folios. Books are made up of multiple quires, stacked and stitched together.

3. Write your text
- Prepare your quill, which may be a goose feather and can be sourced from the bank of a lake in late summer when they moult. The wing your feather comes from will be the opposite from the hand you write with. In Latin, *penna* (wing) is the root of our word 'pen'. Incidentally, it's also the root of 'penne' pasta which, like a quill, is a hollow cylinder!
- It will need regular sharpening with your pen-knife (which is the origin of the modern term).
- Prepare your ink, perhaps a dark ink made from oak galls.
- Decide in advance or on-the-go where to leave gaps for illustrations and decorative initials. Making a note of the page order, you may want to separate your *bifolia* so that you have a single-layer, flat surface to write on.
- Choose your script. Scripts in the Middle Ages were very prescribed (excuse the tautology). What you use will vary according to the time and area in which you live (maybe half-uncial in 8th-century Northumbria, English Caroline minuscule in late 10th-century Winchester) and the nature of the book (majuscule, minuscule, cursive and so on).
- Start writing! You may be copying meticulously from an exemplar.

4. Decorate!
It is unusual for manuscripts to be the product of a single person's labour. Certainly at the decorating stage, multiple hands are likely to be at work.
- Do under-drawings in crayon or lead-point and outline.

- Apply gesso (a mixture containing gum) to areas intended for gilding. This might be stained red.

[Illustration]
In a 12th-century image of the angel appearing to the shepherds, the red gesso is visible through the worn gilding: Cotton MS Caligula A VII/1, f. 6v.

- Carefully apply the fragile gold leaf and burnish (polish). The gold will stick to gesso, the red tone of which enhances its warm glow.
- Apply pigments made from organic (usually plant-based) and inorganic (mineral) ingredients, suspended in a water soluble medium such as egg yolk.

5. Bind your book
- Sew along the spine of each gathering.
- Now, sew your quires together at evenly spaced sewing stations along their spine (see drawing of binding process) and affix long cords across to them.
- Sew end bands to the top and bottom for extra reinforcement.
- Source your book-boards for the front and back covers. In Northern Europe, book boards were commonly made from quarter sawn slabs (see drawing of tree-trunk) of dense, durable timbers such as oak and beech.
- Thread the cords into holes and channels in your two book-boards, binding them to the edges of the spine.
- Cover with leather and hide the cut edges on the inside covers with paste downs. Odds and ends from around the workshop will do.

[Illustration]
Notice how the ends of the boards of this 12th-century binding show short sections of the growth rings of the tree. Cutting the board this way ensured the least amount of warping as the wood dried: Add MS 46487.

Optional Extra: decorate your binding
- Sheets of precious metal, ivory plaques, roman gems and jewels will enhance your binding no end. But be warned, these rarely stand the test of time, being a particular favourite of plundering invaders, wont to rip treasure-encrusted bindings from their pages. *The 12th-century binding of Add MS 46487 has been carved to receive a plaque or some other decoration. At some point in the later 13th century, this was replaced with a small Limoges enamel, affixed upside down.*

And *voilà*, you should now have made your own medieval manuscript. Easy, isn't it?

INTERESTED IN LEARNING MORE?

Book Recommendations

Anne C. Bromer and Julian I. Edison, *Miniature Books: 4,000 Years of Tiny Treasures* (Harry N. Abrams, 2007).

Geraldine Brooks, *People of the Book* (Penguin, 2008). [Fiction about a rare fifteenth-century illuminated book, a contemporary curator/conservator, and the book's journey through history.]

Father Michael Collins, *Remarkable Books: The World's Most Beautiful and Historic Works* (Penguin Random House, 2017).

Christopher de Hamel, *Meetings with Remarkable Manuscripts: Twelve Journeys into the Medieval World* (Penguin, 2016).

David Diringer, *The Book Before Printing: Ancient, Medieval and Oriental* (Dover; original ed.: *The Hand-Produced Book*, 1953, repr. 1982).

Stephen Greenblatt, *The Swerve: How the World Became Modern* (W.W. Norton, 2012).

Martin J. Hopkinson, *Ex Libris: The Art of Bookplates* (The British Museum Press, 2011).

Keith Houston, *The Book: A Cover-to-Cover Exploration of the Most Powerful Object of Our Time* (Norton, 2016).

Ross King, *The Bookseller of Florence: The Stories of the Manuscripts That Illuminated the Renaissance* (Atlantic Monthly Press, 2021).

Merilyn Simonds, *Gutenberg's Digital Fingerprint* (ECW Press, 2017). [Simonds explores the printing process, contrasting letterpress printing with digital.]

M.B. Brown and P. Lovett, *The Historical Source Book for Scribes* (London, 1999).

Krystyna Wasserman, *The Book as Art: Artists' Books from the National Museum of Women in the Arts*, 2nd ed. (Princeton Architectural Press, 2011).

Chapter Seven

The Printing Press

*"All the world acknowledges that the invention of Gutenberg
is the greatest event that secular history has recorded.
Gutenberg's achievement created a new and wonderful
earth, but at the same time also a new hell."*
—Mark Twain, "The Work of Gutenberg," published in Hartford
Daily Courant, *June 27, 1900, 7.*

Mark Twain (1835–1910) knew a thing or two about printing presses. On July 6, 1862, he began reporting for the *Territorial Enterprise* in Virginia City, Nevada, using his *nom de plume*. His colorful stories sold papers, and he gathered material for his notable books and stories (James; This Day in History). Contemporary visitors to the historic *Territorial Enterprise* building and museum can view Twain's desk as well as an antique printing press. A few years later in 1866, he visited the Sandwich Islands (Hawaii), where the printing press had a remarkable impact. (More on that extraordinary development to come; see below.) He used the articles he wrote describing the islands to augment his personal account of the West in *Roughing It* (1872).

At the same time as Twain was writing for the newspaper, which churned out pages one at a time, William Bullock (1813–67) developed the modern printing press, patented in 1863. Bullock's invention came about around four centuries after Gutenberg's foundational achievement, the first rotary printing press that could "self-feed the paper, print on both sides, and count its own progress—meaning that newspapers, which had until then relied on an operator manually feeding individual sheets of paper into a press, could suddenly increase their publication exponentially" ("Baldwin Modern Printing Press"). The same rotary system was used in child-sized printing press "toys" introduced in the 1950s by Superior Marking Company of Chicago, the "Cub," so that anyone could be a cub reporter (Kennard; Moxon).

Bullock's press revolutionized newspaper production. Unfortunately, his own machine killed the inventor when he kicked at it, catching his foot in a mechanism, which then entangled his leg. Surgical procedures were not well advanced at the time, and he expired during the amputation. No one stopped the presses. Newspapers rolled out at increasing speeds, contributing to improved literacy and mass communication. As award-winning novelist Paulette Jiles (b. 1943) recounts in *News of the World* (2016), a person could make a living traveling around frontier Texas in 1870 reading the latest newspapers to audiences who paid a dime to hear updates from all corners of the globe. It is the need for information that brings people in the novel to hear Captain Jefferson Kyle Kidd deliver the news that he has culled and compiled for an evening's entertainment.

THE HISTORY OF PRINTING

Until Johannes Gutenberg's innovative printing press, books were written primarily by hand. Yes, there were printing presses, but each "page" was produced largely one at a time through carving, as in woodblock printing, which started around 200 CE. Asia was at the forefront of printing for several centuries. Over a span of a dozen years, beginning in 971, the emperor of China commanded the printing of the complete scriptures of Chinese and Tibetan Buddhism. It required 130,000 printing blocks—one block for each page—which were delivered to the capital of Kaifeng for production. A special storage building was constructed, divided into 130 sections, and approved staff did the actual printing of this sacred text, called a *Dazangjing* or *Tripitaka* (Museum of Far Eastern Antiquities, Stockholm). Printing and books were an expensive proposition, restricted largely to nobility and clergy.

More typically, scribes—monks or nuns—wrote books by hand. A really good scribe could write 200 words in the space of an hour. A single book most likely took about a year to produce, with the writer using a quill pen, ink (often carried in an ink horn on the person's belt), and parchment. Paper was still rare in Europe in the Middle Ages, and more often than not, the skins of animals provided the surface material. Parchment reflected the condition of the skin, and on occasion it had a hole that had been present in the hide. Most of the works produced were in the service of spiritual needs: bibles, prayer books, church services. Some were scientific treatises.

They did not have the attributes of books that we take for granted now: no chapters or chapter headings, no page numbers, perhaps no title pages, and certainly no index for easy reference to look up topics. Instead, large, colored decorations denoted the start of sections. These may or may not have been the work of the scribe but more likely saved for an illustrator or illuminator.

One version of the Bible that was not completed in just a year is the fascinating *Devil's Bible*, the largest extant medieval manuscript in existence, housed in the King's Library in Stockholm (see Figure 7.1). The lore surrounding this book is that the monk who completed it—and analysis on the manuscript supports the notion that it was a single person—made a deal with the Devil to produce the work overnight in exchange for the Devil being featured prominently in a picture. A full-page portrait of the fork-tongued fiend is prominent in this three-feet-long, 160-pound tome, officially termed the *Codex Gigas* (Giant Book). It includes not just the text of the Bible but also incantations (e.g., exorcisms), scientific treatises, and a history of the Jewish people by Flavius Josephus (fl. first century CE). Its completion probably took 20 years, the lifespan of the scribe; he also incorporates a section on his multiple sins. The *Devil's Bible* included both spiritual and secular sections, indicating that a standard was not yet set for what was considered a bible. It was produced in a monastery in Bohemia but became part of the Swedish loot from the Thirty Years' War. Some time later, when the Swedish palace where it was housed was burning, the *Devil's Bible* was saved when it was thrown over the castle wall. According to lore, a passerby was killed when it dropped on him.

Figure 7.1
The Devil's Bible/
Codex Gigas.

Figure 7.2
Chained Book.

While this bible was gigantic, other books were miniscule. As discussed in Chapter Six, noble ladies sometimes carried tiny books at their waists: *Psalms*, a book of hours, prayer books. They drew on these books to say prayers in honor of the Virgin Mary at set hours. A scribe writing such small script might use a magnifying glass to complete the task. Feast or holy days were noted in the calendar in red ink, which is the origin of the phrase "red letter days." The term *rubric*, which we tend to think of in education as an evaluation standard, referred in these books to lines of writing in red, usually instructions or spiritual guidance. Devotional books were often richly illustrated and contain some of the most stunning works of art from the Middle Ages.

Because books were so rare and valuable, when owned by a church or family, they were usually on display but often chained so that they could not be stolen (see Figure 7.2). Books had to be protected from things other than theft, too, so they were bound most typically between wooden bookends, which included metal protectors on the corners where they were most likely to be damaged. Locks and clasps kept the pages of the book secure between the binding, as the parchment could swell with humidity. A well-placed knock on a book corner unlatched the clasp. The German expression *ein Buch aufschlagen*, which is still used today, literally means to "knock open a book" and originates from this ancient technique (Basel Paper Museum).

This was the state of books in the fifteenth century: limited numbers of books, perhaps as few as 30,000 in all of Europe; access restricted to nobility and clergy; a focus primarily on liturgical works; inconsistency from one version of a book to another; lengthy production times; expensive materials. All of that was set to change with Gutenberg and his many inventions that combined to make books more consistent and available, but at a huge cost to the inventor himself.

GUTENBERG'S PRINTING PRESS

Mass printing is attributed to Johannes Gutenberg, who lived in Mainz, Germany, where a museum is testament to his invention. He began using movable type, key to the transformation, around 1440, but the first books did not roll off the press until more than a decade later. Throughout that time, he kept the process highly secretive, as any good inventor would do to protect innovative technology. In Gutenberg's case, it also was a matter of life and death. The Church or fellow citizens might suspect any new product of being the result of dark forces or magic. If so, the person could be branded a heretic and put to death. Étienne Dolet (1509–46), a printer in Lyon, France, was accused of atheism and burned at the stake in Place Maubert in Paris.[1] Gutenberg and his workers literally put their lives on the line to make a new kind of bible.

The development of a consistent printing process required many long years, as several aspects had to be invented or perfected. The press itself was derived from wine and cheese presses. But it was not simply the press itself that Gutenberg designed; the production of a book required a host of inventions. First, there was the type itself. It is *movable type* that is the extraordinary development. This innovation required experimentation with metals, script (typeface or font), and casting. It is most likely that Gutenberg drew on metal casting from jewelry makers or coin minters. He needed typeface that would stand up to the enormous pressure of the printing process. He also required a script that printed well and was easily readable. Monastic scribes used various scripts until the ninth century when Charlemagne regularized script, and thus comprehension and transmission, with Carolingian

---

1 From a pamphlet, "Follow in the Footsteps of Lyon's Printers," from the Musée de l'Imprimerie et de la Communication Graphique, 2018.

Minuscule, which evolved into Gothic Minuscule.[2] Secular writing by hand employed what was termed a *humanist script*, so named because it was about human rather than spiritual subjects.[3] Gutenberg employed Peter Schoeffer, a scribe, to help develop a workable typeface, which resulted in *Textura* font.[4]

The creation of a typeface began with carving individual letters, numbers, and punctuation marks. The *punch* depicted each character in reverse so that when it was pressed into a softer metal such as copper, the letter came out correctly. The recessed cavity piece—termed a *matrix*—was then placed in a steadfast *caster* so that hot metal, a combination of antimony, lead, and tin, could be poured into it. When it cooled, the type was removed and smoothed. The type that passed inspection was then placed in segmented cases, capital letters going in the upper cases and the other letters in lower cases—hence the terms *upper case* and *lower case* letters. The letters, numbers, and punctuation marks were organized by popularity of use so that the person setting a line of type had the most-used characters closer to hand.

A total of 290 characters populated the type case, because in addition to the 26 letters of the alphabet needed in both upper and lower case, Gutenberg also had made commonly used joined letters, termed *ligatures*, to save space and ensure that lines were *justified*—even on both sides. Contemporary computer users can simply click on left, right, or full justification. In Gutenberg's day, justification was the job of the typesetter, who used a composing stick to create a line of type. If the line needed to be shorter or longer, then the typesetter could use ligatures or additional spaces. When the line was set, then it was put into a galley, which would provide the page to be printed. Each page had two columns of 42 lines, and each bible had 1,282 pages, typically assembled as 2 volumes. Gutenberg's are thus termed "B42," which denotes the lines per page.

The galley of typeface was then placed on the printing press. Gutenberg's innovations also included ink and "paper." He determined a mixture of soot, linseed oil, and resin for ink that would stick on the parchment but not soak through. (Gutenberg's innovation also meant that pages could be printed on *both sides*.) Ink balls made from dog hide (which has no pores) and stuffed with horsehair were used to apply the ink, with the inker wielding two at once. The paper or parchment had to be slightly damp to absorb the ink. Once printed, pages were hung to dry. To begin, only the black lettering was printed, and the "red lettering" typical to a bible, as well as any decoration,

---

2 The study of ancient scripts is termed *paleography*.

3 Gothic Antiqua or Early Cursive script is the term for humanist script. Petrarch, the famous Italian writer of sonnets, popularized it in the fourteenth century.

4 The historical fiction work *Gutenberg's Apprentice*, by Alix Christie (2014), imagines Schoeffer as a major contributor to the printing revolution fostered by Gutenberg.

was left blank for the individual owner to have finished. In a later innovation both colors could be used to obtain finished products that looked the same from book to book.

Parchment or vellum was the common writing material of the day, and 30 of the 180 bibles that Gutenberg produced were on this substance. A single bible required 160 skins. The rest of the print run was made on paper, which was manufactured using cloth rags. The books were not bound but packed in book barrels and floated by river barge to markets such as Frankfurt, where they were on display for sale or subscription. To this day, Frankfurt has one of the most important book fairs in the world.

The Gutenberg Bible was the first complete book *printed* with movable type. It has been called "the book that changed the world" (Andrews).[5] Books had been printed on presses before, in China and Korea, with wood and bronze type, but Gutenberg used metal type. He revolutionized the process of printing, bringing together multiple innovations that literally changed the world. In 1997, *Time* magazine called Gutenberg "Man of the Millennium" and his invention the most important in a thousand years. It made the primary works of the Church accessible but also increased the number of secular works. The Pharmacy Museum, housed in the castle in Heidelberg, Germany, attributes standardized formulas for medicine and the more precise depiction of botanicals to the printed book. In all walks of life, printed materials created better sharing of information. Books opened the way for a revolution in science and religion and paved the way for the Renaissance.

Ironically, Gutenberg did not profit from this extraordinary invention. He was up to the hilt in debt, having financed his work through loans, primarily from Johannes Fust (c. 1400–66), a wealthy trader, who gave him 1,600 guilders (about a million dollars in contemporary money). When Gutenberg kept delaying repayment, Fust took him to court—and won. As a result, Gutenberg lost the contents of his printing workshop. Fust and Schoeffer set up their own printing business and started an industry that spread quickly, some of Gutenberg's other workers moving to countries beyond Germany to set up their own printing companies. Early printed works prior to 1500 are called *incunabula* and highly valued as they represent the *cradle* of printed books. Only 49 Gutenberg Bibles survive today, and many of them only sections of a whole book. The Bible continued to be the primary book printed for distribution for several centuries. Notable examples include the Baskerville Bible (1763), produced by Cambridge University printer John Baskerville (1707–75), distinguished for its beautiful fonts and ease of reading.[6]

---

5 To trace the history of just one copy of the Gutenberg Bible, read Margaret Leslie Davis's *The Lost Gutenberg* (2019).

6 The Museum of Printing in Haverhill, Massachusetts, owns a Baskerville Bible.

Figure 7.3   Death and the Printers. From *La Grande Danse Macabre* (Lyon, France, 1499).

The earliest known depiction of a printing shop was published in Lyon, France, in 1499. "Death and the Printers" (see Figure 7.3) shows that printers were not immune from the ravages of the Black Death or plague. The compositor, who "composes" the type, is at the left and two pressmen in the middle. At the right and through a window are the storehouse of books that have been printed and its manager.

THE PRINTING PRESS IN ENGLAND

William Caxton (1422–91) is credited with printing the first book in English. A stained-glass window in London's historic Guildhall honors his accomplishments as one of the most influential people in British history (see Figure 7.4). He learned the trade in Europe, working as a printer in Bruges, Belgium, where he produced the first book in English, a history of Troy (1475), which he himself translated from French (British Library Board). He was encouraged in his work by Margaret of York, Duchess of Burgundy (1446–1503), for whom he served as secretary. Typical of early printers, he was also a scholar, translator, and editor.

Figure 7.4
William Caxton,
Printer. Stained
Glass, Guildhall,
London.

Figure 7.5
William Caxton
Printer's Mark.

At his press near Westminister, he produced more than one hundred books, two that have been influential in literature: Chaucer's *Canterbury Tales* and Sir Thomas Malory's *Morte d'Arthur*, the epic of King Arthur and the Knights of the Round Table. He also published work by Christine de Pisan (1364–c. 1430), one of the most notable women writing in the Middle Ages. His press had such a monopoly at the time that books were commonly referred to as Caxtons. His printer's mark, which is also called a device or colophon, printed at the back of books, shows his initials flanking what is apparently the numbers 4 and 7 (see Figure 7.5). It's thought that 1447 and 1474 are both benchmark dates in his career, the former being the date on which he obtained freedom from his apprenticeship with a mercer (in the textile trade) and the latter the date of publishing his first book.

The charmingly named Wynkyn de Worde, a German immigrant, served as assistant to Caxton, and after the master's death, he moved the press to the old city of London in an area that became renowned for writing—Fleet Street—in the churchyard of St. Bride.[7] He greatly expanded Caxton's work, printing hundreds of books, notably producing schoolbooks for children. In fact, he was "the first English publisher to make printed school books the financial basis of his business" (British Library Board 89).

John Day (1552–84) proved to be an influential printer during the English Reformation. According to William E. Engel, Day was responsible "for the look, style, and authorized content" of the times, serving as "printer, author, and stationer" who contributed in the same way that printers of Gutenberg's time did, not only printing but also distributing through his shop. He served as head of the "Stationers' Company,"[8] the guild of printers and publishers in London, which had been established in 1403. His legacy included a "clear italic font . . . and eye-catching illustrations."

A final English printer to note is George W. Jones (1860–1942), called "Printer Laureate" for his excellent work. William Morris of the Arts and Crafts Movement was influential, but Jones used the Morris aesthetic paired with technology. He was an early adopter of Linotype machinery. His printer's mark integrated the sign of the dolphin with his initials in the great tradition established by early printers such as Caxton and Basel's Johann Froben (c. 1460–1527), whose device was designed by no less an artist than Hans Holbein (c. 1497–1543). Notably, Jones expanded the inventory of typefaces with the addition of Granjon, Baskerville, Estienne, and Georgian, producing beautiful books that became collectors' items.

HAWAIIAN PRINTING PRESSES

Of all the printing presses around the world that resulted from Gutenberg's invention, the ones in the garden paradise of Hawaii may be some of the most interesting. By 1860, the literacy rate in the Hawaiian Islands—also known as the Sandwich Islands, named as such by Captain James Cook (1728–79) in his voyages of 1778—exceeded that of New England. Just a few short decades earlier, Hawaii had no written language and therefore no books produced in the native language. How did such a remarkable transfor-

---

7   St. Bride Library, opened in 1895, contains one of the world's most significant collections of books about printing, typography, graphic design, and papermaking as well as printing equipment. Notable holdings include a section of Caxton's *Consolation of Philosophy* and William Morris's *Kelmscott Chaucer*.

8   The formal name is the Worshipful Company of Stationers, although "Newspaper Makers" was added in 1937.

mation take place in such a short period of time? Credit the printing press and the groups behind it: Boston missionaries, a royal family supportive of schools and universal literacy, and committed natives who took to reading and writing like Duke Kahanamoku took to water.[9]

Printing presses were shipped to Honolulu on Oahu in 1822, as well as to Lahaina on the island of Maui about ten years later. They were descendants of Gutenberg's press. Their purpose was to produce religious tracts, government documents, and schoolbooks. The presses were already well used when they arrived in the islands, but they helped revolutionize literacy. A replica of the Maui press is housed in the original printing house, Hale Pa'i—now a museum—on the grounds of the old mission school that is currently a thriving and highly regarded secondary and boarding school. It produced the first newspaper west of the Rockies on Valentine's Day, 1834: *Ka Lama Hawaii* (*The Light of Hawaii*), a weekly for the students. The 200 copies of each of four pages were printed one page at a time, the paper being placed on the *tympan* and secured with an overlaying plate called a *frisket*. Sticks of type were composed and placed in the *stone* and then inked by hand. The apparatus with the paper was then laid over the type, becoming a *coffin* that was slid forward under the *platen* so that it could be cranked to lower it and press the paper downward onto the inked type. Tourists visiting the Lahaina museum now can take home a copy of the front page that was produced for them.

The initiative to bring Christianity to the peoples of Hawaii was rooted in a young Hawaiian orphan, Opukaha'ia, who sailed to the east coast of the mainland at 15 and was "discovered on the steps of Yale College in Connecticut, weeping because 'nobody gave him learning'" (Day and Loomis, preface). Yale students took him in, tutored him, and converted him to Christianity. Baptized Henry Obookiah, he was an apt and devout pupil. His goal was to return to his native islands and share the gospel. Although Hawaiian had no written language at the time, he worked to translate the Bible, starting with Genesis, in 1816. He also wrote his memoirs, which were published in 1818, following his untimely death that year from typhus. He was inspirational for those involved in the Foreign Mission School, which launched the Protestant Mission service under the sponsorship of the American board of Commissioners for Foreign Missions (ABCFM). The missionaries—and their press—arrived just two years following the earnest young man's death.

In order to complete the written Hawaiian language, spelling and grammar necessarily had to be developed. Drawing on phonetic translation, the missionaries simplified the Roman alphabet, reducing it from 26 letters to 12.

9 Duke Paoa Kahinu Mokoe Hulikohola Kahanamoku (1890–1968) was a Hawaiian competitive swimmer and surfer.

The vowels remained: a, e, i, o, u. They were joined by consonants h, k, l, m, n, p, and w. *Owhyee* became *Hawaii*. Some accent marks were added, which complicated printing. But with an alphabet, translation could begin. One of the problems faced by the printers was the mismatch of typeface between English and Hawaiian. Yes, the newly created language included characters from the Roman alphabet, but not at the same frequency. Printers found them notably short of k and a. "To be fully useful for printing Hawaiian text, a font needed 4,000 additional A's and 3,000 additional K's" (Day and Loomis 9).

While the missionaries were translating the Bible from Hebrew and Greek over a period of 17 years, Hawaiians were learning to read (Vowell 99). The first "job" off the printing press in 1822 was a spelling lesson. Shortly thereafter, a primer for schools was printed, drawing on Webster's work on spelling along with punctuation rules, numbers, scripture, and poetry (Day and Loomis 10). The ramshackle printing press produced 20,000 copies of the primer in 1825, importing paper from China. According to museum curators in Hawaii, "between 1822 and 1842, the mission presses put out over 113 million sheets of printed paper, virtually all of it in Hawaiian" (Vowell 100).

The demand for books increased dramatically as the literacy rate of Hawaiians soared. Instruction in reading and writing took off due to the support of the royals and high chiefs (Vowell 133). Having an education became social capital for all. Many native Hawaiians rose to positions of importance in education and government—not necessarily the ministry desired by the missionaries. One of them, David Malo (1795–1853), captured Hawaiian customs and beliefs in his book *Hawaiian Antiquities*. Another book, *Mo'olelo Hawaii*, published in 1838, is a history of Hawaii, written in the language by Hawaiians. Missionaries such as Hiram Bingham II (1831–1908), the father of the explorer who discovered Machu Picchu, compiled Hawaiian hymnals that were also used as readers. Setting notes on a printing press was exceedingly difficult. Bingham said that printing in the native language was crucial to "give them letters, libraries, and the living oracles in their own tongue" (Day and Loomis 30). The missionaries were so successful in their quest for improved literacy and the development of skilled printers, graphic artists, and bookbinders that the local population easily took over the printing presses when the mission was closed.

A sequel to the story of the successful Hawaiian printing press occurred in the Northwest Territory among the Nez Percé nation. A local missionary, Henry Spalding (1803–74), tried to write a book in the tribe's language in 1837, but it was unsuccessful. Two years later, the mission in Hawaii, having received a new printing press, sent an older one to the Oregon missionaries. It, along with printer Edwin Oscar Hall (1810–83), arrived in Lapwai (near Lewiston, Idaho[10]) in May, 1839. Within days, the missionaries had printed 400 copies of an eight-page reader, the first book printed in Oregon, using an adaption of the Hawaiian alphabet. Later books used the Nez Percé language, which was itself not easy to encode in writing. This historic press is on display at the Oregon State Historical Society (Just; National Park Service Whitman Mission National Historic Site).

WOMEN AND PRINTING

As with most occupations, men dominated printing. However, a few notable exceptions exist. Charlotte Guillard (1485–1557), twice widowed by printers, took over the printing press *Soleil d'Or* from 1537 to 1557, located on the Rue Saint-Jacques in Paris. Guilds made an allowance for a woman running a business *if* her husband had died. Guillard was a skilled publisher, proofreading Latin manuscripts with a level of care that won the admiration of the ruling clergy. This was an important time in the history of ideas, and her press published Erasmus, scientific work, and important Greek texts. She was an apt businesswoman, overseeing a bookshop, several printing presses, and a couple of dozen workers (Beech, Jimenes).

Stell writes about a second woman printer, Yolande Bonhomme (c. 1490–1557), a contemporary of Guillard, in a blog post for the Library of Congress. Uncovering women's history is a continuing challenge, but these women's imprints continue to exist on books housed in archives around the world. Similarly, earlier women typographers' names have been noted in the colophon (publication details) of books—Anna Rügerin in Augsburg, Germany, and Anna Fabri in Sweden, both from the fifteenth century—but Guillard was the first influential woman printer and publisher in Europe.

In colonial America, women also took over printing and publishing, often as widows, in a heady time when news and broadsides were filled with angst and rhetoric about the potential of breaking away from Mother England. As more scholars uncover women's history, these stories of women setting type, printing, and collecting bills are coming to the fore in books such as Susan Henry's *Anonymous in Their Own Names* (2012), Carol Sue Humphrey's *The American Revolution and the Press* (2013), Maurine Beasley's *Women of the Washington Press: Politics, Prejudice and Persistence* (2012), and Elizabeth F. Ellet's three-volume work, *The Women of the American Revolution* (reprinted from 1849–50).

Women of the press included Clementina Rind (1740–74), a Virginian, who published Thomas Jefferson's *A Summary View of the Rights of British America*; Hannah Bunch Watson (1749–1806), who took over two Connecticut papers

---

10 Idaho was part of the Oregon Territory until 1863, when it became its own territory.

when she was 27, following the smallpox death of her husband; Ann Catherine Green (1720–75), who published the *Maryland Gazette* and reported on the Boston Tea Party; Elizabeth Timothy (1702–57), who took over the *South Carolina Gazette*; Ann Franklin (1693–1763), sister-in-law to Ben and publisher of the *Rhode Island Gazette*; and Mary Katherine Goddard (1738–1816), who "won the contract to publish the first signed Declaration of Independence in 1777" (Springen 38). These women not only oversaw the printing establishment but also were responsible for their families. Green, for instance, had 14 children, of whom 6 survived. Goddard was not only a printer but also Baltimore's first postmaster, a position in which she served 14 years. Springen notes in her article about colonial printers that these women were the forerunners of nineteenth-century writers and publishers, such as Josephine St. Pierre Ruffin (1842–1924), who in 1886 launched *Women's Era*, the first newspaper published by and for African-American women, which also advocated for voting rights (38). Women like these empowered later twentieth-century icons such as Katherine Graham (1917–2001) of the *Washington Post*.

THE EDICT OF NANTES

Cultural, social, legal, and religious standards had a tremendous effect on the publishing business in the Renaissance. A country's openness to difference allowed for creativity and economic benefits. In France, the Edict of Nantes, authorized by King Henry IV (r. 1589–1610) in 1598, gave Protestants rights in a Catholic-majority country. Massacres of Huguenots (Calvinist Protestants) in France were felt to be justified, as they were believed to be heretics. Being able to live and work safely was an economic boon to them and the country. When Louis XIV (r. 1643–1715) revoked the Edict of Nantes in 1685, Protestants fled to more open countries such as the Netherlands, which benefitted from this Renaissance "brain drain." Religious wars took place not just on the battlefield but also in the printing industry. As well as in France, this also happened in England during the divisive reigns of Henry VIII (r. 1509–47) and, later, of his daughters, Mary (r. 1553–58) and Elizabeth (r. 1558–1603), as the country oscillated between Catholicism and Anglicanism. It is an important lesson to remember that the free flow of ideas is essential to a country's well being.

BEFORE GUTENBERG

While we celebrate Gutenberg and the tremendous accomplishment he engineered, it should be noted that movable type in Korea predated his accomplishment. At Heungdeok Temple in 1377, metal movable type was used to print the sacred Korean Buddhist text *Baekun Hwasang Chorok Buljo Simche Yojol*, which is abbreviated as *Jikji*. The Early Printing Museum in Cheongju honors this site and accomplishment (see Figure 7.6). Since the museum opened at the beginning of this millennium, South Korea has worked to establish itself as having printed by movable metal type the oldest extant book in the world. Unfortunately, the book itself is not held in its home country but in France, at the National Library in Paris. As with Gutenberg's Bible, the work is in two volumes, only the latter one surviving. The work is available digitally (see https://gallica.bnf.fr/ark:/12148/btv1b10527116j. r=jikji?rk=21459;2).

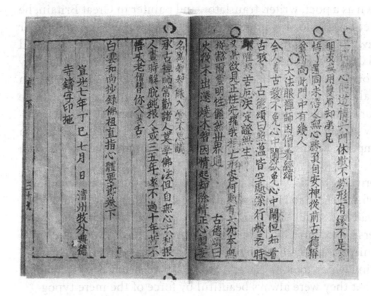

Figure 7.6
Jikji pages.
Early Printing
Museum,
Cheongju,
South Korea.

As with Chinese writing, the text is written vertically and reads from right to left. The vertical orientation is a hallmark of early Asian writing that first was made on strips of bamboo.

How did this sacred text travel from Korea to France? A French diplomat in the nineteenth century serving in the Korean court purchased the volume and returned with it to France, where it eventually entered the Bibliothèque Nationale de France. A work of historical fiction, *The Court Dancer* (2018), by Kyung-sook Shin, translated from the Korean, includes this remarkable story. The novel is about an extraordinarily graceful dancer in nineteenth-century Korea who is "collected" by a French diplomat and taken with him to Paris. When they visit the Louvre, and she sees items from other countries, she asks if there's anything from Korea here, and he says no, but there is something in the National Library—and he put it there: this important fourteenth-century book. South Korea sent a petition to France with hundreds of thousands of names to have it returned, but the French said *non*.

PUSHBACK ON INDUSTRIALIZED PRINTING

The Industrial Age, which took off in the late nineteenth century, pushed the mass production of written materials and made information more readily accessible and less expensive. Dime novels and penny dreadfuls offered leisure reading with action adventure and lurid tales. These low-quality stories on cheap paper had a foe: William Morris (1834–96). A Renaissance person known as a poet, writer, translator, and painter in Great Britain, he may be better known for his interior decoration, textiles, and wallpaper designs today. Along with like-minded colleagues and friends, he launched the Arts and Crafts Movement, which featured artisan workers and socially conscious working standards. He advocated, as a part of this movement, a return to quality printing and employed letterpress techniques. It might be added that for each enterprise he took on, he first mastered the process himself—notably learning Icelandic to translate folk tales. He started his own printing company, Kelmscott Press, named after his manor home. He said:

> I began printing books with the hope of producing some which would have a definite claim to beauty while at the same time they should be easy to read and should not dazzle the eye, or trouble the intellect of the readers by eccentricity of form in the letters. I have always been a great admirer of the calligraphy of the Middle Ages, and of the earlier printing which took its place. As to the 15th century books, I had noticed that they were always beautiful by force of the mere typography, even without the added ornament, with which many of them are so lavishly supplied. And it was the essence of my undertaking to produce books which it would be a pleasure to look upon as pieces of printing and arrangement of type. (Morris 1)

The books he published were on handmade paper or vellum and were beautifully illustrated, drawing on the style of illuminated medieval manuscripts. While stunning in design, they were also expensive, which was contradictory to Morris's support of lower socio-economic classes. The colophon for the press is illustrative of the ornate style of art favored by Morris (see Figure 7.7).

In the United States, Elbert Hubbard (1856–1915), influenced by Morris, started a similar letterpress printing company, Roycroft (named after

Figure 7.7
Colophon for the
Kelmscott Press.

two seventeenth-century London printers) in East Aurora, New York, near Buffalo. Although Hubbard and his wife, noted women's rights author Alice Moore Hubbard (1861–1915), perished in the sinking of the *Lusitania* in 1915, the Roycroft campus and community continue, dedicated to artisan quality work.

CONCLUDING THOUGHTS

Developments in printing advanced beyond Gutenberg's movable type and the press repurposed from winemaking equipment. Lithography was developed in the late eighteenth century and used chemical processes to create a plate that can be inked and printed. It further developed into a technique called offset printing, in which the image is transferred to another medium before the final printing surface. In 1886, the day Ottmar Mergenthaler (1854–99) demonstrated the first linecasting machine to the *New York Tribune*, Whitelaw Reid (1837–1912), the editor, was delighted: "Ottmar," he said, "you've cast a line of type!" The editor's words formed the basis for the business's name, the Mergenthaler Linotype Company, and marked the beginning of Linotype's success story. This "hot metal" press meant that type could be set much faster. It was particularly effective for the dailies that had to start the presses quickly to get the news out to people.

The twentieth century saw tremendous advances in printing and copying. When I first began teaching, handouts were copied on mimeograph machines and carbon paper was used in typewriters to produce more than one copy. It was a careful process of lining up the mimeograph paper and securing it to the drum before starting the roller. The photocopier was a tremendous advance.

Individual printers attached to a personal computer also provided incredible freedom for writers. Our first efforts at our university writing program in 1984 to integrate computers resulted in students writing on what was termed a dumb terminal networked to a mainframe, with their work being spewed out of a dot matrix printer on very wide green-and-white paper. Laser and inkjet printers replaced dot matrix, and digital printing gained popularity thereafter. Desktop publishing transferred the power of document production from professional typesetters to individuals. 3D printing now offers amazing opportunities in the twenty-first century to produce physical objects.

No doubt technological changes will continue to influence printing. These changes are rooted in the fifteenth century, when Johannes Gutenberg developed the movable-type printing press and printed what is considered to be the first book in the West: the Bible. If one of the rare volumes that survived were put on the auction block today, it is estimated that a com-

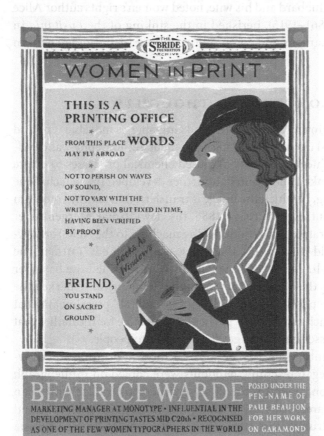

Figure 7.8
Beatrice Warde, "This Is a Printing Office," designed by Pam Smy & Ness Wood (2019). St. Bride Library, London, England.

plete copy could "fetch upwards of $35 million" (Andrews). The impact of Gutenberg's invention to humanity? Priceless. Gutenberg was recognized as the most influential person of the second millennium and his invention as the most important of the same era (1000+ People). Printing presses helped spread information much more quickly, which, in turn, spurred a rise in literacy. This medieval machine literally started the Renaissance.

Beatrice Lamberton Becker Warde (1900–69), a noted twentieth-century historian of typography and a designer herself, wrote the text seen in Figure 7.8, which is posted in Washington, DC, at the Government Publishing Office (GPO), as well as on the walls of many, many printers.

The printed word focused not just on religious texts but, increasingly, on scientific information, philosophy, government, and even literature. As Twain pointed out, it made accessible both worthy and weak texts, leaving their interpretation in the hands of readers.

QUESTIONS TO CONSIDER

1. Noted author William Dean Howells (1837–1920) chronicles the history of "The Country Printer" in his essay of 1896, recalling his childhood experiences of his newspaper-editor father. (The story is accessible online.) Howells's comment that girl apprentices worked at the paper to make a living while male apprentices worked there to make a life (24) no doubt raises the eyebrows of contemporary readers. The country newspaper and printing office still exist in some places. Take, for instance, the *Benton County Enterprise*, published in Warsaw, Missouri, founded in 1879, that continues to put out a weekly paper. The original Washington hand press that printed the paper is still on display. Do you know of a "country paper" that is still in operation? Consider investigating its history and importance to its community.

2. In Europe, some children's books focus on Gutenberg, not just on his history (e.g., Georges Bischoff) but also as a character in fiction. For instance, *Gutenberg et le secret de la Sybille* by Vincent Wagner and Roger Seiter is a graphic book that tells the story, set in 1438, of a poem "Sybille," considered heretical, that is circulating in Strasbourg, and every copy is the *same*—unheard of in this pre-printing-press era. What magic is at work? Who is responsible? Graphic books are a worldwide phenomenon. How do authors of history use the graphic book format to appeal to younger readers?

3. Blogger Jennifer Kennard, in the essay reproduced below, recalls what she terms an "adorable little toy printing press," drawing on several

resources including eBay and YouTube. Do you have memories of tools for writing, or particularly for printing, from your own childhood?

4. In the illustration from the *Swiftset Rotary Printers' Journal*, "Making Type 'Talk,'" users of the Cub printing press are advised that type-face can "do something" for the copy (see the Kennard essay online). Varying typeface can improve the message and influence readers. The point of the advice was to upsell users to order more varieties of typeface; however, from your own experiences, what do you know about how typeface can influence users? (The illustration of the monocled and Bowler hat-wearing figure in the illustration would have been a clever joke recognized by readers of the mid-twentieth century, a famous "dummy" of the time, Charlie McCarthy, managed by ventriloquist Edgar Bergen.)

5. The American Printing History Association published an article on "The Toy Press with a Journal that Means Business" (Moxon; https://printinghistory.org/swiftset-journal/). Compare this scholarly article to the blog by Kennard. How are they similar? How do they differ?

DO-IT-YOURSELF HANDS-ON ACTIVITY

The experience of printing on a letterpress can be exciting. Workshops or classes in letterpress may be available, and there may be a source on a campus or printing shop. It's even possible to build a letterpress. Not surprisingly, the internet has several resources for doing just that. DIY letterpress is increasingly popular in wedding invitations and other handmade writing.

INVITATION TO REFLECT AND WRITE

In the For Further Reading section that follows, Jennifer Kennard reviews and analyzes a 1950s-era child's toy—a printing press. In the chapter on the pencil, David Rees deadpans his way through instructions on sharpening a pencil. Both of these writers look afresh at behaviors associated with writing. What is an unanalyzed aspect of writing—historical or contemporary— that you might see and write about from a new or different perspective? What form might that perspective take? Multimedia? Poetry? News article? Consider how various genres might contribute to looking anew at a writing activity or implement.

FOR FURTHER READING

Jennifer Kennard, The Printing Press as Child's Play, "Press Kit"

The "Cub," an adorable little toy printing press from the Superior Marking Equipment Company (SEMCO) of Chicago, was marketed to young children for a good part of the early 20th century [see Figure 7.9]. It, along with many other rotary press models like it, had all the markings of a great educational tool for young boys and girls alike. Various model press kits included tiny rubber type, spacers, ink, adhesive back picture dies, tweezers for handling type, an inking brush, ink ribbon, mounting slugs, the rotary press and paper. Instruction manuals encouraged kids to print up handbills and postcards to advertise their yardwork and baby-sitting services, and to write and publish home, school and club activities in newspapers. These toy rotary presses actually worked as advertised, yet required a great degree of perseverance and tireless dedication on the part of the budding young printer. This was not a toy for the high-strung or overactive child, as they would quickly grow weary and impatient. The process was not terribly difficult; it was just tedious.

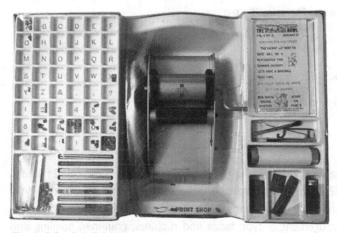

Figure 7.9 Cub Printer.

Working with delicate pieces of rubber type smaller than the size of a chocolate chip, and not nearly as tasty—young composers with nimble fingers would have to pry the letters apart and sandwich them into place with tweezers.

This 1951 ad for the Cub model Superior press appeared in *Popular Science* magazine [see Figure 7.10]. These rotary presses were often the first introduction to relief printing for many, and helped to determine the direction of countless careers in the printing trade.

Toy Press Prints Type

ANY child who can read can set type on this printing press. The rubber type snaps into slots on the press and is so grooved that it is impossible to set characters upside down. Made in three sizes by the Superior Marking Equipment Co. of Chicago, the press will also print pictures.

Figure 7.10   Superior press.

For those determined young typesetters and printers who could manage the tools, SEMCO offered cold cash prize money for inventive and artfully crafted printing examples. Neatness counted...as did "artistic taste in selection and arrangement of type faces and pictures, grammar, spelling and appropriateness of copy." A junior pressman in training was cut no slack.

The bi-monthly *Swiftset Rotary Printers' Journal* was a subscription newsletter published by the Superior Marking Equipment Co. This sample copy [in Figure 7.11] was included in my own "Cub" Superior press kit, given to me by a good friend. A subscription could be had for 25¢ per year in 1951.

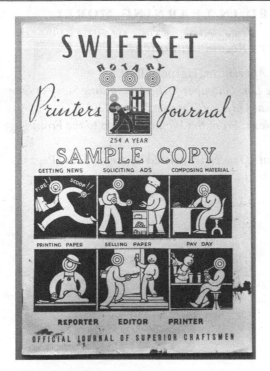

Figure 7.11 Toy printer tasks.

The 1951 instruction manual included an order form for these affordable "picture dies." Each picture set was 50¢, while assorted type fonts cost between 50¢ and $1. The "Cub" press price was $2.25 and the largest model, the "Ace", was $8 with all postage paid.

I admit, I'm somewhat tempted to fire up my own little "Cub" press at times, though the rubber tires on either side of the drum have hardened considerably. Many of these toy presses can still be found in reasonable condition and price on auction sites and elsewhere. Some even come with printed job work from previous owners such as this fun discovery. Somewhere there must be a rotary toy printer group willing to participate in an invitational postcard print-off show sometime. If not, it's time there was. Meanwhile, this PRESS RELEASE: A television advertisement from the early 1960s showcases another style of toy printer modeled on a litho press. Made by toy manufacturer, Ideal, it originally cost $11.44 when first released.

INTERESTED IN LEARNING MORE?

Book Recommendations

Alix Christie, *Gutenberg's Apprentice* (Harper, 2014).

Margaret Leslie Davis, *The Lost Gutenberg: The Astounding Story of One Book's Five-Hundred-Year Odyssey* (TarcherPerigee, 2019).

Kay Mills, *A Place in the News: From the Women's Pages to the Front Page* (Columbia UP, 1990).

Kyung-Sook Shin, *The Court Dancer,* translated by Anton Hur (Pegasus Books, 2018).

Chapter Eight

Punctuation

> *"Sometimes you get a glimpse of a semicolon coming, a few lines*
> *farther on, and it is like climbing a steep path through woods and*
> *seeing a wooden bench just at a bend in the road ahead,* **a place**
> **where you can expect to sit for a moment,** *catching your breath."*
> —*Lewis Thomas, "Notes on Punctuation"*

How do you regard punctuation? Is it an exercise in anxiety, wondering if it is it's or its? Is it a pleasure to consider how a dash might enliven a text? Do you use the Harvard (or Oxford) comma? Do you relish introducing a list with a colon? Do you gasp at signs that say tomato's in the supermarket? Are you a grammar sheriff who notes the wayward apostrophe in business names, advertisements, or signs? Do you believe that the punctuation is a fading concern in the face of text language and social media? Have you a mug with there/they're/their? Do you get excited about celebrating National Punctuation Day each September 24?

> Let's eat Grandma.
> Let's eat, Grandma.
>
> Punctuation saves lives.

Punctuation and its use seem to create a line in the sand, with some writers who fret about what mark to insert where and others who enjoy imbuing a text with meaning through a variety of marks. Perhaps writers would be better off with no punctuation marks at all:

as noted writer and memoirist Russell Baker said when speaking aloud you punctuate constantly with body language your listener hears commas dashes question marks exclamation points quotation marks as you shout whisper pause wave your arms roll your eyes wrinkle your brow in writing punctuation plays the role of body language it helps the readers hear the way you want to be heard

How did Baker punctuate this text? If you and other readers were to compare notes on your own punctuation of this text, would it match? Is it incorrect if it does not? In some cases, punctuation is a matter of author preference. A dash may be used rather than a comma to point to or to introduce. On the other hand, a direct quotation from someone like Baker would be wrapped in quotation marks.

HOW PUNCTUATION DEVELOPED

If you were an actor in ancient Athens, then the playwright might have included marks on the script cuing performers about how to deliver the lines, something close to punctuation. If you were in Ancient Rome, then the text to be read might look something like this:

ARCHAICLATINWASWRITTENPRIMARILYINSCRIPTIOCONTINU-
AWHICHMEANSNOWORDBREAKSORPUNCTUATIONBETWEEN-
WORDSONOCCASIONTHEINTERPUNCTWOULDBEUSEDWHICHISA-
DOTORWHATWEMIGHTCALLAMIDLEVELPERIODTHATWASUSED-
TOSEPARATEWORDSTHEINTERPUNCTMIGHTEVENBETRIANGLE-
SHAPED

A•TEXT•WITH•INTERPUNCTS•MIGHT•LOOK•LIKE•THIS

Contemporary readers might be surprised to learn that word spacing is a kind of punctuation, even if there is no punctuation mark. With Latin forming a good portion of the basis for Western languages, how did punctuation marks arise? During the Dark Ages of Europe, when marauders were rampant, the plague was decimating populations, and starvation was a fact of everyday existence, Irish monasteries and their monks were more secure. Speaking Gaelic, these monks took on the task of replicating the manuscripts and books that scholars escaping Europe brought with them, but a Latin with no word spacing nonplused them. This innovation of putting spaces between words for better readability was the innovation of the monks. The downside was it was more expensive, as the spaces meant more paper to be used.

The *punctus* was a point[1] (period- or comma-shaped) used to indicate a pause or break in the text, particularly when reading. Imagine a monk reading a text during mealtime to those assembled. The point could be elevated, placed midway, or sit at the base of the line. The *punctus elevatus* looked like an upside-down semicolon (twelfth to fifteenth centuries) and functioned quite like the semicolon of today. The *punctus interrogativus* indicated a question and could look like a mark, tilde, or slash above a period.

Another ancient punctuation mark is the *diple* (>), used in Greek manuscripts to draw attention or to mark quotations with a notation in the margin. It moved in the Middle Ages to the text itself, noting that it was set off and eventually evolved into quotation marks. With the printing press, punctuation marks became more regularized as they, too, had to be cast into type, eventually resulting in the shapes on view today. Scribal idiosyncrasy simply wouldn't work. The punctuation marks had to be interpreted in a standardized way. The marks also moved to helping readers—who were reading silently rather than aloud—to understand the text. The printing press meant increased readership and also increased literacy, as more people had access to books and read alone.

For the most part, there are about a dozen punctuation marks that are typically used. One infographic[2] depicts punctuation in order of how often they are used and how difficult they should be to learn: period (.), question mark (?), exclamation point (!), asterisk (*), en dash (–), semicolon (;), brackets [ ], parentheses ( ), ellipsis (…), em dash (—), quotation marks (" "), colon (:), hyphen (-), apostrophe ('), and comma (,). Not included is the slash (/), also called a virgule, from the Latin *virgula*, meaning "little rod." This should come as no surprise: there are no necessarily hard-and-fast rules in punctuation, or often in grammar.[3]

---

1 Before the term punctuation came into use around the sixteenth century in English, the term used was *pointing*, as it was the use of points that guided reading aloud and inflection. Thus, monks would "point" a passage rather than "punctuate" a passage.

2 Source: https://thevisualcommunicationguy.com/2014/06/05/the-15-punctuation-marks-in-order-of-difficulty/.

3 To clarify, grammar, usage, and mechanics refer to different aspects of language. Grammar is the structural underpinnings of a language; usage is literally how the language is used, and it can change; mechanics refers to the nuts and bolts of writing: capitalization, spelling, and punctuation. Here's just one instance of how language changes: the National Council of Teachers of English (NCTE) in its Gender-Fair Use of Language Policy Statement declared that the plural "they" can be used with the singular "everyone" in order to avoid the traditional use of the male singular pronoun "his." Everyone and their do not agree "in number," but the result is fairer to all people.

The period (or full stop) is the oldest punctuation mark, migrating on the line from low to high, depending on how long the reader was to pause, and finally settling on the base to mark a sentence's end. It also took on the role of showing that words were left out, so when three periods are placed together, the ellipsis is the result. Of course, periods are also used for abbreviations, such as Mr., Mrs. (but not Ms), and Jr. These do not affect syntactic structure, though.

The question mark began as the *punctus interrogativus*, but it evolved to the form known now fairly late, probably in the seventeenth century, as the content of the sentence was indicative of a question. The exclamation point also arrived during the seventeenth century. For Spanish speakers, both the exclamation mark and question mark also appear at the beginning of a sentence but inverted (¿ ¡), which was an eighteenth-century refinement, offering the reader a preview of the meaning.

A quirky punctuation mark unlikely to show up in any most-used list is the interrobang, which is a question mark superimposed on an exclamation point (‽). The interrobang was popular during the 1960s but never caught on as a standard mark of punctuation. Its purpose, as envisioned by its creator Martin K. Speckter (1915–88), was to express both surprise and a question.

The semicolon is a "misunderstood" punctuation mark, according to Cecelia Watson, whose book on the subject was published in 2019. It can be used as an emoticon to show winking or crying, of course, but its meaning as a punctuation mark is more complex. Aldus Manutius the Elder (1450–1515), who introduced italics to printing at his Venice establishment, is also responsible for the semicolon. Lynne Truss, the author of the best-selling *Eats, Shoots & Leaves*, admires him so much for his accomplishments that she volunteered to have "his babies" (xii), which, admittedly, would be a neat trick across the centuries. I wouldn't go that far, but I do admire the semicolon, as it elegantly separates and joins two independent clauses— what could stand alone as sentences. I particularly like it when a conjunctive adverb is employed to show the relationship between the two ideas: I wanted to read the best-selling *Eats, Shoots & Leaves*; however, was a book on grammar truly going to be entertaining? (An aside: does a rhetorical question require a question mark?) The second nifty use of the semicolon is to set off items in a series that are too complex for just the lowly comma. For instance, Sparkle, the cat who came to stay; Whiskers, the dog that loved too much; and Roger, the rogue squirrel—these are the animals that made up my summer's distraction.

If there's a semicolon, then surely there must be a full colon. I must admit that a list in a sentence preceded by a colon, but in which the colon is not introduced by a full sentence, is annoying. If there's no full sentence, then the colon is unnecessary. The sentence simply flows into the list. Take this sentence, for instance:

This fall semester, I'll enroll in chemistry, physics, Aikido for exercise, and the odd Honors course.

In contrast, the colon does duty like this:

This fall semester, I'll enroll in the following classes: Chemistry, Physics, Aikido for exercise, and the odd Honors course.

The colon has several other uses, too, but none really have a major effect on sentence meaning.

Quotation marks are most often known for—surprise—setting off quotations. I sometimes wish that English used the more exotic *guillemets*, also called French quotes, which are used in other languages. I do think the chevron more attractive: « ». The quotation marks that English speakers are accustomed to—" "—have migrated up and down the line, much as periods/punctus did. The practice of setting off text to indicate its importance—which may have been a quotation—is quite old. Recall the diple. Another wrinkle in quotations is quoting a quotation within another quotation, which calls on "single quotation marks" (the apostrophe in masquerade). This creates a rather complex set of conventions regarding punctuation marks—inside or outside, depending on your country of origin.

In addition to setting off titles of poetry, song, and short stories (in other words, "short works"), quotation marks can have attitude. In speech, people may make air quotation marks to denote a quotation or a snarky comment. The same is true in print. Do words being defined as words go in quotation marks or italics? I'm of the latter school, personally. A terrific source for checking such issues of usage and mechanics is Purdue University's Online Writing Lab (OWL), which originated during the administration of Muriel Harris, legendary director of the institution's Writing Lab.

The crossbar line, the hyphen, joins words. Grammar checkers on word processors seem to go back and forth if two words should be hyphenated or stand apart. The hyphenation generally comes into play when the two words serve as descriptors of another word, functioning as adjectives: mad-as-hell network anchor has an epiphany or twenty-first-century pen-and-ink supplies.

The longer crossbar, the dash, seems a debonair mark of punctuation that interrupts a sentence or offers a touch of flair at its end. My friends—bar none—think I'm the queen of exotic greens. Or, I'm the queen of greens—mesclun, arugula, kale, chard, peppercress, mustard, and more. Admittedly that dash could have been a colon, but the dash lends a certain *savoir-faire* when the tone is so admittedly over the top. Before word processing, dashes were simply an elongated hyphen in handwriting. The examples here are termed the em dash, which refers to its length, an em being the same length as the font's height. Its cousin, the en dash, is half the width of an em dash. Whereas there are no spaces prior to an em dash, the en dash is open or spaced on both sides. For those who publish—whether in the United Kingdom or the United States—this is a serious matter, as the style requires using one or the other, which can result in quite a bit of copy-editing work.

Even with the rather fraught nature of dashes, they are used rarely enough that they do not approach the complexity of the comma or the apostrophe, two similar marks placed at different levels on the line. The modern comma could be a variation on the punctus marks, depending on its placement on the line—base, mid, or high—indicating the length of the pause. Our good friend, the printer Aldus Manutius, once again gets the credit for using the comma as known today. How many uses does the comma have? (There's another rhetorical question.) Let me count the ways:

- The comma, along with a conjunction, punctuates a compound sentence. [Note that the ingenious semicolon may replace this structure.]
- The comma separates items in a list of three or more, such as eats, shoots, and leaves [if the Harvard or Oxford comma is employed].
- The comma can introduce a quotation.
- The comma bookends an appositive that interrupts the sentence, as in "Jesse, my daughter, is debating which college to attend."
- The comma comes after an introductory phrase or clause prior to the main sentence.
- The comma separates multiple adjectives.

This busy punctuation mark also does mechanical duty after a salutation of a "friendly letter," as well as in dates, names of city and states, and large numbers. There are so many ways to go wrong with a comma. A typographer/designer told me that she used this lesson to emphasize how a comma could change meaning:[4]

The Oracles at Delphi had a nifty ploy to keep their cushy jobs as soothsayers. If asked by a man pondering whether to join an armed

---

4   Gail Griswold, personal communication, 4 August 2019.

conflict, they would write an answer like this. The Oracle's prediction was always right, depending, of course, upon where the comma was placed.

Go not in battle shall you die

A second popular example of demonstrating the importance of punctuation to the meaning of a sentence is this one:

Woman without her man is nothing.

Commas? Colon? Dash? What do you think?

But topping the list for misuse is the apostrophe, and no wonder: its uses are diverse and rather divisive. It is used when letters are missing from a word such as don't (do not) or it's (it is), but the apostrophe offers a possessive quality so that the girl's dog or the dogs' owner are also in play. But then, just to confuse writers, some words are innately possessive—like its—the gender-neutral possessive adjective/pronoun, as in "You can't tell a book by its cover." A book has no gender or sex, so it needs a sexless pronoun: it. Likewise, the plural theirs has possession built in.

BRITISH AND AMERICAN PUNCTUATION

I sometimes tell my students that we fought a war over whether the period at the end of a sentence should go inside the quotation marks or outside. North Americans place the period inside the quotation marks while British put the period outside. The same is true for the comma. The British refer to the period as a "full stop," but note that when email addresses or domain names are spoken, the term is "dot." As George Bernard Shaw quipped, "The British and the Americans are two great peoples divided by a common tongue." And, there I've just demonstrated I'm an American as I put the period inside the quotation mark! [Which certainly called for an exclamation mark.]

IS PUNCTUATION A JOKE?

For some reason, jokes about grammar and punctuation are popular.

• The exclamation point says to the question mark, "I'll never date another apostrophe. The last one was too possessive."

- The comma says to the period, "Let's slow down for a second here," to which the period replies, "We better just stop right now."[5]
- As we saw earlier, "Let's eat Grandma!" or "Let's eat, Grandma!" Punctuation saves lives.
- When grammarians BBQ: Well done? Well-done? Or well, done?"
- What's a prisoner's favorite punctuation mark? A period, as it marks the end of a sentence.
- I was a surgeon with bad punctuation. I got fired for leaving out a colon.
- I took all the punctuation marks off the judge's keyboard. I expect a long sentence.
- The exclamation point says to the question mark, "Must you question everything?" to which the question mark responds, "Why are you always yelling?"

Is the death of punctuation, as described by some pundits due to its inaccurate use on social media, exaggerated, or is it alive and well? (Another rhetorical question!) According to Gretchen McCulloch, internet linguist and author of *Because Internet: Understanding the New Rules of Language* (2019), typographical marks in internet text may be leading to more precise use of punctuation. Authors of brief texts may think carefully about how to punctuate in order to indicate tone, irony, or emotion. In fact, ironic punctuation has a long history. Henry Denham, a printer in sixteenth-century England, proposed the "percontation point," a backward question mark (⸮), to denote irony. Later, it became known as the rhetorical question mark but lasted only a century. The latest punctuation mark may be the emoji, which inflects emotion in any text. Why is an exclamation mark needed if the emoticon shows excitement?

Is punctuation dead? Not if book sales are an indication of life and success. In addition to McCulloch's book on punctuation and the internet (which according to the most current AP rules is no longer capitalized), an entire book is devoted to the semicolon, as we saw above. Will it

---

5 Cecil B. Hartley, a nineteenth-century writer, is known for his book *The Gentleman's Book of Etiquette and Manual of Politeness* (1860), but he also wrote *The Principles of Punctuation* (1818), which included this poem that specified the amount of time for pauses for each punctuation mark (really):

The stop point out, with truth, the time of pause
A sentence doth require at ev'ry clause.
At ev'ry comma, stop while *one* you count;
At semicolon, *two* is the amount;
    A colon doth require the time of *three*;
The period *four*, as learned men agree.

make a splash the way *F***ing Apostrophes*[6] by Simon Griffin did? Or the multi-million-seller by Lynne Truss, *Eats, Shoots & Leaves*, which asks the perennial question: did the bear do it? Mary Norris, the self-professed Comma Queen of *The New Yorker*, has an encore career in writing about her work as a copy editor and then her foray into the Greek etymology of words. What might appear to be a "dry" tome with a stiff-back title, *Dreyer's English: An Utterly Correct Guide to Clarity and Style*, is actually not only proper but also delightful. Grammar Girl Mignon Fogarty has a following online as well as in her cheeky *The Grammar Devotional*, suggesting that daily grammar study may be as valuable as daily meditation or prayer. Of course, these follow on the popular vampire-themed grammar guides of the 1980s by Karen E. Gordon. But still standing is Strunk and White, *The Elements of Style*, first published in 1918 and considered the foundation of clear, concise, writing.

In the end, writers care deeply about punctuation, as these little marks contribute a lot to the meaning of text, serving both the writer and the reader.

QUESTIONS TO CONSIDER

1. That famous philosopher Matthew McConaughey said, "Life is a series of commas, not periods." What witticism might you coin that involves one or more punctuation marks?
2. Where do emoticons fit with punctuation or typographical symbols?
3. Read Lewis Thomas's essay, "Notes on Punctuation," that appears below. How would you classify this essay? What is its tone? When did you realize this about the essay?

DO-IT-YOURSELF HANDS-ON ACTIVITIES

1. In this chapter, you learned about the Interrobang, the question mark paired with the exclamation point to show a question with a note of surprise or wonder. With text language, marks to indicate emotion or style have increased, and many of them are creative. If you had the option of creating a new punctuation mark, what would it be and why? Design that punctuation mark.
2. In honor of National Punctuation Day, September 24, design an activity focusing on punctuation. For instance, there are possible cooking opportunities such as the punctuation meatloaf featured on the National Punctuation Day website, but perhaps cookies or cake might

---

6 The correct name of this book title appears in the References section, in case you can't figure it out!

be another possibility. Another possibility is posting punctuation marks in random places and awarding prizes for those who find them.

3. Collect punctuation errors in print in media, commercial establishments, and public signs.

INVITATION TO REFLECT AND WRITE

1. Claim a punctuation mark or typographical symbol/glyph from the list below. Investigate its history, development, and use. Consider explaining the mark or symbol in an illustrated talk.

> comma
> apostrophe
> hyphen
> colon
> quotation mark
> em dash
> en dash
> ellipsis
> parentheses
> brackets
> curly brackets or braces or squiggly brackets
> semicolon
> asterisk
> exclamation point
> question mark
> percontation point
> period
> interrobang
> ampersand (&)
> pilcrow (¶)
> @ symbol
> pound sign/octothorpe (#)
> backslash (\)
> angle brackets (< >)
> copyright symbol ©
> bullet point •

2. What is your relationship with punctuation? That may sound like an odd question. Do you have a favorite punctuation mark? Those that are avoided? Consider how you use—or don't use—punctuation. This reflection and critique of your relationship with punctuation can be

another section added to the writing autobiography/autoethnography.

3. Annually, the National Punctuation Day folks hold an essay contest. In 2019, the topic was this: "What punctuation error annoys you the most? Find an online meme that illustrates the one punctuation error that sets you off, that makes you scream, that gets you into correction mode. Write a short essay in response."

FOR FURTHER READING

Lewis Thomas, "Notes on Punctuation," from *The Medusa and the Snail* (103–06)

There are no precise rules about punctuation (Fowler lays out some general advice (as best he can under the complex circumstances of English prose (he points out, for example, that we possess only four stops (the comma, the semicolon, the colon and the period (the question mark and exclamation point are not, strictly speaking, stops; they are indicators of tone (oddly enough, the Greeks employed the semicolon for their question mark (it produces a strange sensation to read a Greek sentence which is a straightforward question: Why weepest thou; (instead of Why weepest thou? (and, of course, there are parentheses (which are surely a kind of punctuation making this whole matter much more complicated by having to count up the left-handed parentheses in order to be sure of closing with the right number (but if the parentheses were left out, with nothing to work with but the stops we would have considerably more flexibility in the deploying of layers of meaning than if we tried to separate all the clauses by physical barriers (and in the latter case, while we might have more precision and exactitude for our meaning, we would lose the essential flavor of language, which is its wonderful ambiguity)))))))))))).

The commas are the most useful and usable of all the stops. It is highly important to put them in place as you go along. If you try to come back after doing a paragraph and stick them in the various spots that tempt you you will discover that they tend to swarm like minnows in all sorts of crevices whose existence you hadn't realized and before you know it the whole long sentence becomes immobilized and lashed up squirming in commas. Better to use them sparingly, and with affection, precisely when the need for each one arises, nicely, by itself.

I have grown fond of semicolons in recent years. The semicolon tells you that there is still some question about the preceding full sentence; something needs to be added; it reminds you sometimes of the Greek usage. It is almost always a greater pleasure to come across a semicolon than a period. The period tells you that that is that; if you didn't get all the meaning you wanted or expected, anyway you got all the writer intended to parcel out and now you have to move along. But with a semicolon there you get a pleasant little feeling of expectancy; there is more to come; to read on; it will get clearer.

Colons are a lot less attractive for several reasons: firstly, they give you the feeling of being rather ordered around, or at least having your nose pointed in a direction you might not be inclined to take if left to yourself, and, secondly, you suspect you're in for one of those sentences that will be labeling the points to be made: firstly, secondly and so forth, with the implication that you haven't sense enough to keep track of a sequence of notions without having them numbered. Also, many writers use this system loosely and incompletely, starting out with number one and number two as though counting off on their fingers but then going on and on without the succession of labels you've been led to expect, leaving you floundering about searching for the ninethly or seventeenthly that ought to be there but isn't.

Exclamation points are the most irritating of all. Look! they say, look at what I just said! How amazing is my thought! It is like being forced to watch someone else's small child jumping up and down crazily in the center of the living room shouting to attract attention. If a sentence really has something of importance to say, something quite remarkable, it doesn't need a mark to point it out. And if it is really, after all, a banal sentence needing more zing, the exclamation point simply emphasizes its banality!

Quotation marks should be used honestly and sparingly, when there is a genuine quotation at hand, and it is necessary to be very rigorous about the words enclosed by the marks. If something is to be quoted, the *exact* words must be used. If part of it must be left out because of space limitations, it is good manners to insert three dots to indicate the omission, but it is unethical to do this if it means connecting two thoughts which the original author did not intend to have tied together. Above all, quotation marks should not be used for ideas that you'd like to disown, things in the air so to speak. Nor should they be put in place around clichés; if you want to use a cliché you must take full responsibility for it yourself and not try to fob it off on anon., or on society. The most objectionable misuse of quotation marks, but one which illustrates the danger of misuse in ordinary prose, is seen in advertising, especially in advertisements for small restaurants, for example "just around the corner," or "a good place to eat." No single, identifiable, citable person ever really said, for the record, "just around the corner," much less "a good place to eat," least likely of all for restaurants of the type that use this type of prose.

The dash is a handy device, informal and essentially playful, telling you that you're about to take off on a different tack but still in some way connected with the present course—only you have to remember that the dash is there, and either put a second dash at the end of the notion to let the reader know that he's back on course, or else end the sentence, as here, with a period.

The greatest danger in punctuation is for poetry. Here it is necessary to be as economical and parsimonious with commas and periods as with the words themselves, and any marks that seem to carry their own subtle meanings, like dashes and little rows of periods, even semicolons and question marks, should be left out altogether rather than inserted to clog up the thing with ambiguity. A single exclamation point in a poem, no matter what else the poem has to say, is enough to destroy the whole work.

The things I like best in T.S. Eliot's poetry, especially in the *Four Quartets*, are the semicolons. You cannot hear them, but they are there, laying out the connections between the images and the ideas. Sometimes you get a glimpse of a semicolon coming, a few lines farther on, and it is like climbing a steep path through woods and seeing a wooden bench just at a bend in the road ahead, a place where you can expect to sit for a moment, catching your breath.

Commas can't do this sort of thing; they can only tell you how the different parts of a complicated thought are to be fitted together, but you can't sit, not even to take a breath, just because of a comma,

INTERESTED IN LEARNING MORE?

Book Recommendations

Jeff Deck and Benjamin Herson, *The Great Typo Hunt: Two Friends Changing the World, One Correction at a Time* (Crown, 2011).

Keith Huston, *Shady Characters: The Secret Life of Punctuation, Symbols, and Other Typographical Mark* (Norton, 2013).

Mary Norris, Selections from *The New Yorker* or the books listed in References.

Cecelia Watson, *Semicolon: The Past, Present, and Future of a Misunderstood Mark* (HarperCollins, 2019).

Lawrence Weinstein, *Grammar for a Full Life: How the Ways We Shape a Sentence Can Limit or Enlarge Us* (Lexigraphic, 2020).

Also see the various titles listed earlier in the chapter.

Chapter Nine

Gods, Goddesses, Muses, and Patron Saints of Writing

"Maybe the muse has stepped out back for a smoke."
—*Ann Patchett*

Tucked away in a drawer in my house is a rolled page of black construction paper with gold figures from the London Brass Rubbing Centre at the St. Martin-in-the-Fields Church that depicts the Virgin Mary with her mother, St. Anne (see Figure 9.1). The tag reads, "This is a brass rubbing of St. Anne teaching the Virgin to write. Even for a Saint with a divine pupil, it was darned hard work. That's why St. Anne is the Patron Saint of all writers and writing teachers. You deserve a Patron Saint." The rubbing was a gift from one writing teacher to another. I learned later that the image is about teaching Mary not to write but to read. It's a common image in a canon of works noted as "The Education of the Virgin." Medieval folklore portrayed Mary as very pious and desirous of learning the scriptures; her mother was her teacher.

While St. Anne really is not the patron saint of writing, it makes a person wonder why writers or writing teachers need a patron saint. Writing or teaching writing is definitely hard work. Patron saints serve as role models and heavenly advocates. They may be able to intercede when a person is experiencing writer's block. Within the Catholic Church, there truly exist patron saints for writers and those whose professions are connected

Figure 9.1
Saint Anne teaching
Mary to write—or to
read?

to writing. They acquired their affiliation with writing by having a link to words, writing, or books. As role models, they are to inspire. This chapter provides a catalogue of the remarkable number of saints, gods, goddesses, and muses associated with writing.

PATRON SAINTS

St. Brigit (also Brigid) of Ireland, who lived from 451–525, is the patron saint of printing presses and poets. A contemporary of the better-known St. Patrick, she established a monastery for women, which included a school of art, which became famous for its illuminated manuscripts, particularly the *Book of Kildare*. Following St. Brigit in Ireland is St. Columba (521–597), who transcribed over 300 books before there was a printing press. He is a patron saint of bookbinders and poets. Another patron saint of poets is St. David of Wales, a contemporary of St. Columba.

Printers have patron saints also in St. Augustine, who lived from 354–430 in North Africa and was a prolific writer, as well as St. Genesius of Rome, who was martyred by Emperor Diocletian in 303. Yet another patron saint related to printers and booksellers is St. John of God (1495–1550), who sold books and preached about their subjects.

St. Lucy or Lucia (282–304) is probably best known now for her role in Sweden's annual St. Lucia Day, when a chorus of youngsters in white gowns greets Nobel Prize winners early on December 10, singing the song that all Swedes known by heart, "Santa Lucia." She is certainly an appropriate saint for the Nobel Laureate in Literature, as she makes an appearance in Dante's *Inferno*. Better known as the patron saint of the blind, she is also a patron for writers.

As literacy grew, particularly in wealthy families and monastic communities, scholars and students turned to patron saints Scholastica (480–543) and her twin brother Benedict (480–547). The two of them enjoyed discussing sacred texts, resulting in both being associated with books, reading, and school. Bookbinders have a patron saint in the only pope to ever resign, Pope Celestine V (1215–96; r. 1294), who is always depicted with a book. A true believer in the maxim that "idle hands are the devil's work," he was a prolific copier of books.

St. Francis de Sales of France lived from 1567–1622 and is regarded as a patron saint of writers and journalists. As a priest, he wrote many religious leaflets by hand and several books, including *Introduction to the Devout Life* (1608). During his lifetime, Gutenberg's printing press was invented. St. John Bosco (1815–88) is considered the patron saint of editors and publishers. A native of Italy, he founded schools and orphanages for boys, where he taught them how to run a printing press.

The Venerable Bede (672–735) belongs only to English writers as a patron (see Figure 9.2). A remarkable scholar, he wrote the *Ecclesiastical History of the English People*, which really was a monumental undertaking. His secular work includes books on rhetoric, orthography, and grammar for the abbey school. These works were influential in what is known as the Carolingian renaissance, the first of three such movements in the Middle Ages, which reflects cultural activity that helped move society to the actual Renaissance. This included adopting a Carolingian[1] script, which was easier to read as it included lower-case letters, and preserving classical texts.

Figure 9.2 The Venerable Bede.

---

1 The term *Carolingian* is derived from the ninth-century joint reign of Charlemagne and Louis the Pious of France. Charlemagne ordered that schools be established to improve the literacy levels of his subjects.

It should be noted that Protestants generally neither venerate saints nor turn to them to intercede on their behalf. The feeling is that applying to saints as intercessors comes close to idolatry, when only God should be consulted. In the Middle Ages, the worship of the Virgin Mary reached such heights that it was termed *Mariology*. A backlash occurred when it was perceived that she was worshipped more than her son or God. Critics called this *Mariolatry*, inappropriate devotion.

GODS AND GODDESSES

Before there were patron saints, ancient civilizations in Egypt, Greece, and Rome turned to gods and goddesses. They were used to explain creation myths, the world people inhabited, and the relationship of people to religion. We are interested here in those gods and goddesses associated with writing in particular.

Nisaba (also Nidaba) is the Sumerian goddess of writing, and she served as scribe of the gods. Originally a goddess of grain, she later became associated with writing. Cuneiform in ancient Sumer (3500–3000 BCE) developed as a result of the desire to record transactions, and the buying and selling of grain would have been an important business deal. She became known as "The Lady—in the places where she approaches there is writing" (Monaghan 8). She is depicted holding a gold stylus and clay tablet, according to Kramer (*Sumerians* 138). Although actual symbols (pictographs) of the object being traded were used originally, eventually scribes used a stylus to make wedge-shaped forms on wet clay tablets, the wedges being the origin of *cuneiform*.

As it was common for people to adopt a god or goddess for their professions, the new class of scribes latched upon Nisaba. She became "the goddess of literacy and patroness of the craft of writing" (Mark). Monaghan notes that practice tablets at the scribal schools (c. 2000 BCE) invoke her name: "Praise be to Nisaba!" and "I am the creation of Nisaba" (9). Mark says that "in composing a written work, an author was honoring with the gifts she had given." A Hymn to Nisaba describes her as a "Lady colored like the stars of heaven, holding a lapis-lazuli tablet!" and concludes with this tribute:

O Nisaba, good woman, fair woman, woman born in the mountains. Nisaba, may you be the butter in the cattle-pen, may you be the cream in the sheepfold, may you be keeper of the seal in the treasury, may you be a good steward in the palace, may you be a heaper up of grain among the grain piles and in the grain stores! (Electronic Text Corpus)

Figure 9.3 Cuneiform tablet about Nisaba by Jeremiah Peterson, PhD.

A modern cuneiform artist, Jeremiah Peterson, makes new tablets based on ancient texts (see Figure 9.3). In this one, which was part of a hymn praising the Larsa king Sin-iddinam, Nisaba is praised for the gift of beautiful handwriting to the diligent scribal student:

> The (scribe) who does not neglect his/her work, who perfectly executes the counting (of the proper number of lines of text on the tablet) and incising (of the sings), Nisaba the lady (possessing cunning wisdom, will give perceptiveness to him. She will bestow upon him very beautiful handwriting, the alluring feature of the scribal art! (Peterson)

A temple dedicated to Nisaba and guarded by a pair of lions was excavated in 1945 at Tell Harmal near Baghdad, Iraq (see jstor.org/stable/community.11655566). Her Egyptian counterpart was Seshat, whom we will meet shortly. But, first, what happened to Nisaba? Hammurabi, famous for his law code, preferred male deities. As a result, Nabu became the patron of writing and scribes, and they turned to him for inspiration, while his wife (or perhaps consort), Nisaba, took a secondary role, was relegated to keeping the records and library of the gods (Mark). Eventually, she may have been replaced by another wife, Tashmet. Nisaba has yet another literary connection: her sister, Nunsun, is the mother of Gilgamesh, about whom one of the most famous stories in the ancient world was written. Nabu's name, though, is the one that is most likely to be remembered. In 2018, the Nabu Museum opened in Lebanon to exhibit antiquities and contemporary art. The three men who founded the museum named it after Nabu, whom they know as the "ancient Mesopotamian patron god of literacy, the rational arts, scribes and wisdom," as well as the god of cuneiform writing (Povolny).

The other major civilization to engage early in writing was, of course, Egypt, which had its own gods and goddesses that scribes could patronize. Both Nisaba and Nabu could have migrated to Egyptian culture and shown up, perhaps, with different names, although it's thought that Nabu was himself worshipped. Egyptian gods generally had the heads of animals on human bodies. Thoth's head was that of an ibis, although sometimes it was a baboon. More important for our purposes, though, is that he gets credit for inventing hieroglyphics, the Egyptian form of writing, and he served as scribe in the underworld, responsible for keeping records. In the Egyptian *Book of the Dead*, the scribe proclaims in Thoth's honor, "I am thy writing palette, O Thoth, and I have brought unto thee thine ink-jar" (Stadler). Note that scribes were not using cuneiform and clay tablets but (reed) pen and ink to write.

Seshat—"She who is foremost in the house of books"—appealed to me immediately when I traveled in Egypt. I found her relief at the Luxor Temple on the back of the throne of a seated statue of Ramses II (thirteenth century BCE) as well as on an exterior wall at the Karnak Temple. The "house of books" is the library where scrolls were kept. I was taken aback at the tiny room at Abydos, said to be the library. As we see in Figure 9.4, Seshat's headdress is a seven-pointed leaf symbol, which looks somewhat like a cannabis leaf but more likely represents papyrus, from which proto-paper was made, and she holds a writing implement in her right hand and a rod in her left (she's also the goddess of architects). As with Thoth, she is given credit

Figure 9:4
Seshat, Egyptian Goddess of Writing.

for inventing writing. Some authorities posit that Seshat invented writing but that Thoth taught Egyptians to write. Seshat is variously seen as the female version of Thoth, his wife, or his daughter. She was the scribe of the pharaoh, recording his accomplishments. This goddess was given new life in 2011 when the Seshat Global History Databank was founded to compile the "most comprehensive body of knowledge about human history in one place"—particularly ancient history. Its aim is to "separate history from legend" and try to "pin down why civilisations rose and fell" (Spinney). Ironically, although her name and figure are prominent on the databank website, her presence is not explained. Perhaps all of those involved know that she is the goddess of writing and books.

In Persia, Tahmuras, who served as its third Shah, became adept at writing in 30 different languages. How? He waged war against demons, won, and as his enslaved peoples, they were charged with teaching him the various scripts. Tahmurath (alternative spelling) is one of a dozen important figures connected with writing that are included at the Library of Congress in Washington, DC, on the brass doors of the John Adams Building.

Greeks and Romans adopted some earlier gods into their own worship. Hermes Trismegistus is a combination of Hermes and Thoth and author of the *Hermetic Corpus*, sacred texts organized as a teacher-and-pupil dialogue (second century CE). Hermes, the son of Zeus, was "God of the Word," as his winged physique makes it possible to carry words quickly. The contemporary word *hermeneutic* relates to interpretation of texts, as Hermes was noted for speech, writing and eloquence. Perhaps J.K. Rowling considered this god in naming Hermione, the female form of Hermes, in the *Harry Potter* volumes. The Romans called this messenger god Mercury.

Cadmus, in Greek mythology, was the founder and king of Thebes. While better known for slaying monsters, he was also said to have brought the Phoenician alphabet to his people, which then was adapted to form the Greek alphabet. Lebanon continues to celebrate Cadmus as the "carrier of the letter" to the world (Menoni 11), and a contemporary publishing house has adopted his name. Philyra, a Thessalian, gets credit as a goddess of writing and the inventor of paper. She was also the mother of Chiron, the King of the Centaurs.

The Muses form a collective group of Greek goddesses,[2] the nine daughters of Zeus and Mnemosyne. (Mnemosyne is the goddess of memory and the source of the term *mnemonic*—a device to help remember rules such as "i before e except after c.") The daughters were conceived on nine consecutive nights. They were sources of inspiration, dedicated to the arts and writers,

---

2 Greek mythology contains several sets of pseudo-goddesses. The Muses form one set, but there are also the Fates, the Graces, the Furies, the Seven Heavenly Virtues, and the Titanides.

and lived on Mount Helicon, where they particularly influenced the poet Hesiod, who tended sheep below and codified the muses in his *Theogony* (700 BCE), which outlines the genealogy of the gods. For the purposes of this chapter, Calliope is of most interest, as she is the Muse of epic poetry and is shown holding a writing tablet. The others focus more on history, comedy, tragedy, and dance. While the Muses were credited with inspiring the arts, they could also be vengeful. The singer Thamyris was so proud of his ability that he boasted that he could outperform the Muses, but he was defeated. They not only blinded him but also took away his ability to play the lyre or compose poetry. In another act of cruelty, the Sphinx learned from the Muses the riddle that she used to challenge Thebans—but Oedipus solved it, thus making him the first traveler not to be devoured.

Authors in ancient times invoked the Muses when writing poetry, epics, or drama, and these invocations are evident in both Homer's and Virgil's work as well as later in Dante, Chaucer, and Shakespeare. Robert Graves suggests in *The White Godddess*, published in 1948 and originally entitled *The Three-Fold Muse*, that worship of a single goddess, who oversees creativity, knowledge, and nature has been in place since the Neolithic Age: "language of poetic myth... was a magical language bound up with popular religious ceremonies in honour of the Moon-goddess, or Muse, some of them dating from the Old Stone Age, and that this remains the language of true poetry."

Turning to the Muse for guidance is a tradition that continues for contemporary writers, although some have noted that "butt in the chair" is an effective strategy too. Flannery O'Connor is reputed to have said, "I don't know if the muse is going to show up on any given day, but I'm going to be at my desk every day from 8 to12 every morning in case she does." The term *Muse* has influenced language use in many ways, including as the lower-case verb *muse*, as in to ponder or think. Muse is the origin of the word *museum* (house of knowledge). Adobe adopted the title *Muse* for one of its products, a website-builder app popular during its 2012–20 lifespan due to its ease of use in not requiring code. More successful, Project Muse is a non-profit collaboration between libraries and publishers, an online database of academic journals and electronic books, providing humanities and social sciences content.

Somewhat related to Muses are personified figures that appear to assist or oversee humans. In the city of Le Puy-en-Velay, France, the *Chapelle des Sacrements* of the Cathedral includes a fifteenth-century fresco depicting Grammar, Logic, Rhetoric, and Music—all women—seated above male counterparts (see Figure 9.5). The first three are considered the trivium[3] of learning. As we learned in an earlier chapter, the quadrivium joined these

---

3 The trivium is joined by the quadrivium to compose the seven liberal arts, "liberal" as they represent what an educated free—liberated—person should know.

Figure 9.5   Grammar, Logic, Rhetoric, and Music. Le Puy Cathedral, France.

three to form the seven liberal arts. Logic carries a lizard and a scorpion engaged in combat, representing debate. At the feet of Logic is Aristotle sitting on a stool and arguing, noting each point on his fingers. The Latin motto that is included, "*Me sine doctores frustra coluere sorores,*" means, according to Edward Evans, that "the sister arts cultivate dialectics in vain without the aid of the doctors or men of learning" (154). At the feet of Grammar is Priscian, the author of the *Institutes of Grammar,* the standard text for studying Latin in the Middle Ages, and two boys with open books learning their lessons are to her side. Rhetoric holds a metal file in her hand, and Cicero, the most famous orator of the ancient world, sits at her feet, book in hand, which is ironic given that he would have used a wax tablet and was the master of the art of memory. Why a file for Rhetoric? Typically, she is shown with a sword or caduceus. Perhaps it represents honing or sharpening an argument? John Walters speculates that it could refer to "an artful, cunning, or shrewd person" as noted in the *Oxford English Dictionary.*[4] Ben Jonson (1572–1637), a contemporary of Shakespeare, uses *file* in a way that suggests tongues could be sharpened—or not—as in this line from *Masque of Gypsies*: "From a tongue without a file, Heapes of Phrases, and no Stile" (vol. vi, p. 113). While the female figures are personifications of concepts, they might also be termed *allegories* of the trivium or perhaps *emblems.*

In prehistoric Ireland, Ogma is said to have invented letters and designed the Gaelic alphabet. Farther north, Odin is the originator of written communication in Norse mythology.

Gods and goddesses or other legendary figures of writing are not limited to Western civilization. In China, Cangjie (2640 BCE), who is reputed to

---

4 Personal communication, 13 March 2019.

have had four eyes, created Chinese characters, revising a Quipu[5] or rope-knot-tying method of recording information. He was said to have been inspired by the pattern of veins on a turtle. The Chinese often used turtle shells for writing, as in oracle bones. A competing legend says that Fuxi (also Paoxi) and his sister Nüwa created the system of Chinese characters (2000 BCE). He's also said to be the author of the *I Ching*, a divination text that is the oldest of the Chinese classics.

When scholars and students in China need help, they turn to Wenchang Wang, a Taoist deity known as the god of culture and literature, who is compassionate and helps rich and poor alike. A similar deity in Japan is Tenjin (745–903 CE); temples in his honor provide places where students (and their parents) may pray for success on exams. The village of Echizen has its own goddess, Kawakami Gozen (400 CE), who is credited with teaching its citizens how to make paper (Simonds 23). A shrine and annual festival honor her, and a Cultural Museum of Paper details the history of the high-regarded *washi* paper produced there.

In India, Ganesha, the elephant-headed god, is worshiped by Hindus. Before beginning to put ink to paper, writers invoke Ganesha's help to remove any obstacles to their task and ensure success. He is said to have been the scribe for one of the major Sanskrit epics of ancient India, the *Mahābhārat*. Sarasvati (also Saraswati in Bali), the Hindu goddess of learning and the arts, is credited with inventing Sanskrit. She is depicted riding on a white goose or swan and holding a book. Brahma, the supreme god, is credited with bringing the knowledge of letters to the human race.

For Islam, the Quran notes that writing comes directly from god: "Read in the Name of thy Sustainer, who has created man out of a clot. Read—for thy Sustainer is the Most Bountiful One who has taught the use of the pen" (96:1–5). The Prophet Mohammed revealed verses such as this to scribes who recorded them early in the seventh century CE, as he himself could not read or write.

In Mesoamerica, Mayan culture looked to Itzamná as the deity who provided the foundations of civilization: writing, calendars, medicine, worship rituals, and agriculture. In addition to inventing writing, this benevolent god was also responsible for creating books and the calendar. His depiction as a toothless but wise old man with a large nose signaled that he was not to be feared, an important characteristic for someone promoting writing. Find him on the temple at Palenque, an archeological site in Mexico. For the Aztecs, Quetzalcoatl, the serpent god, is the founder of culture, inventing writing, books, and the calendar, serving the same function as Itzamná.

---

5   Quipu is most often associated with South American Andean groups. For more information on the figures in these paragraphs, consult my source: mythopedia.com.

In North America, Indigenous peoples came to writing quite late. Sint-Holo, an invisible horned serpent that lived in an underwater cave, is the god of writing, language, and literature, worshipped by those known as the "Civilized Tribes": Cherokee, Creek, Chickasaw, Choctaw, and Seminole. He is believed to have inspired Sequoyah, who developed the Cherokee alphabet.

TALISMANS

Some writers may turn to magical objects for inspiration and help. *Talisman* is derived from an ancient Greek word, *telein* (to fulfill, bring to an end), which became *tilsam* in Arabic and migrated to French (*talisman*), Italian (*talismano*), and Spanish (*talismán*). It was an object that—like an amulet—protected the bearer, averting evil and causing good fortune. It has the power to have a miraculous effect. Naturally, it was popular in the age of medieval medicine, when science had not yet triumphed over magic.

A commercial business, 13 Moons Magical Supplies, offers a talisman for poets and writers that draws on ancient (but updated) Celtic symbols, as poets were held in high regard in this culture. Its advertisement copy describes how the symbols are linked to the writer: "Concentrating on the endless knot work of the six-pointed star will intensify natural inspiration and assist in all of your writing endeavors... poems, plays, and books, even your personal journal! Anyone wishing to embark on a career in radio, television, stage or screen will find the 'Talisman for Poets and Writers' a powerful, inspirational Tool." Another supplier, Magickal Needs, advertises a similar product that creates "a powerful magic to help one find the right word at the most opportune moment." The "Seal of Eloquence" may decorate the reverse of the talisman.

For those not wishing to spend twenty dollars or more on a talisman, it is possible to create one. Often the base will be a stone that has a positive association for the writer. Then, according to advice from Faena Aleph, a website devoted to fantasy and mysticism, the object should be imbued with positive energy daily through meditation. Through this action, the object becomes "the physical representation of an intention." The talisman, in effect, serves as a battery to provide energy to the individual. Fingering the talisman focuses the individual on the task at hand.

A student in one of my classes, Kaitlin Conlin, described how crystals, a kind of talisman, work for her:

> For me, crystal work means using different combinations of crystal in
> order to help myself. I struggle with severe anxiety and major writer's

block; I feel a lot of pressure to produce a great piece. To counteract this, I put together a bag of three crystals. For example, if I'm experiencing negative thoughts about my writing, I include a hematite, a black stone that is supposed to repel negative energy. If I'm experiencing anxiety about producing a piece, I include an amethyst, a purple stone that is supposed to reduce anxiety and be calming. If I need to feel more optimistic about my writing, I include a fluorite, either a purple or green stone that is meant to promote optimism and positivity. I then place these three crystals in my pocket or sweatshirt hood to keep them close to me. If I want to feel particularly close to the crystals, I'll hold them in my hand while I brainstorm or write. I do not necessarily believe that crystals and stones have magical power; however, these crystals with their meanings are a physical reminder of a certain quality or mindset I'd like to achieve.

For this writer, crystals provide a kind of talisman that makes personal goals more tangible. Finally, turquoise, named by the French as "Turkish stone," is said to have power to cure writer's block, as it assists in clear thinking and communication.

INSPIRATION AND INTERCESSION

This chapter includes a pantheon of gods, goddesses, muses, and saints. What drove their creation by humans? How have they functioned across time and civilizations? Worship and religion were important to early peoples. In their minds, gods and goddesses controlled almost every aspect of their lives and the world around them. Reverence for them occurred in the home, shrines, and temples. Priests served as the medium between the deities and people. This mythology served to organize the social fabric of a civilization, provide answers, and account for rituals, customs, and festivals. Early civilizations featured deities for every aspect of life, and some religions contained multiple divine figures while Christianity was monotheistic. Catholicism, for instance, created a secondary tier of saints who could be role models and intercessors. Over 10,000 saints and beati, the latter having attained the status of being termed "blessed" and deserving of some religious honor, exist today, as the practice started about a century after the death of Jesus Christ. Important feast days to celebrate divine beings allowed for festivities in societies where daily life was often hard work. From a more cynical viewpoint, these divinities also provided financial support to religious institutions, because people paid (literally) tribute to gods and goddesses or bought indulgences or pardons.

Gods, goddesses, and saints exist on a higher plane than ordinary humans. Their prayers on behalf of people or their intercessions are thus assumed to be more effective. For the deities associated with a particular profession—like writing—they serve as special protectors. Journalists and writers, for example, consider St. Francis de Sales as a patron.

The Muses are a special case and have evolved into one overarching Muse who continues to be thought of as providing inspiration, motivation, and ideas. Writer after writer refers to the role of their Muse in the work done—or not done. Stephen King said in his excellent book *On Writing*, "Amateurs sit and wait for inspiration, the rest of us just get up and go to work." Author and farmer Wendell Berry says there are two Muses: "the Muse of Inspiration, who gives us inarticulate visions and desires, and the Muse of Realization, who returns again to say, 'It is yet more difficult than you thought.'"

Even award-winning writers experience easy writing tasks as well as difficult ones. *The Writer's Almanac* tells the story of how Robert Frost wrote "Stopping by Woods on Snowy Evening." He had stayed up all night working on "New Hampshire," a poem that probably is not familiar to many readers. He'd never worked all night on a poem before, and he went outside to watch the sun come up on a June morning. The idea for "Stopping by Woods" came to him as he stood there; he rushed into the house and wrote the poem that everyone knows, "almost without lifting his pen from the page." He said, "It was as if I'd had a hallucination" ("Robert Frost"). An example of the Muse at work. On the other hand, Pulitzer-Prize–winning author John McPhee, who began contributing to *The New Yorker* in 1963, details his writer's block in an article in 2013: "Block. It puts some writers down for months. It puts some writers down for life." He recounts "four months and nine days of staring" into a computer monitor. The Muse was not at home with him.

Some of the best advice about writing and the Muse comes from Ann Patchett, author of *Patron Saint of Liars*. She says that "Logic dictates that writing should be a natural act, a function of a well-operating human body, along the lines of speaking and walking and breathing" (21). It is not. When she had difficulty with writing, putting the butt in the chair, she used a suggestion from a composer friend to post a sign-in sheet on her door, noting the time she started writing and the time she ended. She vowed to get in a minimum of an hour each day. She says, "The journey from the head to hand is perilous and lined with bodies. It is the road on which nearly everyone who wants to write—and many of the people who do write—get lost.... Maybe the muse has stepped out back for a smoke" (25–26).

Perhaps the inscription on the St. Anne and the Virgin brass rubbing was right. Writing *is* hard work. Everyone deserves a patron saint, god, goddess, talisman, or muse to help them with the task.

QUESTIONS TO CONSIDER

1. Noted film critic Roger Ebert said, "The Muse visits during the act of creation, not before. Don't wait for her. Start alone." This is just one of many, many quotations about Muses and writing. What others can you find?

2. Why do you think writers turn to talismans, saints, goddesses, or a Muse?

3. Gods, goddesses, muses, and patron saints are often depicted in art and architecture. I've mentioned how I found Seshat, the Egyptian goddess of writing, at Karnak and Luxor Temples. What images of these deities can you find, either in person or through an Internet search?

4. The Muses have been said to be the result of the god Zeus and the goddess of memory, Mnemosyne, having a "torrid nine-night fling that resulted in nine babies." In New Orleans, there are streets named after all nine muses, but they are pronounced in the local dialect. When city planner Barthélemy Lafon laid out the streets in 1810, Ancient Greek was very much in vogue. How could he have known that the locals would develop their own pronunciations? Calliope, the Greek Muse of heroic poetry is pronounced like this, kə-ˈlī-ə-pē, according to Merriam-Webster. In New Orleans, it's only three syllabus: kal-ee-ope. Can you locate information about these street names that honor the Muses? (If you'd like to know more, New Orleans' newspaper, the *Times-Picayune*, published an illuminating article by MacCash on these unique pronunciations.)

INVITATION TO REFLECT AND WRITE

Who or what would be your deity or talisman for writing? Describe that divinity or object.

FOR FURTHER READING

Following are two readings: a brief one from the ancient world that explains what happens when a mortal messes with the Muses, and one from contemporary times that addresses writer's block.

1. Thamyris and the Muses[6]

In Greek mythology, Thamyris, son of *Philammon* and the nymph Argiope, was a Thracian singer who was so proud of his skill that he boasted he could out-sing the Muses. He competed against them and lost. As punishment for his presumption they paralysed him, and took away his ability to make poetry and to play the lyre. This outline of the story is told in the *Iliad*.

> Men from Pylos, lovely Arene, Thryum,
> by Apheus ford, well-built Aipy, Cyparisseis,
> Amphigenea; Pteleum, Helos, Dorium,
> where the Muses met the Thracian Thamyris,
> and stopped his singing—he was coming back
> from Oechalia, from the court of Eurytus the king,
> having boasted his singing would surpass the Muses,
> daughters of aegis-bearing Zeus, should they compete,
> so in their anger the Muses mutilated Thamyris,
> taking away his godlike power of song,
> and making him forget his skill in playing the lyre.
> (Homer, *Iliad*, Book 2)

This allusion is taken up in Euripides' *Rhesus*, in the Library attributed to Apollodorus, and in the Scholia on the *Iliad*. These later sources add the details that Thamyris had claimed as his prize, if he should win the contest, the privilege of having sex with all the Muses (according to one version) or of marrying one of them (according to another); and that after his death he was further punished in Hades. The story demonstrates that poetic inspiration, a gift of the gods, can be taken away by the gods.

2. Ann Patchett, from "The Getaway Car"

At the head of this chapter, an epigraph is included, a quote from award-winning author Ann Patchett, that ponders if "the muse has stepped out back for a smoke." Inspiration is not always omnipresent with writers; sometimes, they get stuck. I recall reading the research by Linda Flower and John Hayes in which they found that the writing process includes *incubation*,

---

6   From http://www.hellenicaworld.com/Greece/Mythology/en/Thamyris.html.

thinking about writing. What a relief! All this time, I had been blaming myself for procrastination. Ann Patchett has been there and understands. In the following excerpt from her essay "The Getaway Car," she talks about writer's block, which should resonate with all writers.

Writer's block is a topic of great discussion, especially among young writers and people who think I should write their book for them. I understand being stuck. It can take a very long time to figure something out, and sometimes, no matter how much time you put in, the problem cannot be solved. To put it another way, if it were a complicated math proof you were wrestling with, instead of, say, the unknowable ending of chapter seven, would you consider yourself "blocked" if you couldn't figure it out right away, or would you think that the proof was difficult and required more consideration? The many months (and sometimes years) I put into thinking about a novel before I start to write it saves me considerable time while I'm writing, but as Elizabeth McCracken likes to point out, it's all a trick of accounting. There may be no tangible evidence of the work I do in my head, but I've done it nevertheless.

Even if I don't believe in writer's block, I certainly believe in procrastination. Writing can be frustrating and demoralizing, and so it's only natural that we try to put it off. But don't give putting it off a magic label. Writer's block is out of our control, like a blocked kidney. We are not responsible. We are, however, entirely responsible for procrastination and, in the best of all possible worlds, should also be responsible for being honest with ourselves about what's really going on. I have a habit of ranking everything in my life that needs doing. The thing I least want to do is number one on the list, and that is almost always writing fiction. The second thing on the list may be calling Verizon to dispute a charge on my bill, or cleaning the oven. Below that, there is mail to answer, an article to write for a newspaper in Australia about the five most influential books in my life and why. What this means is that I will zoom through a whole host of unpleasant tasks in an attempt to avoid item number one—writing fiction. (I admit this is complicated, that I can simultaneously profess to love writing and to hate it, but if you've read this far you must be pretty interested in writing yourself, and if you are, well, you know what I'm talking about.)

The beautiful thing about living in Provincetown in the winter, and having no money and no place to spend it even if I did, was that there was rarely anything in the number-two spot on my to-do list. There was really nothing to distract me from the work I was there to do, and so the work got done. The lesson is this: the more we are willing to separate from distraction and step into the open arms of boredom, the more writing will get on the page. If you want to write and can't figure out how to do it, try picking an amount of time to sit at your desk every day. Start with twenty minutes, say, and work up as quickly as possible to as much time as you can spare. Do you really want to write? Sit for two hours a day. During that time, you don't have to write, but you must stay at your desk without distraction: no phone, no Internet, no books. Sit still quietly. Do this for a week, for two weeks. Do not nap or check your e-mail. Keep on sitting for as long as you remain interested in writing. Sooner or later you will write because you will no longer be able to stand not writing, or you'll get up and turn the television on because you will no longer be able to stand all the sitting. Either way, you'll have your answer.

I once gave this entire explanation to an earnest group of college freshmen who had all suffered cruelly from writer's block. When I finished, one girl raised her hand. "Clearly, you've just never had it," she said, and the other students nodded in relieved agreement. Maybe not. [...]

I've been at this writing job for a long time now, and yet for the most part I still solve my problems in the same ways I first learned to solve them as a college student, a graduate student, a waitress. There are certain indispensable things I came to early, like discipline. But other things, like serious research, I came to later on in my career. I have never subscribed to the notion of "writing what you know," at least not for myself. I don't know enough interesting things. I began to see research as both a means of writing more interesting novels and a way to improve my own education. Case in point: I didn't know a thing about opera, so I figured that writing about an opera singer would force me to learn. Conducting research, which had never even occurred to me when I was young might be part of writing, has turned out to be the greatest perk of the job. I've read Darwin and Mayr and Gosse to get a toehold on evolutionary biology. I've floated down the Amazon in an open boat just to see the leaves and listen to the birds. I've called up the head of malaria research at the Bethesda Naval Hospital in Maryland and asked if I could spend the day following him around. He said yes.

As much as I love doing research, I also know that it provides a spectacular means of procrastination. It's easy to convince myself that I can't start to write my book until I've read ten other books, or gone ten other places, and the next thing I know a year has gone by. To combat this, I try to conduct my research after I've started writing, or sometimes even after

I've finished, using it to go back and correct my mistakes. I try to shovel everything I learn onto the compost heap instead of straight into the book, so that the facts just become a part of my general knowledge. I hate to read a novel in which the author had clearly researched every last detail to death and, to prove it, will force the reader to slog through two pages describing the candlesticks that were made in Salem in 1792.

No matter how far I venture outside my own experience, I also know that I am who I am, and that my work will always reflect my character regardless of whether I want it to. Dorothy Allison once told me that she was worried she had only one story to tell, and at that moment I realized that I had only one story as well (see: *The Magic Mountain*—a group of strangers are thrown together...), and that really the work of just about any writer you can think of can be boiled down to one story. The trick then is to learn not to fight it, and to thrive within that thing you feel deeply and care about most of all...

As much as I love what I do, I forever feel like a dog on the wrong side of the door. If I'm writing a book, I'm racing to be finished; if I'm finished, I feel aimless and wish that I were writing a book. I am vigilant in my avoidance of all talismans, rituals, and superstitions. I don't burn a certain candle or drink a certain cup of tea (neither a certain cup nor a certain kind of tea). I do not allow myself to believe that I can write only at home, or that I write better when I'm away from home. I was once at a writers' colony in Wyoming and the girl in the studio next to mine dragged her desk away from the window the minute we arrived. "My teacher says a real writer never has her desk in front of a window," she told me, and so I dragged my desk in front of the window. Desk positioning does not a real writer make. I had a terrible computer solitaire problem once. I decided that my writing day could not begin until I won a game, and soon after that I had to win another game every time I left my desk and came back again. By the time I had the game removed from my computer I was a crazy person, staking my creativity on my ability to lay a black ten on a red jack. I missed computer solitaire every day for two years after it was gone. Habits stick, both the good ones and the bad.

I've spent long periods when I've written every day, though it's nothing that I'm slavish about. In keeping with the theory that there are times to write and times to think and times to just live your life, I've gone for months without writing and never missed it. One December my husband and I were having dinner with our friends Connie Heard and Edgar Meyer. I was complaining that I'd been traveling too much, giving too many talks, and that I wasn't getting any writing done. Edgar, who is a double bass player, was singing a similar tune. He'd been on the road constantly and he was nowhere near finishing all the compositions he had due. But then he told me a trick: he had put a sign-in sheet at the door of his studio, and when he went in to compose he wrote down the time, and when he stopped composing he wrote down that time, too. He told me he had found that the more hours he spent composing, the more compositions he finished.

Time applied equaled work completed. I was gobsmacked, and if you think I'm kidding, I'm not. It's possible to let the thinking about process become so overly analyzed that the obvious answer gets lost. I made a vow on the spot that for the month of January, I would dedicate a minimum of one hour a day to my chosen profession. One hour a day for thirty-one days wasn't asking so much, and I usually did more. The result was a stretch of some of the best writing I'd done in a long time, and so I stuck with the plan past the month of January and into the rest of the year. I'm sure it worked in part because I already had the story in my head and I was ready to start writing, but it also worked because my life had gotten so complicated and I was in need of a simple set of rules. Now when people tell me they're desperate to write a book, I tell them about Edgar's sign-in sheet. I tell them to give this great dream that is burning them down like a house fire one lousy hour a day for one measly month, and when they've done that—one month, every single day—to call me back and we'll talk. They almost never call back. Do you want to do this thing? Sit down and do it. Are you not writing? Keep sitting there. Does it not feel right? Keep sitting there. Think of yourself as a monk walking the path to enlightenment. Think of yourself as a high school senior wanting to be a neurosurgeon. Is it possible? Yes. Is there some shortcut? Not one I've found. Writing is a miserable, awful business. Stay with it. It is better than anything in the world.

Chapter Ten

QWERTY

TYPEWRITERS AND COMPUTERS

> *"We must see to it that in the diversity of interests one*
> *class of the blind is not overlooked for the sake of another,*
> *or any part of the work undervalued."*
> *—Helen Keller, 1907*

The extraordinary Helen Keller (1880–1968), who is dramatized in the play *The Miracle Worker*, achieved much during her lifetime: the first deaf-blind person to obtain a baccalaureate degree; a staunch disability rights advocate for both children and adults;[1] a prolific writer who made much use of both the Braille typewriter and a traditional model. Keller's family's affluence meant that she had the advantages of a tutor—the remarkable Annie Sullivan—when still a child. Most children did not. In a speech on the centenary to honor Louis Braille, she called Braille the "magic wand of the blind."

Louis Braille's accomplishments were introduced in Chapter Three. Through Braille, which she learned at the Perkins Institute, Keller read and wrote. She used a Braille typewriter, first developed in 1892, which had keys corresponding to the six dots of the Braille code, plus keys to space, backspace, and line space. The resulting raised or embossed dots then were easier to read and decode as opposed to a handwritten version. Keller also typed on a traditional QWERTY typewriter and produced many

---

1 It was not until 1990 that the Americans with Disabilities Act (ADA) was made into law.

Figure 10.1
Helen Keller
seated at a desk
in front of a
braille typewriter.

books and articles as well as numerous letters. Technological innovation was a boon to her writing. Although the typewriter was developed in the nineteenth century, and Milwaukee is cited as the birthplace of the first practical typewriter in 1869 (Wisconsin Historical Society), its use was not widespread until the first part of the twentieth century. Although it may seem that typewriters have been replaced by digital writing machines, they have retained an iconic status.

THE TRENDY TYPEWRITER

Typewriters are celebrated annually at the Museum of Printing in Haverhill, Massachusetts, with its QWERTY Festival. What do the hundreds of participants do at a QWERTY party? Here's a list of attractions from the 2018 event:

- Presentations on typewriter history, maintenance, and applications.
- Participate in workshops on typewriter adjustment and repair.
- Learn who actually invented the typewriter (it was not Mr. Remington).
- Peruse 20 tables of typewriter repair services, typewriter suppliers, and typewriter-related publications and products.
- Buy a typewriter for someone you love.
- See the exhibit of over 40 of the Museum's typewriters, many specialty typewriters.

- Learn about "cold type" proportional-type typewriters such as the Varityper, Justowriter, and IBM Composer.
- See rare office machines, from the very first Mimeograph to Gestetner and Ditto, and more.
- View demonstrations of the Linotype machine, which was invented because of the typewriter.
- Cast your name in hot metal, then print your certificate naming you a genuine "slugcaster."
- Type on a vintage Royal manual typewriter with more fingers than just your thumbs. (Museum of Printing)

A special performance by the Boston Typewriter Orchestra (BTO) was to be the big draw at the 2020 QWERTY festival. An orchestra of typewriters? Unusual, but true. Combining satire and an amazing sense of rhythm on typewriters, they tinkle the (typewriter) keys on tunes such as "Entropy Begins in the Office," "Angry Factory," and "Break Time." Naturally, their music can be purchased on vinyl, although they are investigating cassette tapes (Boston Typewriter Orchestra). One of the band members says that he plays a "Tenor Smith Corona" (Playing Against Type).

For some, the nostalgia of the click, clack, and zing of manual typewriters almost does sound musical. Award-winning actor and author Tom Hanks is one of them. He says, "I write without caring about typos, xxxx'ed out words, goofy syntax, & bad spelling because the feel & sound of a typewriter is satisfying in ways that can't be matched." Hanx Writer is an Apple app that provides the satisfying sounds of a vintage typewriter, perhaps emulating the experiences of famous writers such as Agatha Christie, Maya Angelou, Helen Keller, or Dr. Seuss (Miss Cellania). Ray Bradbury found that typewriters encourage the "truth of swiftness," this from an author who composed *Fahrenheit 451* in a library basement on a rented typewriter. Admittedly, an office full of these dinosaurs would have been hard on the ears during the heyday of the typewriter, when "pools" of secretaries produced reams of typewritten paper. In the 1920s, typewriter manufacturers were aware of the cacophony that hundreds of machines in one room could produce. The Remington 12 model typewriter "speaks only in a whisper but will be heard around the world," according to an advertisement in the *Saturday Evening Post*. Remington claims that it "pleases both the executive and the operator" and "scores with the 'boss'" (see Figure 10.2).

Figure 10.2
Saturday Evening Post
ad for Remington
Typewriter.

THE ORIGINS OF TYPEWRITERS

Before there was a machine called a typewriter, it was actually a term for a person. The goal of the typewriter was to produce print, much like Gutenberg's printing press but by a single person. Gutenberg's approach was to take type and assemble or compose it into words. The typewriter used fixed type that was set into motion by a person hitting the keys in order. Rather than write by hand, a writer could produce a professionally printed document. Attempts to design such a machine were recorded as early as the eighteenth century. In England, Henry Mill (c. 1683–1771) took out a patent on a machine in 1714; it is credited as the first license, but the machine itself never took hold. The keys were in alphabetical order. The tale of a successful typewriter is related in the novel *The Blind Contessa's New Machine* by Carey Wallace (2010), set in nineteenth-century Italy, in which Pellegrino Turri creates a machine for his friend Countess Carolina Fantoni da Fivizzano to communicate with.

Many other inventors around the world turned their attention to developing a machine. The designs varied enormously. One machine might be quite tiny, while another might be huge. The typograph pictured in Figure 10.3 features beautifully long keys as well as what appears to be a fairly standard keyboard (although not a QWERTY style).

Figure 10.3
Mergenthaler Linecasting
Machine. Museum of
Applied Arts & Sciences
(2021).

George C. Blickensderfer (1850–1917), an inventor and salesperson, realized that a portable writing machine would be extremely useful to the traveling sales force that crossed the United States by train, so he created a typewheel struck by keys. The 1897 model pictured in Figure 10.4 was unusually lightweight. Again, note that the keyboard had not yet settled into the QWERTY standard but featured numerals, symbols, and a CAPS key.

Christopher L. Sholes (1819–90), a writer in Milwaukee, invented a typewriter and its QWERTY keyboard, the keys arranged logically to prevent the type bars from sticking together. When that happened, the writer had to physically unlock two keys and put them back into place. When I was learning to type on a manual typewriter in the late 1960s, the issue of "sticking keys" was still problematic. Sholes partnered with Carlos Glidden (1834–77) and others to bring out a typewriter in 1874 that set standards for the industry (see Figure 10.5).

Figure 10.4
Blickensderfer Typewriter. The Lightner Museum, St. Augustine, Florida.

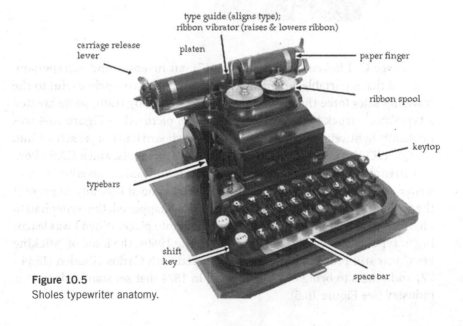

Figure 10.5
Sholes typewriter anatomy.

Mark Twain, ever an adventurer, purchased a Sholes and Glidden machine and reputedly submitted the first typewritten manuscript ever to a publisher. When Sholes and Glidden sold to Remington, which was better known for its firearms and sewing machines, the typewriter took off in popularity. Twain moved on to the enhanced Remington. He stopped writing letters on the machine, however, when the responses demanded a description of the typing process, and he said as much to the Remington Company in a letter of 19 March 1875 that asked, "Please do not use my name in any way. Please do not even divulge the fact that I own a machine."

Early typewriters from Sholes and Glidden and then Remington were mounted on sewing machine tables and even featured a treadle, which was common to the sewing machine. The treadle, which moved the carriage, disappeared, according to the history provided by the Virtual Typewriter Museum, but the sewing cabinet remained.

How does a typewriter work? The writer strikes a letter, number, or symbol on the keyboard, which then causes the typebar, an arm manipulated by a system of levers, to move up and strike the platen, which is a metal tube covered by a rubber sleeve. A piece of paper would have been rolled into the machine so that the type at the end of the bar first hits the ribbon that carries the ink and then makes an impression on the page. The movable carriage advances automatically. The typist must be aware of coming to the margin of the page and then pulling on a lever, the carriage return, to begin the next line. A "shift" key changes the typebar to a different position so that a capital letter can be imprinted. Setting the margins—metal tabs—allowed the typewriter to anticipate the end of the line with a "ding" sound, which signaled the typist to make a carriage return. The platen would then move back to the start and down one line. Double spacing required two returns. The typist had to be ever alert, as mistakes required reinserting a page and starting over. Much later, the typewriter eraser came on the scene, an eraser with an attached

Figure 10.6   Claes Oldenburg and Coosje van Bruggen, Typewriter Eraser (1999). National Gallery of Art Sculpture Garden, Washington, DC.

brush to clear away the debris so as not to foul the machinery. Sculptors Claes Oldenburg and Coosje van Bruggen created a huge version of this implement in 1999; one is in the Sculpture Garden of the National Gallery of Art in Washington, DC. The object will be unrecognizable for those born in the computer age (see Figure 10.6).

Portability was a goal for some typewriter companies. The Bennett typewriter, developed by Charles Bennett in the early 1900s, featured a modified QWERTY keyboard with the space bar inserted not at the bottom but at the top. The advertisement promised that it "Writes Like a $100 Machine," but it sold for only $18 in 1910 (*Saturday Evening Post*).

Typewriter companies soon proliferated; 89 companies existed by 1909, but eventually a few dominated. The Underwood Portable was advertised as having wings and had the tagline "Gives Wings to Words." Using an Underwood helped a writer's imagination to soar: "from its keys words leap in swift flight; ... all that lives in heart and mind is given freest expression" (*American Magazine*).

SOCIAL IMPACT OF TYPEWRITERS

Although women's right to vote in the United States would not be recognized until 1920 with the 19th Amendment, typewriters contributed to women's liberation. In 1838, Catherine Beecher suggested in her *The Moral Instructor for Schools and Families: Containing Lessons on the Duties of Life* that teaching was a natural profession for women and would free them from hard factory work or employment in genteel poverty as governesses. That was just one professional opportunity. With the rapidly increasing use of the typing machine, typewriters—people—were needed. But first they had to learn how to type. As with any innovation, various methods for understanding how to type and accomplishing the act were promoted. Schools of typing opened. The New York YWCA offered typing instruction in 1881. Those skilled in typing didn't have to follow the hunt and peck method, jokingly termed the "Columbus Method": find a key and land on it. By the 1920s, typing pools were common in businesses, and being a secretary became a gendered profession. The job offered women a profession and a way to be economically independent. Certainly the wages would not have been generous, but there would have been opportunities for advancement with additional proficiencies of shorthand and interpersonal communication skills. In fact, shorthand was a skill that predates typewriters but was used primarily by men who served as secretaries—until typewriters came on the scene.

Women working in offices became the norm. By 1910, 81 percent of secretaries were female, and women formed a professional organization for

Figure 10.7
Postcard "We are working under great pressure at the office." Virtual Typewriter Museum.

secretaries in 1942. Their status sometimes was precarious, as male supervisors could prey upon them. Postcards and cartoons depicted the boss seducing the secretary and being caught by his wife (see Figure 10.7). The song "Take a Letter, Maria," by R.B. Greaves (1969) tells the story of a man who worked nights and did not pay sufficient attention to his wife; after he sees his wife with another man, he asks his secretary, Maria, to "take a letter"—in shorthand—to be sent to his wife, before asking his secretary out for dinner.

Typewriters went to war in the 1940s. Manufacturers prepared US Army green models for the use of soldiers managing the war. Orders were typed, not handwritten. Ribbon was available in black or other colors. One favorite was a two-toned black and red.[2]

Manual typewriters have continued to have a fan club, even after electric typewriters and computers were introduced. Danielle Steel, who has authored over 180 books, is devoted to her Olympia typewriter and unabashedly notes that she is a technophobe. In a blog on her website she describes her adored writing machine:

---

2 Poet May Swenson (1913–89) used the red-and-black typewriter ribbon as the cover design of her 1970 collection of poems, *Iconographs*, verses composed spatially to represent the subjects.

My head is spinning a bit, and I had to share it with you. I think I've mentioned to all of you before that I am deeply, powerfully, and sincerely technologically challenged. I write on a 1946 manual typewriter that seems modern to me. I paid $20.00 for it a million years ago, at the beginning of my career, in a second hand typewriter store. And I love it. I can't write on anything else, and wouldn't try. I could never even write on an electric typewriter that takes off at the merest touch. And I can't write on a computer. It just doesn't work for me (except for email). And I'm happy this way, unchallenged, unconfused, and entirely unmodern. It also semi-hides the fact that I am completely confused by technology. And the thought that a computer would EAT 3 chapters of a book, or all of it, is horrifying to me. So I'm definitely sticking to my ancient typewriter, still going strong (best investment I ever made, 116 books later), which very politely only eats what I feed it. My typewriter's name is Ollie (an Olympia, a German hand made table top manual typewriter, which weighs as much as I do. It is an incredibly fine machine. And I'm happy to say it's older than I am). (Steel)

Figure 10.8
Olivetti Valentine
Typewriter and Case.
Design Museum, Ghent,
Belgium (2018).

Steel also has a great comeback when someone asks her if she is "still writing": "What this does is that it immediately puts my writing into the category as a hobby. As in, are you still taking piano lessons, doing macramé, have a parrot? I don't have a huge ego about my work, but let's face it, for me it is a job. A job I love, and I have been doing it since I was 19 years old.... I never say to guys, 'So are you still a lawyer?... A doctor?... A brain surgeon?'"

If ever there were a love affair with a typewriter, surely it had to be with Olivetti's sleek and sexy Valentine model, which burst onto the staid typewriter scene in 1970 (see Figure 10.8). Designed by Ettore Sottsass (1917–2007), the Valentine came with its own elegant carrying case. It is a common fixture in design museums. The manual called it a "brite writer" that is always "travel ready." It also described the rather cumbersome procedure of changing out the ribbon when it ran out of ink. The orange caps on the ribbon cartridges reflected the pop art style of the time. Olivetti is the only typewriter company still standing as of this writing.

ELECTRIC TYPEWRITERS

Thomas Alva Edison predicted that typewriters would use electricity soon after their acceptance and growing popularity. Although the Blickensderfer Electric came out in 1902, it took some decades for electric typewriters to become widespread. Two world wars certainly impeded invention and development. International Business Machines (IBM) invested heavily in typewriter research and tackled the nagging problem of jammed typebars. The solution was the "golf ball" style printing element. The ball could be changed out for various fonts, which had been anticipated by the nineteenth-century Hammond machine.

Listening to feedback from typists, IBM also enclosed its ribbon in a cartridge that could be lifted out and replaced easily, without messy ink smudges. Another important innovation was the ability to correct type. The Selectric from IBM had these features and more. From 1961 to 1971, the Selectric was continuously refined, and IBM made a strategic marketing decision to put these models in schools for typing instruction. (At the time, instruction was given, particularly to girls, in secretarial skills such as dictation shorthand, typing, and bookkeeping.) The Selectric II debuted in 1984, but by that time its days were limited, as the personal computer was beginning to make inroads.

INTERNATIONAL TYPEWRITERS

As we've seen, scripts are not the same around the world; as a result, typewriters differed also. An Arabic typewriter was created in 1914 by Philip Wakid and Selim Shebly Saad Haddad, who were Lebanese immigrants to Egypt. The British Museum features a 1922 typewriter, "Writing Machine Egypt," that was produced by Smith Premiere in Syracuse, New York. It was a heavy machine, made out of iron to withstand the climate.

An even more difficult challenge was the Chinese typewriter (see Figure 10.9). With thousands of characters to include, it had to be large. The designers had to figure out how to include sufficient characters to be efficacious. With 2,000 characters needed on a typewriter—which is still short of the 6,000 used in daily newspapers—there is no keyboard to strike. Instead, the "typist" moves a lever to pick up a character, which is then moved to the paper, where an impression is made. It functions something like a jukebox, picking up a record and putting it in the player. A skilled operator can type 20 characters per minute.

Figure 10.9
Chinese Typewriter.
Museum of
Communication,
Nuremberg,
Germany.

In his book examining this amazing and large machine, Thomas S. Mullaney discusses not just the design challenges of the Chinese typewriter but also the cultural imperative of saving a character-based, non-alphabetic language. When much of the world was invested in QWERTY-style typewriters, how might the Chinese language engage, a question that had implications for economics and trade? Obviously, China is a global leader now, but not so many decades ago it was still somewhat isolated. Mullaney believes that the trials and errors of engineering a Chinese typewriter anticipated technologies of smartphones and other digital devices.

When the computer rose to power in the 1980s, the fate of the Chinese characters was once more at stake. There was simply no way the computing power at the time could contain 70,000 Chinese characters. It was thought that "Computers are the gravediggers of Chinese characters" (Adler). Would China finally be forced to reform its writing system? Professor Wang Yongmin undertook the conundrum and assembled 120,000 notecards of all Chinese character parts. Over the course of five years, he reduced these to 125, which, finally, would fit on a QWERTY style keyboard—rather like flip phones that featured three letters on a number key, but his system placed about five on any one key. Using these character components, what he termed the Wubi Method, a person could type on a standard QWERTY keyboard, but the result would be Chinese characters, a process he demonstrated in 1984 before the United Nations. Amazingly, competing input methods for Chinese characters based on phonetics arose in the 1990s; as a result, it is entirely possible that multiple approaches to typing on a QWERTY keyboard exist for Chinese writers.

TYPEWRITER NOSTALGIA

Danielle Steel is not the only person to cling to a manual typewriter. Actor Tom Hanks collects vintage typewriters the way Jay Leno collects classic cars. Carl Dietz's collection of over 100 machines is housed in the Milwaukee Public Museum, the city of Christopher Sholes, designer of the first truly successful typewriter. What is the attraction? Typewriters are cult objects. They provide tactile and auditory sensations for writers, as they physically engage with the keyboard and the return carriage, and listen for the friendly ding, the reminder that it's time for a new line. It's more than likely that there's no correcting function for the vintage machine, so words must be chosen carefully the first time. It might seem that it's older users, nostalgic for what was perceived to be a kinder, gentler time, who yearn for the QWERTY machine that's not digital, but culture vultures find that millennials are entranced by the notion of producing poetry, stories, or letters with this form of slow writing (Hill). Afrose Fatima Ahmed opened Poem Store, where she produces impromptu typewritten poems for strangers at whatever price they deem fit. She travels the United States and sets up shop in parks and on street corners. She calls it a "common quest for belonging" ("Typewriter Poetry").

Qwerkywriter offers a typewriter-inspired mechanical keyboard that connects to a tablet via a USB port. The aesthetically pleasing keyboard even offers the option of a carriage return—or the user can simply press the Enter key.[3] Qwerkywriter is similar to Hanx Writer in recreating the experience of a typewriter—but with the convenience of a smartphone—for those who want that old-school experience.

The nostalgia for vintage typewriters was apparent in a 2017 obituary in the *New York Times*: "Mary Adelman, 89, Fixer of Broken Typewriters, Is Dead" (Barron). How many fix-it-shop owners rank an obituary in the *Times*? She and her husband—both survivors of the Holocaust—provided "an emergency room for typists with bent keys, problematic platens and ruined ribbons." The literary lights that frequented the shop included Nora Ephron, Philip Roth, and Isaac Bashevis Singer. Adelman felt that typewriters contributed to the craft of writing and thought that personal computers "made writing too easy."

THE DIGITAL REVOLUTION

Four significant markers in human communication are language, writing, the printing press, and the digital revolution. One moment in the latter occurred in March 1975, at the first meeting of the Homebrew Computer Club. Modeling on the trend to brew one's own beer, this group started meeting in Menlo Park, California, to trade circuit boards and to figure out how to turn the huge, ungainly mainframe computers into personal computers—something like moving from printing press to typewriter. Two high-school students joined in: Steve Jobs and Steve Wozniak. They were inspired by these electrical and computer engineers and hobbyists and eventually shared a machine they were working on that they dubbed the Apple.

Early computers filled entire rooms and performed rather basic calculations. Alan Turing (1912–54), part of the British team in World War II that broke the German Enigma Code, was credited with the concept of a computer. The Colossus was a one-ton machine made up of fragile thermionic valves used in 1943 at Bletchley Park, the top-secret site for the code breakers. Rapid development was driven by "military necessity," according to the Design Museum of London. The term *computer* applied generally, though, to people who "computed." The revealing film *Hidden Figures* (2018) included a group of women mathematicians who were "computers." In the course of the story, they teach themselves coding so that they can program the mainframes that appear at NASA.

Grace Hopper (1906–92) enlisted in the Navy Reserves, as she was deemed too old at 34 to join the Navy itself. With a PhD in mathematics

---

3 See https://www.qwerkywriter.com/.

from Yale and experience as a Vassar professor, she joined the Harvard Mark I team in 1944 and five years later transitioned to the Eckert-Mauchly Computer Corporation as part of the team that developed the UNIVAC I computer. She was an adept programmer and insisted that computer language should be written in English, not just binary numbers of zeroes and ones. COBOL was one result, which refers to "common business oriented language." Hopper is most famously known as the person who created the term computer "bug" when a moth was stuck in the machine. Her fascinating life story is told by Kurt W. Beyer in *Grace Hopper and the Invention of the Information Age.*

Early computers were huge and expensive and were operated by trained specialists. Data cards were fed into computers (such as the one in Figure 10.10), and operations could run all night. Students working on large amounts of data for theses and dissertations in the 1960s queued for computer time. Silicon Valley inventors, like those in the "Homebrew Club," changed the landscape from the behemoth computer to the personal computer in the 1970s and 1980s. Their innovations are common now but were revolutionary then. Take the mouse, for instance. Douglas Engelbart (1925–2013) patented the computer mouse on November 17, 1970. Located at the Stanford Research Institute, Engelbart was fascinated with making technology more

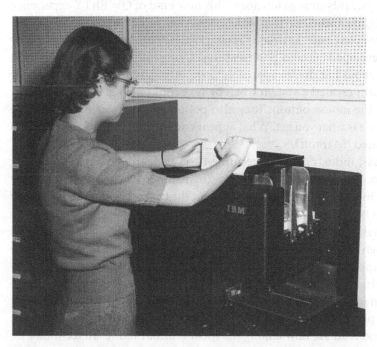

Figure 10.10 Young Woman Working on IBM Computer, 1950s.

intuitive for its users. His background as a Navy radar technician in World War II had given him experience in "reading and manipulating symbols on a screen" (Molella and Karvellas 25). Of the innovations developed, including the joystick, it was the "X-Y Position Indicator for a Display System" that won out. The crude instrument included two wheels with a wooden shell and a selection button that could be used to input information. The cord connecting the instrument to the computer kind of looked like a mouse's tail, hence the moniker. Additionally, the computer's on-screen cursor was referred to as CAT (Metz, "William English"). What could be more appropriate than CAT and Mouse? Prior to the mouse, all commands and movements were made through typed commands. According to the story of the mouse's origin on The Writer's Almanac, "Englebart never received any royalties, and SRI ended up licensing the mouse to Apple for a mere $40,000" (Keillor). Refined by researchers at Xerox PARC (Palo Alto Resesarch Center), the mouse was released in 1984 with the Apple Macintosh.

Integrated circuits and microprocessors made smaller computers possible. Robert Noyce (1927–90) invented the microchip, what has been termed "the electronic backbone of all modern computers and digital devices, from smartphones to digital watches" (Molella and Karvellas 22). Computer screens became windows, and icons—clickable pictures—helped novice users navigate this strange territory. This new kind of QWERTY experience differed significantly from that of the typewriter. Other innovators made the experience even easier. Lawrence Tesler (1945–2020), another Silicon Valley fixture, developed cut-and-paste features. Using information provided by a secretary about her dream approach to inputting and revising text, Tesler and his team created a system whereby text could be highlighted by holding down the mouse button. They also popularized the term WYSIWYG: what you see is what you get. What appears on the screen will look the same when printed (Markoff).

Business, industry, and government took advantage of the computer revolution. The newspaper industry, for instance, turned to compositor machines in which a single person could set the type. This efficiency replaced numerous typesetters.

Personal computers took one of two roads: PCs and Apple. The latter is most closely associated with the wunderkind Steve Jobs (1955–2011). The friendly Apple computer appealed to novice users and young people in particular. Jobs organized the company but left in 1985, returning in 1997 to once again innovate. Industrial design became increasingly important to set off Apple products from PCs. The results were transformative: iMac, iPod, iPhone, and iPad are now among the most familiar names in technology.

HOW COMPUTERS CHANGED WRITING

I am going to look at the history of writing in a QWERTY world through a personal lens. As a high-school student in the late 1960s and early 1970s, I enrolled in typing class even though access to these machines was limited to school. It was the rare family that had a typewriter at home. It was deemed a necessary skill, particularly for girls who might find themselves doing office work post-graduation. Although my older sister had also completed shorthand instruction, I opted to avoid that skill. I wrote my major research paper for a college-prep English class in longhand and then typed it, the first assignment for which I did so. The typewriters I used featured the return bar. We rolled a piece of typing paper into the machine, around the platen, securing it in place with a bar. Then Mrs. Campbell—whom we all feared as a stern taskmaster—directed us in learning to type. Memorizing the QWERTY keyboard was essential. We practiced "The quick brown fox jumps over the lazy dog," a sentence that contains all letters of the alphabet.[4] We took dictation. We referred to text set up adjacent to our machines and were counseled not to look at the keys. We developed muscles in our pinkies that had to stretch for the +, !, 1, =, ?, z, or the shift key. The arrival of the IBM Selectric (1961–84) in schools was a terrific advantage. Margins were set by adjusting tabs above the keyboard. Typing was a dream compared to the older models. The golf ball-shaped changeable type meant that keys would no longer stick or jam.

In college, I was fortunate that my roommate, Bonnie, had purchased an Olivetti typewriter, which she allowed me to use, but most of my essays and research papers were submitted in longhand. Eventually, I purchased my own, a 20-pound red machine that hardly met "portable" status. As an English major in college, I used a lot of footnotes in my literary analysis papers. MLA did not yet allow endnotes. Woe be to the writer who didn't leave sufficient space at the bottom of the page for these documentation notes. I created a separate page for footnote guidelines, using black marker pens (which had only come on the market in the previous decade) to mark lines for 1, 2, 3, or 4 footnotes. Then when typing, I squinted to see these demarcations through the page. If I wanted a copy, then that meant inserting carbon paper between two sheets of paper. Fortunately, correcting paper and fluid came on the market for fixing errors. Prior to that, I used a special typing eraser that included a brush to whisk away the remains. At the conclusion of my doctoral work, I hired a typist for the dissertation, as rec-

---

4   This pangram that uses all letters of the alphabet first appeared in 1885. The epistolary
    novel *Ella Minnow Pea* (see Chapter XX) deifies the author of "The quick brown fox" in a
    funny satire.

ommended by the graduate school of my institution. Each page cost $1.00. Imagine my enormous relief when the dissertation checker of the graduate school, a legendary stickler for correctness, delivered only one half-page of corrections on a sheet of yellow legal-pad paper.

In my first professorial job in 1979, I continued typing, producing copies for my students on a mimeograph machine, which always resulted in blue ink stains. Using an A.B. Dick machine was an important skill. In my second position at a different university, I headed the Writing Center and the Writing Program. Most students submitted their work in longhand, with only a few typed essays. I had a vague notion about computers. At the 1983 meeting of the National Council of Teachers of English (NCTE), I learned about a new computer-based analysis program for writers called Writer's Workbench (WWB). A product of Bell Laboratories, WWB was being piloted at Colorado State University. Simultaneously, WANDAH—Writer's Aid aND Author's Helper—was being trialed at UCLA. The former ran on a UNIX mainframe, while the latter used personal computers (PCs). In the van en route home from the conference, the head of English at the local high school and I plotted how we would integrate these computer programs into our writing curriculum. Eager to get on board, she lobbied her administration for a dedicated Writing Lab with PCs for a class of high-school students. At my university, the mainframe solution with "dumb" terminals in a former classroom adjacent to our Writing Center proved to be the pathway.

I'd not had any real experience with computers prior to this time, not even a Commodore 64, the IBM PC, or the Macintosh 128k. I hadn't used an Atari for playing games. Unlike PCs with their WYSIWYG screens, mainframes required commands for formatting using a text processor. Thus, a .P indicated *paragraph*. WWB offered 32 different analysis programs for students' writing, and we were quite fond of the "find to be" function that identified conjugations of the verb to be with the rationale that we could attack these and insert more active verbs. In the beginning, students ran all 32 analysis programs, sometimes on a single-page essay. The output appeared on a large line printer on paper that must have been at least twenty inches wide with perforated sides. As neophytes, we learned on the job. For instance, we had set up the screen terminals adjacent to each other without considering that students needed to have their handwritten essays near to hand to transcribe. (No one was composing at the computer in those days.) Upright stands to hold pages were added to the setup.

Although I was learning along with my students, who, by the way, rebelled against the machines—"Is this a writing class or a computer class?"[5]—I had

---

5 This would be an apt place for the interrobang punctuation mark introduced in Chapter Eight: ?.

the advantage of having my own personal terminal at home. Purchased for $60, the machine without a brain could actually connect to the main-frame on campus through a telephone line. The chief advantage was that I could continue to prepare materials for the university's writing program after regular work hours. In the 1980s, I began writing professional articles about integrating computers into writing programs, drawing on my own experience and that of my colleagues in the high schools. Serendipitously, I discovered electronic mail (email), and we began to communicate with our students with this newly found method. Email allowed us to commu-nicate with our students beyond class hours; additionally, they could trade essays and offer peer critiques via email. I wrote about this pedagogical strategy in what has been called the first professional article on email in teaching (Kinkead, "Computer Conversations"). In fact, I was publish-ing on computers and writing at the time (see also Kinkead, "Wired"). It was something of a brave new world for us as writing teachers. humanists embracing the machine.

Thankfully, the UNIX approach to teaching writing didn't last long, and our institution turned to PCs. Word-processing systems such as WordStar and then WordPerfect came on board; floppy disks evolved to hard disks. Although bulky, laptops became more common in the 1990s; I had sprung for one in 1988–89 at $1,000, a significant investment at the time, for a sabbatical leave in a remote location. On a later research leave in 1996, a colleague told me that she'd heard about something called the World Wide Web (WWW). A year later, I, like many others, was scouring the Inter-net for information. Not long after, I had a Palm Pilot, a Personal Digital Assistant (PDA), a handheld computer for email, calendars, and notes that anticipated smartphones. I graduated to a BlackBerry and then to other devices through the iPhone.

The necessary equipment for my teaching and research lives now includes an elevated desktop computer at work with a dual monitor, both on a stand-up desk. At home: a laptop and another dual monitor as well as a laptop for travel or meetings and an e-reader that can serve as a writing device in a pinch. The smartphone is with me almost always; my colleagues are wearing their Dick Tracy-style communicators on their wrists. For those too young to know, the comic strip of the clever detective that debuted in 1931 featured a two-way wrist radio beginning in 1946 (Blakemore, "How Dick Tracy").

I've come a long way from leaning over the typewriter to "white out" an error and correct. The ability to revise easily, look up information quickly, and transmit documents electronically has been a sea change over my life-time. What's your story on how technology has affected your writing life?

VOICE-TO-TEXT TECHNOLOGY

Speech-recognition technology is used widely, as in the Siri or Alexa applications that listen to input and then respond. Although software for voice-to-text transmission has been in development for decades, it is only in the 2010s that significant advances were made that could be of widespread benefit (accessibility is an important goal throughout writing). Voice-to-text technology has tremendous benefits for writers, particularly for those with learning disabilities or physical limitations that include blindness, deafness, and paralysis. Ironically, repetitive injuries can occur from using computers, making this technology a way to write without pain (Owens and Van Ittersum). Imagine the cumbersome processes that Helen Keller undertook in order to put words on paper. Speech-to-text technologies can shape writers and their writing. Owens notes that when turning to voice-recognition technology because of pain from tendonitis, there will always be "both opportunities and limitations." This technology brings in both aspects of rhetoric: writing and speaking.

Colton and Walton argue that digital design with disability in mind is a social justice issue. Historically marginalized groups have been challenged by a single approach to writing, and few had Helen Keller's advantages and privilege. Technology has the potential to level the playing field, but it requires everyone being conscious of barriers and working to eradicate them.

CONCLUDING THOUGHTS

Gutenberg's printing press basically did not change much for 400 years. In contrast, technology has transformed dramatically in a short period of time. Although Mark Touhy wasn't talking about writing digitally in an NPR story on robot delivery of food on college campuses, his comment seems applicable: "I think like most technologies, they'll quickly become taken for granted and just a part of our everyday lives" (Madden). If we consider writing overall as a technology, then that rings true for all: a ubiquitous act that is rarely even noticed.

QUESTIONS TO CONSIDER

1. Technology for writing changes rapidly. What has been your personal journey through technology over your lifetime, in terms of how the act of writing has evolved? Refer to particular artifacts from the material culture of writing.

2. It's said that typing on a manual or electric typewriter can be exciting for young people who never had the experience. How do you explain this phenomenon?

3. In yet another testimonial to the lasting interest in vintage typewriters, the Lego Company revealed on June 9, 2021 the addition of a typewriter to its product line. Designed by a Lego fan, Steve Guinness, the concept was submitted through Lego's Idea platform. The model is based on a typewriter owned by Lego founder Ole Kirk Kristiansen. Lego is betting on the "cult following" of typewriters for sales (https://www.lego.com/en-us/aboutus/news/2021/june/lego-typewriter/). Including over 2,000 pieces and costing $200, this Lego product quickly sold out at its introduction. Would you find this an attractive purchase, and would you enjoy the "mindful process of building with Lego bricks"?

4. Typewriter Rodeo is a group of poets who write custom poems on vintage typewriters. Why do you believe this is popular with audiences?

5. Vintage typewriters are appearing at parties as a novelty item so that guests can type messages or content. For instance, at a graduation party, guests might type messages to the honoree. At weddings, guests can type notes to the couple instead of a guestbook. How might you use a vintage typewriter as an idea for a gathering?

6. When did the tradition of supervisors giving work to secretaries to type draw to a close? Interview a family member or friend and ask them to reflect about the historic transition from typewriter to computer.

7. What did it mean for individuals to be able to print work of their own? While Gutenberg's printing press remained unchanged for almost 400 years, the typewriter and then the computer offered independence. Speculate on what the impact was for individuals to have this power.

8. In this chapter, Danielle Steel is quoted about how perturbed she becomes when someone asks her if she is "still writing," as it seems to suggest that writing is a hobby, not a profession. Why do you think writers might be categorized as not being in a serious profession? What might that say about the perceived value of writing?

9. What jobs arose out of the typewriter industry? One was typewriter repair, and people who are passionate about their vintage typewriters must take them somewhere when needing a fix-it job. The *New York Times* obituary for Mary Edelman described her shop as an "emergency room for typists with bent keys, problematic platens and ruined ribbons" (Barron).[6] She and her husband Stanley fixed the typewriters of the literary world. Yet another job is typewriter forensic specialist.

---

6 As an aside, obituaries are wonderful respositories of history.

Peter Tytell (1945–2020) was known as the "typewriter whisperer" for his ability to determine the machine that had created the typewritten document. His skills solved several forged document cases and lawsuits (Sandomir). What other jobs might have been created by the typewriter industry? What are the gains and losses when a major writing instrument is superseded by new technology?

DO-IT-YOURSELF HANDS-ON ACTIVITIES

1. In an essay in the *New York Times*, "How to Speak a Book," award-winning novelist Richard Powers shares his writing process, which does not include touch typing on a keyboard but dictation using speech-recognition technology. He also reviews a history of writers who have dictated their work. Have you tried dictating your words with speech-recognition technology? Perhaps you do this regularly when composing a text or an email message. What is it like to dictate an essay, a story, or even a paragraph? Try it. Focusing on at least paragraph length, "write" using voice-recognition technology. Track what decisions you made in order to accomplish this task. How does it differ from writing or typing by hand? What did you have to do in terms of thinking about your topic? Reflect on these processes and then weigh in on your preferences. What are the opportunities and the limitations of such an approach?

2. In my class on the history of writing, when we focused on typewriters, the two clever students teaching the Hands-on Activity brought three manual typewriters so that everyone could experience typing on these machines. They created a contest in which the three rows of students, each with a typewriter, wrote stories, one sentence at a time by an individual author. The last student in the row concluded the story. Then they were read aloud—although the print was not always legible given the "skill" of the typists—and the group voted on best story. It was a charming way to give everyone a chance to try their hand with these twentieth-century machines. It quickly became clear how much muscle a typist needs even in the pinky finger to reach those corner keys. If you have access to manual or even electric typewriters, try your skill at typing. Even inserting the paper at the platen may seem foreign.

INVITATION TO REFLECT AND WRITE

Reflect on your own use of digital devices—and typewriters, if that's the case. How did you learn to type? How did learning keyboarding for writing affect the curriculum? Did it replace something? Were there challenges in learning to use digital devices for writing? Do you have a catalog of devices that you use, perhaps matching the equipment to the task? Do you make use of voice-to-text technology? This reflection may be later integrated in the larger writing autobiography/autoethnography. Use illustrations as needed.

FOR FURTHER READING

Two pieces are presented below. Both come from the *New York Times*. In the first, Gretchen McCulloch argues that writing is allowing emotion to show through via typographical symbols and formatting. In the second, Tom Hanks articulates his love of vintage typewriters, already addressed in this chapter.

1. Gretchen McCulloch, "We Learned to Write the Way We Talk"

McCulloch is author of *Because Internet: Understanding the New Rules of Language* (2019). This piece is from the *New York Times* and offers a summary of some of the themes of her book.

It's an internet tradition, when humor or sarcasm goes astray online, to apologize by saying something like, "You know, it's just impossible to convey tone in writing."

But what I've noticed as the 2010s come to an end is that this apology isn't needed as much as it once was—not because people have strangely become fans of misconstrued irony, but because the circumstances aren't arising as much. Whether through big flourishes like "That's very ~on brand~" and "y.i.k.e.s." or subtler ones like "that's a Bold choice" and "Wowwwww," we can now convey a full range of emotions in writing.

The reason we once found speech easier for imparting emotions isn't an inherent property of sound waves and voice boxes. Rather, it's that we're more used to employing a broad range of styles in face-to-face communication. An expansive palette of possibilities lets us convey nuanced meta-messages like solidarity (by converging toward someone else's linguistic style at a given moment) and double meaning (by noticing when *what* someone is saying doesn't match with *how* they say it).

Sometimes the "how" is purely derived from context (saying "What a beautiful day!" when facing a windowful of sleet), but many times paralinguistic cues like intonation or facial expression also help us get there (saying "Wonderful" in a flat, clipped tone). This tension between the "what" and the "how" forms the "double" part of "double meaning," and from it a listener can infer gloriously complex sentiments like humor or irony or reluctance or passive aggression.

Writing, by contrast, is something we learn primarily from an educational authority, rather than a layered social context. This authority teaches us a single way of spelling and punctuating and choosing words, a formal style that aims to remove the author as much as possible from the text. Just as news anchors are trained to report the news, not *be* the news, young essay writers are told not to begin their book reports with "I really liked (or hated) this book."

A formal, disembodied style does have a place in the pantheon of linguistic genres. But the problem with this tradition is that it's a jealous god—rather than say, "Here is a style that's useful sometimes," it says, "Here is the only correct way to write, and any variation from it is Bad and Wrong."

But subjectivity is sometimes exactly what we want. I don't need National Geographic to start replacing its photojournalism with selfies, but when my friends go on vacation, I want to see the trip filtered through their eyes—their semi-ironic selfie in front of the Eiffel Tower or the tiny cafe they found on a rainy afternoon means more to me than a generic landmark photo, however beautiful. What's more, if there's only one style, there's no opportunity for meaning-doubling or style-shifting, the richest social parts of a conversation.

As writing has been expanding online into the informal conversational domains where speech used to be primary, the generations who spent their formative years online started expanding writing's muted emotional range. Sure, quotation marks can indicate reported speech, and capitals can indicate proper nouns, but we gain a sense of the writer's personality when they're also available for use as "scare quotes" and Ironic Capitals.

Similarly, in contexts like texting or chat, where the default way of breaking up utterances is with a new line or a new message, the period takes on connotations of seriousness and formality, a slight deepening of the voice at the end of a sentence. Thus, a period can reinforce a negative message ("that's rough.") but undermine a positive one ("that's fine."). The latter style reads to many younger people as passive-aggressive, a sign that the writer could have used a sincere exclamation mark ("that's fine!") but decided not to.

Yes, it's a lot of meaning to infer from a dot, but it's socially useful to be able to convey a nuanced level of reluctance, one that's not strong enough to be worth registering as a full complaint but is nonetheless not quite full-throated enthusiasm.

In other words, we've been learning to write in ways that communicate our tone of voice, not just our mastery of rules. We've been learning to see writing not as a way of asserting our intellectual superiority, but as a way of listening to one another better. We've been learning to write not for power, but for love.

The closest to love that an external list of rules can offer is a feeling of besieged camaraderie, a unity against a perceived common enemy. But it's a miserly form of affection to care for some people only by despising others. It's a perilous form of community, where your membership is always conditional, where you know that your supposed friends in matching "I'm silently correcting your grammar" T-shirts are liable to turn on you without constant vigilance.

If rules vigilantism is all that a love of language can offer, we might as well also consider "Mean Girls" a guide to healthy relationships.

But language snobbery is not inevitable. It's not that people who cling to lists of language rules don't want love as well. It's that they've been sold a false bill of goods for how to get it. In high school English classes and writing manuals, we've been told that being "clear" and "correct" in language will help people understand us.

But understanding doesn't come from insisting on a list of rules, shouting the same thing only louder like a hapless monolingual tourist in a foreign country. Understanding comes from meeting other people where they are, like being willing to use gestures and a handful of semi-remembered words and yes, even to look like a fool, to bridge a language barrier with laughter and humility.

We've been taught the lie that homogeneity leads to understanding, when in truth, understanding comes from better appreciating variety. If I write a sentence like "My brand is strong" using the default settings on my phone's keyboard, I look like a corporate sellout, but if I can write it with subversive capitalization, like "my Brand is Strong," I can convey something quite different, a signal that I'm not taking myself too seriously, that I have an ordinary internet user's ironic ambivalence toward the idea of a personal brand.

Having emotionally real conversations takes vulnerability. In a world where so many of us have been taught to write according to a list of rules, disregarding them is a way of extending trust. As an internet linguist, I often hear from younger people that they want to help the older people in their lives understand a fuller, more flexible range of expression, rather than assume that complex nuances of humor or ambivalence are impossible to write.

Younger people may not enjoy older people muscling in on and misusing their particular trendy words (see the recent driving into the ground of "ok boomer"), but they do desperately want to be able to have emotionally real conversations in text with the people who matter to them.

When we write in ways that a red pen wouldn't approve of, we give our interlocutors the chance to show that they care more about us as a living human presence than they do about some long-dead or absent authority, by not derailing the conversation with moralizing "corrections"—or better yet, by replying with the same vulnerability. In return, being more open and flexible with language rewards us with the capacity to convey the humor and irony and double meaning in writing that we've been craving for so long.

Questions

1. What are ways in which you or others imbue additional meaning or irony into written language through use of spacing, Ironic Capitals, punctuation, or formatting? These may derive from social media. List some in your response.
2. As a linguist, McCulloch is interested in how language develops and changes. Why, for instance, did emoji become immediately popular? What do you think?
3. McCulloch says that "Writing has become a vital, conversational part of our ordinary lives.... We write all the time now." Count how many times you write each day and classify it as informal (e.g., texts, chats, posts) or formal.

2. Tom Hanks, "I Am TOM, I Like to TYPE, Hear That!"

Hanks is a passionate advocate for typewriters. In 2013, he penned—no, typed—this opinion piece for the *New York Times* on why he prefers typing on a manual machine.

BECAUSE Mike McAlary started reporting on cops for the New York tabloids in 1985, Nora Ephron's play "Lucky Guy," which recently completed its run, featured word processors on the newsroom desks rather than typewriters. Too bad. We in the ensemble would have loved to pound on bulky desk-crowding typewriters for the sound alone.

Well, I would have, as I am well versed in the focus-stealing racket one can make with a vintage manual typewriter. I use a manual typewriter—and the United States Postal Service—almost every day. My snail-mail letters and thank-you notes, office memos and to-do lists, and rough—and I mean very rough—drafts of story pages are messy things, but the creating of them satisfies me like few other daily tasks.

Keeping score at a baseball game with a typewriter is not only possible but is also a much more detailed record of the match. (ORTEGA. Full count! Fouled back three in a row...OH, THAT BALL'S LANDIN' WHERE THE FANS ARE STANDIN'!!! Walk. Off. Home. Run. Thanks for your attendance and drive safely.)

I confess that when real work has to be done—documents with requirements equal to a college term paper—I use a computer. The start and stop of writing begs for the fluidity of modern technology, and who doesn't love choosing a new font like Franklin Gothic Medium, Bernard MT Condensed or Plantagenet Cherokee?

For less important doodles in text, the kind that go no farther than your desk or refrigerator door, the tactile pleasure of typing old school is incomparable to what you get from a de rigueur laptop. Computer keyboards make a mousy tappy tap tappy tap like ones you hear in a Starbucks—work may be getting done but it sounds cozy and small, like knitting needles creating a pair of socks. Everything you type on a typewriter sounds grand, the words forming in mini-explosions of SHOOK SHOOK SHOOK. A thank-you note resonates with the same heft as a literary masterpiece.

The sound of typing is one reason to own a vintage manual typewriter— alas, there are only three reasons, and none of them are ease or speed. In addition to sound, there is the sheer physical pleasure of typing; it feels just as good as it sounds, the muscles in your hands control the volume and cadence of the aural assault so that the room echoes with the staccato beat of your synapses.

You can choose the typewriter to match your sound signature.

Remingtons from the 1930s go THICK THICK. Midcentury Royals sound like a voice repeating the word CHALK. CHALK. CHALK CHALK. Even the typewriters made for the dawning jet age (small enough to fit on the fold-down trays of the first 707s), like the Smith Corona Skyriter and the design masterpieces by Olivetti, go FITT FITT FITT like bullets from James Bond's silenced Walther PPK. Composing on a Groma, exported to the West from a Communist country that no longer exists, is the sound of work, hard work. Close your eyes as you touch-type and you are a blacksmith shaping sentences hot out of the forge of your mind.

Try this experiment: on your laptop, type out the opening line of "Moby Dick" and it sounds like callmeishmael. Now do the same on a 1950s

Olympia (need one? I've got a couple) and behold: CALL! ME! ISHMAEL! Use your iPad to make a to-do list and no one would even notice, not that anyone should. But type it on an old Triumph, Voss or Cole Steel and the world will know you have an agenda: LUGGAGE TAGS! EXTENSION CORDS! CALL EMMA!

You will need to make space for a typewriter and surrender the easy luxury of the DELETE key, but what you sacrifice in accuracy will be made up in panache. Don't bother with correcting tape, white-out or erasable onionskin paper. There is no shame in type-overs or XXXXXXiing out a word so mistyped that spell-check could not decipher it. Such blemishes will become the personality of your typing equal to the legibility, or lack thereof, of your penmanship.

The physicality of typing engenders the third reason to write with a relic of yesteryear: permanence. Short of chiseled words in stone, few hand-made items last longer than a typed letter, for the ink is physically stamped into the very fibers of the paper, not layered onto the surface as with a laser-printed document or the status-setting IBM Selectric—the machine that made the manual typewriter obsolete. Hit the letter Y on an East German Erika typewriter—careful now, it's where the Z key is on an English language keyboard because German uses the Z more often—and a hammer strikes an ink-stained ribbon, pressing the dye into the paper where it will be visible for perpetuity unless you paint it over or burn the page.

No one throws away typewritten letters, because they are pieces of graphic art with a singularity equal to your fingerprints, for no two manual typewriters print precisely the same. E-mails disappear from all but the servers of Google and the N.S.A. No one on the planet has yet to save an Evite. But pull out a 1960s Brother De Luxe 895, roll in a sheet of paper and peck out, "That party was a rocker! Thanks for keeping us dancin' till quarter to three," and 300 years from now that thank-you note may exist in the collection of an aficionado who treasures it the same as a bill of sale from 1776 for one dozen well-made casks from Ye Olde Ale Shoppe.

The machine, too, may last as long as the rocks of Stonehenge. Typewriters are dense things made of steel and were engineered to take a beating, which they do. My dad's Underwood, bought used just after the war for his single year at U.S.C., had some keys so worn out by his punishing fingers that they were misshapen and blank. The S key was a mere nib. I sent it to a shop for what was meant to be only a cleaning, but it came back with all the keys replaced. So long, Dad, and curse you, industrious typewriter serviceperson.

STILL, I have the machine and it works, as do most of the typewriters that take up space in my office, home, storage facility and trunk of my car, a collection that started when, in 1978, the proprietor of a Cleveland business machine shop refused to service my mostly plastic typewriter. "A worthless toy!" the man yelled. Yes, yelled. He pointed to shelves full of his refurbished typewriters—already decades old yet all in perfect working order. A typewriter was a machine, he yelled, which could be dropped from an airplane and still work! He gave me a deal on a Hermes 2000 ("The Cadillac of typewriters!"), which featured a knob that adjusted the tension on the keys and the crispest, straightest line of type possible. I've since added the 3000, the Baby and the gloriously named Hermes Rocket to my shelves. Cadillacs, every one!

There is no reason to own hundreds of old typewriters other than the sin of misguided avarice (guilty!). Most can be had for 50 bucks unless, say, Hemingway or Woody Allen typed on them. Just one will last generations—if it is cleaned and oiled every once in a while. The ribbons are easy to find on eBay. Even some typewriters made as late as the 1970s can be passed on to your grandkids or encased in the garage until the next millennium, when an archaeologist could dig them up, hose them down and dip them in oil. A ribbon can be re-inked in the year 3013 and a typed letter could be sent off that very day, provided the typewriter hasn't outlived the production of paper.

Come to think of it, I'd better start hoarding stationery and pray the post office survives.

INTERESTED IN LEARNING MORE?

Book Recommendations

Dennis Barron, *A Better Pencil: Readers, Writers, and the Digital Revolution* (Oxford UP, 2009).

Kurt W. Beyer, *Grace Hopper and the Invention of the Information Age* (MIT Press, 2012).

Shane Borrowman, ed., *On the Blunt Edge: Technology in Composition's History and Pedagogy* (Parlor Press, 2012).

Matthew G. Kirschenbaum, *Track Changes: A Literary History of Word Processing* (Belknap Press, 2016).

Gretchen McCulloch, *Because Internet: Understanding the New Rules of Language* (Riverhead Books, 2019).

Thomas S. Mullaney, *The Chinese Typewriter: A History* (MIT Press, 2017).

Chapter Eleven

Writing as Art

> *Elizabeth, the wife of Emmanuel Lucar,*
> *In whom was declared the goodnesse of the Lord,*
> *With many high vertues, which truely I will record....*
> *Three manner hands could she write, them faire all....*
> *Of women, few like (I thinke) in all this Nation....*
> *Latine and Spanish, and also Italian,*
> *She spake, writ, and read, with perfect utterance;*

These lines from the epitaph on the tomb of Elizabeth Withypoll Lucar (1510–37) of England speak to her numerous talents, including the ability to write in three different scripts and also in four languages: English, Latin, Italian, and Spanish. She was reputed to have written the first essay on calligraphy when she was only 15 years of age, according to Carvalho.

Calligraphy as a term is derived from the Greek *kalligraphia*, from *kalligraphos*, a person who writes beautifully, from *kallos* (beauty) and *graphein* (write). The art of beautiful writing has existed for centuries; Elizabeth Lucar was a skillful purveyor. Elegant lettering gives the reader an enhanced experience, just as a lovely work of art does. Calligraphy is found in many, many places around the world, perhaps most famously in Asian and Islamic cultures.

This chapter focuses on writing as art and includes a discussion of calligraphy, typography, and illuminated (illustrated) texts.

CALLIGRAPHY

The earliest writing in China during the Shang Dynasty appeared on oracle bones (see Chapter Two). The marks on these divination materials eventually evolved into calligraphy, an artistic medium that continues today. In Asia, the "Four Treasures of the Study"—ink brushes, ink, paper, and inkstone—are the calligrapher's tools. The brushes vary greatly in size, and the hair chosen determines the quality of the stroke. Calligraphers select their equipment carefully, depending on the purpose of the writing. The ink stick in Asia often features lovely forms, the ingredients of soot and glue being cast in a mold that aesthetically enhances the writer's tool and makes it a true "treasure." The inkstone provides a base where the ink stick is ground into a powder and then mixed with water to make functioning ink. These stones, too, can be works of art. Given the investment in these three tools, it is unsurprising that the quality of the paper is also high. Early forms were silk or bamboo, but with the invention of paper in China, macerated plant-based products became the norm; these also have diverse varieties, depending on the use. A long scroll with only one or a few characters may be an artistic wall hanging, while book-size paper offered longer texts such as chronicles, reports, and narratives.[1]

Yet another extraordinarily beautiful instance of this art is Islamic calligraphy, which uses Arabic letters. In part, because Islam prohibits images of people in art, geometric forms and writing developed to a high level. As with the sacred documents produced in the Western world by medieval scribes, writing is intimately linked to spiritual beliefs and religion. Sayings from the Quran—proverbs, for instance—are often depicted in beautiful calligraphy and decorate homes and businesses. In Figure 11.1, we see three photographs from Morocco. The photo at the bottom shows the artist at work, and the pieces above are examples of his calligraphic art, the top one the classic geometric shapes and the middle one shapes with Arabic writing.

In the Western world, beautiful writing was promoted in the influential and popular writing manuals by George Bickham (1684–1758) that included *The Universal Penman*; *The British Penman*; and *Penmanship in its Utmost Beauty and Extent* (Carvalho). *The Universal Penman* is a compilation of exemplars from two dozen of the leading calligraphers of the day. In English "round-handwriting," an ornate style popular in the eighteenth century, copper plates were engraved for printing, but it is possible for a calligrapher to replicate them using a dip pen.

---

1 I am grateful to Chong Ho Kim of South Korea for a demonstration of the art of calligraphy in his home and to Dr. Jeong Tai-Soo (pen name: Sam-Do-Heon), Chairperson of the board of directors of the Association of Daegu-Kyoungbuk Calligraphers, for a personal tour of a calligraphy exhibit.

Figure 11.1
Collage of calligraphy with
artist, Casablanca, Morocco.

Exquisite writing continued to be promoted in manuals such as Earl A. Lupfer's *Ornate Pictorial Calligraphy* in the early nineteenth century: "The law of harmony in flourishing is the same as in love. As long as everything goes along smoothly, harmony prevails. But as soon as some rival crosses the pathway, especially in a diagonal way, there is likely to be trouble in camp. Therefore, see that the lines run nearly parallel or cross nearly at right angles."[2] Following in the footsteps of Platt Rogers Spencer (1800–64), who developed the "gold standard" for handwriting instruction, Lupfer

---

2 Tattoo artists rely on these types of manuals for instruction and models.

(1890–1967) was the last principal of the Zanerian College, an institution in Columbus, Ohio, dedicated to *engrossing,* a word medieval in origin, meaning to write in large (gross) script that is clear and attractive. Engrossed documents were often the last formal version of the text, as in diplomas, marriage certificates, or a last will and testament. Zanerian was founded in 1888 by Charles Paxton Zaner (1864–1918) and prepared students for careers as penmen. Business and industry employed the graduates. *The Zanerian Manual of Alphabets and Engrossing* (Lupfer; first published in 1895, revised in 1924) noted in its preface that "The amount of engrossing done in this country today runs into hundreds of thousands of dollars annually, and it is rapidly increasing year by year.... [S]killed engrossers [can] receive upward of $5.00 an hour for their efforts.... Persons who make the proper use of this book will find it a money maker."

The college also sold materials—pen, ink, paper—and trained teachers of penmanship. A "landmark text," *The Zaner Method of Arm Movement* (1904), was used widely in elementary schools. This book "applied the findings of psychologists who had discovered that young children completed manual tasks more easily if allowed to use the large arm movements that were natural to them at their early stage of motor skills development" (Zanerian College). Being a penman (and it was largely a male occupation) was a lucrative profession—until the typewriter gained prominence. The legacy of the Zanerian College is evident in the International Association of Master Penmen, Engrossers, and Teachers of Handwriting (IAMPETH), founded in 1949, which is a "leader in calligraphic education" and seeks to "restore the teaching of penmanship in schools" (Zanerian College).

Has beautiful handwriting gone out of style? Employment in calligraphy is still feasible. The White House, for example, has a Chief Calligrapher who works in the Graphics and Calligraphy Office and is responsible for all official and social documents. The same holds true in the United Kingdom, which has an office of scriveners to the Crown. Queen Elizabeth II offered her official consent to the marriage of her grandson, Prince Harry, to Meghan Markle in a highly ornate document decorated and written on vellum and enclosed in a case (Reuters).

Beautiful writing for weddings isn't dependent on the royal status of a couple, however. Calligraphy for social invitations, particularly weddings, has seen a fascinating rise in the twenty-first century. Calligraphers are making a living through their art and craft. In my research methods course, students are asked to come up with three questions focused on writing about which they are curious. One student, Deidre Hall, asked this question: Why is there an increase in calligraphy on wedding invitations when it is expensive? She drew on personal experience, having received numerous invitations. Her study revealed that wedding invitations might be considered a genre that has particular rhetorical and cultural functions, indicating the status of the couple and family, subtle expectations for behavior by guests, and the tone for the event (D. Hall). While envelopes are the primary material for the calligrapher's art, her participants reported other wedding documents were sometimes handwritten: place cards, seating chart (on display), menus, escort cards, and programs. For a $35,000 wedding—the average price in the United States—about $400 goes to the calligrapher. Handwritten envelopes range from $2–5 each. Custom ink, special paper, and flourishes may increase the cost. Calligraphers may be certified and certainly will have a portfolio of work for review. The number of manuals available to learn calligraphy indicates its popularity, particularly among the DIY crowd.

The rise of calligraphy as a valued art form in the United States is not paralleled in all parts of the world, including those for which calligraphy has been a venerated art form and a noble profession for centuries. In India, where calligraphy has been practiced for hundreds of years, only a handful of calligraphers in the Old Delhi Bazaar persist.[3] Katib Mohammad Ghalid—*katib*, which is Urdu for calligrapher—still gets work from a madrassa, an Islamic seminary (Kishore). In the early days of his work, he was inundated with jobs "from offices to newspapers—every type of design" (Ghal). Thousands were employed as calligraphers prior to 1990. What happened? As is so often the case, the answer lies in technology. Quite simply, computer-generated script is more efficient and less costly. Traditional calligraphy doesn't seem to be enjoying the same resurgence—or staying power—in India as it is in the United States.

Margaret Shepherd, author of *Learn Calligraphy* and *The Art of the Handwritten Note*, believes that "the handwritten note does more than inspire the reader who reads it; it inspires the writer who writes it.... [T]he act of writing... enables you to choose better words... the flowing line of pen and ink lets you express yourself in ways that key tapping just doesn't allow." She would approve of Elizabeth Lucar's "faire" hand and suggest that current writers follow in this 500-year-old (or more) tradition.

BEAUTIFUL BOOKS

Calligraphy was influential in William Morris's drive to counteract cheap, industrialized production of books in the nineteenth century with elegant and lovely volumes. He established Kelmscott Press in London for this purpose as part of the reformist Arts and Crafts Movement:

---

3 I visited the Old Delhi Bazaar in November 2018, but none of the three remaining calligraphers were at work in their makeshift office spaces.

I began printing books with the hope of producing some which would have a definite claim to beauty while at the same time they should be easy to read and should not dazzle the eye, or trouble the intellect of the readers by eccentricity of form in the letters. I have always been a great admirer of the calligraphy of the Middle Ages, and of the earlier printing which took its place. As to the 15th century books, I had noticed that they were always beautiful by force of the mere typography, even without the added ornament, with which many of them are so lavishly supplied. And it was the essence of my undertaking to produce books which it would be a pleasure to look upon as pieces of printing and arrangement of type. (Millesgården)

Morris (1834–96) was a master printer who developed his own fonts and flourishes for the works he printed. Prior to undertaking printing, though, he was a well-known writer and poet. He learned Old Norse to translate Nordic sagas to English. The concept was for the outer book to reflect its contents. Recovered stories from earlier times with gallant heroes and lovely ladies were embellished in style. The illustrations and binding were of the highest quality. Since the Middle Ages, books had not been so "painstakingly produced and richly illustrated" (Millesgården). Other presses were influenced by his work, and contemporary letterpress printing is in the Morris tradition.

What were the traditions of the Middle Ages that Morris hoped to recreate? Works were crafted by hand using natural materials. Illuminated manuscripts were richly decorated. Images in the handwritten books, which typically used vellum or parchment for the pages, were called *illuminations* because they literally glowed with color, silver, or even gold. The purpose was to illuminate the glory of God.[4] Once the text was written, leaving spaces for the drawings, the artist outlined the pattern. Gold leaf was affixed using a type of glue and then rubbed to create a shiny surface. On top of this the image was painted, using colors mixed with egg whites to create tempera. Not all images had such expensive treatment, though. Chapters typically began with the first letter written large and richly illuminated with flourishes. *Rubrication*, which is the use of red ink, marked headings and ends of sections. This tradition originated around 500 CE and extended, not surprisingly, until the advent of the printing press, roughly 1600. Irish and British monasteries were particularly adept at producing these beautiful books, resulting in such works of art as the *Book of Kells* (800) and the

---

4   Persian miniatures are another type of illuminated manuscript that came into fashion in the thirteenth and fourteenth centuries with the goal of delighting the eye; as a result, more realistic figures and fewer spiritual topics were the subject of these illustrations. Muslim artists also used illuminations in texts.

Figure 11.2
A month from *Les Très Riches Heures du Duc de Berry*.

Lindisfarne Gospels (700). Viking raids at monasteries, including Iona and Lindisfarne Priory, resulted in the deaths of dozens of monks, the scribes and illustrators responsible for beautiful books.

In addition to sacred texts, bestiaries—books with illustrations of animals both real and imagined—were popular. The *Westminster Abbey Bestiary* (1290) is perhaps the best known. The "king of illuminated manuscripts" is the *Les Très Riches Heures du Duc de Berry* (1412–16 and 1485–89), its production interrupted by the plague. Each hour of the day had a text for worship (see Figure 11.2).

A notable author and illuminator at this time was the Frenchwoman Christine de Pisan (1364–1430), considered to be the first woman to earn a living as a professional writer (National Geographic Society; Palumbo). Atypical for the time, she was educated, along with her brothers, in Greek,

Latin, literature, history, philosophy, and medicine. Her library was in the royal palace of the Louvre, where her father worked as court astrologer to King Charles V (r. 1364–80). When widowed, she opted not to remarry but to earn a living through writing. As she put it in her diary, "I had to become a man." She managed a scriptorium, overseeing the work of the artists who painted miniature images. She authored poetry and also what could be considered a feminist work, *Le Livre de la Cité des Dames* (*The Book of the City of Ladies*), profiling women who were leaders or intellectuals, thus providing a history of important female figures.

While books were written primarily by hand, a few books were actually printed prior to Gutenberg. These early printed books prior to 1501 are known as *incunabula*, derived from the Latin for cradle, referring to the first stages of development. Thus incunabula are produced in the infancy of printing.

Illuminated books largely disappeared with a notable exception: *The Saint John's Bible*, an illuminated volume commissioned remarkably in the late twentieth century, some 500 years after the last such work. The work is the brainchild of English calligrapher Donald Jackson (b. 1938). He found partners in the monks of Saint John's Abbey, located in Collegeville, Minnesota, as unlikely a site as one might suggest. Living according to the principles of St. Benedict, the monks had the skills necessary for the job, and Saint John's University included a calligraphy collection in its Hill Museum & Manuscript Library, demonstrating the value placed on these works of theological art. The process is almost overwhelming, as the creators had to envision what would happen when and how it would look over many years. They began with an illumination schema in 1996, which provided the initial materials for a commission of the book and fundraising. Artists, medievalists, theologians, biblical scholars, and art historians populate the committee that oversees decision making. As with the monks of the Middle Ages, the primary purpose was to glorify God, but the goal of the *Saint John's Bible* was not simply to be a recreation of a medieval work but also to have a contemporary vision and concomitant aesthetic look. According to the informative web home of the Bible, contemporary images are integrated: satellite photos of the Ganges River Delta, photos from the Hubble telescope, and strands of DNA.

On March 8, 2000, Jackson wrote the first words, "In the beginning was the Word." Over the next seven years, the Bible grew apace, with separate volumes being completed. As with the *Devil's Bible*, the largest extant manuscript of the Middle Ages (see Chapter Seven), the *Saint John's Bible* is large, two feet by three feet, actually somewhat larger than the thirteenth-century volume. Many of the medieval traditions continue: the use of calfskin vellum, gold leaf, hand-cut quills, Chinese ink ground in an ink stone, natural pigments mixed with egg yolk and water. The stencils and stamps are made from computer images, though, using modern technology. Another contemporary technology is the reproduction of original manuscript pages. A heritage edition of the seven volumes includes 299 sets, which are primarily housed in museums, monasteries, and university libraries, and costs $145,000. A smaller version is available for $500.[5]

TYPOGRAPHY

Both calligraphy and typography share a common goal to be well designed; however, the former is accomplished by hand and the latter by machine. According to Clayton, typography has the additional goal of being legible for clear communication. The flourishes common to calligraphy focus more on the ornamental and the decorative aspects of the artform.

Do you have a favorite typeface to use when writing with a keyboard? Typeface can imbue meaning in writing, depending on its design. Some people are passionate about typography and how it communicates. Take the Society of Typographic Aficionados, an organization of "graphic designers, typographers, new media artists, calligraphers, sign painters, printers, software developers, illustrators, writers, and photographers" who share a common "passion for type and typography." The study of type and its history and development truly is fascinating. But, first, some definitions.

- *Glyph* is the term given to individual letters, numbers, punctuation marks, or other symbols that comprise a family of symbols. When a designer plans type, every one of these elements must be included for a complete set.
- *Typeface* is a font family with a common design. Almost anyone can design a typeface.
- *Font* originally comes from Middle French *fonte*, meaning something that is a casting, having been melted. Originally, in metal or wood typesetting, it referred to the size, weight, and style of the typeface: 10-point, 12-point, bold, italic, narrow. With digital type, font and typeface are often used interchangeably. Literally, thousands of fonts exist.
- *Typography* is the art and science of arranging type to be legible yet also attractive, which means selecting typeface, point size, line length, and spacing of both lines and letters.

---

5 A 2019 book, *The Lost Gutenberg: The Astounding Story of One Book's Five-Hundred-Year Odyssey*, by Margaret Leslie Davis, tells the exciting story of a private collector purchasing #45 Gutenberg for an astoundingly low $70,000 in 1950. The next owner, Keio University Library in Tokyo, paid $5.4 million.

- *Serifs* and *sans serif* refer to the small strokes attached to the larger strokes of letters. Serif type has these strokes; sans serif does not (*sans* is French for "without"). Traditionally, it was believed that serif typefaces were easier to read in books. On the other hand, sans serif may be easier to read on a computer screen.
- *Kerning* refers to adjusting spaces between letters to make the text look more regularized, increasing or decreasing the area. For instance, "W" is a wider letter, so the space around it may need to be adjusted.

Gutenberg gets the credit for innovations that produced movable metal type. The designer of the font itself was most likely Peter Schoeffer, a former scribe, who is characterized in the novel *Gutenberg's Apprentice* as a reluctant convert to mechanized print. Designing typeface is both artistic and scientific. Designers can look to a few decades prior to Gutenberg for exacting language on how letters should be formed. The German painter Albrecht Dürer (1471–1528) laid out precise instructions in his *On the Just Shaping of Letters* (published posthumously in 1535) that define a geometric and mathematical approach resulting in beautiful letters. His intent is to provide assistance and standards for the self-taught. He says in the preface, "Wherefore I hope that no wise man will defame this laborious task of mine, since with good intent & in behoof of all who love the Liberal Arts have I undertaken it: nor for painters alone, but for goldsmiths too, & for sculptors, and stonecutters, and woodcarvers, and for all, in short, who use compass, and rule, and measuring line—that it may serve to their utility." The products of Dürer's pen, ink, and rule are very much like the Times Roman font commonly used today.

By Dürer's time, script had already made several transitions: from the thick Merovingian script of the eighth century to the more commodiously spaced Carolingian script of Charlemagne of the ninth century, and then on to the twelfth-century transition to Gothic Minuscule and, a couple of centuries later, Gothic-Antiqua, which was more legible (Basel Paper Mill). After Gutenberg, innovations in type continued. Venice, which was a commercial center due to its location, was an ideal place for "the leap in culture started by Gutenberg's invention" (Silver), as the city-state promoted freedom of the press. Creative printers began experimenting with fonts other than Gutenberg's Gothic, including *aldino*, what is known as italics—named for its origin in Italy—which made the text more elegant and readable.

Typeface Design

Over centuries, typeface has been refined to enhance readability and aesthetic reaction. Rhetorically, typeface is influenced by audience and purpose. Typeface triggers responses. Will you purchase this car? Will you enjoy this book? Do you recognize this business or organization? Contemporary fonts are often based on older forms. Typefaces are designed by individuals or a group of people and have stories and histories. Here are some of the most influential.

Claude Garamond (1510–61) produced an elegant, easy-to-read Renaissance font, a new type of Antiqua that became the leading typeface for books in Europe after 1620. Garamond remains popular today in many variants and as a digitalized font because of its lightness and elegance.

John Baskerville (1707–75) created a typeface so impressive that he was appointed printer to the University of Cambridge. Baskerville was admired by Benjamin Franklin, who also admired Bodoni typeface.

Giambattista Bodoni (1744–1813) created Antiqua, a serif typeface, in many versions after 1791. It is reminiscent of the writing in Roman monuments and was a popular book typeface for a long time. Many digital fonts are available under the collective name Bodoni.

Stanley Morison (1889–1967), typographer, at Monotype Corporation, developed in 1932 for *The Times* newspaper (London) a new layout with lean, space-saving Antiqua typeface reminiscent of baroque forms. The font is immediately recognizable as it is pre-installed on all computers today as Times New Roman.

The ever-popular Nancy Drew books used a humanist sans serif typeface, Lydian, named after designer Warren Chappell's wife, Lydia, and created in 1938. The term *humanist* means that it "gives the impression of being written by a human hand" but without "flourishing strokes" (Tiffany). It was also popular in so-called pulp novels. Although it went underground for some time, it has reappeared in the twenty-first century, perhaps due to its use on International Baccalaureate documents, which Tiffany says gives it an "academic implication," although she finds it gives a certain "smirk" to text and ad copy.

In view of the success of sans serif fonts in advertising, Max Miedinger (1910–80) designed a clear, universally all-purpose sans serif that also went well with other fonts. It began its worldwide march to triumph in 1960 under the name Helvetica. Called the "world's favorite typeface," Helvetica was redesigned in 2019 as Helvetica Now.

Inspired by gravestone lettering in a Florence cemetery, Hermann Zapf (1918–2015) designed a distinctive, elegant Antiqua without serifs that is used in advertising—especially for luxury goods—or in public spaces for memorial or monuments. In addition to the sans serif Optima, he designed Aldus, Palatino, and Zapfino. His wife, the long-lived Gudrun Zapf-von Hesse (1918–2019), was also a typeface designer, and her fonts include Diotima, Columbine, Alcuin, Ariadne, Carmina, Christiana, and Shakespeare Roman. The latter was used by Hallmark. In honor of her 100th birthday, Monotype released the typeface Hesse-Antiqua. She was also a bookbinder and calligrapher. It was rather rare for a woman to design type in a male-dominated industry, but she learned punchcutting.

Zapf-von Hesse is one of only three women to be honored with the Frederic W. Goudy[6] Award for Typography, which is given annually through the Rochester Institute of Technology (RIT). Others are Kris Holmes (b. 1950), who has designed over 75 fonts, including Leviathan, ITC Isadora, Sierra, Lucida, and digital fonts for Apple Monaco and Chancery, and Claire Van Vliet (b. 1933) for Janus Press.

Mail Art is a collaborative art network in which the works of art are sent by post. In 2004, Keith Bates of Liverpool, England, called on artists to design a letter and send it to him; 130 artists responded, giving birth to this font, which is available free of charge.

In 2019, the behemoth typography company Monotype brought out a new typeface, Ambiguity, designed by Charles Nix, with five different "states": Traditional, Radical, Thrift, Generous, and Normate. According to the company, "it offers a range of perspectives across the spectrum from conformist to contrarian" (Mallalieu). Its creation may have arisen from the decidedly contentious interchanges happening online since the 2016 US election.

Typeface also has the possibility of improving lives. In 2018, Japanese designer Kosuke Takahashi created a new typeface that pairs Braille with English and Braille with Japanese characters. As a result, both sighted and non-sighted readers can comprehend the message, and sighted people can even learn Braille (see Figure 11.3). The Braille Neue typeface was to debut originally in signage at the 2020 Tokyo Olympics and Paralympics (Stewart).

---

6 Fredric W. Goudy (1865–1947) is rightly honored for his typography and writing (see *The Alphabet*, 1918). His wife, Bertha M. Sprinks Goudy (1869–1935), was an American typographer and printer. Together they founded Village Press in 1903. One of their first print jobs was William Morris's essay "Printing." *Time* Magazine called her "the first lady of printing" ("Type Couple"). *Bookmaking on the Distaff Side* (Rogers) honors her, and her husband named his hundredth typeface, Bertham, after her. She is yet another example of a woman in typography whose history is not well known.

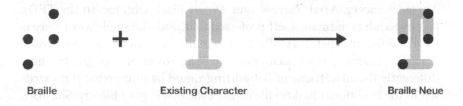

Figure 11.3   Braille Neue typeface combining Latin alphabet and Braille.

Bespoke Typeface

Some organizations commission custom-designed typeface. The term *bespoke* originally referred to custom-made, tailored suits, particularly in Great Britain, but has now evolved to mean made-to-order for almost any product. NASA commissioned its own typeface, as have CNN, Google, and Netflix. Corporations seek to brand themselves with a certain "look," as Goldman Sachs did in 2020 by launching Goldman Sans, a typeface that is meant to evoke a "casual Friday" look and feel but also accommodate numbers more efficiently on its spreadsheet: they "wanted all numbers, from a skinny *1* to an obese *8*, to line up perfectly in a financial table" (Wagner and Stein). Although Beatrice Warde noted in "The Crystal Goblet" that print should be invisible, typeface is important to consumers' first impressions, perhaps not consciously but intentionally.

CONCLUDING THOUGHTS

Reflect on the power of the look of writing, not just how it reads. We translate letters as sounds, but we are also taking in meaning from appearances—what may be termed "extralinguistic." Subliminal messages can be communicated through typeface. Take a look at the following typefaces and consider what those subconscious reactions might be:

Take a look at this typeface.
Take a look at this typeface.
Take a look at this typeface.
Take a look at this typeface.
Take a look at this typeface.

These are five distinctive typefaces, and yet I've pulled down just a few instances from the "A" list of fonts: American Typewriter, Apple Casual,

Apple Chancery, Arial Narrow, and Avenir Black Oblique. In the TEDx talk by Sarah Hyndman, a self-professed fonthead, the single word *story* is used in different typefaces to illustrate beautifully a summary of *Star Wars*. Another presenter, Mia Cinelli, notes in "The Power of Typography" how differently the advertisement Babysitting would be interpreted if it's written in the traditional Baskerville or the evocatively gory Bloody. She asks, "Which babysitter would you hire?"

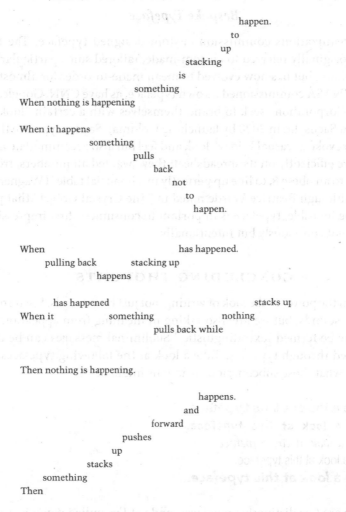

Figure 11.4   May Swenson, "How Everything Happens" (1967).

Noted poet May Swenson used typography in arranging poems, particularly those collected in her fourth volume, *Iconographs* (1970), that use type and the space on the page itself to create images that represent the subject of the poem. In an essay on Swenson's "How Everything Happens," Michael Spooner presents the poem as it was published in an 8.5 x 11 inch format in portrait style (see Figure 11.4). Had it been published in "landscape" format, or, as Spooner suggests, "seascape," then its similarity to waves would be much more evident. Other poems written to conform to the shapes of their subjects include "The Blue Bottle" and "The DNA Molecule," the latter, naturally, in a double helix shape. Although set in type, these poems and their representations suggest a calligraphic approach.

From the *Book of Kells* to NASA, which created its own branded typeface, the appearance of writing has an influence. As you read, consider not just the overt message but also the possible subtext.

QUESTIONS TO CONSIDER

1. Jake Weidmann is a twenty-first-century master of the pen who delivered a 2014 TEDx talk on the importance of handwriting, linking the physical act of writing with a pen with learning. He believes that the pen carries "our cultural heritage." He became the youngest person to receive a Master Penman certificate. His work, which includes flourishes, hand lettering, and calligraphy, is housed on the very modern medium of the Internet: https://www.jakeweidmann.com/. If you have the opportunity, watch his TED talk. What are the elements of his argument? Do you concur? Why or why not? If you cannot watch the talk, then consider what the arguments are for maintaining handwriting and even for cultivating beautiful penmanship.

2. Prior to round writing, *insular* script flourished in the British Isles after the Roman occupation and prior to the Norman Conquest of 1066. (During the Roman era in Britain, lettering was more of a square shape.) *Uncial* script had more rounded strokes and became the favorite of scribes. Insular took the uncial (or half-uncial) and made it more cursive, linking letters. To see examples of these early calligraphic forms, look at the *Book of Kells* (Irish) or the *Lindisfarne Gospels*. These, and other historic exemplars, are online, or replicas may be housed in a local library. Tilghman argues in a scholarly article that embellished letters and words are more than sounds but carry "extra-linguistic" meaning: "some letters could carry iconographic meaning along with their phonological valance" (294). How might that happen? What do you think it means?

3. Trace the history of a "beautiful book," such as *The Lost Gutenberg* noted on p. 243, note 5.

4. Graphic designers in the past have been overwhelmingly male (Zuzana Licko [b. 1961] being atypical), but the gender imbalance is beginning to be addressed (Morley). A notable exception is Beatrice Lamberton Warde (1900–69), a scholar of typography and marketing manager for the British Monotype Corporation (Garfield 57–61). She was an arbiter of printing taste and served as the foremost (and probably only) women typographer in the world. In her speeches to colleagues, she maintained that the best typeface communicates the idea and doesn't draw attention to itself—no longer a principle that is believed. The broadside that she produced to show off Eric Gill's new typeface, Perpetua, is still visible in printing offices around the United States (I saw it posted in the Palace of the Governors Printing Office in Santa Fe). What is your reaction to Warde's assertions? Why would printing offices continue to post this nearly a century after it was written? (The text of Warde's philosophy statement appears at the end of Chapter Seven.)

DO-IT-YOURSELF HANDS-ON ACTIVITIES

1. Bullet journals are contemporary ways for people to record their daily lives, but in a beautiful way. It's a To Do List that can also be a work of art. Tutorials on learning calligraphy brush lettering are available online for novices. Try your hand at writing calligraphy. What do you notice as you write in this form? Do you find the concept of the bullet journal attractive?

2. Asemic writing is "a-semantic" writing, signifying that it doesn't necessarily have meaning (see Figure 11.5). It's wordless, an effort to prove that meaning doesn't come from the words but rather the context. It is, in short, writing without language; viewers are asked to consider meaning. This postmodern approach to writing has gained popularity in the twenty-first century. Look at examples online. Authors of asemic writing include Rosaire Appel, Cecil Touchon, and Michael Jacobsen. Try your hand at asemic writing. When finished, what is your response to it? Is it writing? Is it art?

Figure 11.5
Example
of Asemic
Writing
by Kaitlin
Johnson.

3. Try your hand at making illuminated letters. You'll need paper, a ruler, and a pen. The reading that follows offers directions ("Illuminated Lettering"). You can also find online tutorials.

Made by Marzipan: How to Draw Illuminated Letters

Illuminated letters are colorful, illustrated letters that are decorated with gold or silver. In early manuscripts, they served as placeholders in the text and added interest to documents. Illuminated letters were traditionally created using real gold in the form of a fine powder. You can still purchase real gold powder or gold leaf. However, this technique is expensive and complex. Luckily, there's an easier way to achieve the metallic appearance of gold.

Supplies

- white cardstock
- Sumo Grip® mechanical pencil
- transparent ruler
- masking tape (optional)
- Pigma Micron® pens
- Gold or Silver Pentouch® in fine or extra fine point
- Use this downloadable template for practice.

Supply Tips

1. We'll be using a gold Pentouch®, made by Sakura. This is a pen with paint-like ink, that covers beautifully and has the bright shine we want. Choose either a fine or extra fine nib size.
2. You'll also need a pencil with a good eraser. I prefer Sakura's Sumo Grip®, which is comfortable to use and has an extendable eraser.
3. I'm using Sakura's Pigma® Micron® pens to outline and add color to my letters. These come in a variety of nib sizes and shades.
4. Finally, you'll need a transparent ruler. I bought mine in a pack of three from the dollar store. You can add a masking tape tab to one end to easily lift it without the risk of smearing freshly drawn lines.

How To

Sketching the Letters

1. Today I'm going to demonstrate a few different styles of the same letter. You can draw endless variations by mixing and matching different serifs, themes, and patterns. I'm going to draw a grid of squares to make a series of mini canvases for my letters. An inch and a half is a good size.
5. This first letter is inspired by the Roman alphabet. It features straight lines and triangular serifs. You can add dimension by drawing interior triangles at the end of each stem. Connect the center point of the triangles with a center line. Divide crossbars with a center line, then connect to the stem's center line at a diagonal. Shade the right half and bottom segments. Draw a flower behind the letter.
6. This next letter will have curved ball serifs. Add a curved crossbar with a center point. Give the illusion of depth by drawing slits in the stem and making the crossbar extend behind the letter.
7. Here are additional ideas for decorating your letter:
- Use geometric shapes.
- Add jewels, cuffs, or beads.
- Hooks and spurs add interest to the outline of a letter.
- Flourish a tail or intertwine a crossbar.
- Make an inline border and fill the shape with a pattern, such as harlequin diamonds or filigree.
- Draw inspiration from traditional lettering styles, such as Gothic, Blackletter, or Celtic.

- Illustrate with a theme, such as birds and feathers, fruit and flowers, ribbons, vines, or rope, or biblical motifs
- The square background is often a part of the illustration. You can fill it with a pattern or add a border.

Outlining

8. Now that you've seen how you can add variety to your letters, I'm going to switch over to a sketch I've done of the entire alphabet. I'm going to color this one and turn it into a PDF that you can print and use for reference. I'm starting by outlining everything with a black Micron® pen.
9. Erase the pencil lines within your letters.

Adding Gold Ink

10. Next we'll add the gold ink, using a Pentouch®. Shake the pen and depress the nib on a piece of scratch paper to get the ink flowing.
11. Choose which areas of your letter you'd like to emphasize, and color with the Pentouch®. This gold ink catches the light beautifully!

Adding Color

12. Finally, add color to your letter with Micron® pens. I'm sticking with primary colors, plus green.

INVITATION TO REFLECT AND WRITE

Typography is a complicated subject, as the history of typefaces extends over centuries. They are classified by era or characteristics of design, for instance, serif and sans serif. Typeface is a part of writing that we often take for granted. In fact, in 1930, noted typography historian and designer Beatrice Warde gave an important speech, "The Crystal Goblet: Why Printing Should be Invisible," in which she argued that the font should not even be noticed by readers.

Fonts or typeface are numerous. A list below is just a partial accounting. Choose one to study and research. Once you have adopted a font, then do the background research to find out when it was created, by whom, and its history. Consider that each font was designed by an individual. Who was that person? Note that typeface designed by women is more difficult to find;

however, as noted earlier in the chapter, Gudrun Zapf-von Hesse is one exception. She won the Fredrick W. Goudy Award for type design. Another woman typeface designer is Kris Holmes, who designed Shakespeare Roman for Hallmark Cards. Typeface designed by women and people of color are difficult to locate but a worthy goal.

Here is a list, a fraction of the possibilities to investigate. The results may be presented in an essay or an illustrated talk, the latter appropriate for a visual medium.

Antiqua	Goldman Sans
Arial	Goudy
Baskerville	Granjon
Bauhaus	Helvetica
BBC Reith	Humanist
Block Up	IBM Plex
Bodoni	Impact
Choc	Lydian (for Nancy Drew fans)
Coco	Mail Art Typeface
Comic Sans	Optima
Courier	Palatino
Doves Press	Papyrus
Franklin	Rockwell
Futura	Times and Times New Roman
Garamond	Univers
Georgia	Verdana
Gill	Wingdings

FOR FURTHER READING

The two articles that follow address typeface design in more detail: one about women designers (and the lack of them), and the other about revitalizing a centuries-old typeface.

1. Lauren Elle DeGaine, "The 'eBay Archive': Recovering Early Women Type Designers"

In the following article, a contemporary researcher of typeface finds hidden women designers through an unusual archive: eBay.

Southern Vancouver Island's 100-kilometer-long BC-14 Highway slides predominantly east to west along British Columbia coastline through traditional Coast Salish territory. Beneath the old-growth trees that are the marrow of this lush ecosystem is the small, unincorporated community of Shirley, and the Cook Kettle Press. Though small, the press is a regional hotbed of letterpress activity. As a print shop, it provides opportunities for artists to use its space and equipment. It also acts as a restoration shop that revamps antique printing equipment for universities, the International Printing Museum in California, as well as private printers and bookmakers. Lloyd Bowcott oversees the press's restoration work and Facebook group, PNW Letterpress, which connects printing communities around the world.

In late 2017, I was part of an all-woman collective printing poetry chapbooks at Cook Kettle. In the spirit of our collaboration, I wanted to use a metal typeface designed by a woman. But what metal typefaces are designed by women? This question spurred my Master's research into the role of women in type design and the recovery of such work through commercial sites like eBay, which serves as an unofficial "archive" of work mostly missing from institutional collections.

There are conflicting numbers for how many women had their typeface designs cast into metal for letterpress printing prior to the rise of digital foundries. In the pre-digital printing industry, women worked as printers and typesetters, as well as in type drawing offices. However, very few women had typeface *designs* credited to them. There is interest among printers and typographers about the history of early women type designers;[7] however, the subject is yet to be comprehensively studied by the broader academic community.

I define "early women type designers" as women designers of alphabetic typefaces that were *cast into metal* by commercial foundries for use in letterpress printing between 1900 and 1960. According to my preliminary research (which I will continue at the University of Victoria this fall), there are seven women who fit these parameters, including Franziska Baruch, who designed a Hebrew typeface in 1920s Germany. Perhaps the most well-known of these women is Elizabeth Friedlander, whose biography was published by Incline Press in 1998. Gudrun Zapf-von Hesse, whose typeface Diotima was digitized in 2017 (the year she turned 100) is another relatively well-known figure in the community.

The field of women's typographical work is more obscure when we look beyond Friedlander and Zapf-von Hesse, but even these two "known" figures

---

7 [See, for example, this article: http://www.alphabettes.org/first-female-typeface-designers/.]

are studied far less than their male counterparts. Take the influential discussions by Robert Bringhurst (*The Elements of Typographic Style*, 1992, 3rd ed., 2008) and Alexander Lawson (*Anatomy of a Typeface*, 2005): of the 107 designers in Bringhurst's 2008 index, three are women—and two of these created *digital* fonts. Lawson's book mentions only one woman designer—in relation to her husband's work, rather than her own.

The fact that there is no comprehensive scholarly resource on early women type designers has led to gaps in our understanding of women's roles in modern print culture. For example, a museum exhibit from 1947 lists Elizabeth Colwell as the *only known* American woman type designer, but Princeton University Library's "Unseen Hands" lists Bertha Goudy (also an American) as "type designer." (Goudy has no typefaces attributed to her, but she *was* an essential collaborator in her husband Fred's work.) Such discrepancies show competing claims of authority around women's type casting, and suggest the need for wider academic investigation and recovery. Elizabeth Colwell represents a prime figure for my preliminary research in this field, since there is significant (though not comprehensive) primary source material related to her work. Moreover, some, if not most, of her work exists in vulnerable places like commercial sites where it is bought and sold by collectors, which gives the material an online presence that for better or worse remains outside academic discourse and sites of preservation.

"Proof to the Contrary"

Elizabeth Colwell was born in Bronson, Michigan in 1881. She remains the only known American woman type designer of her generation; her typeface, Colwell Handletter and Italic, was commissioned by the American Type Founders Company (ATF) in 1916, and it is unknown how many sets are still extant. In addition to her successful career in hand-lettered advertisements, Colwell was also a woodcut artist and poet. She studied at the School of the Art Institute of Chicago (AIC) and under American artist B.J.O. Norfeldt. Her success in advertising is particularly remarkable; her hand-lettered advertisements for the Cowan Company furniture store and Marshall Fields are considered to be some of her best work.

The only thorough consideration of Colwell's work is a March 1913 article in *The Graphic Arts*, an early 1900's magazine on "the craftsmanship of advertising." The author, Alice Rouillier, provides insightful and eloquent analysis of Colwell's work; she notes, "[Colwell's] letters are clear cut, her arrangements dignified and full of grace, bearing always the stamp of originality." There is a clear similarity between the hand-drawn letters in Colwell's department store advertisements and the shapes and forms of the Colwell Handletter characters. Rouillier's remark that Colwell "leaned to the use almost exclusively of *natural* forms" (emphasis mine) is likely a reference to her use of floral motifs, but is also an indication that Colwell trusted her own well-trained aesthetic.

Colwell's significance to women's history in printing was recognized in her lifetime. Henry Lewis Johnson, the Editor of *The Graphic Arts*, wrote of Colwell that, "[i]t has been an axiom among designers, although just why it is hard to say, that women cannot do good lettering. Miss Colwell, with many other women designers, offers direct proof to the contrary."

"A Letter in Pure Form"

Colwell Handletter, published by ATF in 1916, is a Roman typeface in the Jenson style. Jenson-style typefaces, taking their name from the fifteenth-century Venetian printer, Nicolas Jenson, have a uniformity and evenness of character that makes them exceptionally legible, while subtly evoking the gracefulness of calligraphy. The thickness of the line is similar to a pen-stroke, so that the characters are substantial without being chunky, and economical use of tapering ensures that the characters are aesthetically pleasing without being overwrought. When William Morris set out to create a perfect Roman typeface—in his words, "a letter in pure form"—he turned to the Jenson style.

The *1923 American Type Founders Specimen Book and Catalogue*, which advertised ATF's typefaces and provided recommendations for how to use them, describes Colwell's design in this way: "Pleasing and attractive are the graceful lines and flowing style of hand-drawn letters and few typefaces can convey these characteristics so faithfully as the Colwell Handletter and Italic." The diction of this marketing material feminizes Colwell's typeface, and the ATF suggests using Colwell Handletter in "announcements, holiday printing, and commercial work." The relationship of these uses to traditionally secretarial or feminine domains (event planning, sending greeting cards, and shopping for craft goods) is interesting considering Colwell Handletter was the only typeface ATF published that was designed by a woman. My graduate work will explore whether Colwell Handletter was designed with an intentional bias toward the feminine, if it was feminized by ATF after the fact because of its creator, or if ATF recognized an opportunity in their market and commissioned a woman to create the typeface specifically to speak to their women customers.

Colwell's typeface is representative of her unique position as the singular American woman typeface designer of her generation. In his preface to the digitized version of ATF's 1923 specimen book, David Armstrong of Sevanti Letterpress writes, "With the *arts & crafts* and *art deco* movement in full swing, the book ended up being a snapshot of life in the Americas in the 'roaring 20s.' This book is a fascinating glimpse of a bygone age." Colwell's typeface is a contribution to this "fascinating glimpse." In fact, as the only woman contributor to the 1923 Specimen Book, her typeface is essential, an important historical artifact.

Colwell in the Library and the Print Shop

Artists and scholars have continued to value traditional printing and book-making methods, perhaps utilizing them with even more fervor as e-readers and other digital forms of reading have become ubiquitous. This is reflected in the hands-on book arts programs at universities across North America (such as Texas A&M's Book History Workshop, the BookLab at UMD, and the Center for the Book at the University of Iowa) as well as public-facing projects such as the Book Arts Collaborative (Muncie, IN), the annual Ladies of Letterpress Conference (St. Louis, MO), and the annual Wayzgoose Book Arts Fair at the Grimsby Public Art Gallery in Ontario. Here in the Pacific Northwest we are fortunate to have a sizeable community of independent printmakers selling commercial products like greeting cards, business cards, and wedding invitations. The University of Saskatchewan's SSHRC-funded Safer Printmaking website states, "Printmaking is evolving as a vital, dynamic, and pluralistic form of Canadian contemporary art-making." Letterpress printed materials have a superior tactility, which brings a different quality of pleasure to the reading or viewing experience, and the conservation skills that often dovetail with traditional bookmaking are relevant to the preservation of historic materials that happens in libraries and archives.

In late 2017, I purchased a set of 36-point Colwell Handletter Italic on eBay for $114. I am unable to determine how many cases of her type are still in existence, but eBay provided a rare collection of antique equipment. At Cook Kettle Press, I used the typeface to letterpress print the covers of the poetry chapbook *When You Let the Morning In*. Our small feminist printing collaborative created a Kickstarter campaign to self-publish the chapbook by creating Pop Bottle Press. I was able to share Colwell's work—and the work of three other contemporary women artists—with 58 readers in seven countries. Feminist projects like this are reminiscent of early-twentieth-century initiatives—such as Elizabeth Yeats's women-run Cuala Press, founded in 1908—to promote women's work and equality.

The "eBay archive" allows women's work to be recovered from the margins and provides a piece of the story of the role of women in design, print culture, and book history. Such commercial sites comprise a kind of extra-institutional international finding aid that has become an important scholarly mechanism for recovering research material currently missing from institutional archives. At the same time, it also highlights the instability of material culture traded in the open market. In collaboration with a university library, I am in the process of digitizing Colwell's typeface for further research. I'm also looking forward to my next trip to Cook Kettle Press where the story of this typeface continues to be inked.

2. Anne Quito, "What Would Justus Do? The Graceful Restoration of a 200-Year-Old Serif Typeface Shows the Problem with Digital Fonts"

To see the illustrations, go to https://qz.com/quartzy/1310669/.

In the early 1800s, a talented German punchcutter by the name of Justus Enrich Walbaum created a typeface that signaled modernity. A departure from the Blackletter fonts that were common in German books at that time, Walbaum designed a "warm and stylish" Roman typeface that would become a favorite of publishers for its readability. Walbaum Antiqua, as it was called, was so superior that Johann Wolfgang von Goethe insisted that his books be printed in this typeface.

Despite its technical excellence, Walbaum has largely been forgotten, eclipsed by similar high-contrast serifs such as Didot and Bodoni, which are still commonly used in books and fashion magazines today. Apart from a few logos and publications, Walbaum isn't exactly the top-of-mind font for most graphic designers.

While Roman style letters flourished in France and Italy in the 1800s, most books in Germany were still set in Blackletter type.

"Walbaum has gotten the short shrift," says Monotype's Charles Nix, who collaborated with fellow type designers Carl Crossgrove and Juan Villanueva to properly restore the 200-year-old font for 21st-century users.

Walbaum Antiqua's relative obscurity is also due to the political climate in the 1800s, Nix explains. Unfortunately for Walbaum, French forces, under Napoleon's command, invaded and occupied Prussia around the time he introduced his French-style letters. Germans dismissed Walbaum Anti-qua, which was inspired by the French designer Firmin Didot's eponymous typeface, as anti-patriotic.

Describing the project as a labor of love, Nix says he, Crossgrove, and Villanueva wanted to "do right" by the German designer, who they greatly admired. "As type designers and font geeks normally do, we professed our mutual love of Walbaum and how it's been overlooked," says Nix, describing his first meeting with Crossgrove in 2015. "We made a pinky pact that we would get to it."

After over two years of work, the three designers unveiled a remastered version of Walbaum last month—posited to be the most extensive restoration of the under-appreciated serif. Like restoring a painting, remastering a classic typeface requires both detective work and artistry. First, designers scour libraries and archives to collect old samples of the typeface in various sizes and weights. They take high resolution photos and trace letterforms digitally, often smoothing out shapes to eliminate rough details from the ink gain and paper fibers. Sometimes, designers are required to infer an entire alphabet based on a few letters. They prepare the bold, italicized styles, upper and lower case letters, numerals, and punctuation marks, and create character sets for various languages.

Using type specimens from 1803 and 1812, Nix, Crossgrove and Villanueva sought to extrapolate from Walbaum's original intent, using the mantra, "What would Justus do?"

The result: Sixty-nine Walbaum variations optimized for size—from 6pt footnote text to massive marquee lettering—that work well on print and digital displays.

Why Fonts Need to Be Restored for the Digital Age

This isn't the first time someone has attempted to remaster Walbaum for digital applications. In fact, several Walbaum variations were already available. But most of them lack the finesse of the original, explains Crossgrove. "Most of the available digital versions were lacking something—some of them were incomplete or uninspiring," he says. The problem is in what's called "optical sizing." Before computers allowed us to change a font's point sizes instantly, type designers had to create variations of the same typeface in different sizes. In this process, they were also able to make important adjustments, such as adding more space between letters in small text, or making the letterform openings a bit larger to increase legibility.

All this was lost when typefaces were digitized in the 1980s and 1990s. For efficiency's sake, digital type foundries choose just one size master as a basis for each typeface, then size it up or down, often losing the nuances the designer had originally created. "Users gained the ability to scale a font for any setting, but lost the type maker's size-specific optimizations," explains Stephen Coles on Typographica. "This newfound freedom altered the typeface's intended appearance and, in many cases, its integrity. Fonts made for small text looked clunky and inelegant when enlarged. Fonts made for headlines became anemic and unreadable when reduced for body."

Nix illustrated the point with an analogy: "Imagine if we all decided that 10-year-old boys would be the optimal human form," he says. "Rather than having babies, we just shrunk 10-year-old boys to baby size, and enlarge them to the size of a full grown man. That's kind of what we're combatting."

Walbaum originally developed 28 size variations of the serif in the 1800s—including numerals, decorative ornaments to separate blocks of text, and mathematical symbols—but most digital revivals prior to Monotype's restoration were based on just one master. "This is something endemic when the digital type revival happened," says Crossgrove, referring to the era in which the works of famous typographers such as John Baskerville, William Caslon, and Claude Garamond were recreated in pixel versions for use on PCs. "It probably has to do with marketing or cost of manufacture.... There are a lot forces sweeping aside all the additional rich material that you can have."

But this one-size-fits-all approach is changing, says Crossgrove. "[Type designers] have been restoring the idea that type can be made for a specific size use.... It's not a new thing to do that but it's one of the things that was lost in these technological changes."

And why do type restorations matter for non-font geeks? For those of us who do extended reading on our various screens and media devices (basically, all of us) ease of reading can make a big difference. "The legibility is improved dramatically," says Nix, referring to the restored Walbaum font. "My experience as a book designer and as a reader, it's very obvious that the careful attention to the spacing, the shape of the form of those smaller sizes, the adjustment of serif length and overall aesthetic in addition to that—make for a much better reading experience."

INTERESTED IN LEARNING MORE?

Book Recommendations

Simon Garfield, *Just My Type* (Gotham/Penguin, 2011).
Sarah Hyndman, *Why Fonts Matter* (Gingko Press, 2016).
———, *The Night the Fonts Farted* (Type Tasting, 2020). [Children's book.]
Peter Schwenger, *Asemic: The Art of Writing* (University of Minnesota
   Press, 2019).

Film Recommendations

Helvetica, directed by Gary Hustwit (2017), https://www.hustwit.com/
   helvetica.
Typeface, directed by Justine Nagin (2009), https://kartemquin.com/films/
   typeface.

Chapter Twelve

Writing Letters

THE EPISTOLARY TRADITION

> *"How can I exist without writing to you?"*
> —*Goethe*

> *"Letters are what history sounds like when it is still part*
> *of everyday life."*
> —*Lisa Grunwald and Stephen J. Adler*

In February 1781, Johann Wolfgang von Goethe (1749–1832), perhaps the most famous author in German literature, left behind a pair of gloves as a love token after visiting Charlotte von Stein, a married lady-in-waiting. She returned them to him, and he thanked her in a short note, or *billet*. In it, he describes the inherent contradiction of letter writing: lovers can share their thoughts, but they cannot be together. How are they to endure that state of existence? For 10 years, Goethe and von Stein exchanged countless letters, sometimes just short notes. Sometimes the poet wrote several times a day. He even felt that he was afflicted with a "Billet sickness." Did their love affair go beyond this epistolary relationship? Whatever the case, the lady was severely put out when Goethe decamped to Italy for two years without telling her—even though he continued to write. She requested her letters to be returned and burned them. Goethe kept his own copies and eventually published them!

While this epistolary exchange seems extreme, it was not out of the ordinary. The eighteenth century became the century of the letter. Because of compulsory school attendance, literacy increased across social classes in Germany. But the letter has a much longer history. It was, in fact, the primary genre in writing for many centuries and was present in the civilizations that are known for the origin of writing: Sumer, Egypt, and China. The first recorded handwritten letter, around 500 BCE, was reputedly by Persian Queen Atossa, the mother of Xerxes, according to the ancient historian Hellanicus (Roberts). Xerxes (519–465 BCE) himself, as king of the Persian empire, realized the importance of correspondence and maintained roadways, particularly the Royal Road, anticipating more modern postal systems.

Even before Atossa, though, letters were important, particularly in diplomatic relationships. These letters, however, were not "handwritten," so to speak, but set in clay by scribes, which is why they exist today. Letters were of particular importance in diplomatic relationship as emissaries traveled among the various civilizations. One of the most famous sets of these missives is the Amarna Letters of the fourteenth century BCE, discovered in the late nineteenth century. Almost 400 tablets offer clues to diplomatic relations between Egypt and other kingdoms. The letters themselves provided the communication system needed for peace and security within the region. Amarna was the city founded by Akhenaten (also known as Amenhotep IV), the father of Tutankhamen. Akhenaten was considered a heretical leader, as he believed in monotheism rather than the pantheon of gods traditional to Egyptian worship. As a result, his city did not survive, the seat of government returned to Luxor/Thebes, and the tablets were kept intact for hundreds of years until looters and archaeologists discovered them.[1]

In the Bible, 21 of the 27 books of the New Testament are actually epistles. The word *epistle* comes from the Greek word *epistole* and means letters or messages. Paul was particularly prolific in using this genre, contributing 13. In his letters, he addressed specific churches or individuals. Others were authored by Peter and John as well as Jesus' half-brothers, James and Jude. Letters were the most common form of communication in that time. The papal brief (from Latin *breve*) started in the fifteenth century and was a letter

---

1   William Moran translated 350 letters from cuneiform into English for the first time in 1992: *The Amarna Letters*. William M. Schniedewind and Zipora Cochavi-Rainey offer an updated edition, *The el-Amarna Correspondence* (2014).

from the sitting pope that stated a new or revised policy. For instance, Henry VIII was given a papal brief so that he could marry his brother's widow, Catherine of Aragon (1485–1536), necessary at the time as she would have been considered his *sister*, although no blood relation.

WHAT IS A LETTER?

Each fall on my campus, incoming students share a common reading of a book in a program called "Connections." The idea is to connect students to various aspects of the campus. At the conclusion of the program, when the speaker associated with the book has finished, we ask students to connect back to home by sending a postcard to family or friends. During the first year of this activity, we quickly learned that we had to also teach postcard conventions. Many students had never written or mailed a postcard. Perhaps some have never written a letter.

Correspondence has conventions on how it is formatted. The formal letter includes several parts, most of which were created as conventions centuries ago. The first is the return address: your name and address. This is followed by the date. After a blank line, the name and address of the recipient is added. Then the salutation provides the prescribed greeting, typically "Dear" followed by the person's first or last name, depending on the relationship. The body of the letter conveys the message, and the sender closes with a polite word or two such as "Sincerely," "Thank you," or "Best wishes." Then the writer signs the letter. The envelope follows the conventions of a return address in the upper left corner and the recipient's address centered on the envelope, leaving room for postage.

Envelopes arose in the nineteenth century; before that, letters were often simply folded and sealed with wax, although they could be protected by more intricate means. Mary, Queen of Scots (1542–87) sealed her last letter prior to beheading on the orders of her cousin, Queen Elizabeth I, with a "butterfly lock." Queen Elizabeth herself used a triangle lock to secure her messages. Cross-hatch marks covered the blank margins of the letter so that others could not later add words to her texts. A dagger-trap actually included a booby trap in case an unauthorized person tried to gain access to the contents. Jana Dambrogio, a conservator at MIT Libraries, made it her business to decode letterlocking, practices enacted prior to the envelope (Cain, "Before Envelopes"; see Figure 12.1). Keeping written conversations secure has been important ever since the first diplomatic clay tablets were transported among ruling parties.

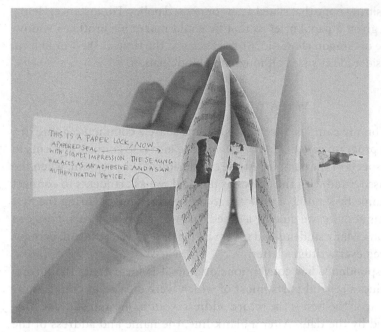

Figure 12.1   Letterlock. MIT Libraries.

The format of a letter varies somewhat depending on its purpose. The letter described above is usually called a formal or business letter. Letters to friends may be more casual in format. On the other hand, letters of application for jobs or inquiry, for references, or to complain, or a letter to the editor, should retain standard features. The diverse variety of letters includes Dear John/Jane letters to break up a relationship, poison pen letters[2] that are malicious and usually anonymous, love letters, cease and desist letters to order an activity to stop, chain letters that are to be copied and sent to others in a pyramid-type scheme, thank-you letters, and letters of sympathy. A letter of resignation may include a rationale for leaving the job, although the 1974 letter by President Richard M. Nixon addressed to Secretary of State Henry Kissinger simply said, "I hereby resign the Office of the President of the United States." Advice on writing each type of letter can be found through the Internet and manuals.

---

2   Called "The Early 20th Century's Strangest Crime Wave," poison pen letters (also written on the increasingly popular typewriter) "could not only hurt but in some cases kill" (C. Evans).

LETTER-WRITING MANUALS

Letters are often of a private nature and are traditionally handwritten to one or more recipients, which will be transported some distance. Letters have a longer life than, say, a scribbled note. Some might say they don't require much time to write. On the other hand, the famous quote "I would have written a shorter letter, but I did not have the time"[3] suggests that the well-crafted letter requires thought and consideration.

Because letters were an essential part of societies from ancient times, guides on how to write good letters proliferated. In ancient Greece, Demetrius Phalereus (c. 350–c. 250 BCE) divided letters into types, with rules governing each: friendly, commendatory, reproving, objurgatory, consolatory, castigatory, admonishing, threatening, vituperatory, laudatory, persuasive, begging, questioning, answering, allegorical, explanatory, accusing, defending, congratulatory, ironic and thankful (Saintsbury 8). Having instructions and models for each type of letter provided efficiency, particularly important given the materials available for writing at the time. Demetrius also noted that letters revealed the author's character, an important aspect that continued in manuals—being aware of how one is perceived through letters.

Ancient Rome outdid Greece in letter writing. As a master of writing and speaking, Cicero was known for his excellent letters, which were collected and published. Pliny the Younger (61–c. 113 CE) and Seneca (c. 4 BCE–65 CE) also contributed letters to the record, and it is through letters such as these that much is known about the history of the time and place. As scholars Lisa Grunwald and Stephen J. Adler note, "Letters are what history sounds like when it is still part of everyday life" (1). Enos and Robinson analyzed a very early Roman letter, a birthday party invitation written when Rome controlled Britain, said to be the first written in Latin by a woman's hand.

In the Middle Ages, letters became more important for documentation, much like the collected epistles of St. Paul, and they tended to be the province of clergy and governments, as well as nobility. Bizzell and Herzberg (492) put forward a monk, Alberic of Monte Cassino, as an early author of manuals for letter writing. In two manuals produced early in the eleventh century, Alberic defined four parts of a letter: exhortation, narration, argument, and conclusion, drawing on Cicero's guidelines. He refined the exhortation, however, to be a salutation. These instructions were calls *ars dictaminis*, the art of composing letters. Following Alberic, another manual

---

3   Typically attributed to Mark Twain, this sentiment was actually written by French philosopher Blaise Pascal (1623-62) but has been used by John Locke (1632-1704), Benjamin Franklin, and Woodrow Wilson (1856-1924), among others. Even Cicero is reputed to have written a version of it (The Quote Investigator, https://quoteinvestigator.com/2012/04/28/shorter-letter/).

by an anonymous writer of Bologna (translated by James J. Murphy) laid out the definition and parts of a letter: "An epistle or letter, then, is a suitable arrangement of words set forth to express the intended meaning of its sender. Or in other words, a letter is a discourse composed of coherent yet distinct parts signifying fully the sentiments of its sender.... There are, in fact, five parts of a letter: the Salutation, the Securing of Good-will, the Narration, the Petition, and the Conclusion." The writer defines appropriate wording for each part. Among the multiple suggestions for salutations is this one from a teacher to a pupil:

> N—, promoter of the scholastic profession, wishes N—, his most dear friend and companion, to acquire the teachings of all literature, to possess fully all the diligence of the philosophical profession, to pursue not folly but the wisdom of Socrates and Plato.

While this salutation might seem rather flowery by contemporary standards, the relationship between pupil and professor in the Middle Ages was a sacred one in which a shared goal of education was deemed noble. The manual also includes suggestions on grammar and style.

In the Renaissance, humanism, a belief that people are important and that there should be concern for people and their welfare, was in the ascendency. Organized religion began to be scrutinized rather than accepted without question. Martin Luther (1483–1546) led the revolution, protesting practices of the Catholic Church, that led to Protestantism. The printing press, as has been discussed in another chapter, ushered in more attention to scientific and philosophical writings, such as those by the prolific Erasmus.[4] With this increased emphasis on people, letter writing became more attractive, as individuals penned missives to one another. Paper was more available—although still expensive. Printed books proliferated after Gutenberg's invention, and some of these books populated classrooms as texts for teachers and students. The eloquence and style of classical writers such as Cicero were introduced to young scholars, who copied letters in their copybooks, following a pedagogical principle that good models influence novice writers positively. It was believed that good letter writers were good writers overall.

No one epitomizes the emphasis on letters and their importance more so than Madame de Sévigné of France (see Figure 12.2). Marie de Rabutin-Chantal, the Marquise de Sévigné (1626–96), is distinguished for her seventeenth-century letters, which number more than a thousand. Her cor-

---

4 Erasmus even suggested that schools should be places where students "enjoy their lessons" rather than the torture chambers he felt they were (Lancy, *Anthropology of Childhood* x). This is just one example of a humanistic approach.

respondence is considered so witty and detailed that it rises to the level of literature. The recipients of her letters were many, as she was well connected; however, she wrote a phenomenal number of letters to her daughter, who moved to Provence with her husband, some distance from Madame de Sévigné's home in a chateau near Vitré in Brittany. An independent and cultured woman, she socialized with other aristocrats and enjoyed intellectual salons of the time. Her husband died in a duel over his mistress. Perhaps ironically, biographies of this lettered woman note that although she was only 24, she never married again. Her letters are filled with details about the spa she visits at Vichy when ill, her estate, her social life, and significant events of the day.

Figure 12.2   Madame de Sévigné and Souvenir Quill Ink Pen, 2018. Purchases from the Vitré Chateau Museum shop, France, 2018.

In 1677, Madame de Sévigné moved to Paris to the impressive palace the Hôtel Carnavalet; 200 years later, it became a museum focused on the history of the city.[5] Her letters were considered such marvelous reading that they were published, at first without her knowledge and then, later, with her consent. It is said that she wrote the history of Paris in her letters. She recounted the outcomes of battles between France and Holland, described the confession and execution of a woman of nobility who had poisoned family members, and shared what she was reading. These volumes of letters were read eagerly, and not just in France. They served as models for the elite. In the

5   To read more about the amazing Madame de Sévigné, turn to Frances Mossiker's biography, *Life and Letters*.

early twentieth century, for example, Englishman George Saintsbury (1845–1933), writing in his introduction to *The Letter Book* (1922), notes that it is not affectation that makes readers admire Madame de Sévigné so much but rather her "absolute non-pareility in almost every kind of genuine letter" (vii).

Earlier in this chapter, the eighteenth century was noted as the "century of the letter," a golden age of letter writing. The practice bloomed during this period, and the materials needed to write letters also exploded. Konstantin Dierks counted hundreds of penmanship manuals, spelling books, grammar books, and dictionaries produced in the colonies/United States between 1750 and 1800 (32). The British Library calls eighteenth-century writing manuals "an early form of self-help book" (Morton). They certainly helped members of the middle class understand how to pen an endearing eloquent note, which could lead to a favorable courtship, a job offer, or a rise in social status. "By demystifying the rules and conventions of letter writing, a social practice traditionally symbolic of power, authors of familiar letter manuals helped middling families pursue their claims to social refinement and upward mobility," according to Dierks. Samuel Richardson (1689–1761), who was one of the first British novelists, known for his epistolary tales *Pamela* (1740) and *Clarissa* (1748), also authored *Letters Written to and for Particular Friends* (1741). Templates for letters with various purposes were included in the manual. How do I write a love letter? How do I propose an entrepreneurship opportunity? How do I chastise a wayward adult child? While people in the upper social register might not require such form letters, with the increased accessibility to education and writing materials, the middle and working classes did.

Letters thus diversified beyond official correspondence among governments and businesses. The art of letter writing extended to family and friends, and, notably, among women, as it became important to stay in touch. The collected letters of Jane Austen (1775–1817) offer insight into the content of letters of the period. Although it is believed that she wrote several thousand letters, only 161 survive, as her family destroyed many. Her letters reveal her interactions with family and friends and detail her surroundings and current events. Slightly gossipy at times, but also witty and amusing, the letters offer such trenchant comments as this one from December 24, 1798: "I do not want people to be very agreeable, as it saves me the trouble of liking them a great deal." Or this one from September 23, 1813: "He seems a very harmless sort of young man, nothing to like or dislike in him—goes out shooting or hunting with the two others all the morning, and plays at whist and makes queer faces in the evening" (Le Faye). Most of Austen's letters are written to her sister Cassandra (1773–1845), who was also the culprit in destroying or censoring so many.

Throughout the nineteenth century, letter writing remained an important means of communication. Increased literacy and improved transportation—

along with the rise of national postal services—meant that more people could write, send, and receive letters. Correspondence became more equalitarian, not just the province of officialdom or the rich. An 1878 manual by William Johnson Cocker, *Hand-book of Punctuation, with Instructions for Capitalization, Letter-writing, and Proofreading*, shows that correct format became as important as eloquence and style, which is suggested in the title itself that places letter writing third in the series of four items. The *Hand-book* directs writers to place the first paragraph directly "under the comma or the dash of the salutation" and to start new paragraphs "whenever a new subject is introduced," indenting the first line slightly to the right of the margin (95). The manual also emphasizes an increasing interest in business letters.

LETTERS AND WAR

The Civil War

When Ken Burns was organizing his incredible documentary *The Civil War* (1990), he was frustrated by the lack of first-person accounts. A historical advisor sent him the extraordinarily moving letter from Sullivan Ballou (1829–61) that follows.

July 14, 1861
Camp Clark, Washington

My very dear Sarah: The indications are very strong that we shall move in a few days—perhaps tomorrow. Lest I should not be able to write again, I feel impelled to write a few lines that may fall under your eye when I shall be no more....

I have no misgivings about, or lack of confidence in the cause in which I am engaged, and my courage does not halt or falter. I know how strongly American Civilization now leans on the triumph of the Government and how great a debt we owe to those who went before us through the blood and sufferings of the Revolution. And I am willing—perfectly willing—to lay down all my joys in this life, to help maintain this Government, and to pay that debt....

Sarah my love for you is deathless, it seems to bind me with mighty cables that nothing but Omnipotence could break; and yet my love of Country comes over me like a strong wind and bears me unresistibly on with all these chains to the battle field.

The memories of the blissful moments I have spent with you come creeping over me, and I feel most gratified to God and to you that I have enjoyed them for so long. And hard it is for me to give them up and burn to ashes the hopes of future years, when, God willing, we might still have lived and loved together, and seen our sons grown up to honorable manhood, around us. I have, I know, but few and small claims upon Divine Providence, but something whispers to me—perhaps it is the wafted prayer of my little Edgar, that I shall return to my loved ones unharmed. If I do not my dear Sarah, never forget how much I love you, and when my last breath escapes me on the battle field, it will whisper your name. Forgive my many faults and the many pains I have caused you. How thoughtless and foolish I have often times been! How gladly would I wash out with my tears every little spot upon your happiness....

But, O Sarah! If the dead can come back to this earth and flit unseen around those they loved, I shall always be near you; in the gladdest days and in the darkest nights ... always, always, and if there be a soft breeze upon your cheek, it shall be my breath, as the cool air fans your throbbing temple, it shall be my spirit passing by. Sarah do not mourn me dead; think I am gone and wait for thee, for we shall meet again....

Ballou was killed at the Battle of Bull Run a week after writing this letter, which was never delivered. Instead, it was collected with his other personal effects by the governor of Rhode Island, who traveled to the battle site in its aftermath to collect the belongings of those citizens of the state who had fallen (PBS).

Equally moving is the letter from Frederick Douglass (c. 1818–95), who escaped from slavery in 1838, to his former master Thomas Auld, which was published in Douglass's abolitionist newspaper, *The North Star*, in 1848. It's worth noting that Douglass taught himself to read and write after his flight from Maryland. He became one of the most eloquent speakers and writers of his time. Sullivan Ballou was influenced by letters such as this one to believe that the cause for which he fought was just.

To Thomas Auld
September 3d, 1848

Sir:
1. ...
2. I have selected this day on which to address you, because it is the anniversary of my emancipation; and knowing of no better way, I am led to this as the best mode of celebrating that truly important

event. Just ten years ago this beautiful September morning, yon bright sun beheld me a slave—a poor, degraded chattel—trembling at the sound of your voice, lamenting that I was a man, and wishing myself a brute. The hopes which I had treasured up for weeks of a safe and successful escape from your grasp, were powerfully confronted at this last hour by dark clouds of doubt and fear, making my person shake and my bosom to heave with the heavy contest between hope and fear. I have no words to describe to you the deep agony of soul which I experienced on that never to be forgotten morning—(for I left by daylight). I was making a leap in the dark. The probabilities, so far as I could by reason determine them, were stoutly against the undertaking. The preliminaries and precautions I had adopted previously, all worked badly. I was like one going to war without weapons—ten chances of defeat to one of victory. One in whom I had confided, and one who had promised me assistance, appalled by fear at the trial hour, deserted me, thus leaving the responsibility of success or failure solely with myself. You, sir, can never know my feelings. As I look back to them, I can scarcely realize that I have passed through a scene so trying. Trying however as they were, and gloomy as was the prospect, thanks be to the Most High, who is ever the God of the oppressed, at the moment which was to determine my whole earthly career. His grace was sufficient, my mind was made up. I embraced the golden opportunity, took the morning tide at the flood, and a free man, young, active and strong, is the result.

3. I have often thought I should like to explain to you the grounds upon which I have justified myself in running away from you. I am almost ashamed to do so now, for by this time you may have discovered them yourself. I will, however, glance at them. When yet but a child about six years old, I imbibed the determination to run away. The very first mental effort that I now remember on my part, was an attempt to solve the mystery, Why am I a slave? and with this question my youthful mind was troubled for many days, pressing upon me more heavily at times than others. When I saw the slave-driver whip a slave woman, cut the blood out of her neck, and heard her piteous cries, I went away into the corner of the fence, wept and pondered over the mystery. I had, through some medium, I know not what, got some idea of God, the Creator of all mankind, the black and the white, and that he had made the blacks to serve the whites as slaves. How he could do this and be good, I could not tell. I was not satisfied with this theory, which

made God responsible for slavery, for it pained me greatly, and I have wept over it long and often. At one time, your first wife, Mrs. Lucretia, heard me singing and saw me shedding tears, and asked of me the matter, but I was afraid to tell her. I was puzzled with this question, till one night, while sitting in the kitchen, I heard some of the old slaves talking of their parents having been stolen from Africa by white men, and were sold here as slaves. The whole mystery was solved at once. Very soon after this my aunt Jinny and uncle Noah ran away, and the great noise made about it by your father-in-law, made me for the first time acquainted with the fact, that there were free States as well as slave States. From that time, I resolved that I would some day run away. The morality of the act, I dispose as follows: I am myself; you are yourself; we are two distinct persons, equal persons. What you are, I am. You are a man, and so am I. God created both, and made us separate beings. I am not by nature bound to you, or you to me. Nature does not make your existence depend upon me, or mine to depend upon yours. I cannot walk upon your legs, or you upon mine. I cannot breathe for you, or you for me; I must breathe for myself, and you for yourself. We are distinct persons, and are each equally provided with faculties necessary to our individual existence. In leaving you, I took nothing but what belonged to me, and in no way lessened your means for obtaining an honest living. Your faculties remained yours, and mine became useful to their rightful owner. I therefore see no wrong in any part of the transaction. It is true, I went off secretly, but that was more your fault than mine. Had I let you into the secret, you would have defeated the enterprise entirely; but for this, I should have been really glad to have made you acquainted with my intentions to leave.

4. You may perhaps want to know how I like my present condition. I am free to say, I greatly prefer it to that which I occupied in Maryland. I am, however, by no means prejudiced against the State as such. Its geography, climate, fertility and products, are such as to make it a very desirable abode for any man; and but for the existence of slavery there, it is not impossible that I might again take up my abode in that State. It is not that I love Maryland less, but freedom more. You will be surprised to learn that people at the North labor under the strange delusion that if the slaves were emancipated at the South, they would flock to the North. So far from this being the case, in that event, you would see many old and familiar faces back again to the South. The fact is, there are few

here who would not return to the South in the event of emancipation. We want to live in the land of our birth, and to lay our bones by the side of our fathers'; and nothing short of an intense love of personal freedom keeps us from the South. For the sake of this, most of us would live on a crust of bread and a cup of cold water.

5. Since I left you, I have had a rich experience. I have occupied stations which I never dreamed of when a slave. Three out of the ten years since I left you, I spent as a common laborer on the wharves of New Bedford, Massachusetts. It was there I earned my first free dollar. It was mine. I could spend it as I pleased. I could buy hams or herring with it, without asking any odds of any body. That was a precious dollar to me. You remember when I used to make seven or eight, or even nine dollars a week in Baltimore, you would take every cent of it from me every Saturday night, saying that I belonged to you, and my earnings also. I never liked this conduct on your part—to say the best, I thought it a little mean. I would not have served you so. But let that pass. I was a little awkward about counting money in New England fashion when I first landed in New Bedford. I like to have betrayed myself several times. I caught myself saying phip, for fourpence; and at one time a man actually charged me with being a runaway, whereupon I was silly enough to become one by running away from him, for I was greatly afraid he might adopt measures to get me again into slavery, a condition I then dreaded more than death.

6. I soon, however, learned to count money, as well as to make it, and got on swimmingly. I married soon after leaving you: in fact, I was engaged to be married before I left you; and instead of finding my companion a burden, she was truly a helpmeet. She went to live at service, and I to work on the wharf, and though we toiled hard the first winter, we never lived more happily. After remaining in New Bedford for three years, I met with Wm. Lloyd Garrison, a person of whom you have possibly heard, as he is pretty generally known among slaveholders. He put it into my head that I might make myself serviceable to the cause of the slave by devoting a portion of my time to telling my own sorrows, and those of other slaves which had come under my observation. This was the commencement of a higher state of existence than any to which I had ever aspired. I was thrown into society the most pure, enlightened and benevolent that the country affords. Among these I have never forgotten you, but have invariably made you the topic of conversation—thus giving you all the notoriety I could do. I need not tell

you that the opinion formed of you in these circles, is far from being favorable. They have little respect for your honesty, and less for your religion.

7. But I was going on to relate to you something of my interesting experience. I had not long enjoyed the excellent society to which I have referred, before the light of its excellence exerted a beneficial influence on my mind and heart. Much of my early dislike of white persons was removed, and their manners, habits and customs, so entirely unlike what I had been used to in the kitchen-quarters on the plantations of the South, fairly charmed me, and gave me a strong disrelish for the coarse and degrading customs of my former condition. I therefore made an effort so to improve my mind and deportment, as to be somewhat fitted to the station to which I seemed almost providentially called. The transition from degradation to respectability was indeed great, and to get from one to the other without carrying some marks of one's former condition, is truly a difficult matter. I would not have you think that I am now entirely clear of all plantation peculiarities, but my friends here, while they entertain the strongest dislike to them, regard me with that charity to which my past life somewhat entitles me, so that my condition in this respect is exceedingly pleasant. So far as my domestic affairs are concerned, I can boast of as comfortable a dwelling as your own. I have an industrious and neat companion, and four dear children—the oldest a girl of nine years, and three fine boys, the oldest eight, the next six, and the youngest four years old. The three oldest are now going regularly to school—two can read and write, and the other can spell with tolerable correctness words of two syllables: Dear fellows! they are all in comfortable beds, and are sound asleep, perfectly secure under my own roof. There are no slaveholders here to rend my heart by snatching them from my arms, or blast a mother's dearest hopes by tearing them from her bosom. These dear children are ours—not to work up into rice, sugar and tobacco, but to watch over, regard, and protect, and to rear them up in the nurture and admonition of the gospel—to train them up in the paths of wisdom and virtue, and, as far as we can to make them useful to the world and to themselves. Oh! sir, a slaveholder never appears to me so completely an agent of hell, as when I think of and look upon my dear children. It is then that my feelings rise above my control. I meant to have said more with respect to my own prosperity and happiness, but thoughts and feelings which

this recital has quickened unfits me to proceed further in that direction. The grim horrors of slavery rise in all their ghastly terror before me, the wails of millions pierce my heart, and chill my blood. I remember the chain, the gag, the bloody whip, the deathlike gloom overshadowing the broken spirit of the fettered bondman, the appalling liability of his being torn away from wife and children, and sold like a beast in the market. Say not that this is a picture of fancy. You well know that I wear stripes on my back inflicted by your direction; and that you, while we were brothers in the same church, caused this right hand, with which I am now penning this letter, to be closely tied to my left, and my person dragged at the pistol's mouth, fifteen miles, from the Bay side to Easton to be sold like a beast in the market, for the alleged crime of intending to escape from your possession. All this and more you remember, and know to be perfectly true, not only of yourself, but of nearly all of the slaveholders around you.

8. At this moment, you are probably the guilty holder of at least three of my own dear sisters, and my only brother in bondage. These you regard as your property. They are recorded on your ledger, or perhaps have been sold to human flesh mongers, with a view to filling your own ever-hungry purse. Sir, I desire to know how and where these dear sisters are. Have you sold them? or are they still in your possession? What has become of them? are they living or dead? And my dear old grandmother, whom you turned out like an old horse, to die in the woods—is she still alive? Write and let me know all about them. If my grandmother be still alive, she is of no service to you, for by this time she must be nearly eighty years old—too old to be cared for by one to whom she has ceased to be of service, send her to me at Rochester, or bring her to Philadelphia, and it shall be the crowning happiness of my life to take care of her in her old age. Oh! she was to me a mother, and a father, so far as hard toil for my comfort could make her such. Send me my grandmother! that I may watch over and take care of her in her old age. And my sisters, let me know all about them. I would write to them, and learn all I want to know of them, without disturbing you in any way, but that, through your unrighteous conduct, they have been entirely deprived of the power to read and write. You have kept them in utter ignorance, and have therefore robbed them of the sweet enjoyments of writing or receiving letters from absent friends and relatives. Your wickedness and cruelty committed in this respect on your fellow-creatures, are

greater than all the stripes you have laid upon my back, or theirs. It is an outrage upon the soul—a war upon the immortal spirit, and one for which you must give account at the bar of our common Father and Creator.

9. The responsibility which you have assumed in this regard is truly awful—and how you could stagger under it these many years is marvellous. Your mind must have become darkened, your heart hardened, your conscience seared and petrified, or you would have long since thrown off the accursed load and sought relief at the hands of a sin-forgiving God. How, let me ask, would you look upon me, were I some dark night in company with a band of hardened villains, to enter the precincts of your elegant dwelling and seize the person of your own lovely daughter Amanda, and carry her off from your family, friends and all the loved ones of her youth—make her my slave—compel her to work, and I take her wages—place her name on my ledger as property—disregard her personal rights—fetter the powers of her immortal soul by denying her the right and privilege of learning to read and write—feed her coarsely—clothe her scantily, and whip her on the naked back occasionally; more and still more horrible, leave her unprotected—a degraded victim to the brutal lust of fiendish overseers, who would pollute, blight, and blast her fair soul—rob her of all dignity—destroy her virtue, and annihilate all in her person the graces that adorn the character of virtuous womanhood? I ask how would you regard me, if such were my conduct? Oh! the vocabulary of the damned would not afford a word sufficiently infernal, to express your idea of my God-provoking wickedness. Yet sir, your treatment of my beloved sisters is in all essential points, precisely like the case I have now supposed. Damning as would be such a deed on my part, it would be no more so than that which you have committed against me and my sisters.

10. I will now bring this letter to a close, you shall hear from me again unless you let me hear from you. I intend to make use of you as a weapon with which to assail the system of slavery—as a means of concentrating public attention on the system, and deepening their horror of trafficking in the souls and bodies of men. I shall make use of you as a means of exposing the character of the American church and clergy—and as a means of bringing this guilty nation with yourself to repentance. In doing this I entertain no malice towards you personally. There is no roof under which you would be more safe than mine, and there is nothing in my house which

you might need for your comfort, which I would not readily grant.
Indeed, I should esteem it a privilege, to set you an example as to
how mankind ought to treat each other. I am your fellow man, but
not your slave,

During the Civil War, letters could not be sent via the post office, as mail
service to the South was suspended (Burke). After the war, many veterans
found work as letter carriers. The adhesive stamp was developed in the
1850s so that people didn't have to go to the post office to mail letters. As a
result, the postal service began installing mailboxes in urban areas. Prior
to 1863, letter carriers delivered letters and were paid by recipients, generally a penny or two, not by the post office. According to the Smithsonian
National Postal Museum, in 1863, a Cleveland postal worker, Joseph Briggs,
noticed long lines of women and children checking for letters from loved
ones away in the war. He convinced officials to try out free home delivery,
which was an immediate success. The service expanded exponentially as
letters became easier to send and receive, and the revenue generated funded
the employment of thousands of carriers, particularly helpful to the veterans
who returned home maimed.

World War I

My research for this book took place over several years, but in the fall of
2018 I had the pleasure of living in France in the weeks leading up to the
November 11 celebration of the end of World War I. In almost every village
I visited, the exhibitions on the Great War focused on letters to and from
the front. Letters provided a lifeline between loved ones back home and
the soldiers in the battlefields, as well as the women tending the wounded
and driving ambulances. The Polish Library on the Ile Saint-Louis in Paris
featured just such an exhibit. The same was true for Rochefort, the charming
naval history town on the Atlantic. The historic paper mill in Angoulême
took a somewhat different approach. A wonderful stop-action animated film
that used paper for all of the characters and settings, *Lettres de Femmes*,
featured the battlefield nurse using strips of love letters as bandages. It was
amazingly effective and touching.

Prior to the advent of electronic mail, letters provided—and often still
do—a lifeline between military personnel and their friends and families.
"Mail call" has been eagerly anticipated in the United States since the Con-
tinental Post was established in 1775. During World War I, over a period of
just one year, the Post Office dispatched 35 million letters to the American
Expeditionary Forces. During the Korean War, over 11 tons of mail were

delivered to the multinational forces. Sending letters to military personnel requires only the domestic rate, no matter the location of the soldier's posting. The International Red Cross was instrumental in supplying writing materials to soldiers, particularly those in hospitals, and the organization also delivered mail to those who had been captured and held prisoner. Unless the mail brought a "Dear John" letter breaking off a relationship, letters were almost always a morale booster.

POSTING LETTERS

As already noted, King Xerxes kept roads in Persia in good shape for the transport of mail. The Roman emperor Trajan (r. 98–117 CE) commanded that *positus* (carriers) be stationed at regular distances with chariots waiting to transport important documents; the word *post* is derived from these carriers.

In the American colonies, Francis Lovelace (1621–75), the British governor of New York and New Jersey, attempted in 1673 to set up postal service between New York City and Boston. The King's Best Highway followed trails created by Indigenous peoples, and postal riders notched trees along the 268-mile journey. Eventually, it became known as the Boston Post Road and then US Route 1. Until the Civil War, letters were delivered by courier, coach, or horse rider. The cost, paid by the recipient, varied by distance and number of pages. The United States introduced a limited postal service in August 1842, followed by a uniform 5-cent charge in 1845 and standardized stamps in 1847.

In May 1840, Great Britain introduced the first prepaid stamp for nationwide postal delivery service, the Penny Black stamp, using the portrait of the young Queen Victoria, for letters under half an ounce, and the Twopenny Blue stamp for letters over that weight. Other countries adopted this system soon after. Even before this time, though, London was at the forefront of organized mail delivery. A historic sign in the "Old City" section of London notes the original Letter Office and the fact that postmarks were being stamped as early as 1661 (see Figure 12.3).

One of the most fascinating stories in mail delivery is the Thurn-und-Taxis family, who made a fortune from starting the first successful European postal delivery.[6] The family, who lived in Regensburg, Germany, created a

---

6   Thomas Pynchon's novella *The Crying of Lot 49* (1966) focuses on a woman, Oedipa Maas, possibly unearthing the centuries-old conflict between two mail-distribution companies, Thurn-und-Taxis and Trystero (or Tristero). The latter is Pynchon's invention.

Figure 12.3
City of London
Historic Sign on
first postmark.
2019.

postal delivery system for Europe in 1806, a private enterprise that lasted until 1867. But this royal family had previous experience, having served since the sixteenth century as the Imperial Courier of the Holy Roman Empire. The Imperial Postmaster became a hereditary position in the von Taxis family. The postal service was sold for three million Thaler[7] to the government. The financial benefits of this enterprise is evident in the 500-room "home" of the family in Regensburg. The current occupant, Princess Gloria (b. 1960), earned notoriety during the 1970s for wild parties. Known as Princess TNT, she said at one time that her castle "makes Buckingham Palace look like a hut" (Silva).

Now, for something entirely different: Rural Free Delivery (RFD). The US Postal Service began experimenting with free delivery to farms in 1896 and institutionalized the practice in 1902. When I was growing up on a Missouri farm, our address was Racket Star Route. Others living in the country had Route One or the like, but ours seemed different, even special. I didn't know the backstory until visiting the marvelous National Postal Museum in Washington, DC, a part of the Smithsonian Institute. The legislation establishing new mail service in 1845 called for contractors to carry the mail with "celerity, certainty, and security." Weary of repeatedly writing these words in ledgers, postal clerks substituted three asterisks—* * *—and the phrase "Star Route" was born. Private contractors delivered (and in some places in the United States, they still do) the mail to remote sites by vehicles,

---

7 The currency of the Holy Roman Empire and Hapsburg Monarchy at the time.

boat, dogsleds, and airplanes. One of the most charming delivery systems is a burro pack train that travels eight miles down the Grand Canyon to the village of Supai, Arizona (see Figure 12.4).

Figure 12.4   Burro Mail Train for Supai Village. Grand Canyon, Arizona (2012).

THE EPISTOLARY NOVEL

Given the importance of letters, perhaps it should not be surprising that when the English novel form developed, the narrative was told through the medium of letter writing: the epistolary novel. Samuel Richardson, who was a printer by trade but who also authored a manual on letter writing, is credited with the first novel in English, *Pamela; or, Virtue Rewarded* (1740), the story of a girl from the country who becomes a servant in London in the household of Mr. B. Although he tries time and time again to seduce her, she resists, and eventually, he sees his error and marries her—thus *Virtue Rewarded*. The character in Richardson's follow-up novel, *Clarissa*, did not fare as well, and the conclusion of that lengthy story has Clarissa in her coffin. The emphasis on virtue and then marriage between two social classes that was highly unlikely in the day was deemed a sham by Henry Fielding (1707–54), author of *Moll Flanders* and *Tom Jones*. He turned out a vicious satire of Pamela, called *Shamela* (1741), also in epistolary form;

in it, Squire Booby is the one entrapped, as the country girl is actually the daughter of a prostitute. Fielding followed *Shamela* with the equally outra- geous and entertaining *Joseph Andrews* (1742), about a pure country lad who has to fight off the advances of Lady Booby. Who says eighteenth-century England was not lively?

That keen letter writer Goethe also used the form in his romantic and melancholy *The Sorrows of Young Werther* (1774). In France, the work that was brought to the stage and screen in the 1980s to great acclaim, *Les liaisons dangereuses*, began as an epistolary novel, written by Pierre Choderlos de Laclos (1741–1803), in 1782. The allure of the epistolary novel is that it provides an intimate look into the mind of the character, and in the case of novels where multiple narrators are at work, into the minds of more than one character. Because of this, epistolary novels are sometimes considered psychological novels, allowing the reader to be a voyeur of the interior lives of the characters.

The novel turned to other formats after the eighteenth century, but the epistolary form never went away entirely. It's made notable appearances in these titles: *The Color Purple* (1982) by Alice Walker; *The Perks of Being a Wallflower* (1999) by Stephen Chbosky; *The Guernsey Literary and Potato Peel Pie Society* (2008) by Mary Ann Shaffer and Annie Barrows; and *Old Lovegood Girls* by Gail Godwin (2020). For young people, the Vietnam War is explained in an interchange of letters between a pacifist and a girl in *Until Tomorrow, Mr. Marsworth* by Sheila O'Connor (2018). Perhaps the height of the epistolary novel occurs when the books contain physical letters and envelopes. *The Jolly Postman or Other People's Letters* by Janet and Allan Ahlberg (1986) features a British mail carrier on his bicycle who delivers letters to several well-known fairy-tale characters, including Cinderella and the Big Bad Wolf. At crucial points in the narrative, the reader stops and extracts a letter from an envelope on the page. Another popular interactive book is *Griffin and Sabine: An Extraordinary Correspondence* (1991), the first in a trilogy by innovative author Nick Bantock, who provides adults with a titillating window onto a passionate, but distant, relationship. As with *Pamela* and *Shamela*, *Griffin and Sabine* also has its parody: *Sheldon and Mrs. Levine: An Excruciating Correspondence* (1994), by Sam Bobrick and Julie Stein.

A long-running play, *Love Letters*, written in 1989 by A.R. Gurney (1930–2017) allows audience members to eavesdrop on the correspondence between a man and a woman over their 50-year, long-distance relationship. A fascinating turn in the epistolary format is the novel written entirely in instant messaging, popularized in the "Internet Girls" series by Lauren Myracle, beginning with *ttyl* (2004), *ttfn* (2007), *l8r, g8r* (2008), and *yolo*

(2014). Knowing that "talk to you later," "Ta ta for now," "later, gator," and "you only live once" are the translations of these titles is helpful; in fact, the reader needs to be familiar with an extensive lexicon of text speak that goes in and out of style. At the moment that I am writing this, FOMO—fear of missing out—is insanely popular on social media. Myracle also offered *bff* (2009) as an opportunity for "best friends forever" to write their own book.

ELECTRONIC MAIL

The instant messaging novels noted above came about as a result of the computerization of correspondence. Email revolutionized letter writing and might even be called the second golden age of correspondence. Although electronic mail existed as early as the 1960s, I first encountered it in 1984 when my university opened its UNIX mainframe computers for use in the Writing Program. A side benefit was email. All faculty were given usernames of five letters/numbers that started with "FAT." I was grateful to be FATCG while a friend of mine was FATCW. Imagine the humiliation! Student usernames started with SL.

Email made correspondence so much more efficient than traditional paper and pen or typewriter. It was instantaneous, and it could be global. In the twenty-first century, other forms of electronic conversation compete with email: texting, social media, and instant messaging. Email has become something that perhaps only an older generation might prefer, although it is still extensively used. Email also means that there is no down time from work; employers can be in touch night and day, which can lead to a 24/7 work assignment. For professionals, this can mean 100 or more messages in any one day. Coupled with advertisements and spam, email can detract from "real" work. Additionally, privacy issues have come to the fore. How secure is a person's email? Does it belong to the company? Can it be tracked even when deleted? Such questions have made email a contested space, but it continues to be an efficient, if unstable, mode of communication. It may even be responsible, in part, for a return to the handwritten letter, as the follow ditty suggests:

Snail Mail

Email rushes to and fro
Since paper letters seem too slow
But we prefer the status quo
Our cards are sent by escargot.

Figure 12.5
Snail mail.

POSTSECRET

To engage in truly confidential missives, a person might explore PostSecret. In 2004, Frank Warren began his PostSecret project. He handed out postcards near the National Postal Museum in Washington, DC, and left them in public places. The postcards were addressed to him, and the rules were that the writer should write a true secret that had never been shared before and that it must be anonymous (see Figure 12.6). Since that time, he has received hundreds of thousands of postcards. The secrets range from acts of kindness to shocking revelations. The postcards provide a safe method of revealing untold stories and perhaps beginning reflection, recovery, or realization for the writer. As a community mail project—a website provides a venue for the postcards—PostSecret offers an opportunity to empathize, understand, and connect. In addition to the website (https://postsecret.com), Warren has published several volumes of the postcards.

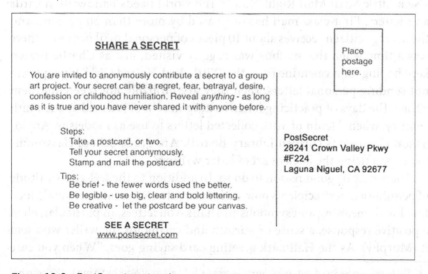

SHARE A SECRET

You are invited to anonymously contribute a secret to a group art project. Your secret can be a regret, fear, betrayal, desire, confession or childhood humiliation. Reveal *anything* - as long as it is true and you have never shared it with anyone before.

Steps:
　Take a postcard, or two.
　Tell your secret anonymously.
　Stamp and mail the postcard.
Tips:
　Be brief - the fewer words used the better.
　Be legible - use big, clear and bold lettering.
　Be creative - let the postcard be your canvas.

SEE A SECRET
www.postsecret.com

Place postage here.

PostSecret
28241 Crown Valley Pkwy
#F224
Laguna Niguel, CA 92677

Figure 12.6　PostSecret postcard.

DEAD LETTERS AND THE DEATH OF LETTERS

Is there anything sadder than a letter written but not received? Letters that are undeliverable in the United States end up in the Dead Letter Office, where clerks may open them to seek clues for addresses, but the contents remain private. According to the National Postal Museum, between 1871 and 1900, over 11.7 million immigrants arrived in the United States, settling in cities as well as the farmlands of the Midwest. A limited command of English meant that some addresses were undecipherable.

Dead letters are at the center of Terry Pratchett's satirical book (and the steampunk film made from the fantasy), *Going Postal* (2004), one of a series set in Discworld. The story features a towering relic of a post office filled with undelivered letters. When the newly designated postmaster, who wears a hat adorned with Mercury's wings, delivers just one letter that unites a couple, he vows to deliver the tons of missives that have piled up. Perhaps dead letters are not a problem, though, if no one is writing letters anymore. With letters, too, their demise has been mourned for some time. In his 1922 book on the art of writing letters, George Saintsbury noted that it was felt at the time that the penny post had killed letter writing (2), presumably because the inexpensive stamp made letter writing accessible to lower socio-economic classes, which was off-putting for those of higher status.

But is it possible that the handwritten letter is not truly dead? As Mark Twain is reputed to have said, "My death has been greatly exaggerated." In a *New York Times* article in 2018, Susan Shain suggests that "We Could All Use a Little Snail Mail Right Now."[8] The world needs handwritten cards and letters. First-class mail has decreased by more than 50 percent, and the average citizen receives about 10 pieces of personal mail per year. There was a time when the mailbox was eagerly visited, just as Charlie Brown kept hoping for a valentine from the "Little Red-Haired Girl." If people are not sending personal letters, then they are probably not receiving them either. The days of practicing letter writing in school is as old as the ninth century, when Alcuin of York collected letters to use as models in Anglo-Saxon classrooms (British Library Board). Are grade-school classrooms today practicing the ancient art of letter writing?

There may be good reason to do so. In addition to the feel-good attitude of penning a letter, recipients now see handwritten letters as a personal touch filled with meaning and symbolism. Thank-you letters, in particular, elicit a positive response, a sense of warmth and caring for the writer who sent it (Murphy). As the Hallmark greeting card saying goes, "When you care

---

8   Shain references an edited collection of letters called *Letters of Note* by Shaun Usher, who has compiled "letters deserving of a wider audience" for British and American audiences.

enough to send the very best." In fact, a handwritten letter may outclass a greeting card, which does the work for the sender with the pithy sentiment or empathetic response. And the icing on the cake may be the stamp that is picked out especially for the occasion: Celebrate, Love Forever, Breast Cancer Research Support, Cartoons, Vintage Cars, Sports, and National Parks are just a few examples. Additionally, research suggests that writing by hand helps a person's thinking. The physical act of putting pen to paper has benefits. There is the aesthetic benefit when using quality pen and ink and paper and the tactile sensation that comes from using excellent materials. As the author of *The Art of the Handwritten Note* stresses, "Do not write with a pencil or use blue-lined school paper, especially not notebook paper with holes punched in it. That's like going out dressed only in your underpants" (Shepherd 41).

This concluding section of the chapter has focused on dead letters and the death of the letter. But what about the connection between letter writing and death itself? Dr. VJ Periyakoil, a geriatrics and palliative care doctor, recommends that people write a "last letter" while they are still healthy. The Stanford Friends and Family Letter Project provides guidance to those who wish to write to friends, families, or those from whom they are estranged so that they can acknowledge important people in their lives, relate essential memories, apologize to those whom they may have hurt or forgive those who have hurt them. In essence, they are saying goodbye. Writing a letter that reviews one's life doesn't have to be a near-death experience; it can happen at any time or anywhere. The only time it's inappropriate is when it's too late.

Letters can be powerful means of communicating with others—or even with yourself. "A handwritten note is like dining by candlelight instead of flicking on the lights" (Shepherd, xv). Send them. Receive them. Keep them.

QUESTIONS TO CONSIDER

1. Letters appear often in works of art, such as Vermeer's "Girl Reading a Letter at an Open Window" (1657-59) held by the art museum in Dresden, and his "Woman Reading a Letter" (1663-64), located in Amsterdam. Others include "A Girl Reading a Letter by Candlelight, with a Young Man Peering over Her Shoulder" (1762), by Joseph Wright of Derby, Anna Paik's "The Letter," and Kenny Harris's "Woman Reading a Letter" (on a phone). Reading and writing letters have been consistent themes in paintings. Why might a painter be attracted to this subject?

2. Letter writing manuals continue to be popular: *The Art of the Handwritten Note: A Guide to Reclaiming Civilized Communication* by Margaret Shepherd; *To the Letter: A Celebration of the Lost Art of Letter*

Writing by Simon Garfield; and *Snail Mail: Rediscovering the Art and Craft of Handmade Correspondence* by Michelle Mackintosh. These titles suggest that letters are a "civilized" way to communicate with others. Why do you think these authors are keen on letter writing?

3. In addition to epistolary novels such as *The Color Purple, Letters from Yellowstone*, and *Pamela*, nonfiction titles also focus on letters. Martin Ganda and Caitlin Alfirenka described their pen-pal experience in *I Will Always Write Back: How One Letter Changed Two Lives* (2015). The classic exchange of letters *84, Charing Cross Road* by Helene Hanff (1970) features 20 years of correspondence between Hanff, a freelance writer living in New York City, and a used-book dealer in London. Who writes such extended correspondence? How and why are letters saved? What are the implications that so much correspondence is now done electronically?

4. Instruction in handwriting has become a hotly debated topic in the twenty-first century. What are the arguments for and against continuing instruction in cursive writing? Drawing on your own personal experience, what have you seen as positive and/or negative attributes depending on whether you use cursive and/or print?

5. In 2020, during the coronavirus crisis, language scholar Deborah Tannen noted that salutations and closings in correspondence—particularly email—changed to reflect the times and became less formulaic, as "How are you?" did not quite suffice. Analyze your own correspondence during this time. Did your salutations and closings change to reflect the circumstances?

DO-IT-YOURSELF HANDS-ON ACTIVITIES

1. Before there were envelopes, letter writers could exercise caution that their epistles would stay confidential by using the technology of letterlocking. *The Dictionary of Letterlocking*, by Dambrogio and Smith, offers several examples of techniques to secure letters. Over 80 videos on letterlocking exist on YouTube on a dedicated channel. Pick one letterlocking technique that interests you and give it a try.

2. What archival letters do you have in your life? Are there letters from your birth, letters from soldiers, love letters? In my own personal archive, I have the letter written to my mother by a cousin on my father's side suggesting that I be named "Jane," in honor of a Civil War ancestor who bravely saved one of her sons wounded by vigilantes; another son was murdered.

My husband has the touching correspondence that his grandfather wrote at the end of World War II, when he came out of hiding with his wife in Budapest, finally safe from the Nazis. The eldest daughter and her family were murdered in Auschwitz-Birkenau, but another daughter escaped with her husband through Turkey to Australia. His son, my husband's father, got one of the very few passes to travel to the United States.

This may be an opportunity to talk to your family about important letters. If you do find an archive of letters that should be saved, then the National Postal Museum offers advice on preservation. As the museum notes, "Letters, documents, and photographs give us windows into our past. They carry both the individual stories of our families and the broader historical narrative of local, national, and global communities." Their advice includes the importance of having clean hands; removing letters from envelopes and flattening them carefully, but keeping letters together with their envelopes, as important information is stored in both; organizing documents; and storing or displaying carefully. Letters, documents, and photographs may also be scanned to archive digitally.

3. National Letter Writing Week is celebrated in the United States in the second week of January, an auspicious time to remember to write thank-you letters for the holidays just past. Or you might choose National Letter Writing Day, celebrated on December 7. Either reflecting on the year past or anticipating the new year offers content to consider for the text of the letter. It provides a way to reconnect with others. It may also be an opportunity to think about the aesthetics of the letter: fine paper or envelopes, letterpress-printed notecard, interesting stamps, even sealing wax. Other recipients may be strangers. Operation Gratitude seeks letters written to those in the service, veterans, or first-responders (https://www.operationgratitude.com/express-your-thanks/write-letters/). A poster from World War II Veterans of Foreign Wars said to "Keep 'em Smiling with Letters from Folks and Friends!" The Academy of American Poets has a "Dear Poet" program each April during National Poetry Month that invites young people (grades 5-12) to write to a poet (https://poets.org/national-poetry-month/dear-poet). You might assist a younger family member or friend to do so.

4. Each year the Washington Calligraphers Guild, in partnership with the National Association of Letter Carriers, hosts a "Graceful Envelope Contest," with the goal of "transforming an ordinary envelope into a work of art." It requires artistic lettering or calligraphy coupled with effective use of color and design. What envelope design would you want to submit? Each year features a different theme. Past years' entries are viewable online and are highly entertaining. Check out the contest here: https://www.calligraphersguild.org/envelope.html.

5. Engage in "Slow Writing." As with the Slow Food movement, slow writing encourages people to connect and to be mindful of how they are living. The tactile feel of pen, ink, and paper can be very satisfying. The nature of writing is tied to its origins in divination and communication with the gods. It was considered holy or magical, and those who wrote were held in high regard. Through thousands of years, this notion of writing may have dimmed, but it's never gone away entirely. The materials writers used, by extension, may be imbued with reverence as well. Fountain pen aficionados may lust after the latest prestigious model at $8,000 or perfumed ink at $80 a bottle, or consider the devotees of Moleskine notebooks. It's not necessary to spend a lot of money in order to connect with writing and its implements. Handmade paper and a good pen are places to begin. Try being mindful and composing a letter. As the very expensive Laban Pen Company suggests, "Refill your soul by writing."

6. The World Needs More Love Letters[9] is an initiative designed to provide letters of hope and encouragement to those who need them. Its website proclaims, "Snail mail is for the cool kids." Individuals and their stories are posted, and writers choose to whom they'd like their letters to be sent, which are then bundled for the recipient. Another group secrets letters in public spaces such as bookstores or libraries. Love Letters, according to an article in the *Salt Lake Tribune* on 9 February 2020, is a pop-up event organized by Culture Collective Events that uses art "to create a world filled with joy, belonging, and human connection" (Manson). Try one of these initiatives to leave the world a better place.

7. During the coronavirus pandemic in 2020, the Smithsonian National Postal Museum offered simple instructions for constructing a time capsule of materials, including correspondence, that could be sealed for future review. The supply list includes the following:

- 6 Business Reply Envelopes
- Ruler
- Fine Tip Marker
- Embroidery Thread
- Needle
- Button
- Glue Stick
- Washi Tape
- File Label Stickers
- Scissors

---

9 http://www.moreloveletters.com/

FOR FURTHER READING

Following is a reading to supplement this chapter on letter writing. A 1902 epistle written by noted activist Ida Wells-Barnett (1862–1931), it reports on the horrific record of racial terrorism against African Americans. This history is memorialized at the Equal Justice Initiative in Montgomery, Alabama, in a monument to "Peace and Justice," which opened in 2018 and honors more than 4,400 individuals who died. Similar to monuments about apartheid and the Holocaust, the lynching memorial acknowledges the appalling past and seeks truth and reconciliation to heal.

Office of Anti-Lynching Bureau
2939 Princeton Avenue
Chicago

To the Members of the Anti-Lynching Bureau:

The year of 1901 with its lynching record is a thing of the past. There were 135 human beings that met death at the hands of mobs during this year. Not only is the list larger than for four years past, but the barbarism of this lawlessness is on the increase. Six human beings were burned alive between January 1st 1901 and Jan. 1st 1902. More persons met death in this horrible manner the past twelve months than in three years before and in proportion as the number roasted alive increases, in the same propor- tion has there been an indifference manifested by the public. Time was when the country resounded with denunciation and the horror of burning a human being by so called christian and civilized people. The newspapers were full of it. The last time a human being was made fuel for flames it was scarcely noticed in the papers editorially. And the chairman of your bureau finds it harder every year to get such matter printed. In other words, the need for agitation and publication of facts is greater than ever, while the avenues through which to make such publications have decreased. Nowhere does this apathetic condition prevail to a greater extent than within the membership of the Anti-Lynching Bureau. When the bureau was first organized three years ago, it was thought that every man, woman, and child who had a drop of Negro blood in his veins and every person else who wanted to see mob law put down would gladly contribute 25 cents per year to this end. There were upward of 300 responses to the first appeal and less than 50 percent renewed at the end of that year. The third year of the bureau's existence is half over and although the chairman has determined to issue a periodical, there are absolutely no funds in the treasury to pay postage much less the printer. Nevertheless my faith in the justice of our cause and the absolute need of this agitation leads me to again address those who have shown 25 cents worth of interest in the matter heretofore. I send with this circular a pamphlet which friends have helped to pay for. It was thought best to begin with what to us was the beginning of history for our race in the United States the Reconstruction period. In view of the recent agitation in Congress and out anent the disfranchisement of the Negro and the causes alleged therefore it was thought best to throw some light on those times and give some unwritten history. This history is written by one who can say with Julius Caesar of the history he wrote: "All of which I saw and part of which I was." He has given his time and money to aid the publication. Will not the members of the bureau bestir themselves to circulate this number and aid in the publication of others. We can only change public sentiment and enforce laws by educating the people, giving them facts. This you can do by 1st, Renewing your membership in the Anti-Lynching Bureau and securing others. 2nd, By paying for the copy sent you and purchasing others to distribute. 3rd. By paying for the copy of the Reconstruction "Review" to your Congressman together with a letter urging the cutting down of the representation in Congress of the states which have nullified the Constitution. It rests with you to say whether the Anti-Lynching Bureau shall be strengthened to do its work for the future.

Jan. 1st, 1902 Ida B. Wells-Barnett, Chairman

INTERESTED IN LEARNING MORE?

Book Recommendations

Margaret Shepherd, *The Art of the Handwritten Note* (Broadway Books, 2002).

Selected Letters of Madame de Sévigné or *Madame de Sévigné: The Life and Letters* (1898).

A series of DIY letter-writing books, including these:

Lea Redmond, *Letters to My Future Self: Write Now, Read Later, Treasure Forever* (Chronicle, 2014).

————. *Letters to My Friend: Write Now, Read Later, Treasure Forever* (Chronicle, 2017).

Film Recommendations

Lettres de Femmes, directed by Augusto Zanovello (2013), https://www. youtube.com/watch?v=FdPEsCCbFAQ&t=13s. [animated film; 10 minutes]

"Missing You—Letters from Wartime, " Smithsonian National Postal Museum (n.d.), https://youtu.be/EtjYFhmEvkE?list=LL [8 minutes]

"125 Years of Delivering for America" (n.d.), https://youtu.be/ AG1wAGRnwwo?list=LL [42 minutes]

Chapter Thirteen

Writing and School

> *The writer should be seated comfortably feet flat on the floor and the desk sloping slightly.... The forefinger should rest on the pencil about one-and-a-half inches from the point, and should point into the paper at an angle of 45 degrees,... [using] a Black Prince pencil, or Platinum fountain pen with medium nib.... The ball point pen is most emphatically discouraged.*
> —*Tom Gourdie,* Ladybird Book of Handwriting *(1968)*

How do children learn to write? According to Tom Gourdie, the author of the British *Ladybird Book of Handwriting*, children learn by sitting, as described in the instructions above. Those directions apply to the physical act of writing and may seem rather like being in a straitjacket. Certainly, learning to write includes mechanistic and physical aspects. While the conditions described by Gourdie seem rigid, at least these schoolchildren had chairs and desks (see Figure 13.1). Perhaps not so for the children who were taught to write when writing was still in its infancy.

To reiterate, writing in ancient cultures was a response to increased complexity in societies that needed to record and account in fixed documents. This required agreement on a set of symbols and principles or rules. To propagate these systems, instruction was required. Thus, schools arose early, most likely as early as 3000 BCE, as scribes needed to pass on their knowledge to a new generation of writers, record-keepers, and accountants.

Figure 13.1
Chandler School
Desk. Source:
*Illustrated Catalogue
of School Supplies,*
1897–98.

ANCIENT SCHOOLS OF WRITING

Instruction in writing covers 5,000 years of history; obviously, a single chapter, perhaps not even a single book, can address the complexity of this history, although James J. Murphy's *A Short History of Writing Instruction* makes a valiant effort. His volume begins with Greek schools, but learning how to read and write was integral to Sumer and Egypt even earlier. Scribal schools in the former, called *eduba*, existed as early as 2500 BCE, which is known due to clay tablets—textbooks, if you will—excavated at Ur and Shuruppak. Boys—and perhaps the rare girl—created their own writing tools by forming a clay tablet, which could be "erased" by dampening and smoothing it, making it ideal for practice texts. The cuneiform tablet shown in Figure 2.4 (see Chapter Two) offers insight into this kind of exercise.

The student had to learn the "intricate cuneiform system," along with various dialects and even the archaic Sumer language, according to Marilyn Kelly-Buccellati (207), and relied on expert scribes and more experienced peers. As an apprentice, the boy mixed clay for the tablets and prepared the stylus. Copying lists was pragmatic work, while literary texts preserved Mesopotamian culture. Schools featured a strict regimen such as drills repeated over and over, copy practice, and understanding of a culture's literature. Students who did not perform well or who acted out were disciplined harshly. One surviving clay tablet from a schoolboy noted that if he is late, "my teacher will cane me."

Learning how to be a scribe ensured a good occupation for the future, as few were literate and scribes were therefore responsible for transcribing correspondence orally and responding. Because writing was closely tied to trading, scribes also had a good knowledge of mathematics, weights, and measurements.

In Egypt, where writing was highly prized, training as a scribe was viewed as a pathway to success. Sons of officials and kings attended scribal training from ages five to ten and then spent another ten years apprenticed to government officials. Schools were known as "Houses of Life" (Eskelson 36). Three different types of writing systems existed: hieroglyphics, which required excellent drawing skills; hieratic script; and demotic script. Greek was yet another required language, evident in the Rosetta Stone. Scribes had to learn hundreds of signs to work among these three systems, with hieroglyphics being the most complicated. The very best students could have futures in writing and illustrating *Books of the Dead*, beautiful papyrus scrolls for funerals that were entombed with the person. A lesser scribe might be reduced to counting cattle or the amount of wheat harvested and recording that information on lists for overseers.

Unlike Sumer, Egyptian students might have had paper-like material, papyrus, and reeds and ink (as opposed to the stylus used to make impressions in clay tablets). Sculptures of the iconic scribe depict him seated, the stiff kilt serving as kind of a desk, perhaps the first "laptop" (see Figure 13.2).

Figure 13.2
Scribe sculpture.
The Louvre, Paris
(2018).

The scribe also kept a palette, which held pens and had hollows for ink. These tools are described in the Egyptian *Book of the Dead*, the scribe proclaiming in Thoth's honor, "I am thy writing palette, O Thoth, and I have brought unto thee thine ink-jar" (Stadler). The god Thoth (recognizable for his head as either an ibis or a baboon) gets credit for inventing hieroglyphics and serves as scribe in the underworld, responsible for keeping records—those lists again.

CLASSICAL GREEK AND ROMAN SCHOOLS AND WRITING

Students in both ancient Greece and Rome were fortunate to study in languages with alphabets with a limited set of letters based on phonemes, unlike cuneiform or hieroglyphics. Recall that both alphabets arose from the writing of Phoenicians, intrepid traders who sailed the Mediterranean. According to Richard Enos, writing began to be viewed as the backbone of "civic power" (6), and because writing was easier to learn due to the reduced number of symbols, more people learned to write. Increased literacy led to a more democratic society and government, as people could more readily participate in it. Citizenship became an important concept. Greek culture also had a literary tradition, based on the works of Homer, Hesiod, and a wide range of other poets.

In Rome, both sides of rhetoric were important: speaking and writing. The city rightly had a reputation for powerful oratory, particularly through the legendary Cicero. Schoolchildren practiced writing on wax tablets using the sharp point of a stylus; when the blunter end was drawn back and forth on the wax, the resulting heat "erased" the text: *tabula rasa*. Memory is one of the five aspects of classical rhetoric, and students were to memorize text that they had written. Tablets "became a common Roman metaphor for how our brains work. They thought, 'the mind is like a wax tablet where you can write and erase and rewrite,'" Stephanie Frampton says in her book, *Empire of Letters* (10).

Rome became an empire, in part due to its high level of speaking and writing, which was bolstered in an educational system that included public schools that required tuition. After they conquered Greece, Romans adopted and refined the tutorial system of the Greeks and integrated their rhetorical and philosophical texts in addition to using conquered Greeks as teachers. Writing had a curriculum and principles. The leading educator of the time, Quintilian (35–100 CE), recommended starting school early in pupils' lives, noting that "memory...not only exists even in small children, but is especially retentive at that age." Again, the importance of memorizing information and texts was stressed. The highest levels of education involved rhetoric and becoming an eloquent orator and writer. At all levels, what we now call the "language arts" were stressed: reading, writing, speaking, and listening. Reading and listening decode language, while speaking and writing encode it. Romans also stressed what might be called the fifth language art: thinking.

Students arrived at higher levels of cognition and philosophical thought through a structured curriculum. James Murphy provides an overview of the Roman teaching methods described in Quintilian's *Institutio Oratoria*, which include five categories: precept, imitation, composition exercises, declamation, and sequencing:

> *Precept* is a "set of rules that provide a definite method and system of speaking." Grammar as precept deals with "the art of speaking correctly, and the interpretation of the poets."
>
> Rhetoric as precept includes the five classical parts: invention, arrangement, style, memory, and delivery. In contemporary pedagogy, "prewriting" functions much like invention—coming up with topics about which to right. Arrangement is the organization of the essay, and style is self-evident. Memory and delivery refer to the oral execution of the writing.
>
> In imitation, students use models to "learn how others have used language." They do so by practicing the following: reading aloud, Master's detailed analysis of text, memorization of models, paraphrase of models, transliteration (prose to verse or Latin to Greek and also in reverse), recitation of the paraphrase or transliteration; and correction of paraphrase or transliteration.
>
> Composition exercises are "a graded series of exercises in writing and speaking themes." Each one built on the last with increasing difficulty for the task.

- Retelling a fable
- Retelling an episode from a poet or a historian
- Amplification of a moral theme
- Refutation or confirmation of an allegation
- Commonplace, or confirmation of a thing admitted
- Encomium or eulogy of a person or thing
- Comparison of things or persons
- Impersonation: speaking or writing in the character of a given person
- Description or vivid presentation of details

- Thesis or argument for or against an answer to a general question that doesn't involve individuals
- Laws or arguments for or against a law.

Declamation or speeches took one of two forms:

1. A deliberative political speech arguing in favor or against an action;
2. A legal speech prosecuting or defending a fictional or historical person in a law case.

Sequencing was the systematic ordering of classroom goals to move from simple to more complex and reinforcement of each lesson as it progressed and became more difficult. (75–76)

Fortunately, these materials on the Roman system of education survived due to monastic scribes copying manuscripts. The Roman Empire did not; it collapsed in the fifth century. Latin, however, endured to become the language of scholars, clergy, and governments.

WRITING AND MEDIEVAL SCHOOLS

The standard textbooks for schools were written in Latin. Priscian, who was a teacher in the sixth century, wrote the grammar book that was to be used for centuries. Grammar was not just rules but also the complex explanation of how language works. Even in the fifteenth century, Priscian was still considered the expert source of grammar, which is why he's depicted in the fresco on the wall of the cathedral in Le Puy. He represents grammar, Aristotle signifies logic, and Cicero embodies rhetoric—the three prime instructional areas of the curriculum, constituting what was known as the trivium, the "big three," if you will.

When the Roman Empire fell, Europe fell apart, too, and the Dark Ages of starvation, disease, and war arose. Charlemagne managed to reunify Europe in the ninth century, becoming the first Holy Roman Emperor, which illustrates the rise of Christianity in the territory. Keen on education, he imported monks from Ireland and England, including Alcuin of York (c. 732–804), a famous teacher and scholar. They brought with them the concept of lower-case letters, and the script used for writing changed from the crabbed hand of the Merovingian dynasty to the more readable Carolingian script. This is one of Charlemagne's great contributions—regularizing writing. Additionally, he decreed in 789 that at least two boys from every village must be educated. While Charlemagne didn't invent school, he ensured that schooling would pervade the country, which was, roughly speaking, France and its surrounding countries.

The increased emphasis on written communication for Charlemagne's empire to ensure the stability of regions at great distances required enhanced and more widespread education and publication of documents and books to carry important messages abroad. The weight placed on education and writing also resulted in the production of more literature and more sophisticated rhetoric. A clergy that had issues with its own literacy had to ramp up its game, as teaching and learning became an important mission for monasteries and cathedrals. Students were to be able to read the Bible and the articles of faith in Latin as well as sing the liturgy. They used wood boards for tablets or an ABC tablet on which they could write the alphabet or notes from readings given by the priest. The teacher had a chair, but the little scholars might have had benches at best at which to sit or write; more likely than not, they sat on the floor (see Figure 13.3).

Figure 13.3
Matthäus Schwarz at 5 years, writing. Start of 15th century. Paris, BNF, ms Allemand 211.5.6. Schwarz, as an adult, is credited with writing/illustrating the first fashion book, cataloguing his own apparel over the decades.

Students entered monastery schools at about six or seven years of age. Depending on the establishment, discipline could be rigorous. Misbehaving students received a tap on the head, hand, or face loud enough to be significant and terrify the other students; in other cases, gentler masters not only were teachers but also consolers of children separated from their families. Three or four masters worked with a dozen students, teaching them to read and write but also about hygiene and good behavior, such as not running or jumping in line and being deferential to elders.

By the end of the Middle Ages, almost all of the little towns in the empire had access to primary education at least, and most people could write their own names, which was the test for literacy. Still, rural populations through the empire and the British Isles at the end of the fifteenth century might have had only a 10-percent literacy rate. Books were increasing in number, but often teachers had to turn to other sources for reading materials. Alphabets were inscribed in embroidery, leather belts, and tile work. Church architecture incorporated stained windows and carvings for storytelling.[1] Only the privileged few had real books; of course, that began to change with Gutenberg's printing press. For urban schools, students might move beyond the rudiments of writing to the *trivium* (grammar, logic, and rhetoric) and *quadrivium* (arithmetic, geometry, music, and astronomy), comprising the liberal arts.

Being literate was very important to people of the Middle Ages in terms of the law, as the term "benefit of clergy" meant that anyone who was literate—particularly the clergy—had to be tried in an ecclesiastical court rather than a civil court. The former generally pronounced less strict judgments, and many were saved from execution by this advantage. Henry II (1154–89) of England ran afoul of the Archbishop of Canterbury, Thomas Becket (c. 1120–70), when he tried to reduce this benefit, and it was not until the Tudors that changes were made, but still, some benefit of clergy hung on for centuries. Literacy could literally save lives.

While scriptures were the first source of textual material in the Middle Ages, they were not as essential for some groups in terms of daily activity or romantic life. People in business needed writing for accounts and records; aristocrats employed secretaries for running estates; and women may have written love letters or poems, particularly at Les Baux in France, which became known in the fifteenth century as a famous site of courtly love, home to poets and troubadours. The Dark Ages were definitely receding. Olson notes that "books designed explicitly for schooling and accompanied by pictures began in the late 15th century in Italy and Germany. Christopher Heuber, a teacher, included pictures in his ABC book of 1477" (289). The

---

1 An exhibition, *L'école au Moyen Âge*, at the Tour Jean Sans Peur in Paris, curated by Danièle Alexandre-Bidon (2007), provided helpful information for this history.

first university in the Western world originated in Bologna in the eleventh century, followed by the University of Paris in the twelfth century—an institution that later became known as the Sorbonne—and then Oxford followed in England. It should be noted that students could enter university at quite a young age if qualified. Charlemagne's renaissance made possible the overall Renaissance of Western Europe.

In nineteenth-century American education, two school books reigned supreme: the *New England Primer* and *McGuffey's Readers*. The latter featured a strong Christian theme and sold over 120 million copies between 1836 and 1960—and is, in fact, still selling some 30,000 copies annually. William Holmes McGuffey (1800–73) promoted moral and spiritual education as well as reading and writing. The books became progressively challenging in learning vocabulary, sentences, and longer texts. McGuffey drew examples from real literature meant to engage children, and he also advocated active learning, with teachers reading aloud and asking questions that complemented the stories. Through lively Readers, his overarching goals were to "improve students' spelling, sharpen their vocabulary, and redevelop the lost art of public speaking" (National Park Service). Following the Civil War, the Readers were revised in 1879 and secularized to support a growing diverse population. (The Christian content has been restored in recent reprints, most likely for home schooling.)

TWENTIETH-CENTURY SCHOOLS AND WRITING

In France, schools and writing instruction remained remarkably the same over some time. We have an in-depth account of *How the French Boy Learns to Write* from 1915, thanks to Rollo Walter Brown, a college professor, who spent a year in France immersed as an ethnographer in classes of 12-to-13-year boys. Note that schooling was segregated by gender; in many ways, the curriculum echoed that of classical Rome.

Writing and the composing of essays and exercises formed the core of the French curriculum in the early twentieth century. Brown observed, "Studies in vocabulary and practice in dictation are carried on constantly in the lower grades in order that the boy may express himself without hindrance when he is old enough to have something of his own to say in organized compositions" (89). Imitation was key to learning to write well, and memorization was also important to developing as a writer. A boy might be called on to recite a poem that was to be memorized, but throughout, the teacher might interrupt, asking other students for clarification of words or comments on structure (53). Personally, I think I might begin to forget the lines of the poem with all those pauses!

Reading materials were designed to develop "the powers of attention and observation, the imagination, and habits of reflection" (89) and were thoroughly discussed in the classroom. Teachers responded to the students' essays orally and in writing, focusing on constructive criticism that provided lessons for all. In other subjects, writing was a means of learning the material. The system encouraged both quality and quantity of writing. Those who thought and wrote well were honored by teachers and classmates (47).

Topics for compositions, even at this distance in time and place, were truly interesting, preparing students not just to write well but in many cases to write pragmatically. At an age of ten years, students were asked to observe and describe such things as an inanimate object or a robin building a nest. Other tasks: explain a game that you play; be sure to speak of the kind of game, whether of skill or of chance; the material employed, and the placing of it; the number of players; and the important rules one must follow. Write a letter to a boy who has recently visited you, and announce the sudden, accidental death of a mutual friend (66). For older students, essays required more imaginative treatment—as in being at a greater distance from the subject. For instance, "Write a letter to the Prefect asking that an old friend who lost an arm in the Franco-Prussian war be put in charge of a tobacco shop that has become vacant." Even older boys, of 15 to 18, were asked to analyze and reflect: "By drawing upon your own experience in the study of philosophic writers of the eighteenth century, write a letter to a young English friend who in his course in French is about to take up the study of Montesquieu" (69). This preparation in writing was crucial for passing the examination for graduation, which he had to complete in three hours, resulting in no more than a dozen pages (71).

While the French approach to teaching writing in primary and secondary school might seem old-fashioned, through the 1970s, scholars such as Edward Corbett, Andrea Lunsford, and Winston Weathers were lauding the utility of imitation as an instructional approach. It was also in the 1970s that a paradigm shift occurred in writing instruction, moving from an emphasis on product to an emphasis on process. This approach to teaching, which embraced education from kindergarten through college, introduced the notion of prewriting, drafting, revising, and editing, acknowledging that the stages were also recursive, looping back and forth among each other. Prewriting drew on invention, as defined in classical rhetoric, but also extended into additional planning with classroom-based activities.

In the twenty-first century, teaching with "mentor texts" has been popularized through the work of Ralph Fletcher, Kelly Gallagher, and others. The foundation of this approach is that students benefit from examples, which sounds much like the educational approaches of classical studies. Teachers using mentor texts are advised to give vocabulary and definitions before reading the text aloud. Then the students respond to content-based questions. After that discussion, the techniques the writer used are discussed. A technique might be how the writer engages the reader or how the writer has used statistics or quotations in meaningful ways as evidence. The students then write their own text drawing on the example set by the mentor text. The teacher reinforces the mentor text during individual conferences or through class discussion. Unlike classical education, teachers are encouraged to practice the exercise themselves to try out strategies.

ABILITY AND DISABILITY

Who is left out of school? Over the course of history, schooling was often reserved for the elite. In the United States, access to education has a checkered history. Horace Mann (1796–1859) notably advocated for free and universal public education, essential to a democratic society. That goal is still evolving, but lawsuits and legislation have resulted in changes. During the twentieth century, progress was made. In 1965, the Elementary and Secondary Education Act included Title 1, committed to supporting low-income students and closing the achievement gap. The purpose of Title 1 funding "is to ensure that all children have a fair, equal, and significant opportunity to obtain a high quality education and reach, at minimum, proficiency on challenging state academic achievement standards and state academic assessments" (US Department of Education).

Children with disabilities may not have had equitable access to schooling. During the early 1950s, ADA activist Judy Heumann (b. 1947) was denied access to school because polio had put her in a wheelchair. She persevered with limited at-home instruction. In 1970, she was denied a teaching license in New York because, so the thinking went, how could a teacher in a wheelchair evacuate children in case of a fire (Girma)?

In 1973, the Children's Defense Fund, directed by Marian Wright Edelman (b. 1939), issued a report about why two million children in the United States were not in school. The trials that Judy Heumann experienced 20 years earlier were still in evidence, but the report had an impact. Ten years after Title 1, the Education for All Handicapped Children Act required public schools receiving federal funds to provide equal access to education. While the 1975 act provided access to education, the Americans with Disabilities Act (ADA) of 1990 ensured that physical barriers like street curbs were removed and that transportation accommodated students.

To assist students with school, and in this case our particular interest in writing, adaptive or assistive technology has been developed. In Chapter Three, we saw how Braille was introduced as a system by which those with visual impairments could read and write. For those with limited vision, screen magnifiers and readers can be helpful. A screen reader may vocalize text or transmit it into Braille. Major software companies—Apple, Google, and Microsoft—have developed programs to assist. Fortunately, the onset of the computer age helped significantly in providing new technologies.

Universal design is the approach to all manner of design in environments, buildings, and products that make them accessible to everyone, regardless of ability level, age, or other factors. How can the most people use products, bearing in mind that not everyone can walk, hear, see, or manipulate objects? Universal design removes barriers to physical movement and learning. Selwyn Goldsmith wrote his influential book *Designing for the Disabled* in 1963. His focus in particular was architecture and how dropped curbs on streets and bus ramps could improve accessibility, but his concepts influenced more than building and infrastructure design. In what other venues do design choices offer accessibility or barriers? Close captioning is one result of acknowledging that a significant population needs assistance to communicate (Zdenek). Captioning, particularly of media, is a significant benefit for communication. The Described and Captioned Media Program (DCMP) offers principles for designing media for students with disabilities based on the belief that every student deserves equal access to learning opportunities. In addition to addressing hearing and visual roadblocks, captioning can aid those with poor literacy skills or those for whom English is a second language. Writing effective captions is a skill, and DCMP provides "keys" to assist, such as mixing case (lower and upper case) and whether or not to transcribe verbatim or as edited text.

Instructors at all educational levels must be sensitive to many areas that could impede student writers, including physical ability, mental health, or learning disability. On my own campus, I receive alerts in advance to students who may require accommodation. A deaf student may need captioning on videos or lectures; a blind student may request large-format texts or use voice recognition technology. Some students may simply need more time to complete writing assignments. How the curriculum is structured can help students achieve their full potential. Universal design for learning principles include the following:

- Provide multiple means of representation
- Provide multiple means of action and expression

- Provide multiple means of engagement
- Steps to an Inclusive Learning Environment
- Focus on essential course elements
- Establish clear expectations and learning objectives
- Design activities specific to the learning objectives
- Encourage self-directed learning and active learning
- Provide information using multiple methods
- Incorporate diverse assessment strategies
- Build in opportunities for feedback.[2]

This brief look at writing and disability can be explored further in the intersection between Disability Studies and Rhetoric and Composition. In 2005, the Modern Language Association, a professional organization of humanists, designated Disability Studies as an area of study appropriate to the discipline. No longer just the province of health or clinical work, Disability Studies became an accepted focus for humanities inquiry. According to the National Council of Teachers of English (NCTE), "disability studies research in the fields of composition, rhetoric, and literacy studies has yielded variations on the composing process, alternative ways of working with students in classrooms and writing centers."

Access to education also has a significant impact on access to meaningful employment and the possibility of economic independence. In short, accessibility is crucial to quality of life.

CONCLUDING THOUGHTS

Throughout the ages, the one consistent theme is that teaching writing is hard work. Teachers invest significantly in preparing to work with students, assigning writing tasks, and responding to them. The effort is equally intensive for the student writers, who move from idea or concept to a finished product. Writers move from simple to complex tasks almost every day, and as they develop from novice to expert, they encounter increasingly difficult tasks that may actually result in a temporary regression in writing skills. Even then, there is no guarantee that the skilled writer produces the same quality each and every time. Writer's block is real, lurking around the corner. Still, the work is worth the effort. And, when it turns out well, then, it's as American writer and humorist Dorothy Parker (1893–1967) wisecracked, "I hate writing, I love having written."

---

2 Utah State University Disability Resource Center, www.usu.edu/drc/faculty/design.

QUESTIONS TO CONSIDER

1. From a 1290 BCE document of a father advising his son: "Be a scribe, it saves you from toil, it protects you from all manner of labor. Be a scribe." Does that advice still fit today? If so, how, and if no, how?

2. Ableism is a prejudice or discrimination toward people with disabilities. In recent years, language has been investigated to see how it may be ableist—often unintentionally—and hurtful to those with disabilities. Examples include lame, crazy, insane, idiot, blind, deaf, idiotic, dump, retarded, spaz. What examples of ableist language can you find in the media or in your own use? Have you considered revising word choice based on an awareness of how ableist language may be perceived?

3. Zdenek suggests that attention to accessibility for those who are disabled should not just be an add-on but integral to planning in writing and communication: "When disability is additive, when it is tacked onto our practices and pedagogies, it tends to reinforce the institutional status quo that positions disability as an exception to the norms of nondisabled bodies and minds" (537). How does this change the approach to writing, design, and schooling?

4. Read reviews of contemporary editions of *McGuffey's Readers* on Amazon, GoodReads, or another review site. What are the attractions of these nineteenth-century school texts to contemporary teachers or parents?

5. How does the architecture of schools relate to or affect students learning to write? Winston Churchill (1874–1965) said, "We shape our buildings; thereafter, they shape us." In the early twentieth century, Booker T. Washington (1856–1915) partnered with philanthropist Julius Rosenwald (1862–1932), president of Sears, Roebuck, and Company, to build schools in the rural south for Black children, as education was severely underfunded and segregated. From 1913 to the early 1930s, 5,000 schools were erected in 15 states; in addition to funding from Rosenwald, the communities themselves were required to invest. The architectural principles included these directions: "The orientation of the buildings and the placement of the windows were carefully thought out so that the sunlight would shine on the students' left side and not be blocked by their right hands while writing" (Wilcox). Think about the places for writing in the schools and libraries where you've been. Consider Writing Centers. What thought was given to how they could be most conducive to teaching and learning writing?

6. Classical scholar Edith Hamilton (1867–1963), who wrote lively books about Greek and Roman mythology, said: "It has always seemed

strange to me that in our endless discussions about education so little stress is laid on the pleasure of becoming an educated person, the enormous interest it adds to life. To be able to be caught up into the world of thought—that is to be educated." What does it mean to you to be "an educated person"? Why is that important?

INVITATION TO REFLECT AND WRITE

Chapter One, the autoethnography, asked you for a personal history of your own writing practices. Reading the brief record of writing teaching and learning in the current chapter, you can contrast and compare it to your own writing instruction. How is your experience different? How is it similar? This is an opportunity to flesh out the schooling portion of the autobiography/autoethnography.

FOR FURTHER READING

The material culture of writing really takes off in school: pencils, crayons, pens, paper, erasers, computers. This academic essay on Moleskine notebooks focuses on how an object can influence writer's identity. As you read, consider if the material culture of your writing identity is similarly influenced by particular objects. Note, too, how the essay is illustrated by particular objects. You may wish to add illustrations to the story of your writing life.

The essay, "The Symbolic Life of the Moleskine Notebook: Material Goods as a Tableau for Writing Identity Performance" by Cydney Alexis, was published in the journal *Composition Studies* in Fall 2017, and can be found at https://compositionstudiesjournal.files.wordpress.com/2019/03/45.2-alexis.pdf.

INTERESTED IN LEARNING MORE?

Book Recommendations

Tariq Ali, *Shadows of the Pomegranate Tree* (Chatto and Windus, 1992). [A novel about Arabic knowledge and the Moorish occupation of Spain when caliphs ruled before the Reconquest.]

Malcolm Bosse, *The Examination* (Square Fish, 1996). [A novel about the Chinese system of meritocracy and government employment.]

Rollo Walter Brown, *How the French Boy Learns to Write* (Harvard University Press, 1915).

Jonathan Green, *Chasing the Sun: Dictionary Makers and the Dictionaries They Made* (Henry Holt, 1996).

Joyce Kinkead, *A Schoolmarm All My Life: Personal Narratives from Frontier Utah* (Signature, 1996).

William Holmes McGuffey, *The Original McGuffey's Pictorial Eclectic Primer* (Winthrop B. Smith, 1835; rpt. Mott Media, 1982).

Stuart A.P. Murray, *The Library: An Illustrated History* (Skyhorse, 2019).

Susan Orlean, *The Library Book* (Simon & Schuster, 2018).

Lydia Pyne, *Bookshelf* (Bloomsbury, 2016).

Lucille M. Schultz, *The Young Composers: Composition's Beginnings in Nineteenth-Century Schools* (Southern Illinois University Press, 1999).

Pip Williams, *The Dictionary of Lost Words* (Ballantine, 2021). [This novel tells the story of the distaff side of the making of the *OED*.]

Simon Winchester, *The Professor and the Madman: A Tale of Murder, Insanity, and the Making of the Oxford English Dictionary* (Harper, 1998).

Film Recommendation

The Professor and the Madman, directed by P.B. Shemran (2019).

Chapter Fourteen

Writing and Work

> *"Writing is consistently at the top of two kinds of lists—the lists that employers say they want and the list of skills employers often complain that recent graduates don't have when they graduate."*
> —Laurie Grobman and E. Michele Ramsey (104)

Writing in the workplace is termed a "threshold skill" for hiring and promotion. A poorly written application is unlikely to result in a job, as it signals a lack of care that may transfer to on-the-job work. Training to "upskill" employees is an unwanted investment for companies and businesses that may cost more than $3 billion annually (National Commission on Writing, *Writing*). More than 90 percent of employers cite the need to write effectively as a skill of great importance in daily work, according to a white paper by The National Commission on Writing in America's Schools and Colleges. A survey of business leaders found that companies produce technical reports, formal reports, memos and correspondence, and presentations. Documentation has become increasingly important, and communication must be crystal clear. Even among non-professional employees, responsibilities for writing exist. Poor writing skills reflect on an individual's competency and credibility. And it's not just about grammar, spelling, and sentence structure; employers look for reasoning, evidence, and organization. In short, writing is an essential skill for everyone.

Writing is one of the essential "soft skills" that employers value: communication—both written and verbal; critical thinking; collaboration or teamwork;

creativity; and computer skills. A survey of 500 US senior executives found that 44 percent think that Americans lack these soft skills (Adecco). "Hard skills" are teachable, technical abilities that may be easier to learn because soft skills are grounded in thinking, experience, personality, and attitude.

WHAT IS WORKPLACE WRITING?

Workplace writing is as diverse as the businesses that exist. Writing done in real estate differs from that in the aerospace industry. On the other hand, genres of workplace writing can be clearly identified, as Grobman and Ramsey have done in this list of 54 types of workplace writing (104):

Activity reports	Marketing plans
Abstracts	Memos
Ad copy	Opinion pieces
Agreements	Pamphlets
Annual reports	Personnel evaluations
Articles	Politics and procedures
Blogs	Policy briefs
Brochures	PowerPoint slides
Business plans	Press releases
Business rules	Product line brochures
Business valuations	Proposals
Contracts	Reports
Direct mail writing	Resumes
Email	Signs
Employee agreements	Social media
Facebook	Software documentation
Grant proposals	Speeches
Grant summaries	Style guides
Health manuals	Technical definitions
Infographics	Technical descriptions
Instructional books	Technical manuals
Instructions	Technical reports
Labels	Trial preparation notes
Legal briefs	Twitter
Letters	Web copy
Loan packages	Websites
Manuals	White papers

While this may seem an exhaustive list, other types of workplace writing exist, such as employee evaluations, scripts, and usability studies. It would be difficult to think of a job in which writing did not play some part. Even in a fast-food setting, employees write requests to their supervisors while shift leaders write descriptions of the shifts, reasons for employee reprimands, or requests for new equipment. Manual workers in carpentry carry special rectangular pencils that won't roll away when placed on a surface. While the pencils' primary use is to mark on surfaces, they are also used to make notes and leave instructions for the laborers and craftspeople.

THE IMPORTANCE OF WRITING IN THE WORKPLACE

Retail may be another segment that is not viewed as requiring much writing, as the focus may seem to be communicating verbally with customers or stocking shelves; however, special orders, restocking notes, and damage reports all require writing. A member of a store's data-entry team may have many more writing tasks. A sporting goods employee, for instance, works from a list of brands and products to find and edit images, create a creative and catchy title for each and a sales pitch description, combined with a bulleted list of features. Products may range from fly-tying feathers to women's apparel or writing different descriptions for dozens of trucker-style hats.[1] Managers do substantial writing, such as scheduling and communicating with employees, designing displays and evaluating products, completing maintenance requests, and creating status reports. In fact, managers in a variety of settings have significant writing tasks for which clear communication is crucial. A manager of an apartment complex with 500 residents sends out email messages that must make sense to everyone about updates, maintenance, cleaning checks, snow removal, and safety. Task lists also become important to ensure processes are followed; the sticky note is a popular format for "to do" activities. An overarching principle with clients or customers is maintaining good relationships, essential to a well-run business.

Likewise, the service industry depends on good rapport with its clients, who value accurate and professional communication. Workers in accounting, for instance, focus on numbers but also on clear notes and updates about accounts. Documenting interactions with customers is important, including what may seem insignificant, such as "Called regarding balance. No answer. Left VM." A company that provides free captioned telephones for the hearing impaired relies significantly on writing. Captioning agents transcribe accounts; others install and train customers on how to use the

---

1 I wish to acknowledge Will E. Walker for this example.

equipment. Contacting customers in this business may be via email or even personal contact at their homes, leaving a door hanger with information if they are not at home. Good communication within a business among its colleagues and outside the business with its clients is a valuable asset to any company and can set job applicants apart from the competition.

An atmosphere in the workplace in which trust, good humor, and high morale are shared is worth gold and can build effective teams. Wardle did a research study on the difficulties experienced by a computer technician when he was hired in a university humanities department that had different communication values. The technician and the academics "were constantly at cross purposes—he did not write in ways the community members saw as appropriate, and he did not view their conventions as ones he should adopt" (527). Discourse communities share common values about writing and speaking, and new workers who succeed are initiated into these communities or learn to adapt. Specific groups may use words common in the field, called jargon or cant, what may be referred to simply as technical terms. In the early days of computers in the workplace, technicians used terms like RAM (random access memory) and ROM (read only memory), just two of the many terms that may have sounded foreign and off-putting to those outside the discourse community. Likewise, acronyms can signal membership in a group; for instance, writing specialists may refer to 4Cs, the abbreviation for their Conference on College Composition and Communication. Knowledge of particular terms can lead to a feeling of insider or outsider status. Being aware of field-specific jargon is important to an individual's success. Sometimes a person may sound as if they are spouting "alphabet soup" of acronyms that are known only to the insiders of that discourse community. Communicating well is a threshold skill for success in personal or professional circles.

Good, clear writing can be the difference between life and death in medical fields. An Emergency Medical Technician (EMT) must write detailed "hand off reports" giving information on baseline vital signs, any interventions, drugs administered, and personal information so that the attending physician has important background information for treatment that needs to be done quickly. Another precise documentation for the medical field is "recording procedures," known as the first line of defense in a court of law if a patient decides to sue. Likewise, obtaining consent to treat is crucial, because again, the patient can sue for compensation if consent has not been properly obtained. Excellent communication is expected even when the situation may be stressful or the participants are tired. Health professionals providing therapy write status and progress reports, particularly for long-term cases. Additionally, these workers must be familiar with law and procedures for everyone, but doubly so for vulnerable groups such as the mentally or physically challenged.

Science is yet another area in which meticulousness counts tremendously. Experiments need to be recorded faithfully in lab notebooks, a hallmark of Responsible Conduct of Research (RCR). Notebooks record dates and procedures, results, errors, accidents, and reflections. A good notebook uses a page per day for easier tracking, not multiple days on any one page. The notebook remains in the lab, and members of the research team can post queries and answers in the book. In a lab, a researcher may then transfer data to spreadsheets for analysis, drawing on information from previous days or weeks.

Quality-control technicians develop certificates of analysis and safety data sheets. The former may guarantee the values of chemicals used, while the latter details the hazards of a particular chemical or product, including instructions if the work goes awry. A system of checks and balances requires a document to be reviewed and assessed by a co-worker, who can grant or withhold their approval and return it for an authenticating signature.

Increasingly, writing is a global activity. One of my students works as a content developer for a global human resources company located in London, but she works from her home and online. She described her work this way:

> Most of my job is updating the company website and running its social media accounts. I also send out a monthly newsletter, detailing what the company has been doing recently. Aside from the occasional meeting or phone call, all of the work I do is writing-based, which allows me to apply aspects of my education in a real-world setting. Collaboration is what my job is reliant on. All of the information I work with has to come from someone else, who generally gets it from someone else, too, and then it's up to me to compile it all and decide what's most important. Most of this collaboration is done via email, which has taught me the value and importance of clear language in communication. Clear language can reduce twenty emails into two, which saves everyone time and patience. (Megan Eralie)

Another student—Sasha—described her work translating documents, as she is fluent in English, French, and Japanese. It must be accurate but also take into account the nuances of a language. For instance, Japanese rarely uses phrases of loss such as "I miss you" or even words of love; as a result, when translating a line from Mozart's *The Magic Flute*, "I cannot bear to live without my Pamina," the closest translation that made sense was "*Pamina ga inai, totemo kanashi,*" which means "Pamina isn't here, it's very sad." As with Megan, collaboration is key. The translators rely on one another to check their work.[2]

While writing is often considered a solitary act, in the workplace it may be more frequently a collaborative or team activity. Presentations, for instance, may have multiple authors and reviewers in order to create the best result. Lunsford and Ede (1990) investigated collaboration in the workplace and found that the ability to work together on projects was extremely important. That is borne out in analysis of employers' wish list for their employees, where adeptness at the soft skill of teamwork is a high priority. While letters or memos might typically feature one author, longer format reports, manuals, case studies, presentations, and newsletters feature multiple writers, each contributing text and also reviewing others' work.

CONCLUDING THOUGHTS

From the earliest days of writing systems, writers have held an important place. Scribes copied documents and took dictation, but they were often considered some of the most learned members of society, attending the rare schools that existed in order to become literate in the profession. Some went beyond being mere copyists and achieved status as teachers, legal experts, religious scholars, and leaders. In the Middle Ages, scribes worked in a scriptorium to copy religious and classical works. With exacting work, these scribes—usually monks and sometimes nuns or unencumbered women— were masters of the technology of writing, using calligraphy and perhaps even illustration and taking care with valuable vellum or parchment.

They evolved over the centuries, and when the printing press came into existence, scribes were not always needed. Scriveners, rather like a contemporary notary public, worked on legal documents such as wills, trademarks, and patents. Secretaries (usually male) continued to work for others of high status or nobility. In contemporary terms, the American Society of Legal Writers took up the term Scribes for their professional organization, with a mission statement "to promote a clear, succinct, and forceful style in legal writing." ScribeAmerica is an organization that helps professional writers in health care to improve their productivity and assists them with critical tasks.

---

2   Many of the examples of workplace writing were obtained, with permission, from my students: Claire Banks, Keenan Bryner, Cameron Cheney, Weston Christensen, Megan Eralie, Dallin Hammond, Lilian Hayes, Sasha Heywood, Kaitlin Johnson, Tristin King, Rob Lehman, Ashlee Richards, Adam Robinson, Will Walker, and Brady Wallis.

Writers today carry with them this legacy of craft and art. Excellent writing has the potential to be a mark of high status; stellar writers can be successful in many venues and are particularly valued in the workplace. Writing has the power to make or break an organization, as words have the power to move colleagues, consumers, and clients. A technical manual that has errors and ambiguities is an aberration in the relationship between the object and its user, according to Robert Pirsig, author of *Zen and the Art of Motorcycle Maintenance* (1974). Writing in the workplace is more than just correct grammar and spelling; developing a philosophy of writing in the workplace and valuing the importance of relationships and rhetoric are a worthy undertaking.

QUESTIONS TO CONSIDER

1. How would you describe the writing in the workplaces that you've been in? What worked in the setting? What didn't work?
2. What is the role of collaborative writing in the workplace?
3. What kinds of writing are expected in your career choice? Several websites offer information about the kinds and amount of writing done in a range of jobs (e.g., https://www.mymajors.com/career-list/). Referencing the career website and what you may know through your major, what are the requirements for writing and/or communication skills in your chosen career? How is your major preparing you for these important skills? How is the rest of your undergraduate coursework preparing you in terms of writing/communication skills? What have been important milestones in your writing development over the course of your undergraduate career?

INVITATION TO REFLECT AND WRITE

Investigate the writing that you do for work. Describe the setting and detail the types of writing. Have mentors at work guided you in writing or improving texts? What models are offered? If you don't write at work, then are there others who do? What types of writing are involved? Is there any collaboration among those at your workplace in terms of writing tasks? Describe that process. What are the opportunities, issues, pitfalls, or challenges? What would you change about workplace writing? In other words, give a window onto the workplace and writing. You may wish to integrate research or data into this response. You could even interview co-workers to obtain their perspectives.

FOR FURTHER READING

The concern about employees' ability to communicate led to the formation of a National Commission on Writing that drew on the expertise of writing specialists as well as government officials. This brief report offers statistical evidence of the power of writing for career success.

Writing: A Ticket to Work...Or a Ticket Out

A Survey of Business Leaders
Report of the National Commission on Writing (2004)
(Abridged)

Summary

A survey of 120 major American corporations employing nearly 8 million people concludes that in today's workplace writing is a "threshold skill" for hiring and promotion among salaried (i.e., professional) employees. Survey results indicate that writing is a ticket to professional opportunity, while poorly written job applications are a figurative kiss of death. Estimates based on the survey returns reveal that employers spend billions annually correcting writing deficiencies. The survey, mailed to 120 human resource directors in corporations associated with Business Roundtable, produced responses from 64 companies, a 53.3 percent response rate.

   Among the survey findings:

- Writing is a "threshold skill" for both employment and promotion, particularly for salaried employees. Half the responding companies report that they take writing into consideration when hiring professional employees. "In most cases, writing ability could be your ticket in...or it could be your ticket out," said one respondent.
- People who cannot write and communicate clearly will not be hired and are unlikely to last long enough to be considered for promotion. "Poorly written application materials would be extremely prejudicial," said one respondent. "Such applicants would not be considered for any position."
- Two-thirds of salaried employees in large American companies have some writing responsibility. "All employees must have writing ability...Manufacturing documentation, operating procedures, reporting problems, lab safety, waste-disposal operations—all have to be crystal clear," said one human resource director.

- Eighty percent or more of the companies in the service and finance, insurance, and real estate (FIRE) sectors, the corporations with the greatest employment growth potential, assess writing during hiring. "Applicants who provide poorly written letters wouldn't likely get an interview," commented one insurance executive.
- A similar dynamic is at work during promotions. Half of all companies take writing into account when making promotion decisions. One succinct comment: "You can't move up without writing skills."
- More than half of all responding companies report that they "frequently" or "almost always" produce technical reports (59 percent), formal reports (62 percent), and memos and correspondence (70 percent). Communication through e-mail and PowerPoint presentations is almost universal. "Because of e-mail, more employees have to write more often. Also, a lot more has to be documented," said one respondent.
- More than 40 percent of responding firms offer or require training for salaried employees with writing deficiencies. Based on the survey responses, it appears that remedying deficiencies in writing may cost American firms as much as $3.1 billion annually. "We're likely to send out 200–300 people annually for skills-upgrade courses like 'business writing' or 'technical writing,'" said one respondent.

Business Roundtable (www.businessroundtable.org) is an association of the chief executive officers of some of the leading US corporations. The chief executives are committed to advocating public policies that foster vigorous economic growth and a dynamic global economy. The Roundtable's members represent corporate leaders in manufacturing, finance, services, and high technology. The Roundtable encouraged its members to participate in the survey, which was developed and administered by the National Commission on Writing for America's Families, Schools, and Colleges.

Introduction

Declaring that "writing today is not a frill for the few, but an essential skill for the many," the National Commission on Writing for America's Families, Schools, and Colleges issued a benchmark report in April 2003, *The Neglected "R": The Need for a Writing Revolution* (see Appendix A for the executive summary).

That document called for a writing agenda for the nation. It promised that the Commission would reconstitute itself to lead an action agenda around writing. It also pledged to issue annual reports to Congress on the state of writing in the United States, both to keep the importance of written communications in the public eye and to ensure that *The Neglected "R"* was not itself neglected on library shelves.

The Commission believes that much of what is important in American public and economic life depends on clear oral and written communication. We are convinced that writing is a basic building block for life, leisure, and employment. I am proud to serve as chair of the follow-on effort led by the National Commission on Writing for America's Families, Schools, and Colleges.

This second report from the Commission summarizes the findings of a major survey of 120 members of Business Roundtable, a survey conducted in the spring of 2004. The Roundtable includes some of the most prominent corporations in the United States and the world. We thank the human resource divisions of these corporations for completing the Commission's survey.

The survey reveals that good writing is taken as a given in today's professional work. Writing is a "threshold skill" for salaried employment and promotion. It is particularly important in services and in finance, insurance, and real estate (FIRE), growing employment sectors that are likely to generate the most new jobs in the coming decade. In a nutshell, the survey confirms our conviction that individual opportunity in the United States depends critically on the ability to present one's thoughts coherently, cogently, and persuasively on paper.

Bob Kerrey
President
New School University
New York, NY

Response Rate and Confidence in Findings

- Of 120 Business Roundtable human resource directors surveyed, 64 responded, for a response rate of 53.3 percent.
- Nonresponding Roundtable firms were somewhat larger, on average, but the difference was not statistically significant.

Discussion:

- Business Roundtable is an association of chief executive officers of some of the leading corporations in the United States.

- Statisticians typically anticipate that a response rate of 40 percent for an elite corporate group of this sort would be acceptable. This survey's response rate of 53.3 percent is very robust. It was made possible by aggressive telephone follow-up encouraging human resource officials to complete the survey.
- The telephone follow-up also provided a rich array of comments and observations from the respondents.
- We can be confident that, overall, the results of this survey represent the opinions of human resource personnel in major American corporations. That confidence does not extend to individual industrial sectors.
- Manufacturing employment, for example, is considerably overrepresented among Roundtable membership. Employment is underrepresented in sectors concerned with construction, mining, wholesale and retail trade, and agriculture, forestry, and fishing. Conclusions about the latter sectors need to be interpreted cautiously. With the exception of wholesale and retail trade, employment in these sectors is considerably lower than employment in services or manufacturing.
- No members of the Roundtable come from government (at any level) or from the small-business community.

How Important Is Writing in the Workplace?

- Close to 70 percent of responding corporations report that two-thirds or more of their salaried employees have some responsibility for writing, either explicit or implicit, in their position descriptions.
- With the exception of mining and transportation/utilities, large majorities of salaried employees in all industries are expected to write.
- Writing is almost a universal professional skill required in service industries as well as finance, insurance, and real estate (FIRE). It is also widely required in construction and manufacturing.
- Among hourly (i.e., nonprofessional) employees, the expectations for writing are not as high. Even among hourly employees, however, between one-fifth and one-third of employees have some writing responsibilities in fast-growing sectors such as services, FIRE, and construction.

Salaried Hourly

Discussion:

- Most growth in the US economy over the next decade is expected to be in service industries. They are expected to create 20.5 million new jobs in this decade. (Berman, Jay M. "Industry output and employment projections to 2010." *Monthly Labor Review*, Nov. 2001, p. 40.) These are corporations (including those in the FIRE category) reporting that 80 percent or more of salaried employees have some responsibility for writing.

- Internationally, functions emphasizing communications (such as customer contact and R&D) are least likely to be outsourced. Payroll and information technology, on the other hand, are most likely to be outsourced. (*CEO Briefing: Corporate Priorities for 2004*. A report from the Economist Intelligence Unit, London, New York, Hong Kong, January 2004, pages 26 and 29.)

Respondents' Comments:

- "In most cases, writing ability could be your ticket in...or it could be your ticket out."
- "All employees must have writing ability. Everything is tracked. All instructions are written out. Manufacturing documentation, operating procedures, reporting problems, lab safety, waste-disposal operations— all have to be crystal clear. Hourly and professional staff go through serious training. They must be able to communicate clearly, relay information, do postings, and the like. As a government contractor, *everything* must be documented."
- "Writing skills are fundamental in business. It's increasingly important to be able to convey content in a tight, logical, direct manner, particularly in a fast-paced technological environment."
- "My view is that good writing is a sign of good thinking. Writing that is persuasive, logical, and orderly is impressive. Writing that's not careful can be a signal of unclear thinking."
- "Most of our employees are hourly...so most of our people don't really write very much."

Is Writing an Important Hiring Consideration?

- More than half (51 percent) of responding companies say that they frequently or almost always take writing into consideration when hiring salaried employees
- Among service and FIRE sector companies, 80 percent or more of

respondents report taking writing into account frequently, or almost always, when hiring salaried employees.

- Transportation/utilities companies are least likely to take writing into consideration when hiring salaried employees (17 percent).
- Writing is not as important a hiring consideration for hourly employees. Only 16 percent of all responding companies report taking writing into consideration frequently, or almost always, when hiring hourly employees.
- Even among hourly employees, however, writing is a significant hiring consideration in the finance, insurance, and real estate (FIRE) sector.

Discussion:

- Overall, writing samples are rarely required from job applicants (just 11 percent of responding companies report they require writing samples from applicants for salaried positions).

Salaried Hourly

- However, in companies where writing is considered part of the job, 54 percent of responding companies require a writing sample, and 71 percent form impressions of applicants' writing abilities based on letters submitted with application materials.
- Fully 86 percent of responding companies report they would hold poorly written application materials against a job candidate, either "frequently" or "almost always."
- Every responding company in the service sector took this position, as did 86 percent of firms in the FIRE sector.

Respondents' Comments:

- Comments from the survey make it clear that interviewers and personnel managers consider poorly written application materials to be a kiss of death in the employment negotiation. They assume that applicants who are careless with important personal communications, such as job applications, are unlikely to be careful with important corporate documents.
- "We are almost always looking for writing skills when hiring, among both hourly and professional employees. It's inherent. We're looking for professionalism in every aspect."

- "Poorly written application materials would be extremely prejudicial. Such applicants would not be considered for any position."
- "We'd frequently hold that against the applicant since it reflects on care and attention to detail."
- "Generally, the staffing office would not pass along a badly written résumé to the hiring divisions."
- "Applicants who provide poorly written letters wouldn't likely get an interview, especially given the large pool who do present themselves well."

What Kind of Writing Is Expected on the Job Today?

- E-mail and oral presentations with visual aids (e.g., PowerPoint) are ubiquitous in the American economy.
- More than half of all responding companies also report the following forms of communications as required "frequently" or "almost always": technical reports (59 percent), formal reports (62 percent), and memos and correspondence (70 percent).
- Whatever the form of communication, it is clear that respondents expect written materials to be accurate, clear, and grammatically correct.
- Accuracy and clarity are particularly valued in the finance and service sectors; conciseness is not universally held to be important, but respondents in construction value it highly. Visual appeal is considered "important," but not "extremely important."

Discussion:

- Corporate respondents make clear distinctions between the different requirements for writing, depending on purpose and audience—e.g., clarity and rigor for financial analyses, and scientific precision for technical reports.
- There is a great deal of corporate interest in how changing forms of communication (e.g., e-mail and PowerPoint) modify writing demands.

Respondents' Comments:

- "Business writing generally calls for clarity, brevity, accuracy, and an appropriate level of detail for documenting."
- "Scientific precision is required almost always for scientists and engineers responsible for preparing formal papers and technical reports."

- "In offices worried about legal issues, communications and human resources, employees must be able to write well."
- "E-mail has had a big effect on how people communicate. It makes communication easy on the job, since everyone has a computer, but there are more messages than anyone needs, and more copies to everyone."
- "In this electronic age, writing skills are critical. Because of e-mail, more employees have to write more often. Also, a lot more has to be documented."
- "We're inundated daily with e-mail, and people have to learn to think in 'core points.' We need presentation skills on the same basis. Most of us have experienced 'death by PowerPoint.' Training should focus on being direct, presenting only what's needed."

Do Employees Have the Writing Skills Employers Seek?

- By a substantial majority, respondents report that two-thirds or more of their employees (current and new) meet company writing requirements (see Table 2).
- Employers in firms in the service, FIRE, and construction sectors (which rely heavily on writing) are most likely to say that two-thirds or more of their employees possess requisite writing skills.
- Despite what seems to be a generally positive picture, a significant proportion of responding firms (about one-third) report that one-third or fewer of their employees, both current and new, possess the writing skills companies value.

Discussion:

- The Roundtable corporations include many of the blue-chip corporations of the United States. They get their pick of the best graduates from the finest colleges and universities in the United States and the world.
- Respondents from the services and FIRE sectors are most likely to screen for writing skills, to use writing as a part of the hiring process, and to refuse to hire someone with clearly inadequate skills.
- Those in the construction sector also report a heavy reliance on writing, and they appear to be satisfied with the writing skills of their employees.
- In brief, responding corporations in the service, FIRE, and construction sectors hire whom they seek: employees who are able to communicate in the ways most valuable to the employer.

- Corporations also express a fair degree of dissatisfaction with the writing of recent college graduates—and also with academic styles of writing, unsuited to workplace needs.
- Since up to one-third of the employees in these blue-chip corporations do not possess adequate writing skills, writing deficiencies may be even more pronounced elsewhere in the broader private sector, particularly among employees of small- and medium-sized businesses.

Respondents' Comments:

- "Almost all our people have the skills at the professional level. We screen for them."
- "Almost all of them have these skills—we wouldn't hire without them."
- "The skills of new college graduates are deplorable—across the board; spelling, grammar, sentence structure . . . I can't believe people come out of college now not knowing what a sentence is."
- "Recent graduates aren't even aware when things are wrong (singular/ plural agreement, run-on sentences, and the like). I'm amazed they got through college."
- "People's writing skills are not where they need to be. Apart from grammar, many employees don't understand the need for an appropriate level of detail, reasoning, structure, and the like."
- "Recent graduates may be trained in academic writing, but we find that kind of writing too verbose and wandering."

Is Writing a Promotion Criterion?

- More than half of all responding companies take writing skills into account in making promotion decisions for salaried employees.
- Corporations in the construction sector are least likely to frequently consider writing in promotion decisions (only 33.3 percent say they frequently or always do so); companies in manufacturing are the most likely (57.5 percent).
- With regard to hourly employees, 95 percent of respondents indicate that writing is "never" or "only occasionally" considered as part of promotion decisions.

Discussion:

- Employers who are most interested in writing are likely to screen for writing skills in hiring and assume these skills are present. In that sense, promotions would not depend on writing skills, since everyone is assumed to possess them.
- A lack of writing ability is more likely to be a factor in termination than in promotion decisions.

Respondents' Comments:

- Survey comments reveal that many personnel officials found it difficult to conceive of salaried employees with poor writing skills reaching the point where they would be considered for promotion.
- "It would be unusual for someone already on the job to be in this position. Writing would have been part of the hiring process."
- "It's more of a negative if missing, than a positive for promoting."
- "Someone who couldn't communicate wouldn't be getting promoted."
- "If someone is up for promotion, it means they do good work on all fronts."
- "Writing is integral in nearly every job. It's really not a promotion issue since you'd never get to the point of promotion without good communications skills. You can't move up without writing skills."

Do American Companies Provide Writing Training? If So, What Does It Cost?

- More than 40 percent of responding firms offer or require training or retraining in writing for salaried employees who need it (see Figure 5).
- Construction and manufacturing are more likely than others to provide writing training to salaried employees who need it.
- All responding mining and service employers report they "never" or "only occasionally" provide employees with writing training.
- Relatively few responding firms provide writing training for hourly employees (81 percent of respondents report they "never" or "only occasionally" provide such training).

Discussion:

- Where employees need training in writing skills and employers provide such assistance, the average cost of such training is approximately $950 per employee across industries. However, comments on the forms indicated that the range of services provided is considerable, from online tutoring programs costing very little to full-scale writing workshops priced in the thousands.
- Extrapolating the findings from Roundtable companies (by industrial sector and hourly and salaried employees), we estimate that annual private-sector costs for providing writing training could be as high as $3.1 billion (see Appendix B).
- The $3.1 billion figure does not include employees of government or the retail and wholesale trade sector, neither of which is represented among respondents. The total cost to the economy of providing writing training is, therefore, likely to be considerably higher.

Respondents' Comments:

- "We're likely to send out 200–300 people annually for skills upgrade courses like 'business writing' or 'technical writing.'"
- "We provide training in business writing and documentation. We don't train in basic writing."
- "We offer in-house programs to improve writing and communications skills. Our company has been running this program for several years. We even brought in a college professor to improve writing, and he developed six courses for us."
- "I estimate the costs to range between $2,500 and $3,500 per individual, when it's absolutely necessary to send people for training. We formerly tried doing it in-house, but found it too complex to do effectively."

Implications

Opinions, even those of high-level corporate executives, should never be the sole basis of policy. Still, three important educational policy implications stand out from the results of this survey.

First, writing appears to be a "marker" attribute of high-skill, high-wage, professional work. This is particularly true in sectors of the economy that are expanding, such as services, and the finance, insurance, and real estate sectors. Educational institutions interested in preparing students for rewarding and remunerative work should concentrate on developing graduates' writing skills. Colleges and university leaders, as well as school officials, should take that advice to heart. The strength of corporate complaints about the writing skills of college graduates was surprisingly powerful.

Second, writing is also a "gatekeeper." The equity dimensions of the writing challenge are substantial. People who cannot write in the United States can clearly find employment. The findings of this survey, however, indicate that opportunities for salaried employment are limited for employees unable to communicate clearly. Of particular concern here is the need to develop the language and communications skills of English-language learners, who are likely to be at a disadvantage in today's workplace. Unless our society pays attention to developing all of the education skills (including writing) of all segments of the population, it runs the risk of consigning many students who are poor, members of minority groups, or learning English to relatively low-skill, low-wage, hourly employment.

Third, the comments provided by the respondents confirm a central argument of the Commission throughout its existence. Writing consists of the ability to say things correctly, to say them well, and to say them in a way that makes sense (i.e., grammar, rhetoric, and logic). Corporate leaders' comments equating clear writing with clear thinking were impressive. Business writing, of course, is only one form of communication. Even so, business writing, at its best, requires effective communication about work that is frequently complex and intellectually demanding. Skill in such communication is not developed by a few school hours here and there devoted to writing. Developing the kinds of thoughtful writers needed in business, and elsewhere in the nation's life, will require educators to understand writing as an activity calling for extended preparation across subject matters—from kindergarten through college.

In *The Neglected "R,"* the Commission stated that writing helps students "connect the dots" in their learning. That metaphor can also stand for career development. In many ways, what this survey tells the nation is that writing helps graduates connect the dots in their careers, as well.

Chapter Fifteen

Social Media

"Disconnect to connect."

"Putting my phone down and picking up my life."

"Make sure you are happy in real life, not just on social media."

"Let it go. Change the channel. Turn it off. Unsubscribe. Unfriend. Unfollow. Mute. Block. Walk away. Breathe."[1]

Social networking got its start supposedly in 1978 when the Computerized Bulletin Board System (CBBS) went online in Chicago. Ward Christensen (b. 1945) and Randy Suess (1945–2019) created this virtual message board, which required dialing in by telephone modem, so that members could post information for one another. The internet was just getting started. The initiative of these computer hobbyists was driven by a massive snowstorm that struck Chicago in January of that year and gave them time to follow through on their idea. Unsophisticated, the system allowed only one user at a time, but it inspired the development of other bulletin board systems. Facebook, Twitter, and YouTube are the legacy of the CBBS that was launched decades earlier (Metz, "Randy Suess").

The intent of social media then and now is to share information and build communities. An important aspect of the applications associated with social

1 Michael Bliss, https://www.perpetualbliss.me/post/185331615877.

media is that they build on Web 2.0 Internet, which relies on user-based or consumer-created content that is easy to submit or upload. Reviews of products on online catalogs, for instance, provide information for others to use in making an assessment. Does the sweater run small? Is the color as featured? How does it fare in the wash? These product reviews, however, generally lack an important feature: interactivity.

In 2020, during the COVID-19 pandemic crisis, Facebook turned to an unusual thread: where to find paper products. Jeff posted, "It's 7:45 am, and I just returned from Lowe's where I found these reusable towels." Kyrsten posted, "Shangri La Health Food got some more toilet paper in—about 18 four-pack rolls." Sierra alerted users, "There's toilet paper at the South Walmart right now!" Alison asked, "Size 1 Huggies? Preferably Little Snugglers, but any is fine." Others focused on pantry essentials such as yeast for baking bread; a responder noted that one grocery store limited purchase to a three-envelope packet per person. Another was "Looking for elderberry herbal tea for my 81-year-old mom." Social media provided opportunities for community building in a stressful time when face-to-face (F2F) interaction was not recommended, when self-quarantine became the rule, not the exception.

IS THERE AN APP FOR THAT?

Software or computer applications (apps) originally were designed to improve the efficiency of email, calendars, and databases and began appearing in the 1970s–1980s. Frances Allen (1932–2020), a rare women in computer design in the 1960s, was particularly interested in how computer programs could be created more easily and then executed speedily. She worked on the top-secret supercomputer project for the National Security Agency and then at IBM. Her idea was to spread "digital tasks across multiple computers," known as parallel computing (Metz). As a result, smartphone apps can be responsive within seconds. She won the Turing Prize (named after Alan Turing, who broke the German Enigma Code during World War II; see Chapter 10), the first woman to do so.

The inventory of app stores that service Android and iOS systems recently exploded with both innovation and demand. In the late twentieth century, people started to IM—Instant Message—and other "Messenger" services followed. LinkedIn debuted in 2003 to connect people professionally in terms of their careers. Skype, which added video to messaging, also appeared. Myspace, a forerunner in social networking, appeared the year prior to the more long-lasting Facebook in 2004, but its popularity decreased significantly after a high volume from 2005 to 2008. On March 21, 2006, Jack Dorsey (b. 1976), co-founder of Twitter, wrote, "just setting up my twttr," thus sending the first tweet and instituting microblogging with a limit of 130 characters and a new use for the octothorpe, more commonly termed the hashtag (#). Twitter also spawned a genre of fiction, including an "Internet girls'" series by Lauren Myracle that includes *ttfn*, tweet language that means "ta ta for now." To understand the story, readers have to be adept at decoding text language such as ROTFL (rolling on the floor laughing), YOLO (you only live once), and 'rents (parents). In Chapter Four, I wrote about "slow writing," the deliberate use of pen, ink, and paper. This chapter, in contrast, features "fast writing."

Smartphone technology allowed social media sites to proliferate. Snapchat (2012) offered video sharing, which anticipated TikTok (2017); Pinterest (2009) allowed users to "scrapbook" information or images to be saved, which could be seen by others; Instagram (2010) provided another forum for visual sharing, with many young people migrating from Facebook to this more trendy site. Dating and "hook up" applications moved from desktop to mobile, notably Tinder (2012), where users could construct their profiles for review and then weigh in on others' profiles by swiping left (to indicate dislike) or right (try for a match-up).

Although smartphones do cost to operate, apps can eliminate what used to be called "long distance charges." (Landline telephone rates varied depending on the time of day. When I earned tenure at my job, I deliberately chose to call my parents in the middle of the afternoon, which I knew would signify that this was Big News.) WhatsApp (2009), for example, owned by Facebook and used internationally, offers multiple functions for communicating, including text and audio messages, phone calls, pictures, and videos.

Blogs, which is a shortened form of "weblog,"[2] offered longer-format writing for people to share information, opinions, and stories. The motivation to communicate with others in this format started with the rising popularity of the internet in the late 1990s and achieved widespread use in the first two decades of the twenty-first century. Unlike a website, a blog has a recognizable structure, with a header, main content, sidebar, and a footer, and content is updated fairly frequently. Food blogs are one of the most popular topics for bloggers and provide a space for people to share recipes and cooking ideas. Over 30 million bloggers were active in the United States as of 2020. Although the accuracy of blogs (like many websites) can vary significantly, they are a source of information, providing user-created content. And they can turn into moneymakers for successful bloggers who include advertisements on their sites.

WordPress is one popular platform or content management system

---

2 Similarly, a vlog is a video blog that uses social media or a personal website.

(CMS) for bloggers. Started in 2003, WordPress offers various "themes" or designs for bloggers. A reluctant blogger, I dithered for years about pursuing a topic that I was invested in and thought was sharable before finally launching *Road Works* in 2011, when I was on research leave from my university and had some time to try it out. My blog is dedicated to providing book titles set in the area where I'm traveling. In a look-back essay, I introduced the history of my idea, which originated in 1994 when I first began a concerted effort to structure a reading list to fit the geography. We were heading from our home in northern Utah to the Santa Fe opera, car-camping much of the way and stopping at archaeological sites en route. Finally, I cracked open Edward Abbey's *The Monkey Wrench Gang* and *Desert Solitaire*. I re-read *Death Comes for the Archbishop* and found a Tony Hillerman mystery set near Chaco Canyon. The reading enhanced the travel significantly, and I thought others could benefit from this approach, which is the motivation of many bloggers—sharing information. Anxious about going public and fearing criticism, I nevertheless felt that communicating to like-minded voyagers was an act of letting others in on this secret. Developing a reading list is part of the joy of planning a trip, and since the advent of e-readers, I no longer have to pack an extra bag of books. Blogs can be shared via Twitter, Facebook, and LinkedIn for additional exposure.

Not surprisingly, businesses got on board with social media to enhance marketing. Advertisements appear regularly on non-commercial sites such as Facebook and show up almost frighteningly when someone has just finished browsing a shopping site. Yes, our behaviors are being tracked. Chatbots are rule-based or artificial intelligence (AI) software applications that allow a "robot" to chat with customers. Companies have found that responses can often be automated, freeing up human customer service representatives to focus on more complex issues and questions. Chatbots are also available 24/7 for quick response to customers. Yes, this means humans are "talking" to technology "bots," who may be anthropomorphized as "Susan" or "Al."

Chatbots are being used in alternative ways and not just for business applications. Dan Shewan offers an analysis of innovative ways in which Chatbots can improve quality of life and be helpful. Chatbots can serve as companions to patients with dementia or Alzheimer's, providing a conversational partner. An app named Casper helps insomniacs get through the night. Medical chatbots offer quick advice on questions. UNICEF uses chatbots to give voice to marginalized communities. Disney uses chatbots to engage children in stories and fantasies.

WHAT DOES IT ALL MEAN?

In the best of all possible worlds, social media provides opportunities for people to connect in multiple ways and formats. A high-school class may anticipate a reunion of graduates but also track celebrations, grandchildren, and deaths. During the 2020 pandemic, families, friends, and colleagues turned to social media to communicate safely.

Does the quality of writing matter in social media? It depends. Shortened text language, misspellings or typos, and even errors can pass between friends. The look of text can also indicate meaning. As one student put it, "My Mom still thinks it's important to include punctuation in a text message." Generational? Maybe. When a writer on social media composes a message, does that person consider audience, humor, irony, satire? Are the deliberations that occur when creating a more formal piece of writing taken into consideration? Is the writing looking for a reaction or an effect? The standard deliberations of a writer—purpose, audience, form, style, organization—may very well still be in play in social media posts.

Once business and other organizations come into the social media arena, darned right that they care deeply about their messages, as this is an important platform for marketing and for cultivating "leads" that will either purchase or sign on to take action. While images are important, a good story has never lost its appeal. As noted in Chapter Twelve, it takes more work to write a shorter letter. The same is true for a Twitter feed: an effective 140 characters (or so) is not easy.

Social media pervades contemporary lives for anyone who is digitally aware and online. While for many this source provides connection and companionship, for others there is a dark side.

DIGITAL DETOX

According to Celeste Headlee, author of *Do Nothing*, looking at a phone screen and scrolling through social media during non-working hours is interpreted as work by the brain. Researchers have found that the mere presence of a smartphone near to hand reduces brain power (Ward et al.). The proximity of the digital device leaves less room for other thinking. It's one reason that digital detox is growing in popularity. The epigraph at the beginning of the chapter offers inspirational advice to focus on connecting with others in person, not electronically. The irony of couples or family eating dinner out but each one focused on a screen rather than on faces is blatant. In short, we should live life through physical activity that doesn't rely on devices.

Paperchase, a store located in the United Kingdom, focuses on the material culture of writing. In a blog published on its website that focuses on World Mental Health Day, the company recommends "writing things down," as journaling has "proven mind and soul benefits" that include "reducing anxiety, helping…focus…thoughts and feelings, improving mental clarity and organizing…thoughts." One idea is to try out digital detox bingo, crossing out social media applications such as Instagram, Pinterest, YouTube, and Facebook (see Figure 14.1). Substituting for screen time is attention to mindfulness, imagination, reflection, quiet, and, of course, writing.

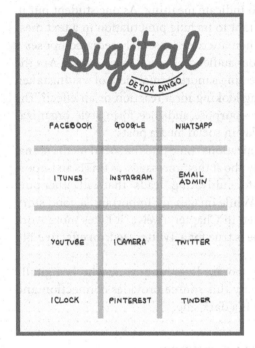

Figure 15.1
Digital Detox Bingo.

Another product offered by Paperchase is the School of Life phone detox flipbook, which brings "sanity to your most intense technological relationship." As the detox guide notes, "The dark truth is that it has become very hard to find anyone (and certainly anything) more interesting than one's smartphone." It advises that there is a "hidden cost" to a relationship with a smartphone, not paying attention to the world around us (School of Life). The company also offers an old-fashioned hourglass with sand that marks 15 minutes to focus on "What Really Matters." We can assume that setting the timer on a smartphone would be antithetical to the detox approach.

The concern about too much technology, particularly for children, is global. A 2018 tabloid report (A. Hall) noted that British families were going to focus on a summer without gadgets and an emphasis on outdoor activity for their youngsters. Smartphones offer weekly analyses of screen time and can even schedule "down time" when only phone calls and specified apps can be used. Self-regulation of time on apps is also feasible. Parents can set up Family Sharing to track a child's screen time and also set parental controls.

What are the issues? Digital devices are seductive and can become an addiction. According to an internet trends report, the average office worker checks email 30 times in any hour, and smart phones are accessed more than 150 times in a day (Meeker). Hours spent on devices per day per adult user in the United States continues to trend upward, for a total of 6.3, of which 3.6 is on a mobile device, 2 on a desktop or laptop, and slightly under an hour on other connected devices (see Figure 15.2).

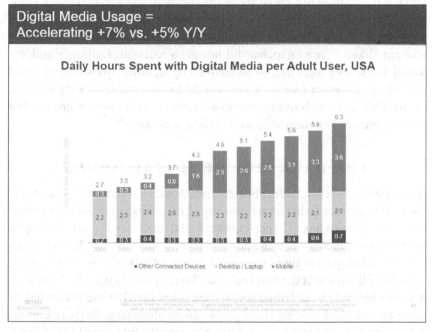

Figure 15.2   Digital Media Use.

So much time spent on digital devices can affect productivity; on the other hand, it's also possible to do work anywhere, anytime—a state of being "always on"—but that can also be a problem. Too much time on digital media means less time for others or for self-care. It can disrupt sleep and affect health and happiness. For those who do want to disconnect or to decrease digital usage, experts recommend planning carefully in order to be successful. Some people do not look at work email on weekends; another tactic is to disconnect on holidays or vacations. Focusing on the self means substituting other activities: exercise, particularly in nature; arts and culture events; cooking; games and sports; quality time with family or friends. A sure way to disconnect is to locate in a geographic area that doesn't have digital access. That's what happened in the small West Virginia town of Green Bank, where an observatory requires a "radio quiet zone," a regulation from 1958 that could not have foreseen Wi-Fi or cell signals. Children and teens read books, do chores, talk with their families, play with friends—without texts, TikTok, or Instagram to distract them (Levin).

Some research has been done on social media abstainers or former users (Bullinger and Vie). Peer pressure encourages people to be consumers of social media. For instance, Facebook encourages sharing of information, and if a friend does not know about the incident, there may be an accusation, "But, I posted it on Facebook." Relationship repair may be required if someone "unfriends" another on Facebook. Or perhaps an Instagram post was not "liked." Or a Snapchat did not get a reaction. Bullinger and Vie found that some people had social media fatigue; others grew disenchanted with the postings on Facebook and sought to tune out negativity, politics, or the TMI (too much information!) syndrome.[3] Still another group cited privacy and safety concerns as well as data security (82).

THE DARK SIDE OF SOCIAL MEDIA

According to novelist Andrea Bartz, crime novels have mined social media for its dark themes. In her own novel *The Herd*, published in 2020, a glamorous character who has a "hyper-curated social media feed" goes missing. In another novel, *Follow Me* by Kathleen Barber, a social media follower turns stalker, and in yet another crime read, Harriet Walker's *The New Girl*, an "online troll" disrupts the heroine's life. Bartz's point is that all is not what it seems behind the polished social media images that are presented by some people. And reading these posts can be alienating. Bartz references several studies, including "Instagram #Instasad?," that found that following Instagram posts of friends can be a positive experience but following strangers can be a negative encounter. Stranger than fiction, perhaps, is this account from my local newspaper's "This Week in Court," about a woman from another state charged with 15 counts of "class-A stalking," a result of sending hundreds of social media messages and sexually explicit photos to

---

3   A student in my research methods course, Emily Abel, found in a study of "Wedding Postings on Social Media by Utah LDS Young Adults" (2019) that viewers tired of seeing too many photographs posted from a wedding: "I don't need to see 10,000 wedding pictures, thank you very much."

a university student with the note that "she is going to have sex with him if he wants to or not." The stalker had purchased a one-way ticket from Florida but was arrested prior to boarding and then extradited to Utah. Not surprisingly, a competency evaluation was recommended.

Aside from fiction, other books have cited the difficulties that can arise with social media. Singer and Brooking argue in *Like War: The Weaponization of Social Media* that hackers and terrorists use Twitter and Facebook to create divisions among people. *War in 140 Characters: How Social Media is Reshaping Conflict in the Twenty-First Century* (Patrikarakos) shows how "the battlefield has moved onto phones," as soldiers and victims turn to Twitter, YouTube, and Facebook. Siva Vaidhyanathan, in *Antisocial Media*, describes Facebook as moving from a friendly gathering to become a behemoth that can undermine society and democracy. Posts can be uncivil, even inflammatory and inaccurate, but widely shared. Similarly, Andrew Marantz's *Anti-Social: Online Extremists, Techno-Utopians, and the Hijacking of the American Conversation* deplores how alt-right exploited what should have been an open, democratic forum for ideas. Jaron Lanier's argument is evident in the title of his book: *Ten Arguments for Deleting Your Social Media Accounts Right Now*. One of the arguments focuses on the enormous amount of data being collected about users and the lack of privacy. Corporate algorithms mine these data for advertising.

Social media use by young people is particularly fraught with peril. Bullying can be enabled through social media. The stories of young people committing suicide as a result of online bullying are well known. Nancy Jo Sales offers numerous examples of young women who try to meet expectations of social media in her *American Girls: Social Media and the Secret Lives of Teenagers*. Their male friends request nude photos, and the young women feel pressure to comply or at least project an image of perfection. If acquaintances are asking for nude photographs, then another threat on social media is the pedophile who preys on young people, exploiting the internet for pictures of children and teens. Clearly, supervision of minors using social media is an issue and a worry for parents.

SOCIAL MEDIA THROUGH THE AGES

Maybe you think social media is a twenty-first-century kind of thing. According to Tom Standage, author of *Writing on the Wall*, it's actually been practiced for two thousand years. He uses social media as a metaphor to describe writing that is shared publicly, commented on, and rated in a system that equates to like/love/haha/wow/sad/angry.

The technology of writing in classical Roman times was the wax tablet used with a stylus. The sender wrote on one side of the book-shaped wax tablet, and when the recipient answered, it was on the facing "page" of the tablet. Papyrus was a bit easier to transport due to its weight, and couriers managed to deliver letters from the Roman capital to the provinces in a remarkably short amount of time. Letters were publicly read, shared, and even copied for distribution. In this way, news and opinions circulated amazingly broadly. Standage quips that "slaves were the Roman equivalent of broadband" (22), as they served both as scribes and messengers.

Standage posits that Martin Luther's revolutionary religious message, the "Ninety-five Theses" that challenged the Catholic Church and were displayed on the door of a church in Wittenberg, Germany, was a "new post." It certainly got people's attention, as Luther made use of the relatively new innovation, the printing press, and he wrote it in the vernacular language of the people rather than in the Church language of Latin. His writings and pamphlets were read widely in guild halls and beer halls and received much acclaim as he argued against Church practices such as "indulgences" that cost even the poor precious funds. Luther's writing was met with responses and debate in other pamphlets that argued for the Catholic Church. Likewise, revolution of a political nature was launched two centuries later in the Colonies by pamphlets that maintained that it was "Common Sense" for those in America to seek its independence. Standage is fond of applying contemporary metaphors to the past. In *The Victorian Internet*, for instance, he compares the telegraph to the internet. The point of *Writing on the Wall* is that humans have a need to connect, share information, and express themselves.

IS GRAFFITI SOCIAL MEDIA?

In Pompeii and Herculaneum, two Italian cities covered by the ash of Mount Vesuvius in 79 CE, walls served as sites for public postings. In addition to erotic art, brothels featured scratched messages on the walls by customers who might give a review of a particular prostitute. These are considered explicit graffiti. Other writings on the wall were as simple as "Gaius was here," rather like the ubiquitous "Kilroy was here" popularized in World War II (see Figure 15.3). Lovers wrote declarations; others carved insults. A catalog of put-downs included *Rusticus est Cordyon*, which meant "Corydon is a clown or country bumpkin," and *Epaphra, Pilicrepus non es*, signifying "Oh, Epaphras, thou art no tennis-player" (LaFrance). Public notices announced gladiator games. In short, these formed something of a social media wall, where everyday life was aggregated with posts. No sign of a hashtag, though.

Political graffiti speaks to discontent and rebellion. Lawrence Durrell, writing of the contested land of Cyprus in his memoir *Bitter Lemons* (1957), saw, scrawled on walls, "Enosis and only Enosis," the joining of Cyprus with Greece, much to the dismay of Turkish Cypriots, and the division eventually led to a divided

Figure 15.3   Kilroy was here graffiti.

country with a border still maintained by United Nations forces. "The Troubles" in Ireland and Northern Ireland featured political graffiti from both sides. The Printing Museum of Haverhill, Massachusetts, hosted an exhibition of "Contemporary Arabic Graffiti and Lettering: Photographs of a Visual Revolution" in 2014 that explored how calligraphic graffiti revealed "political unrest" and raised "questions about established ideologies and beliefs," which may have contributed to the "Arab Spring" demonstrations. "Language becomes a vehicle for social protest, and the re-imagined letter form becomes not only a means, but also a symbol, for envisioning a brave new world," according to the curators.

Graffiti, although Italian in origin, is derived from the Greek *graphein*, which means "to write." The term evolved to include not just writing but also drawing, and in contemporary times, it may be more associated with spray paint, decorated trains, and concrete walls. The Museum of Graffiti opened in Miami, Florida, in 2019 with the objective of preserving graffiti's works of art. Letters are used as "artistic building blocks" (Caramanica) and artists use various styles. Not all viewers praise graffiti writing, though, as it is often done in public spaces, considered a form of vandalism, and can result in criminal charges and fees for cleaning. The founders of the museum argue that graffiti is creative expression by the individual and worthy of preservation and study. Two well-known graffiti artists are Banksy and Basquiat. Although drawings rather than words dominate their work, both employ epigrams to deliver social commentary. One of the former's pieces, "I Must Not Copy What I See on the Simpsons," features a boy with his skateboard copying this phrase multiple times, an ironic allusion to the television show.

What's missing in graffiti and in Standage's historic survey of social media? Digital technology. Social media in contemporary terms is bound to electronics, and its ability to be broadcast can be global.

CONCLUDING THOUGHTS

Although social media on digital devices is less than 50 years old, with an explosion of platforms and applications within the last two decades, it has had an enormous impact on the social, economic, and political fabric of lives around the world. And, clearly, change is innate to social media. What's the next big dating app when Tinder, Grindr, eHarmony, Match, and Bumble fade? No doubt there will be apps as yet unimagined. With one billion smartphones in use, interconnectivity between web and apps will continue, and artificial intelligence (AI) will come into play more frequently, no doubt. An overarching concern is privacy and security of data.

Social media has connected people but also alienated them. It has demonstrated both the best and worst of people, elevating the exceptional and the banal. It has allowed voices to be heard—even voices that are extreme and disruptive to a democratic society. It has tested the limits of freedom of speech. Our networks have the potential to be unlimited and global. What the world will make of social media is still evolving. It's anyone's guess if it will be an asset or not.

QUESTIONS TO CONSIDER

1. Social media allows people to interact with each other by sharing and consuming information. The variety and diversity of these media allow an individual to pick and choose among offerings. Reliability and credibility are factors in making those decisions. What happens when individuals construct an alternative reality from media that is patently false? How do you evaluate and choose which social media "to follow"?

2. Choose a social media page of an individual and evaluate the components and design of the site: profile; followers; hash tags; news feeds; information updates; like buttons; notifications. What makes an effective site?

3. It's said, "the Internet is written in ink," meaning that what is written on social media platforms may last forever. How do you consider the legacy of your postings and make choices on what you post?

4. Social media has been criticized for elevating the banal and praised for its world-altering power. What is your reaction to this kind of evaluation? What do you see on social media that is banal or powerful?

5. What do you see as the future of social media?

INVITATION TO REFLECT AND WRITE

Digital detox[4] is a process whereby users reduce the time spent on devices. This is not a condemnation of digital devices, as technology often makes lives easier; however, concerns have been raised that perhaps they detract from other meaningful activities. Users may already be receiving reports on "screen time" on a weekly basis from devices and be concerned about the number of hours they spend. (The average college student spends four hours daily on a screen.)

Consider a digital detox for a set amount of time and analyze your behavior and the results. This is a time to voluntarily refrain from using devices such as smartphones, computers, even smart watches, and also to reduce time spent on social media platforms. Before going cold turkey, users should decide on goals. Build the detox activity around that. What might substitute for the time gained? Will the detox last a week? A month?

A first easy task is to declutter devices. Can the desktop screen of a computer or smartphone be organized more efficiently? Apps can be deleted or organized. (Settings will inform users of how often or when apps were last used.) What apps add value to your life? Determine an action plan, put it into place, review, and assess through a designated time period. Some users become digital minimalists as they discover gained time.

At the end of the detox period, describe how your digital detox worked, including goals, accomplishments, challenges, frustrations, and the path forward.

FOR FURTHER READING

Two readings provide contemporary perspectives on social media and its use and abuse.

1. Andrea Bartz, "Social Media Fakeness Is Bad for Our Psyches... But Great for Crime Writers"

Andrea Bartz, author of *The Herd* (2020), writes in this brief essay that social media may promote unreal images of people quite different from what they are online. Apparently, several authors of crime novels have latched onto the darker side of social media.

---

4   I am indebted to Megan Eralie for a presentation on Digital Detox that informed this writing assignment.

There's a scene in my sophomore thriller, *The Herd*, in which Hana, the publicist of an elite all-female co-working space, has a rare loss of composure. Hana's glamorous best friend, Eleanor, who founded the company, has just gone missing, and Hana calls up Eleanor's oldest bud, the sweet but hapless Ted. Hana laments that Eleanor's hyper-curated social media feeds offer no clues to her whereabouts, and Ted points out that Eleanor has always been private—maybe she had good reason to disappear.

That's when Hana lashes out. "You know, everyone says that: She's so private, she's so guarded, look at her running a lifestyle blog but hardly ever sharing anything about her own life," she snaps. "People think they're opposite poles: You can be all TMI and post a million no-makeup selfies, or you can be like Eleanor and only post about your professional life. But it's not any different. Eleanor doesn't have *more* secrets than the woman who posts four hundred times a day. She just invests less time in hiding them."

In the era of personal brands and "finstas" and perfect-seeming social media profiles, ones designed to provoke envy and admiration, it's no surprise that suspense writers have found ways to thread the creepiness of curated online lives into their narratives. Witness Kathleen Barber's *Follow Me*, about an influencer whose biggest fan turns into an IRL stalker. Or Harriet Walker's forthcoming *The New Girl*, in which a fashion editor on maternity leave becomes the victim of an online troll—one whose vitriol stokes her fears that everything she's worked for will be yanked from her. Or Janelle Brown's forthcoming *Pretty Things* (out in April), in which an heiress-slash-influencer teams up with a plucky grifter for the scam of a lifetime. Or Caroline Kepnes' smash hit *You*, where a lovable psychopath worships and ensnares young women based on their online presence—only to be devastated when his targets aren't as perfect as their profiles suggest.

And though most of us aren't stealing our crushes' phones and leaving behind jars or urine while we're busy killing their frenemies (anyone?), we've all fallen into the trap of mistaking someone's feed for their life. After all, opening Instagram is like turning on the tap for a deluge of polished pictures. Social media slaps us in the face with impossibly beautiful versions of people's lives, and those rose-colored snaps can make our own existence seem dreary in comparison.

That's likely why research has linked social media with loneliness, envy, and anxiety. In one survey, 60 percent of active social media users said it has negatively impacted their self-esteem, and 80 percent agreed that these apps and sites make it easier for others to deceive them.

Thrillers have always trafficked in secrets and in the cold gap between who we seem to be and who we truly are. Social media provides fertile ground for crime writers because the reality behind the cheery photos and quippy captions is darker, uglier, marbled with shame and skeletons in the closet. Because there's an irony at the heart of social media upkeep, one I explore in *The Herd*. Despite knowing your own social media presence is shiny and fake, we forget that the same is true for others, conflating their updates with their reality...and feeling miserable in comparison.

Another irony: Those who post the most (and seem the happiest) might actually be the least OK. A 2014 study of bloggers showed that people with an anxious attachment style—those who feel less confident and safe in their relationships—tend to reveal the most about themselves online. All those Shiny Happy People who can't shut up about how great their life is *juuust* might be the lady who doth protest too much.

In everyday life, the implication is: Talk to your damn friends. Ask them how life with a newborn is, instead of leading with, "You two are going to so many breweries and doing so many fun things—you are rocking parenthood!" Inquire about the trip that looked 100 percent spectacular online, so that your jetsetting friend can be real about the rental car that died an hour outside the airport in Tulum or the airline drama that made getting home touch-and-go.

It's not just good for your friendship—it's also good for your psyche. A study from Pace University (terrifically titled "Instagram #instasad?") found that following IRL friends on Instagram is associated with fewer depressive symptoms; it's tracking *strangers*, who'll never give you the full, imperfect story, that's linked with depression.

The Herd centers on a group of uber-ambitious, high-achieving women who feel they have to maintain the Instagram-perfect facade not just online but also in their interactions...but of course, the dark secrets won't stay subsurface forever. So for the sake of crime writers everywhere, don't stop showing us that sparkly, perfect veneer. Because we can't wait to write about what happens when the beautiful mask begins to slip.

2. Andrew Marantz, "What the Coronavirus Crisis Has Changed about Social Media, and What It Hasn't Changed."

This article was written at the beginning of the pandemic. What happened in the months that followed?

Elon Musk is good at making electric cars, flamethrowers, and rocket ships; he is bad at making music, choosing friends, and forming opinions in real time. I know these latter, more personal facts about Musk because he has a Twitter account—one of the most popular accounts in the world, with more followers than CBS News, NBC News, and ABC News combined. In 2018, when twelve young soccer players were trapped in an underwater cave in Thailand, Musk, on Twitter, mused about building a rescue vessel. His help wasn't needed, as it turned out, but he did take the opportunity to get into an ugly Twitter spat with a cave diver who was involved in the rescue. (For reasons too complicated to explain here, Musk ended up calling the diver a "pedo guy," and the diver sued him, unsuccessfully, for defamation.) A month later, Musk tweeted, about one of his companies, "Am considering taking Tesla private at $420. Funding secured." This was probably nothing more than a dumb joke—420, in extremely outdated slang, refers to marijuana—but the S.E.C. took it seriously, and the tweet resulted in Musk paying a fine of twenty million dollars, stepping down as chairman of the company, and agreeing to get preapproval from Tesla's lawyers before tweeting anything similar again.

Another kind of person—especially a person with several companies to run and many billions of dollars to manage—might have taken any of these incidents as a perfectly good cue to delete his account. Yet here we are in the grip of a global pandemic, and Musk cannot help himself. Last week, he tweeted, "danger of panic still far exceeds danger of corona imo." (The initialism is sometimes rendered "imho," for "in my humble opinion," but Musk is apparently self-aware enough to omit the "h.") A few days later, one of Musk's followers, a guy whose display name was "bill lee" followed by a smiling-pile-of-poop emoji, tweeted a link to an article called "Stanford Professor: Data Indicates We're Severely Overreacting to Coronavirus." The article was from the Daily Wire, a right-wing blog full of partisan clickbait. "Imo, this professor is correct," Musk replied. In the meantime, he added, he would devote some of his factories' capacity to building ventilators, "even though I think there will not be a shortage by the time we can make enough to matter."

The professor in question was John P.A. Ioannidis, a well-regarded Stanford epidemiologist who is known for precisely this kind of bubble-bursting argument. (His most widely cited publication is called "Why Most Published Research Findings Are False.") Despite the Daily Wire headline, though, Ioannidis wasn't exactly arguing that we *are* overreacting to the virus. He was arguing that we *may* be overreacting, because we don't yet have enough evidence to know whether our "draconian countermeasures" will do "more good than harm." This much is clearly true. Until we're able to test a broad sample of the population, for example, we won't know whether the fatality rate from *COVID*-19 is closer to five per cent or to 0.05 per cent. It's possible that we'll look back in a few months and agree that the worst part about the coronavirus was our panicked response to it. We should be so lucky. For now, I would contend that we have no choice but to act decisively, even without complete evidence.

So far, this might seem like an anecdote about the Internet as a basically functional marketplace of ideas. Professor writes provocative analysis (for STAT, an online publication about the life sciences); extremely online industrialist amplifies said analysis (or, at least, a tweet-size synopsis of it); and here I am, online, lodging my critique. What's not to like? Steven Levy, in *Wired*, recently wondered whether the coronavirus would "kill the techlash"—whether Americans under lockdown, convening on Zoom and stocking home bars via Drizly and socializing distantly on Instagram Live, would start to feel less indignant about our Silicon Valley overlords and more grateful for all the nifty apps they've bestowed on us. But one problem with the concept of the techlash is that it's always been about too many things at once: surveillance capitalism, anticompetitive practices, phone addiction, Mark Zuckerberg's uncanny-valley smile. It's possible to ameliorate one of these problems without broaching the others. Facebook can be the death knell of consumer privacy and also a fun place to share baby photos. Amazon can be a rapacious monopoly and also the most reliable way to get light bulbs in a time of crisis. Twitter can keep us informed (and anxious) about the pandemic, but this doesn't obviate concerns about its long-term effects on our public discourse.

After asserting that Ioannidis "is correct," Musk shared his reasoning: "growth rate of confirmed C19 cases is dropping every day," he tweeted, linking to a bar graph on a C.D.C. site that he thought corroborated this view. In another tweet, Musk predicted that there would be "close to zero new cases in US too by end of April." A Twitter user called Hopeful Pope of Muskanity, referring to Musk as "my liege," asked whether this would happen essentially by magic, in the absence of social distancing and other public-health measures. Musk replied, "Kids are essentially immune."

These claims are wrong, and dangerously so. Most children with *COVID*-19 do seem to experience milder symptoms than adults—but "most" is not "all," and, besides, a metascientist like Ioannidis would caution us against clinging too dogmatically to this preliminary finding, or to any finding, about what is still a novel virus. What we do know is that children can get infected with the virus, and can pass it on to others, which makes them, in the most relevant sense of the word, very much *not* immune. The C.D.C. bar graph that Musk linked to did seem to imply that cases were dropping—but only if you squinted at the graph without bothering to read the words hovering above it, in large type: "Illnesses that began during this time may not yet be reported." One portion of the graph, helpfully shaded gray, clarified that "this time" referred to the most recent stretch of six days—the very days in which cases appeared, misleadingly, to have gone down. As far as anyone can tell, and as dozens of less muddled bar graphs attest, American cases of *COVID*-19 are trending exponentially upward.

I don't mean to imply that Elon Musk is the main problem. There have always been tycoons and celebrities with bad opinions; if this crisis teaches us to pay less attention to them, at least during public-health emergencies, so much the better. And if Musk does end up helping to stave off a shortfall of ventilators, the people whose lives he saves will owe him an incalculable debt of gratitude, and will not particularly care about his shoddy reasoning. Still, Musk is a useful case study, because his combination of characteristics—blithe self-assurance, poor reading comprehension, a proclivity toward the contrarian and controversial, and an apparent willingness to spend ten minutes boning up on a new topic before explaining it to the world—are hardly unique. Rather, they are precisely the characteristics that make him, in a phrase that should only be used in scare quotes, "good at Twitter."

In 2018, Jack Dorsey, the C.E.O. of Twitter, vowed that the company would work to "increase the collective health, openness, and civility of public conversation." (Dorsey, unlike Paul Elie, does not seem to have brushed up on his Sontag recently; he uses the metaphor of "conversational health" almost as a mantra.) Since then, the company has made modest improvements. Harassment, threats, and bots are still rampant on the platform, although their proportions seem to have diminished. But, in this backlash-to-the-techlash moment, Twitter has been enjoying a rare bit of good press. The pandemic, Ben Smith argued in the *Times*, is showing that "Twitter, Facebook, YouTube and others can actually deliver on their old promise to democratize information and organize communities, and on their newer promise to drain the toxic information swamp." Dorsey, in a direct message to Smith, wrote, "Public conversation can help the world learn faster, solve problems better and realize we're all in this together."

In the run-up to the 2016 election, social media was more or less over-run by junk. In the current crisis, social-media companies have been more proactive about preventing the most overt liars and chaos agents—financial scammers, Russian spies, the President of the United States—from monopolizing their platforms. And yet this is where the distinction between disinformation and misinformation, which might normally seem pedantic, becomes relevant. Disinformation means intentional deception (for example, the false insinuation that the coronavirus was created in a Chinese lab). Misinformation is a broader category. Some of it is intentional; some of it isn't. When social-media executives are asked what they're doing to combat misinformation, they often respond by describing what they're doing to combat *dis*information, because disinformation lends itself to simpler, sharper answers. But most people who spread misinformation on social media are not Macedonian teen-agers hoping for a quick payday or Iranian spies trying to meddle in a foreign election. Most people spread misinformation because they are misinformed. This is a much broader problem, and the solution to it, if there is one, is far less obvious. In February, the World Health Organization took to Twitter to debunk a few urban legends ("there is no evidence from the current outbreak that eating garlic has protected people from 2019-nCoV"; "Sesame oil is delicious but it does not kill 2019-nCoV"). Earlier this month, Twitter announced that it would take down tweets containing "denial of established scientific facts about transmission ... such as '*COVID*-19 does not infect children because we haven't seen any cases of children being sick.'" But, when Elon Musk tweeted almost exactly these words, Twitter reviewed the tweet and decided that it "does not break our rules."

Some would argue that the solution here is simple: more aggressive enforcement. Find all the bad tweets and remove them; repeat until all the bad tweeters are gone. But this can't be the whole solution. Enforcement is necessary, but it's not sufficient. Banning the worst of the worst is a relatively easy call, but many of the less egregiously bad tweets—tweets that do not appear to violate any of the platform's rules but nonetheless sow unnecessary fear, or exacerbate distrust, or cause confusion regarding matters of life and death—come from people who are merely trying to be "good at Twitter." Social media was always designed to give us what we want, not what we need. For years, it has incentivized controversy, outrage, and half-baked contrarianism. Now its administrators are starting (inconsistently, half-heartedly) to punish some of the people who have correctly internalized those incentives. This is better than nothing, and it may be cause for one or two celebratory news cycles, but the problem is too systemic to be reversed overnight. A bad tweet, morally speaking, is often a good tweet, judging strictly by the numbers. We will not wake up tomorrow and find that all the bad tweets are gone. In the short term, at least, all we can do is flatten the curve.

INTERESTED IN LEARNING MORE?

Book Recommendations

Celeste Headlee, *Do Nothing: How to Break Away from Overworking, Overdoing, and Underliving* (Harmony, Random House, 2020).

Jaron Lanier, *Ten Arguments for Deleting Your Social Media Accounts Right Now* (Henry Holt, 2018).

David Patrikarakos, *War in 140 Characters: How Social Media is Reshaping Conflict in the Twenty-First Century* (Basic Books, 2017).

Nancy Jo Sales, *American Girls: Social Media and the Secret Lives of Teenagers* (Knopf, 2016).

P.W. Singer and Emerson T. Brooking, *Like War: The Weaponization of Social Media* (Eamon Dolan/Houghton Mifflin Harcourt, 2018).

Tom Standage, *The Victorian Internet* (Walker & Company, 1998).

———. *Writing on the Wall: Social Media—The First 2,000 Years* (Bloomsbury, 2013).

Siva Vaidhyanathan, *Anti-Social Media: How Facebook Disconnects Us and Undermines Democracy* (Oxford UP, 2018).

Film Recommendations

The Social Dilemma, directed by Jeff Orlowsky (Argent, 2020).

The Social Network, directed by David Fincher (Columbia, 2010). [Narrative film about Facebook's origin]

Chapter Sixteen

Writes/Rites of Passage

> *It is not my deeds I write down, it is myself, my essence.*
> —Michel de Montaigne (1595)

Before writing, rites of passage, such as birth, adulthood, and death, were carried out in ceremonies that marked these life-phase transitions. Oral traditions created memorized histories, genealogies, and folk wisdom. Dances and chants also conveyed these important cultural messages. Elders carried these stories with them, passing them through generations. Although cultures vary in emphasis on these transitions, anthropologists have noted typical life phases that include birth, naming, first haircut, school, adolescence, adulthood, marriage, parenthood, and death (Grove and Lancy).

Some cultures continue traditions without relying on writing. In Indonesia, the Toraja Culture had no written script with their language, and that absence continues to show in their rituals, particularly with death. When I visited Sulawesi some years ago, it was to have a look at these fascinating death rituals. We began with baby graves, in which a child who has not yet started teething but dies is wrapped in cloth and placed in a hollowed out space of a tree and then covered with palm basketry. A single tree may house several of these infant graves. Most likely there has been no naming of these children, which would be delayed until the child was older when the family was assured of its longevity. The babies are believed to become part of the tree itself, contributing to its essence.

We also attended a funeral in a village some miles from paved roads. The elderly woman had been "sick" for over a year—actually dead and remaining in her room embalmed and waiting for the family to accumulate enough wealth to hold the funeral ceremony. Only then is the person declared dead. Platforms had been built to accommodate the large group that came to celebrate the passing of the grandmother. Water buffalo and pigs were slaughtered just behind us to provide the feast. At the end of several days, the body is placed to rest in a cave on a cliff, and a carved wooden effigy in the person's likeness is installed on a balcony to watch over the grave. Annually, the bodies of deceased are exhumed by relatives, washed, and outfitted in new clothes. Rather than writing, beautiful woodcarving is a hallmark of Torajan culture. Death is a valued rite in this society, but writing is not necessarily associated with it.

Not far from Sulawesi is Bali, another island of Indonesia. In contrast to the Torajan culture, Bali draws its language and writing system from India, which makes sense as the primary religion is Hinduism. The script is syllabic, and originally it was derived from the Brahmi writing system, although writing in Bali today uses the Latin alphabet. Funerals in Bali use the sacred texts of Hinduism. Two different cultures, yet geographically not that distant. Rites of passage can look different in diverse cultures, and writing may or may not play a role.

WRITING, CULTURE, AND PRESERVATION

Writing overcomes time and distance. It is the rare person today who can recite Homer's *Odyssey*. The transition between oral tradition and written documentation may be most clearly seen in David Malo's work *Hawaiian Antiquities* (1835–36). When Christian missionaries arrived in Hawaii in 1823, the nation did not have a written language, but a mere 40 years later, its people were the most literate in the world, resulting in Hawaiians such as David Malo recording cultural practices. In the introduction to the book, Malo noted that traditions were not definite, as "the ancients were not possessed of the art of letters.... Memory was the only means possessed by our ancestors of preserving historical knowledge; it served them in place of books and chronicles" (19). Sarah Vowell, a popular NPR essayist and author, in her entertaining book *Unfamiliar Fishes*, details the traditions and practices Malo recorded once he did have a written language. In this book, he

> details the impressive variety of fish hooks; burial practices; the codes
> and rituals of the ruling class; the names of a long list of gods, dif-

ferentiating the god worshipped by robbers from the god worshipped by thieves; birth rituals; the kapu system; hula, sports, and games; chants and genealogies; how (and why) to build a house; fascinating and poetic delineations of time and phases of the moon.... (133)

The transition of life phases in contemporary, Western civilizations is marked by multiple documents, beginning with a birth certificate. The practice of certifying a person's birth is both very old and also recent. The original documentarian—a physician or midwife—generally had delivered the baby. In earlier times, births were registered at the community church, and the same was true for other rites of passage such as christenings. In England, Somerset House was the center for birth, marriage, and death certificates beginning in 1837. British mysteries sometimes included a visit to this storehouse of vital records to unravel family connections and solve a murder. "Aha!" the detective might reveal. "We now know that Miss Talbot actually was Mrs. Fotheringham, a relationship she needed to hide in order to marry the wealthy Lord Taylor."

The secular purpose of this "write of passage" (note the intentional pun!) is to integrate the person into the social and legal fabric of a nation or community. It is used for taxation, voting, military service, marriage, and benefits. It is tied to nationality and parentage. Birth certificates can also be contested documents, particularly when the biological sex assigned at birth does not match sexual identification.

In the United States, birth certificates did not gain universal application until World War II, when nationality was important for employment in defense companies. There are two reasons for this record being so late in taking hold: one is that births did not always take place in a hospital, as they could just as likely be in the home; and child mortality was still quite high.

Not having a birth certificate results in barriers to other rites of passage. Tara Westover, in the nonfiction account of her life growing up in a survivalist family in southeastern Idaho, *Educated*, begins with this memory. At seven, she did not exist. She didn't know it at the time, but according to the government, she actually didn't exist. She had no birth certificate or social security number, no piece of paper or database to prove she did exist. So in reality, according to Idaho and the US Government, no seven year-old Tara Westover. The same was true of four of the seven children in the home. When Tara needs to get a birth certificate, a delayed certificate, at nine or ten, her parents are not actually sure of her birthdate. Later, when she needs a passport, she is unable to have one issued, as she cannot confirm her birthdate, and the government cannot issue one without some verification she is really Tara or that a Tara was ever born. The story has a somewhat happy ending. Westover home-schools herself, achieves a college degree, and studies at Oxford. The enthralling account of her life is a bestseller.

Writing during the lifespan may be enacted by the person or enacted on the person. In fact, writing about an individual may occur well before birth. Gender-reveal parties, which became popular in the 2010s, could rely on writing a scavenger hunt, riddles, trivia game, or cards. As a result, before a child writes, family members may write on the person's behalf—sometimes taking it to an extreme. In the "Cherubs" section of David Lancy's *The Anthropology of Childhood*, he recounts the story of the mother who "kept a daily diary" when pregnant to "relate to and communicate with her fetus" (77). She then went on to quit her job when her daughter was born in order to devote herself to scrapbooking the child's life. Obviously qualifying for Lancy's classification of *cherub*, the toddler is memorialized in an average of five volumes per year, the mother devoting 50 hours weekly and thousands of dollars to the task.

SCHOOL

Once a child enters school, or perhaps prior to that depending on the family circumstances, "reading, 'riting, and 'rithmetic"—the three R's—form the nucleus of the curriculum. The language arts include writing, reading, speaking, and listening and are foundational to learning. A popular philosophy is that first children learn to write and read and then they learn through writing and reading. "Writing to learn" is a catchphrase that continues through collegiate education and forms one of the cornerstones of the writing-across-the-curriculum and writing-in-the-disciplines movement. Emergent literacy is a major area of research in Writing Studies.

The importance of school was driven home in my own life when I received a diploma certifying that I had "satisfactorily completed the first day of School" (see Figure 16.1). Note that school is capitalized, signifying its importance. The document anticipates "twelve pleasant and profitable years in public school," followed by "graduation from high school and admission to college." This was forward thinking for 1960. Even when I graduated from high school, I was one of only a few classmates who pursued a college education.

School writing so completely dominates young people's lives that it may be difficult at times to equate writing with anything but school. There are worksheets, book reports, journals, essays, research papers, quizzes, and speeches and perhaps work on a student newspaper or yearbook (print or digital). The extracurricular writing that students undertake is most likely

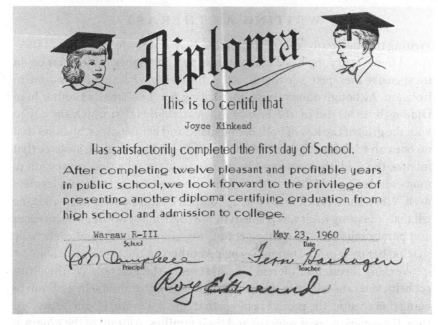

Figure 16.1   Diploma for First Day of School, 1960. Author's personal collection.

more expansive, including various forms of social media, job and college applications, and personal correspondence.

As with the injunction to "read 20 minutes a day" with your child to follow the adage that "reading is FUNdamental," writing consistently is another pathway to success. Families may augment the school curriculum with at-home writing tasks. One family I know asked their son to author three letters to the editor of the local newspaper over the year to practice researching and arguing for a particular issue or stance. Other families may invest in writing helpers such as "My Little Journal of Gratitude." Children may write their "3 positive words to describe my day" or respond to this prompt: "Today, I'm most grateful for...." Part of an approach to focus on positive aspects of lives, gratitude journals name specific people, things, or events for which a person is thankful. According to a Berkeley blog from its Greater Good site, "Writing helps to organize thoughts, facilitate integration, and helps you accept your own experiences and put them in context.... [I]t allows you to see the meaning of events going on around you and create meaning in your own life" (Marsh).

WRITING AS THERAPY

Writing through pain, loss, or depression is an acknowledged form of therapy. Almost everyone has a computer or pen and paper, which can be an inexpensive therapist. Writing is, after all, a personal act generally done in isolation. Although often private, the writing may be shared, as author Joan Didion (b. 1934) did in *The Year of Magical Thinking*, in which she coped with the grief of the loss of both her husband and her daughter. She says that no one can truly anticipate grief and its effects, "the unending absence that follows, the void, the very opposite of meaning, the relentless succession of moments during which we will confront the experience of meaninglessness itself" (189). She wrote to "make sense" of their deaths because as a writer she felt that "meaning itself was resident in the rhythms of words and sentences and paragraphs" (7). In writing about, working through, and eventually sharing her own grief, Didion has helped others in the same situation.

Working through a different kind of trauma, the Veterans Writing Project helps veterans tell their stories through writing seminars. In addition to being therapeutic, the project believes that "great literature" can be derived from the experiences of veterans and their families. Alumni of the program note that they have written themselves "out of a very dark place" and that writing "allows us to shape and control traumatic memories" (Brennan and Shaw). The Greek word *catharsis* means cleansing, releasing, or purifying. Aristotle wrote that art—in his specific case, theatre, through emotion on stage—helped viewers renew and restore themselves. Writing literary pieces or journals can help with this renewal and restoration, too. Some therapy approaches ask writers to focus on positive experiences to re-channel the focus of their lives from the negative or traumatic, while others advise meeting the negative experiences head on. Writing has the potential to allow a person to vent, organize ideas, or refocus from negative to positive. No matter the approach, the product encourages getting thoughts on paper or screen and then reflecting on those ideas, thoughts, and words. Writing as therapy may not be effective across the board for all people, however, and professional guidance may be warranted.

Bullet journals are a special type of planner that may be used for mental and emotional health or simply to be more organized and reflective. The "BuJo" is grounded in the concept of bulleted lists. A "to do" list includes one bullet point for each item. Bulleted lists achieved popularity with word processing when it became easy for writers to insert lists—numbered or "bulleted" with typographical symbol that can vary in shape (e.g., arrow, square, circle). The Bullet Journal Method outlined by Ryder Carroll will "Track the Past, Order the Present, and Design the Future."

LIFESPAN WRITING

Writing follows people through their entire lives, from learning to write to being documented as individuals. Writing is deeply personal and individual. Much attention is given to school writing, but much less so to writing across the decades of people's lives. An international initiative that aims to collect a century's worth of research on lifespan writing was formed in 2016 with the lead of Professor Charles Bazerman. Called the *Writing through the Lifespan Collaboration*, the group includes scholars from around the world. The scholars and researchers hope to "develop a robust, multidimensional understanding of how writing develops from cradle to grave." The scholars themselves range in age, so many of them will not be around to see if the project is successful. Ryan Dippre has developed a methodology and conducted case studies of writers across a range of ages to examine how "literate action" develops over a lifetime. After all, learning to write is a lifelong journey.

For adults, finding a life partner can be an important rite of passage. A traditional wedding ceremony may be quite brief, but if the pair chooses to author their own vows, then that can be a writing assignment fraught with both anxiety and joy. Jewish couples may opt for a formal *Ketubah*, often a lavishly decorated and scripted commitment document that can be framed for display in the home. Artists offer customized designs online so that couples can choose a design and review sample scripts. It may include an introductory paragraph, main text (with option for secular or sacred), poetry, and signature lines for the rabbi, couple, and two witnesses.[1] The document itself can be printed on various papers, including Japanese Washi, bookcloth, cotton, or papercut. Importantly, the historical function of the Ketubah is to enumerate the rights and responsibilities of the groom in order to protect the wife. An earlier format served to seal the "bride price" or dowry to be paid to the parents of the bride. As with other matrimonial documents, the contemporary version has evolved, but its presence in the home reminds couples of their vows and commitment to one another.

In Christian religion, marriage banns, the public announcement of a couple's impending wedding, served to ensure that the marriage would be valid, that no other spouses existed, and that consanguinity (close kinship) was not an issue. This medieval practice served as the initial contract, followed by a marriage license. In this practice, the couple did not compose any text but relied on the religious leader, a priest or minister, to provide

---

1 Source information from Sonia Lancy Bui as well as Jennifer Raichman, artist, at https://www.jenniferraichman.com/.

the public announcement orally and in writing. In contemporary societies, engagement announcements are more likely to be made through social media. This functions as a way to make public a couple's impending marriage but also can serve to gather names and addresses for formal invitations, more necessary for a mobile population that may not be easily tracked through traditional venues.

Divorce decrees have their roots in ancient cultures. Biblical information about divorce occurs in Deuteronomy and notes that the husband must write a certificate of divorce (24: 1–4). A Sumerian husband would use formulaic pronouncements: "You are not my wife." He then cut her garment to show that they were severed, but he also gave her money. It was important that the act be documented in writing. In contemporary dissolutions of marriage, two documents exist: a divorce certificate issued by the state for record keeping and a divorce decree that lays out division of property and, if needed, child custody and support. Unlike with weddings, generally no self-authored text exists, although mutually agreed-upon decisions may bypass legal assistance and draw on templates.

Death has been marked by writing for millennia. In the Old Kingdom of Egypt during the 5th Dynasty (2465–2323 BCE), a pyramid at Saqqara constructed for the pharaoh Unis includes what are known as Pyramid Texts. These formulas carved in the wall detail how a funeral is to be conducted and also include the worship of Osiris, god of death. They later became standard for inscribing on coffins. Epitaphs are short texts that honor the deceased, often placed on tombstones, just like the Pyramid Texts. Edgar Lee Masters's *Spoon River Anthology* from 1916 tells semi-fictional accounts of the former residents of an Illinois small town through epitaphs. Although a commercial and critical success, the book of verse was criticized by townspeople who were the unwitting models for the caricatures. Here's one of the over 200 poems characterizing townspeople of Spoon River, a woman who was abused by her husband, Fletcher McGee. His epitaph and answer to her accusation appears later in the anthology

Ollie McGee

Have you seen walking through the village
A Man with downcast eyes and haggard face?
That is my husband who, by secret cruelty
Never to be told, robbed me of my youth and my beauty
Till at last, wrinkled and with yellow teeth,
And with broken pride and shameful humility,

I sank into the grave.
But what think you gnaws at my husband's heart?
The face of what I was, the face of what he made me!
These are driving him to the place where I lie.
In death, therefore, I am avenged.

Folklorists find that real tombstones speak volumes. The stones may record simple life records of birth and death dates and relationships, but some go beyond to leave a definite impression of the life lived. These are, quite literally, concrete examples of culture (see Meyer). Local cemeteries contain notable examples of personalized epitaphs.

From a cowboy, Russell J. Larsen (Logan City Cemetery):

Two things I love most, good horses and beautiful women, and when I die, I hope they tan this old hide of mine and make it into a ladies riding saddle, so I can rest in peace between the two things I love most.

For a pioneer, Mary Jane McCune (1838–55, Cedar City Cemetery):

Bitten by rabid coyote, developed rabies, became violent, was smothered with feather bed when husband returned. She and her unborn child were dead and buried.

Kathryn Kirkham Andrews's grave marker features a recipe:

Kay's Fudge
2 Sq. chocolate
2 Tbs. butter
Melt in low heat
Stir in
1 cup milk
Bring to boil
3 cups sugar
1 Tbs. vanilla
Pinch salt
Cook to softball stage
Pour on marble slab
Cool & Beat & Eat

Wherever she goes, there's laughter.

Andrews lived from 1922 to 2019 and engraved her recipe three years prior to her death. As with other unique tombstone texts, it shows up on social media and Pinterest, perhaps more long-lasting than the formal obituary.

Cradle-to-grave writing encompasses many, many genres and kinds of writing. The following list gives a hint of just how varied writing forms and formats can be.

application (e.g., job, college, grant)
bad news letter or memo
blog—personal, corporate, etc.
book cover or dust jacket
business card
campaign speech
CD or DVD collection (e.g., the items in the collection—playlist)
census report
chart, diagram, or graph
claims letter
classified ad (e.g., personal, want ad)
collections letter
congratulatory letter
contract
cookbook or recipe collection
declaration
dialogue
diary entry
directory (e.g., staff, telephone, member)
divorce decree
editorial column
email message—personal, customer service, interoffice, etc.
eulogy
eyewitness account
government document
feature article
flyer, pamphlet, or brochure
friendly/personal letter
fund-raising letter
good news letter or memo
government report
grave marker/tombstone
greeting card—birthday, holiday, condolence, thank you, etc.
grocery list
homepage on a website

hospital chart
IM or chat room transcript
interview or interview transcript
letter
letter of recommendation
letter or memo of introduction
log entry
love letter
meeting transcript
memo—departmental or interoffice
memoir
memo of understanding
menu
newsgroup posting or thread
newspaper ad (e.g., full to partial page ad for businesses, etc.)
notebook
obituary
online bulletin board posting or thread
online forum posting
online profile (such as on social media or an app)
online shopping (e.g., eBay) listing
pamphlet
performance appraisal
personal commentary
personal interest article (as in newspapers, magazines, etc.)
photo gallery/album
photograph with caption, keywords/tags, and/or descriptions
police report—CSI-style, coroner's, etc.
postcard
press release
proposal
quiz
ransom note
recipe
religious ceremonies
report card
resignation letter or memo
resume
scrapbook
social worker's report
sports score and story

survival kit
text message
thank you letter, memo, or note
timeline
trading card
transcript of phone call, conversation
trip report
T-shirt message
vlog
video or computer game vignette
voice mail message
wanted poster
web page—personal, corporate, organization, educational
wedding vows
wiki or wiki entry
will
yearbook—spread on student life

Our lives tend to be fully documented. What documents do you keep, treasure, or discard?

QUESTIONS TO CONSIDER

1. The list of types of writing across the lifespan is not complete. What would you add?
2. Which items on this list have you written?
3. Nelson Mandela (1918–2015) said, "A good head and good heart are always a formidable combination. But when you add to that a literate tongue or pen, then you have something very special." Have you considered an epitaph for a tombstone or a phrase or words by which you would like to be remembered?
4. What documents of your early years exist? Are there archives from your school writing? What might you learn by reviewing these texts?

DO-IT-YOURSELF HANDS-ON ACTIVITY

The autoethnography is one genre. What might this piece look like in another format? One possibility is a book, and in this case, perhaps a mini-accordion book. A handmade book can provide a keepsake while it offers also the opportunity to re-think the content of the autoethnography into a shorter, more visual format.

Alisa Golden offers 100+ ways to create your own book in her *Making Handmade Books*, which integrates the accordion format. An accordion book can be as simple or as complex as you desire. Here are some ideas for design.

- Insert printed pages in the accordion book
- Use calligraphy to write on the pages
- Illustrate with pictures or art
- Adapt into a Tabbed Accordion format
- Add poetry
- Include a family tree
- Integrate "rites of passage" documents
- Add ribbon or bookmark
- Add a pocket to hold an item
- Make cut-outs to see through pages
- Add "signatures" (additional pages) to the book
- Using two accordion books, make a back-to-back accordion book (option: with tunnels)
- Use a Circle Accordion format
- Add a closure to secure the book
- Make a box for your accordion book

INVITATION TO REFLECT AND WRITE

1. At the end of Chapter One of this book, you were invited to compose an autoethnography about your writing history, processes, identity, and material culture. Through reading this book, you have also been invited to write short essays about various topics such as writing and work or social media. At this point, review all of these texts and integrate them into a formal autoethnography worthy of standing as a chronicle of your development and identity as a writer up to this point. Take a broad view. Consider that this will be placed in an archive or your own time capsule to be looked back upon in the years to follow. Illustrate, if feasible, with artifacts or photographs of writing moments. Note important rites of passage in which writing played a part. That might be a driver's license, a passport application, a voter registration ID, or a certificate. You might end by reflecting on what the future holds for you in terms of writes/rites of passage.
2. Steve Martin, comic, actor, writer, and banjo player, says, "The real joy is in constructing a sentence. But I see myself as an actor first because writing is what you do when you are ready and acting is what you do

when someone else is ready." What makes you joyful about writing? What is its place in your life?

FOR FURTHER READING

The *New York Times* developed a special section devoted to "Love." In this column, Lois Smith Brady offers advice for those considering authoring their own vows to avoid pitfalls.

Lois Smith Brady, "Before Saying 'I Do,' Define Just What You Mean"

Writing your own vows, Lois Kellerman says, is like making homemade cookies.

"If you can find the right ingredients, the right words in the case of vows, it is almost always better," said Ms. Kellerman, a former leader of the Brooklyn Society for Ethical Culture who has officiated at hundreds of weddings.

Many brides and grooms are choosing to say vows they have written themselves, whether marrying in a meadow or a cathedral. Writing your own vows, then standing up and saying them in front of a crowd definitely heightens the emotions at a wedding ceremony.

"Some couples have stage fright and don't want to get up there and bare it all in public, possibly crying, just being a mess," said Rachael Hofmann, a wedding planner in Boulder, Colo. "It's tough to get that emotional publicly."

But homemade vows can add much to the ceremony. "I think a lot of people overlook the fact that the ceremony should be really lovely and heartfelt," said Amanda Kingloff, 38, a writer who lives in Brooklyn and who wrote her vows for her marriage to Michael Cohen in Garrison, N.Y., in May 2009. "They think more about, 'Should I be serving fish or chicken?' "

"I wanted my vows to be a creative spin on who we are," Ms. Kingloff said. By the time they wed, she and Mr. Cohen, now 42, had lived together two years. Her vows read more like a short story about how, once they started dating seriously, her furniture and various collections had merged with Mr. Cohen's, a metaphor for how their lives had joined.

She made just a few promises in her vows. "I didn't need to say, 'I vow to honor and cherish you' because we already cherished each other," she said. "It seemed obvious."

Brides and grooms began writing their own vows in the mid-19th century, according to Elizabeth Abbott, who has written several books about

WRITES/RITES OF PASSAGE 365

marriage. American feminists and the like-minded men they married were among the first to reword traditional vows.

"They wrote vows together to express a common view of marriage," Ms. Abbott said. "They thought about it really carefully because it was quite radical at the time, whereas today, I would say, it's very personal."

In the 1960s and 1970s, couples often wrote their own vows as a way of rebelling against their parents' marriages, which many brides and grooms then viewed as unequal, unexamined and uncool.

"My first wedding, I performed in 1975 in Santa Barbara," said the Rev. Roger Fritts, who wrote "For as Long as We Both Shall Live," a guide to creating your own vows and ceremonies and who is now the pastor of the Unitarian Universalist Church in Sarasota, Fla. "That summer, I did 27 weddings, and almost all of the couples wanted to write their own vows."

Today's homemade vows rarely aim to change society, but they can be remarkably personal and idiosyncratic. Brides and grooms promise to honor and cherish things like each other's sense of humor, movie preferences, shopping sprees, long work hours, a love of swimming in cold water or of driving old Volkswagens.

"The best vows I've ever heard were at a wedding I thought was just a party, and it ended up being: 'Surprise! We're getting married right here on the spot,'" said Kate Lacroix, 39. She recalls how the groom said, "'I promise I'll never forget your number again'—and he recited her phone number—'and I now know exactly what you like in a Chipotle burrito.'"

Ms. Abbott said couples today place great importance on these kinds of highly personal, carefully crafted vows. "It's a talisman against the misfortunes of marriage," she said.

On the Weddingbee blog, couples share and discuss one another's homemade vows-in-progress. One bride posted vows there that included the lines: "I promise to be corny every chance that I get and to ask you to dance whenever I can. I also promise to laugh and agree with you when you tell me I can't dance."

Also, writing your own vows is in the 'my life is your life' spirit of Facebook, Twitter and reality shows about marriage. "This is just one other way we've broken down the walls and are allowing people to see our humanity," said Ms. Lacroix, who married Joel Barnard on June 29 with homemade vows, in their backyard in Boulder. When composing her vows, Ms. Lacroix did not seek inspiration in novels, poems, wedding books or wedding blogs. The point was to avoid a template. Instead, she relied on a diary she and Mr. Barnard, now 42, had kept together, along with the e-mails and texts they had sent to each other since meeting online.

He began his vows this way: "I, Joel Barnard, am the luckiest man alive. Who would have guessed a few clicks of a mouse could have led me to you? A woman so fascinating, so brilliant, so hilarious, so loving, so utterly bizarre at times."

Ms. Lacroix said she had organized her vows into two sections: How I Knew I Wanted to Marry You, and Here Are My Promises to You. Among those promises: "I vow to at least attempt to stop putting paper towels into the recycling bin, even though it's confusing because of the word 'paper,'" and "I vow to see what the relationship needs and to look deeper than my self-interests."

She avoided anything that resembled pillow talk, that rhymed or that was too precious or poetic. "A marriage is about the day-in-and-day-out workings," she said, something many wedding officiants advise couples to keep in mind when coming up with their vows. "It's not florid and lofty and remarkably romantic. It's 'Hey, Babe, it's your turn to empty the dishwasher.'"

Mr. Fritts even suggested sitting down at the kitchen table to write them. "So many vows have grandiose promises in them, but at the kitchen table, you're more likely to be down to earth, practical, modest," he said.

Ms. Kellerman, an author of "Marriage From the Heart," a book about how to build a healthy and enlightened marriage, encouraged couples to write vows together and to polish them like silver.

"For vows to work properly, they have to be carefully reviewed, discussed, pulled apart, put together again until an 'aha' moment arrives when the couple feels the rightness of what they'll be saying together," she said.

The Rev. Calvin O. Butts, pastor of Abyssinian Baptist Church in Harlem, advised couples to keep the vows succinct, about three minutes each, and to memorize them. "I would like it if they didn't have to pull out a little funky piece of paper or reach down in their bosom," he said.

Ms. Kellerman also said couples must be willing to work hard and dig deep to write strong homemade vows. "If you are not really engaged and just going through the process, it will backfire," she said. "If you have a lot of stress, it's not worth it. I love some of the traditional vows. If you've been married long enough, like me, you're real happy about 'in sickness and in health.'"

Homemade vows are still serious lifelong promises. "These are incredible things people are promising," Mr. Fritts said. "They're saying: 'Look, if we have a child born with a chronic disease, I'm going to be there. If you get hit by a car and you're crippled and in a wheelchair, I'm not going to leave you.'"

Some couples find the words for their vows from movies or television shows like "Girls." (In one episode, the character Marnie said to her boyfriend: "I want to have your babies. I want to watch you die." That would be a wedding vow that would pretty much say it all, in two short sentences.)

Mr. Barnard, who also vowed to help search for Ms. Lacroix's cellphone whenever she loses it (which is often), plans to frame his vows and hang them on the wall above his desk.

"It's easy to forget about them and let them drift off into the ether," he said. "I think it's really important to stay aware of them and keep yourself in check."

Questions

1. In the comments section, one response focused on avoiding "vapid and specious" vows and aiming for "transformative." How could writers of vows achieve meaningful prose or poetry?
2. Another comment noted that same-sex couples have been writing vows for some time, even prior to changes in laws. The author feels that an "outsider" perspective can contribute additional meaning. Weddings occur between a variety of couples, not just of traditional age or match. Can you think of non-traditional ceremonies that were noteworthy?
3. Another comment expresses relief that the Episcopalian faith has a standard ceremony in its *Book of Common Prayer*. Why would some attendees prefer a traditional ceremony?
4. If you are married, did you author vows? Why or why not? If you are not married but anticipate marriage at some point, what do you think you will do in terms of vows?

INTERESTED IN LEARNING MORE?

Book Recommendations

The following are general histories of writing. As mentioned in the Preface, the history of writing and its material culture is encyclopedic. This volume is only an introduction to the fascinating stories that lie behind the history of our everyday activity.

Ewan Clayton, ed., *Writing: Making Your Mark*. [This is the catalog of a wonderful exhibition hosted at the British Library in 2019.]
——. *The Golden Thread: The Story of Writing* (Counterpoint, 2014).
Henri-Jean Martin, *The History and Power of Writing* (University of Chicago Press, 1994). [translated from French]
Martin Puchner, *The Written World: The Power of Stories to Shape People, History, and Civilization* (Random House, 2017).

Glossary

addendum: In the parts of a book, the addendum comes at the end and may include an explanation or commentary.

alphabet: A set of letters or symbols that represent the basis for a writing system. Alpha and beta are the first two letters of the Greek alphabet.

appendix: Additional material that supports the primary text of a book and may provide foundational information that is not necessary to include in the body, such as surveys, documents, or other evidence.

ascenders: Letters of the alphabet that have stems that rise above the line such as b, d, and k; also the name of the vertical stems themselves.

asemic writing: Writing that is not semantic, thus having no meaning, popularized particularly in the twenty-first century.

bamboo: Strips of this wood were used as a writing material, particularly in ancient China.

bark paper, tapa: Before paper, various materials were used as a type of proto-paper, including bark from trees, particularly in Asia and South America, which were beaten to make a surface material for writing.

binding: For the contents of books to be safe from wear and tear, covers or boards enclosed the pages. After a book was printed, a bookbinder enclosed the text, sewing the pages together and securing them to the stable boards and a backbone. This process created the book as opposed to a scroll.

book arts: The process of producing a book in the early days integrated various artisans: printers, illustrators, bookbinders, and artists. In a return to carefully crafted products, book arts focuses on quality rather than mass production, resulting in lovingly created volumes.

Book of the Dead: In ancient Egypt, funerary texts were written to honor the dead and were lavishly detailed and written. Their existence reveals much about the civilization.

Braille: Named after its innovator, Louis Braille, this tactile system of embossed dots allowed the visually impaired to read and write.

calligraphy: The art of beautiful handwriting.

chained book: In the Middle Ages, books were so rare and valued that they might be chained to a library or lectern to avoid theft.

chapter: A division of a book, used beginning in the thirteenth century.

clay tablets: A very early writing medium in the ancient Near East, particularly for impressing cuneiform. Wet clay tablets were written on with a stylus and then dried to form a permanent record. They are important artifacts in the evolution of writing.

codex (pl. codices): The early form of books, handwritten on parchment, paper, or another material and bound together, typically with a single copy made.

colophon: The "finishing touch" or the "last word" of a book or manuscript that includes information on the printer (with the printer's symbol), date of publication, place of printing, typeface, the edition, the number of copies for a limited run. Before the standardization of the title page, the author's name might also appear on the colophon. With increased interest in book arts and letterpress printing, the colophon is making a reappearance.

cuneiform: Wedge-shaped writing originating in Mesopotamia as one of the earliest systems of writing.

dauber: An ink ball used to distribute ink onto the typeface for printing.

demotic script: In ancient Egypt, hieroglyphics was the original writing system, but in order to write more efficiently, scribes developed first hieratic script and then demotic, the latter used for common documents.

descenders: Letters of the alphabet that have stems that descend below the line such as g, j, and y; also the name of the vertical stems themselves.

dictionary: A reference book that lists words alphabetically (usually, although not in the case of ideograms) with their spelling, pronunciation, origin, meanings, and uses. Famous dictionaries for the English language include Dr. Samuel Johnson's in England in 1755 and Noah Webster's in 1828, the latter being the first standard dictionary for American usage. *The Oxford English Dictionary* (OED), a comprehensive work, began appearing in 1884 (Simon Winchester's 1998 book *The Professor and the Madman*, and the subsequent 2019 film, provide a fascinating look at its history).

dip pen or nib pen: This pen has no ink reservoir (which a fountain pen does) and has to be dipped in ink frequently to recharge the metal tip.

Doves Press: Late-nineteenth- and early-twentieth-century printing company in Hammersmith, London, renowned for its typeface design.

dwarsligger: Popularized in the Netherlands, a small, portable book with very thin pages and printing aligned with the spine.

em dash (—): The width of a capital M, the em dash is used to set off a part of the sentence more effectively than with commas.

en dash (–): The width of a capital N, the en dash is used with a range of numbers or pages.

epigraph: A short quotation at the beginning of an article, chapter, or book that has relevance to the text to come. Its origin is the Greek *graphein*, "to write."

eraser: An implement to remove writing marks, particularly pencil, with a rubber material, or chalk with a cloth.

ex libris: Latin phrase for "from the books or library," found on the bookplate inside a book and denoting its owner. As books were expensive and precious to their owners in the early days of printing, bookplates could incorporate family coats of arms and then evolved into decorative, artistic miniature prints.

ferrule: The metal connector that attaches an eraser to a pencil shaft.

flyleaf: The free (not printed) pages at the front and end of a book; endpapers are pasted to the inside of the front and back covers.

folding books: An artistic approach to using an existing book to fold its pages in aesthetic designs.

folio: A sheet of paper folded in half for printing, also meaning a leaf, from the Latin folium. In contrast, a quarto is a sheet of paper folded in fours.

font: The size, weight, and style of a typeface.

fountain pen: A writing implement with a reservoir or cartridge for ink that flows to the nib.

furniture: Wooden blocks of various sizes that secure the form to the printing press so that it is tight and will not move when printing begins.

galley: The form in which the type is set for printing that allows a page to be printed for proofreading.

glyph: A symbol that shows a pictogram or ideogram (e.g., Mayan) or the smallest element of a typeface such as "a" in whatever form its design appears.

gold leaf: Hammered gold applied to illuminated manuscripts in particular to highlight religious or heroic figures, popularized in the Middle Ages.

Gothic script/type: An embellished handwriting or typeface popular from 1150 to 1600 in Europe, it was replaced by simpler, more accessible script or typeface but is still used in calligraphy.

graphite: The mineral that forms the core of a pencil, so named by a German geologist for its use in writing, derived from the Greek word *graphein*, "to write." Originally called plumbago.

gutter: In a book, the trough between the inner margins of the pages.

Helvetica: One of the most widely used typefaces, developed in 1957 as a sans serif design by Max Miedinger of Switzerland.

hieratic script: A cursive form of Egyptian hieroglyphics that was simpler and more efficient for writing but more formal than demotic script.

hieroglyphs: Ancient Egypt developed its writing system based on pictures that could also represent sounds. They were the system designated for royal and spiritual uses in particular.

hornbook: Handheld wooden slate with educational elements for a child's education such as the alphabet, phonics, numbers, and a religious text such as the Lord's Prayer on a page covered by transparent horn to protect the text. A handle may have had a hole for a carrying strap. Popular in schools in England and colonial America.

ideograms: These evolved from pictograms, more realistic representations of items or concepts, and represented more abstract ideas.

illuminated manuscripts: a book with decorations in the margins, borders, and around initial letters of a section, particularly in the Middle Ages.

incunabula: Books produced prior to Gutenberg and movable type, typically before 1501, the origin of the printed book.

ink: Fluid used for writing.

interrobang: A question mark superimposed on an exclamation point, popularized in the 1960s.

irony punctuation: Marks that denote sarcasm or irony.

italics: Developed in Italy (hence the name), a cursive style font that looks like handwriting and is used in English for specially designated purposes such as the title of a book.

Jikji: Korean word for a much longer title of Buddhist writing.

kerning: The adjustment of spaces between letters in typography.

keyboard: A set of keys that are initiated by hand to input letters on a typewriter or computer. The QWERTY keyboard is the standard for English language users.

leaf: A sheet of paper, which has two pages, the first being the verso page and the opposite the recto page.

letterpress: Originated by Gutenberg, the typeface is locked into a form, inked, and then pressed upon the material (e.g., paper, vellum). It was replaced by other, more efficient forms of printing (e.g., offset) but has seen a resurgence in fine printing initiatives.

lexigram: Symbols or figures that represent words, a type of alphabet or communication system.

ligatures: The combining of two or more letters or graphemes into a single glyph for efficiency in printing: e.g., æ, fl, §. As a result, a case of type includes many more sections than just the 26 letters of the alphabet (upper and lower case) when ligatures are included.

linotype: An entire line of type can be produced through hot metal typesetting machinery, negating the need for a "composer" to arrange type letter by letter.

logogram, logograph: A written character to represent a word or phrase, particularly used in Asian characters.

majuscule: Script written in all capital letters.

material culture: The physical objects that contribute to human activity, including implements, tools, buildings, written records, and clothing. In the case of writing, implements and artifacts that are associated with the act of writing.

matrices: In making type, the metal recipient of the punch that forms the letter or symbol in the type.

Mesopotamia: The name means between two rivers (Greek etymology) and represented the area between the Tigris and Euphrates rivers in what is now Iraq. This ancient civilization in southwest Asia included important historic sites in writing, such as Sumer and Babylon.

minuscule: Script written in lower-case letters.

movable type: First used by the Chinese in the eleventh century with porcelain type; Korea printed the first book with movable metal type 75 years prior to Gutenberg. It allowed for flexibility and efficiency in setting the page for printing and could be altered, unlike woodblock printing.

nib: The metal end of a pen that delivers the ink to the writing material.

octothorpe: Symbol (#) also known as hashtag or pound sign.

oracle bones: Writing material used in ancient China for divination.

orthography: The conventions of a written language that indicate the rules of spelling, capitalization, punctuation, and so forth.

page: Originally Latin meaning to fix or fasten, as in papyrus being formed as a page, but later applied to paper as in a leaf or sheet of paper, with page being one side. In computer use, pages are digital, as in home page, web page.

paleography: The study of ancient handwriting.

palm leaves: Writing material used particularly in Asia prior to paper.

paper: Derived from plant-based material that is macerated or pulped; invented in ancient China and transitioned gradually west.

papyrus: A type of proto-paper that was used in ancient civilizations, particularly Egypt. Made from the papyrus plant, a sedge, it is not considered paper, as strips are glued or affixed to form a sheet.

parchment: Historically, animal skin used as a writing material, a high-quality type being vellum.

percontation point: A reverse question mark used for a rhetorical question (sixteenth century).

petroglyph: A rock carving that could be an early system of communication or art among prehistoric or indigenous peoples.

pictograms: Symbols that provide fairly literal depictions of the items to be represented, which later evolved into ideograms; originally, a pictogram of a bird looked like a bird, but then the ideogram suggested the bird and evolved further into more abstract letters.

platen: In a printing press, a flat metal plate; in a typewriter, the roller.

printing press: A mechanical device that imprints ink onto a medium, typically paper. The innovation of the printing press and movable type allowed for mass production of texts.

psalter: A volume containing the Book of Psalms and perhaps additional devotional material, popular in the medieval period.

punch: The metal used in typeface design that is pressed into the matrix to cast a letter or symbol.

punctus: A single dot punctuation mark used in ancient Roman and Greek scripts to denote a pause. Placement low on the line indicated a comma; at mid-range a colon; at the top, a period. This was an early form of a punctuation mark.

quill: A feather used for writing instruments prior to the advent of the nib pen. To make the quills ready for writing, a clarification process was necessary.

quire: A medieval book or pamphlet that could be as small as eight leaves made from four sheets of paper and later enlarged to two dozen sheets. As with quarter, quire refers to four.

quoin: In letterpress printing, an expandable metal lock that allows the type to be secured tightly within a frame for printing. The type itself is surrounded by "furniture" to fill gaps.

ream: Paper comes in reams, which contain 480 sheets or 20 quires. Its origin is from Arabic *rizma*, meaning bundle.

Rosetta Stone: Discovered in 1799 by French engineers and soldiers of Napoleon and covered in three scripts: hieroglyphics, hieratic, and Greek. The combination of the three versions of a single text in one location allowed linguist Champollion to finally crack the code of hieroglyphics.

runes: Angular alphabet used by Germanic peoples (e.g., Scandinavian) in the first and second centuries CE. Rune stones marked important people and places.

scribes: Professional writers that record and copy information. In ancient civilizations, this was a highly regarded career.

script: In terms of history of writing, script records information that can be communicated beyond time and distance. It also refers to alphabets, handwriting, and texts. In the computer age, it became a set of commands.

scroll: A roll of paper, parchment, or papyrus that contains writing and is generally stored rolled. In the computer age, scroll became a verb to advance through a page as if unrolling it.

serif: The curved portion of letters or typeface that extend up or down from the actual letter. Sans serif, or "without" serif, means that these have been removed for a simpler look that may be easier to read.

signatures: A sheet of paper on which a number of pages are printed; these must be in multiples of four, so a sixteen-page signature will include eight pages on one side and eight on the reverse. The pages are laid out so that they will be in the correct order when printed.

slate: Slate was enclosed in a wooden frame for individual students, using chalk or a slate pen to write and then a cloth or sponge to erase. Slate was cheaper than paper and ink as it could be reused. The writing slate, which gained widespread use in the nineteenth century, is in the tradition of the Roman wax tablet and the contemporary individual white board and gel pen.

spine: The back of a book where pages are attached and the title appears. It literally is the backbone of a book that holds it together.

stylus: A pointed instrument used to write. Ancient Egyptians made reed pens that used ink. Romans developed metal styluses with pointed ends that could inscribe writing on wax tablets. Now in the computer age, styluses are used to enter commands on screens.

trivium, quadrivium: Three branches of learning comprise the trivium: rhetoric, logic, and grammar; the quadrivium added music, arithmetic, geometry, and astronomy. These seven are termed the liberal arts.

typeface: The overall design of a family of type; fonts are the variations within the typeface (e.g., boldface, italics, widths).

typography: The art and craft of the design and look of printed materials, including layout. A typographer makes decisions that affect how the viewer sees the end product.

uncial script: Used in Latin and Greek manuscripts (400 800 CE) and featured rounded handwriting. Its etymology may refer to an inch high. Insular script, famous in the British Isles prior to the Norman Conquest, is a type of uncial script.

vellum: Refers to calf and was a high-quality parchment (animal skin) used for writing before the widespread introduction of paper.

volume: In ancient Rome, a reading material (codex or book) was rolled on a rod. A second rod re-rolled the volume as the reader proceeded through its contents. It evolved to be a term that described a book during the Middle Ages and then one in a series of books during the Renaissance.

washi: Japanese paper valued for its cultural heritage and its durability.

wax tablets: Ancient Romans used wax tablets with a stylus for writing. Wax was poured into a frame; the wax surface was typically protected by a wooden covering. The surface was impermanent and could be "erased" by rubbing the blunt end of the stylus across the text.

woodblock: An early printing system developed in China in which wood is carved to make an impression when inked.

writing system: An agreed-upon set of symbols for communication based upon linguistic rules of a language. The symbols may be alphabetic, syllabic, pictographic, or ideographic. Systems are also termed scripts or orthography. Early writing systems include cuneiform and hieroglyphics.

Works Cited and Bibliography

Adecco. "The American Skills Gap is Real." 7 Jun. 2016, http://www.
adeccousa.com/employers/resources/skills-gap-in-the-american-
workforce/.

Adler, Simon. "The Wubi Effect." *Radiolab*, 14 Aug. 2020, https://www.
wnycstudios.org/podcasts/radiolab/articles/wubi-effect.

Adler-Kassner, Linda, and Elizabeth Wardle. *Naming What We Know:
Threshold Concepts of Writing Studies*. UP of Colorado, 2015.

Alexis, Cydney. "The Symbolic Life of the Moleskine Notebook: Material
Goods as a Tableau for Writing Identity Performance." *Composition
Studies*, vol. 45, no. 2, 2017, pp. 32–54.

Alter, Alexandra. "Tiny Books Fit in One Hand: Will They Change the
Way We Read?" *The New York Times*, 29 Oct. 2018, https://www.
nytimes.com/2018/10/29/business/mini-books-pocket-john-green.
html.

American Association of Colleges & Universities (AAC&U). Essential
Learning Outcomes. www.aacu.org/essential-learning-outcomes.

American Magazine. "Gives Wings to Words" (advertisement). Vol. 95,
1923, https://www.google.com/books/edition/The_American_Maga-
zine/NGAwAQAAMAAJ?hl=en&gbpv=1&dq=underwood+gives+win
gs+to+words&pg=RA3-PA183&printsec=frontcover.

Andrews, Evan. "7 Things You May Not Know about the Gutenberg
Bible." *History Stories*. History.com, 23 Feb. 2015, http://www.history.
com/news/7-things-you-may-not-know-about-the-gutenberg-bible.
Accessed 28 Dec. 2017.

Anonymous of Bologna. *The Principles of Letter-Writing (Rationes dic-
tandi)*. Translated by James J. Murphy, http://medieval.ucdavis.edu/
20B/Ars.Dictandi.html. Accessed November 12, 2018.

Aristotle. *Poetics*. Translated by Malcolm Heath, Penguin, 1997.

Azarian, Mary. *A Farmer's Alphabet*. 9th ed., David R. Godine, 2012.

Baker, Russell. "How to Punctuate." *How to Use the Power of the Printed Word*, edited by Billings S. Fuess Jr., Anchor, 1985.

"Baldwin Modern Printing Press." *The Writer's Almanac*. Accessed 14 April 2016, https://www.writersalmanac.org/index.html%3Fp=7855. html.

Barron, James. "Mary Adelman, 89, Fixer of Broken Typewriters Is Dead." *The New York Times*, 24 Nov. 2017, https://www.nytimes. com/2017/11/24/obituaries/mary-adelman-89-fixer-of-broken-type-writers-is-dead.html.

Bartz, Andrea. "Social Media Fakeness Is Bad for Our Psyches...But Great for Crime Writers." *Crime Reads*, 24 Mar. 2020, https://cri-mereads.com/social-media-fakeness-crime-writers/.

Bazerman, Charles. "The Case for Writing Studies as a Major Discipline." *Rhetoric and Composition as Intellectual Work*, edited by Gary A. Olson, Southern Illinois UP, 2002, pp. 32–38.

Beasley, Maurine. *Women of the Washington Press: Politics, Prejudice and Persistence*. Northwestern UP, 2012.

Beech, Beatrice. "Charlotte Guillard: A Sixteenth-Century Business Woman." *Renaissance Quarterly* 36, no. 3, 1983, pp. 345–67. https:// doi.org/10.2307/2862159.

Berry, Mary Elizabeth. *Japan in Print: Information and Nation in the Early Modern Period*. U of California P, 2006.

Beyer, Kurt W. *Grace Hopper and the Invention of the Information Age*. MIT Press, 2012.

Bickham, George, engraver. *The Universal Penman*. 1941. bnpublishing, 2014.

Bischoff, Georges. *Le siècle de Gutenberg* [*The Century of Gutenberg*]. La Nuée Bleue, 2018.

Bizzell, Patricia, and Bruce Herzberg. *The Rhetorical Tradition: Readings from Classical Times to the Present*. 2nd ed., St. Martin's, 2001.

Blakemore, Erin. "How Dick Tracy Invented the Smartwatch." *Smith-sonian Magazine*, 9 Mar. 2015, https://www.smithsonianmag.com/ smart-news/how-dick-tracy-invented-smartwatch-180954506/.

——. "How Lizzie Bennet Got Her Books." *JStor Daily*, 8 Jun. 2018, https://daily.jstor.org/how-lizzie-bennet-got-her-books/.

Boston Typewriter Orchestra. http://www.bostontypewriterorchestra. com/. Accessed 4 Feb. 2020.

Brady, Lois Smith. "Before Saying 'I Do,' Define Just What You Mean." *The New York Times*, 16 Aug. 2013, https://www.nytimes.com/2013/08/18/ fashion/weddings/before-saying-i-do-define-just-what-you-mean.html.

Bréjoux, Jacques. Interview with author. 18 Oct. 2018.

Brennan, Thomas James, and Coban Shaw. "Writing to Calm and Compose the Injured Brain." At War blog, *The New York Times*, 24 Aug. 2012, https://atwar.blogs.nytimes.com/2012/08/24/writing-to-calm-and-compose-the-injured-brain/.

British Library Board. *William Caxton*. British Museum Publications, 1976.

Bromer, Anne C., and Julian I. Edison. *Miniature Books: 4,000 Years of Tiny Treasures*. Harry N. Abrams, 2007.

Brown, Rollo Walter. *How the French Boy Learns to Write*. Harvard UP, 1915.

Bullinger, Cory, and Stephanie Vie. "After a Decade of Social Media: Abstainers and Ex-Users." *Social Writing/Social Media: Publics, Presentations, and Pedagogies*, edited by Douglas M. Walls and Stephanie Vie, WAC Clearinghouse, UP of Colorado, 2017, pp. 69–88.

Burke, Kathryn. "Letter Writing in America: Civil War Letters." Smithsonian National Postal Museum, 2005, https://postalmuseum.si.edu/letterwriting/lw04.html. Accessed 14 Nov. 2018.

Burns, Ken, director. *The Civil War*. Florentine Films, 1990.

Cahill, Thomas. *How the Irish Saved Civilization*. Nan A. Talese, 1995.

Cain, Abigail. "Before Envelopes, People Protected Messages with Letterlocking." *Atlas Obscura*, 9 Nov. 2018, https://www.atlasobscura.com/articles/what-did-people-do-before-envelopes-letterlocking.

———. "Every Page of This Book Is a Slice of Cheese." *Atlas Obscura*, 18 Feb. 2019, https://www.atlasobscura.com/articles/book-made-of-cheese.

Caramanica, Jon. "A Graffiti Museum Where the Writers Are in Charge." *The New York Times*, 4 Dec. 2019, updated 12 Dec. 2019, https://www.nytimes.com/2019/12/04/arts/design/museum-of-graffiti-miami.html.

Carroll, Ryder. *The Bullet Journal Method*. Portfolio, 2018.

Carvalho, David Nunes. *Forty Centuries of Ink*. 1904.

Cerku, Ashley. "The Art and Rhetoric of Letter Writing: Preserving Rhetorical Strategies throughout Time." *Young Scholars in Writing*, vol. 12, 2015, pp. 104–13.

Charles, Ron. "John Green Wants You to Read Tiny Books." *The Washington Post*, 3 Aug. 2018. https://www.washingtonpost.com/entertainment/books/john-green-wants-you-to-read-tiny-books/2018/08/02/3110b5bc-94e6-11e8-a679-b09212fb69c2_story.html?utm_term=.e4ab74c9cccc.

Chen, Dene-Hern. "The Cost of Changing an Entire Country's Alphabet." *BBC News*. 25 Apr. 2018. http://www.bbc.com/capital/story/20180424-the-cost-of-changing-an-entire-countrys-alphabet.

Chesterton, G.K. "The Riddle of the Ivy." *Tremendous Trifles*, Methuen, 1909.

Christensen, John. "The Rag Man." *Utah Stories from the Beehive Archive*, 2017. http://www.utahhumanities.org/stories/items/show/307.

Christie, Alix. *Gutenberg's Apprentice*. HarperCollins, 2014.

Cinelli, Mia. "The Power of Typography." TEDx Talk, 19 Apr. 2016, https://www.youtube.com/watch?v=C_RzDqgGcao.

Clark, Neil. "Paper Detective." *Saturday Evening Post*, 27 Feb. 1954, pp. 124–26.

Clayton, Ewan. "A Short History of Calligraphy and Typography." British Library, https://www.bl.uk/history-of-writing/articles/a-short-history-of-calligraphy-and-typography. Accessed 4 Oct. 2019.

Cocker, William Johnson. *Hand-book of Punctuation, with Instructions for Capitalization, Letter-writing, and Proofreading*. A.S. Barnes, 1878.

Collins, Father Michael. *Remarkable Books: The World's Most Beautiful and Historic Works*. DK/ Penguin Random House, 2017.

Colton, Jared S., and Rebecca Walton. "Disability as Insight into Social Justice Pedagogy in Technical Communications." *Journal of Interactive Technology & Pedagogy*, issue 8, 2015. https://jitp.commons.gc.cuny.edu/disability-as-insight-into-social-justice-pedagogy-in-technical-communication/.

Conlin, Kaitlin. Crystals as Talisman. Personal correspondence, 10 Mar. 2020.

"Contemporary Arabic Graffiti and Lettering: Photographs of a Visual Revolution." Exhibition, The Printing Museum, Haverhill, MA, 31 Mar.–13 Sept. 2014. https://printingmuseum.org/exhibition/contempo-rary-arabic-graffiti-and-lettering-photographs-of-a-visual-revolution/.

Corbett, Edward J. "The Theory and Practice of Imitation in Classical Rhetoric." *College Composition and Communication*, vol. 22, no. 3, October 1971, pp. 243–50.

Council of Writing Program Administrators. *WPA Outcomes Statement for First-Year Composition (3.0), approved July 17, 2014*. http://wpacouncil.org/aws/CWPA/pt/sd/news_article/243055/_PARENT/layout_details/false.

Crip Camp: A Disabilities Revolution. Directed by Nicole Newnham and Jim LeBrecht, directors, Netflix, 2020.

Daley, Jason. "Museum Offers $15,000 per Character to Decipher Oracle Bone Script." *Smithsonian Magazine*, 26 Jul. 2017, https://www.smithsonianmag.com/smart-news/museum-offers-15000-letter-deciphering-oracle-bones-180964213/.

Dambrogio, Jana, Daniel Starza Smith, and the Unlocking History

Research Group. *Dictionary of Letterlocking* (DoLL). 2016. http://letterlocking.org/dictionary, last updated 30 Dec. 2017. Accessed 19 Jul. 2019.

Daniels, Maygene. "The Ingenious Pen: American Writing Implements from the Eighteenth Century to the Twentieth." *American Archivist*, Summer 1980, pp. 312–24.

Davies, Lyn. *A Is for Ox: A Short History of the Alphabet.* Folio Society, 2006.

Davis, Deidre. "Ability & Possibility: A Personal Chronicle of the 20th Anniversary of the Americans with Disabilities Act." DiversityInc, 15 Oct. 2010, https://www.diversityinc.com/ability-possibility-a-personal-chronicle-of-the-20th-anniversary-of-the-americans-with-disabilities-act/.

Davis, Margaret Leslie. *The Lost Gutenberg: The Astounding Story of One Book's Five-Hundred-Year Odyssey.* TarcherPerigee, 2019.

Day, A. Grove, and Albertine Loomis. *Ka Pa'I Palapala: Early Printing in Hawaii.* 2nd rev. ed., Mission Houses Museum, 1997.

DeGaine, Lauren Elle. "The 'eBay Archive': Recovering Early Women Type Designers." *Modernist Archive*, vol. 4, cycle 2, 4 Sep. 2019. https://modernismmodernity.org/forums/posts/ebay-archive.

Devroye, Luc. Gudrun Zapf von Hesse. Type Design Information Page, http://luc.devroye.org/fonts-26296.html. Accessed 10 Mar. 2020.

Didion, Joan. *The Year of Magical Thinking.* Vintage, 2007.

Dierks, Konstantin. "The Familiar Letter and School Refinement in America, 1750–1800." *Letter Writing as a Social Practice*, edited by David Barton and Nigel Hall, John Benjamins, 2000, pp. 31–41.

Dippre, Ryan J. *Talk, Tools, and Texts: A Logic-in-Use for Studying Lifespan Literate Action Development.* The WAC Clearinghouse, UP of Colorado, 2019.

Diringer, David. *The Book Before Printing: Ancient, Medieval and Oriental.* 1953. Dover, 1982.

Dizikes, Peter. "How Writing Technology Shaped Classical Thinking." *MIT News*, 8 Jan. 2019, http://news.mit.edu/2019/empire-letters-writing-technology-stephanie-frampton-0108.

Douglass, Frederick. Letter to Thomas Auld (September 3, 1848). *Frederick Douglass: Selected Speeches and Writings*, edited by Philip Foner, Lawrence Hill Books, 1999, p. 111, https://glc.yale.edu/letter-thomas-auld-september-3-1848.

Downs, Douglas, and Elizabeth Wardle. "Teaching about Writing, Righting Misconceptions: (Re)envisioning 'First-Year Composition' as 'Introduction to Writing Studies.'" *College Composition and Communication*, vol. 58, no. 4, June 2007, pp. 552–84.

Dreyer, Benjamin. *Dreyer's English: An Utterly Correct Guide to Clarity and Style*. Random House, 2019.

Drogin, Marc. *Anathema! Medieval Scribes and the History of Book Curses*. Allanheld & Schram, 1983.

Dürer, Albrecht. *Of the Just Shaping of Letters*. 1805. Translated by R.T. Nichol, Dover Books, 2011. https://www.gutenberg.org/files/37103/37103-h/37103-h.htm.

Durrell, Lawrence. *Bitter Lemons*. Faber and Faber, 1957.

"18 Famous Authors and Their Fountain Pens." LuxiPens, https://luxipens.com/18-famous-authors-and-their-fountain-pens/. Accessed 10 Jan. 2020.

Ellet, Elizabeth F. *The Women of the American Revolution*. 1849. Vols. 1–2, 5th ed., American History Press, 2004.

Ellis, Carolyn, et al. "Autoethnography: An Overview." *Forum Qualitative Sozialforschung/Forum: Qualitative Social Research*, vol. 12, no. 1, 2010, article 10, https://www.qualitative-research.net/index.php/fqs/article/view/1589/3095.

Enchelmayer, Ernest J. "Rhetoric in the Visual Arts." *Conference of the International Journal of Arts and Sciences*, vol. 1, no. 19, 2009, pp. 59–72. http://openaccesslibrary.org/images/AUS182_Ernest_J._Enchelmayer.pdf.

Engel, William E. "The Printer as Author in Early Modern English Book History." *The Academic Minute*, 13 May 2020. https://academicminute.org/2020/05/william-e-engel-university-of-the-south-the-printer-as-author-in-early-modern-english-book-history/.

Enos, Richard. "Ancient Greek Writing Instruction and Its Oral Antecedents." J. Murphy, pp. 1–35.

Enos, Richard Leo, and Natasha Trace Robinson. "Claudia Severa's Birthday Invitation: A Rhetorical Analysis of the Earliest Artifact of Latin Written by a Woman's Hand." *Peitho*, vol. 18, no. 2, Spring/Summer 2016. https://cfshrc.org/article/claudia-severas-birthday-invitation-a-rhetorical-analysis-of-the-earliest-artifact-of-latin-written-by-a-womans-hand/.

Erickson, Lee. "The Economy of Novel Reading: Jane Austen and the Circulating Library." *Studies in English Literature, 1500–1900*, vol. 30, no. 4, Autumn 1990, pp. 573–90, https://doi.org/10.2307/450560.

Eskelson, Tyrel C. "How and Why Formal Education Originated in the Emergence of Civilization." *Journal of Education and Learning*, vol. 9, no. 2, 2020, pp. 29–47. https://doi.org/10.5539/jel.v9n2p29.

Evans, Curtis. "The Poison Pen Letter: The Early 20th Century's Strangest Crime Wave." *CrimeReads*, 10 Mar. 2020, https://crimereads.com/poison-pen-letter/.

Evans, Edward Payson. *Animal Symbolism in Ecclesiastical Architecture.* W. Heinemann, 1896.

Faena Aleph. "5 Steps to Creating a Talisman (to Transform Superstition to Magic)." http://www.faena.com/aleph/articles/5-steps-to-creating-a-talisman-to-transform-superstition-to-magic/. Accessed 8 Mar. 2019.

Filgate, Michele. "Writers and Their Favorite Tools: On Pens, Pencils, and Other Fetish Objects." *Literary Hub,* 13 Aug. 2015, https://lithub.com/writers-and-their-favorite-tools/.

"The First Shape Book: Little Red Riding Hood (1863)." *The Public Domain Review.* https://publicdomainreview.org/collections/little-red-riding-hood-1863/. Accessed 20 Nov. 2018.

Fletcher, Ralph. *Mentor Author, Mentor Texts: Short Texts, Craft Notes, and Practical Classroom Uses.* Heinemann, 2011.

Florey, Kitty Burns. *Script and Scribble: The Rise and Fall of Handwriting.* Melville House, 2008.

Fogarty, Mignon. *The Grammar Devotional: Daily Tips for Successful Writing from Grammar Girl.* Holt Books, 2009.

Form & Function: The Genius of the Book. Exhibition, Folger Shakespeare Library, Washington, DC, 16 Jun.–23 Sep. 2018, https://www.folger.edu/exhibitions/form-function-genius-of-the-book

"Four Treasures of the Study." China Online Museum. http://www.china-onlinemuseum.com/painting-four-treasures.php.

Frampton, Stephanie Ann. *Empire of Letters: Writing in Roman Literature and Thought from Lucretius to Ovid.* Oxford UP, 2019.

Franklin, Benjamin. "A Conversational Pleasantry." *The World's Best Poetry,* edited by Bliss Carman, et al., vol. IX, John D. Morris & Co., 1904. Bartleby.com, 2012, https://www.bartleby.com/360/9/80.html.

Gallagher, Kelly. *Write Like This: Teaching Real-World Writing through Modeling and Mentoring Texts.* Stenhouse, 2011.

Garfield, Simon. *Just My Type.* Gotham/Penguin, 2011.

———. *To the Letter: A Celebration of the Lost Art of Letter Writing.* Avery, 2013.

Geertz, Clifford. *The Interpretation of Cultures.* Basic Books, 1973.

Ghal, Nikita. "The Other Ghalib: Meet One of the Last Calligraphers of Old Delhi's Urdu Bazaar." *Hindustan Times,* 10 Jul. 2017, https://www.hindustantimes.com/delhi-news/the-other-ghalib-meet-one-of-the-last-calligraphers-of-old-delhi-s-urdu-bazaar/story-6FGl-wjigaGCNS1A9GbwPGN.html.

Giesbrecht, Josh. "How the Ballpoint Pen Killed Cursive." *The Atlantic,* 28 Aug. 2015, https://www.theatlantic.com/technology/archive/2015/08/ballpoint-pens-object-lesson-history-handwriting/402205/.

Girma, Haben. "What the A.D.A. Means to Me." *The New York Times*, 20 Jul. 2020, https://www.nytimes.com/2020/07/20/us/judy-heumann-alice-wong-haben-girma-disability-activists.html.

Golden, Alisa. *Making Handmade Books: 100+ Bindings, Structures & Forms*. Lark Crafts, 2011.

Goldsmith, Selwyn. *Designing for the Disabled*. Mc-Graw-Hill, 1963.

Gordon, Karen E. *The New Well-Tempered Sentence: A Punctuation Handbook for the Innocent, the Eager, and the Doomed*. Rpt. Mariner, 2003.

———. *The Transitive Vampire: A Handbook of Grammar for the Innocent, the Eager and the Doomed*. Times Books, 1984.

Goudy, Frederic William. *The Alphabet: Fifteen Interpretative Designs Drawn and Arranged with Explanatory Text and Illustration*. Village Press, 1918.

Gourdie, Tom. *Handwriting for Today*. Pitman, 1971.

———. *The Ladybird Book of Handwriting*. Wills & Hepworth, 1968.

Graves, Robert. *The White Goddess*. Faber & Faber, 1948.

Griffin, Simon. *Fucking Apostrophes*. Icon Books, 2016.

Grobman, Laurie, and E. Michele Ramsey. *Major Decisions: College, Career, and the Case for the Humanities*. U of Pennsylvania P, 2020.

Grom, Brenton. "Slaves of Fashion, Loafers of Industry: A History of Paper Collars and the Men Who Wore Them." *Disposable America*, Dec. 2015, https://disposableamerica.org/course-projects/brenton-grom/.

Grove, M. Annette, and David F. Lancy. "Cultural Views in Life Phases." *International Encyclopedia of Social and Behavioral Sciences*, edited by James D. Wright, 2nd ed., Elsevier, 2015, pp. 507–15.

Grunwald, Lisa, and Stephen J. Adler. *Letters of the Century: America 1900–1999*. Dial Press, 1999.

Hahn, Kimiko. "To a No. 2 Yellow Pencil on May 1, 2020." *Teach This Poem*, 17 Aug. 2020.

Hall, Astrid. "Can't Stop, Won't Stop: Half of Brit Families Going on 'Digital Detox' This Summer—Because Their Kids Won't Get Off Gadgets." *The Sun*, 8 Jun. 2018, https://www.thesun.co.uk/tech/6484064/digital-detox-parents-kids-tech/.

Hall, Deirdre. "Calligraphy and Wedding Invitations." Research project conducted at Utah State University, 2018.

Hamilton, Edith. "The Lessons of the Past." *Saturday Evening Post*, 27 Sep. 1958.

Hanks, Tom. "I am TOM. I like to TYPE. Hear That?" *The New York Times*, 3 Aug. 2013. https://www.nytimes.com/2013/08/04/opinion/sunday/i-am-tom-i-like-to-type-hear-that.html.

Harjo, Joy. "Ancestors: A Mapping of Indigenous Poetry and Poets." 9
    Oct. 2015. Blaney Lecture, Poets Forum, New York City, 23 Nov. 2015,
    https://poets.org/text/ancestors-mapping-indigenous-poetry-and-
    poets.
Headlee, Celeste. *Do Nothing: How to Break Away from Overworking,
    Overdoing, and Underliving*. Harmony, Random House, 2020.
Henry, Susan. *Anonymous in Their Own Names*. Vanderbilt UP, 2012.
Hensher, Philip. *The Missing Ink: The Lost Art of Handwriting*. Farrar,
    Straus and Giroux, 2012.
Heumann, Judith, and John Wodatch. "We're 20 Percent of America, and
    We're Still Invisible." *The New York Times*, 26 Jul. 2020, https://www.
    nytimes.com/2020/07/26/opinion/Americans-with-disabilities-act.
    html.
Hill, Angela. "Millennials (and Tom Hanks) Buying Vintage Typewrit-
    ers." *The Mercury News*, 12 Aug. 2016, https://www.mercurynews
    .com/2015/07/20/
    millennials-and-tom-hanks-buying-vintage-typewriters/.
Houston, Keith. *The Book: A Cover-to-Cover Exploration of the Most Pow-
    erful Object of Our Time*. Norton, 2016.
"How Books Became Cheap: A Timeline of Bookmaking Technology."
    Lapham's Quarterly, 30 Jul. 2020, https://www.laphamsquarterly.org/
    roundtable/how-books-became-cheap.
Humphrey, Carol Sue. *The American Revolution and the Press*. Northwest-
    ern UP, 2013.
Hunt, Will. "Artists of the Dark Zone." *Archaeology*, Nov./Dec.
    2019, pp. 49–53, https://www.archaeology.org/issues/358-1911/
    features/8074-america-southeast-cherokee-caves.
Hunter, Dard. *Papermaking: The History and Technique of an Ancient
    Craft*. 1947. Dover, 1978.
Hurley, Sean. "Boston Orchestra Makes Typewriters Sing."
    NPR, 9 Oct. 2008, https://www.npr.org/templates/story/story.
    php?storyId=95578403.
"A Hymn to Nisaba." The Electronic Text Corpus of Sumerian Literature.
    http://etcsl.orinst.ox.ac.uk/section4/tr4161.htm. Accessed 24 Dec. 2019.
Hyndman, Sarah. *Why Fonts Matter*. Gingko Press, 2016.
"Illuminated Lettering." *Made by Marzipan*. https://www.madebymarzi-
    pan.com/?tutorial=illuminated-lettering.
"Itzamná." *Encyclopedia.com*. 27 Jun. 2018, https://www.encyclopedia.
    com/history/encyclopedias-almanacs-transcripts-and-maps/itzamna.
James, Ronald. "Territorial Enterprise." *Online Nevada*, 20 Mar. 2009,
    http://onlinenevada.org/articles/territorial-enterprise.

Jimenes, Rémi. *Charlotte Guillard: Une Femme Imprimeur á la Renais-sance*. Presses Universitaires de Rennes and Presses Universitaires François-Rabelais, 2017.

Just, Rick. "The Lapwai Press." *Speaking of Idaho*, 11 Jul. 2018, https://www.rickjust.com/blog/the-lapwai-press.

Karant-Nunn, Susan, and Ute Lotz-Heumann. "Confessional Conflict." *After 500 Years: Print and Propaganda in the Protestant Reformation*, University of Arizona Libraries, 2017, https://speccoll.library.arizona.edu/online-exhibits/exhibits/show/reformation/role-of-printing.

Keillor, Garrison. "Computer Mouse." *The Writer's Almanac*, 17 Nov. 2019, http://www.garrisonkeillor.com/radio/twa-the-writers-almanac-for-november-17-2019/.

Kelly-Buccellati, Marilyn. "Apprenticeship and Learning from the Ancestors: The Case of Ancient Urkesh." *Archaeology and Apprenticeship: Body Knowledge, Identity, and Communities of Practice*, edited by Willeke Wendrich, U of Arizona P, 2012, pp. 203–23.

Kennard, Jennifer. "Press Kit." *Letterology*, 3 Mar. 2014, http://www.letterology.com/2014/03/press-kit.html?m=1.

King, Stephen. *On Writing: A Memoir of the Craft*. Scribner, 2000.

Kinkead, Joyce. "Computer Conversations: E-Mail and Writing Instruction." *College Composition and Communication*, vol. 38, no. 3, Oct. 1987, pp. 337–41.

———. "Matching Software and Curriculum: A Description of Four Text-Analysis Programs." *Computers and Composition*, vol. 3, no. 3, Aug. 1986, pp. 33–55.

———. *A Schoolmarm All My Life: Personal Narratives from Frontier Utah*. Signature Books, 1996.

———. "Wired: Computer Networks in the English Classroom." *English Journal*, vol. 77, no. 7, 1988, pp. 39–41.

Kinkead, Joyce, and Cameron Haney. "Touchdown! A Student-Athlete and Mentor Develop a Playbook for Undergraduate Research." *PURM*, vol. 9, no. 1, 2020.

Kinkead, Joyce, and Morgan Wykstra. *The Geography of Writing: Mapping Writing across Time and Place*. 2018, https://geographyofwriting.wordpress.com/.

Kipling, Rudyard. "How the Alphabet Was Made." *Just So Stories*, 1902.

Kishore, Nantha. "Old Delhi's Last Calligrapher." *The Diplomat*, 2 Jul. 2018, https://thediplomat.com/2018/07/old-delhis-last-calligrapher/.

Kittler, Juraj. "From Rags to Riches: The Limits of Paper Manufacturing and Their Impact on Book Print in Renaissance Venice." *Media History*, vol. 21, no 1, 2015, pp. 8–22. http://dx.doi.org/10.1080/13688804.2014.955840.

Kluge, Martin. *The Basel Paper Mill: The Swiss Museum for Paper, Writing and Printing.* Basler Papiermühle, 2014.

Knorovsky, Katie. "Handmade Paper from China." *National Geographic*, 30 Nov. 2007, https://www.nationalgeographic.com/travel/intelligent-travel/2007/11/30/handmade_paper_from_china/.

Kramer, Samuel Noah. "Schooldays: A Sumerian Composition Relating to the Education of a Scribe." *Journal of the American Oriental Society*, vol. 69, no. 4, 1949, pp. 199–215. https://doi.org/10.2307/596246.

———. *The Sumerians: Their History, Culture, and Character.* U of Chicago P, 1971.

Kuh, George D. *High-Impact Educational Practices: What They Are, Who Has Access to Them, and Why They Matter.* Association of American Colleges and Universities, 2008.

LaFrance, Adrienne. "Pompeii's Graffiti and the Ancient Origins of Social Media." *The Atlantic*, 29 Mar. 2016, https://www.theatlantic.com/technology/archive/2016/03/adrienne-was-here/475719/.

Lahaina Restoration Foundation. Hale Pa'I Printing Museum. http://lahainarestoration.org/hale-pai-museum/. Accessed 20 Dec. 2017.

Lancy, David F. *The Anthropology of Childhood: Cherubs, Chattel, Changelings.* Cambridge UP, 2008.

———. "Learning 'From Nobody': The Limited Role of Teaching in Folk Models of Children's Development." *Childhood in the Past*, vol. 3, 2010, pp. 79–106.

Lanier, Jaron. *Ten Arguments for Deleting Your Social Media Accounts Right Now.* Henry Holt, 2018.

Laskow, Sarah. "Protect Your Library the Medieval Way, with Horrifying Book Curses." *Atlas Obscura*, 9 Nov. 2016, https://www.atlasobscura.com/articles/protect-your-library-the-medieval-way-with-horrifying-book-curses.

Leech, Tom, curator and director. "Breakfast with O'Keeffe: The Press of the Palace of the Governors." Georgia O'Keeffe Museum, Santa Fe, NM, 3 Apr. 2019.

Le Faye, Deidre, editor. *Jane Austen's Letters.* 4th ed., Oxford UP, 2014.

Levin, Dan. "No Cell Signal, No Wi-Fi, No Problem: Growing Up Inside America's 'Quiet Zone.'" *The New York Times*, 6 Mar. 2020, https://www.nytimes.com/2020/03/06/us/green-bank-west-virginia-quiet-zone.html.

Lewis, Harry. "Contextualizing Place as Type: Creating an Auburn Typeface." *Xchanges*, vol. 12, no. 2/vol. 13, no. 1, 27 Jan. 2019, https://xchanges.org/contextualizing-place-as-type-12-2-13-1.

López, Alfonso. "Morse Code: Communication Goes Electric." *National Geographic History*, vol. 7, no. 3, Jul./Aug. 2021, pp. 18–19.

Lunsford, Andrea A. "Aristotelian Rhetoric: Let's Get Back to the Classics." *Journal of Basic Writing*, vol. 2, no. 1, 1978, pp. 2–12.

Lunsford, Andrea, and Lisa Ede. *Singular Texts/Plural Authors: Perspectives on Collaborative Writing.* Southern Illinois UP, 1990.

Lupfer. E.A. *Ornate Pictorial Calligraphy.* Dover, 2014. Reprint of *Fascinating Pen Flourishing*, Zaner-Bloser Company, 1951.

———. *The Zanerian Manual of Alphabets and Engrossing: An Instructor in Roundhand, Lettering Engrossing, Designing, Pen and Brush Art, Etc.* 1895. Rev. ed., Zaner-Bloser Company, 1924, https://archive.org/details/Masgrimes_Archive_Zanerian_Manual_1924.

Lyall, Sarah. "Behold, the Tiniest of Books." *The New York Times*, 7 Mar. 2019, https://www.nytimes.com/2019/03/07/books/tiny-books-grolier-club.html. [Also available as "Making It Easier to Hold Infinity in the Palm of Your Hand," *The New York Times*, 8 Mar. 2019, p. C20.]

MacCash, Doug. "Meet the 9 Muses, New Orleans' Unpronounceable Uptown Streets." *The Times-Picayune*, 19 May 2016, https://www.nola.com/entertainment_life/music/article_8dd85826-8c21-51f8-9c0d-3b8493537e93.html.

Mackintosh, Michelle. *Snail Mail: Rediscovering the Art and Craft of Handmade Correspondence.* Hardle Grant Books, 2015.

Madden, Patrick. "College Campus Tries Out Robot Delivery." NPR, 7 Apr. 2019, https://www.npr.org/2019/04/07/710781494/college-campus-tries-out-robot-delivery.

Magickal Needs. Talisman for Poets & Writers. https://www.magickal-needs.com/product/talisman-for-poets/. Accessed March 8, 2019.

Mallalieu, Andy. "Monotype's Next Typeface Ambiguity Is Contentious, Confrontational and Contrarian." Creative Boom, 16 Jul. 2019, https://www.creativeboom.com/resources/monotypes-next-typeface-ambiguity-is-contentious-confrontational-and-contrarian/.

Malo, David. *Hawaiian Antiquities* (*Moolelo Hawaii*). 1898. Translated by Dr. N.B. Emerson, *Hawaiian Gazette*, 1903, http://www.ahamoku.org/wp-content/uploads/2011/12/Malo-David-Hawaiian_Antiquities-Moolelo-Hawaii-translated-by-N-B-Emerson-Honolulu-Hawaiian-Gazette-Co-Ltd-1903.pdf.

Manson, Pamela. "This Salt Lake City Group Writes Love Letters to Strangers." *The Salt Lake Tribune*, 9 Feb. 2020, D1, https://www.sltrib.com/artsliving/2020/02/09/this-salt-lake-city-group/.

Marantz, Andrew. *Anti-Social: Online Extremists, Techno-Utopians, and the Hijacking of the American Conversation.* Penguin, 2019.

———. "What the Coronavirus Crisis Has Changed about Social Media, and What It Hasn't Changed." *The New Yorker*, 26 Mar. 2020, https://

www.newyorker.com/news/daily-comment/what-the-coronavirus-crisis-has-changed-about-social-media-and-what-it-hasnt-changed.

Mark, Joshua J. "Nisaba." *World History Encyclopedia*, 23 Jan. 2017, https://www.worldhistory.org/Nisaba/.

Markoff, John. "Lawrence Tesler, Who Made Personal Computing Easier, Dies at 74." *The New York Times*, 20 Feb. 2020, https://www.nytimes.com/2020/02/20/technology/lawrence-tesler-dead.html.

Marsh, Jason. "Tips for Keeping a Gratitude Journal." *Greater Good Magazine: Science-Based Insights for a Meaningful Life*, 17 Nov. 2011, https://greatergood.berkeley.edu/article/item/tips_for_keeping_a_gratitude_journal.

Marshall, Colin. "A Medieval Book That Opens Six Different Ways, Revealing Six Different Books in One." *Open Culture*, 16 Oct. 2018, http://www.openculture.com/2018/10/medieval-book-opens-six-differ-ent-ways-revealing-six-different-books-one.html.

Martínez, Ma. del Carmen Rodríguez, et al. "Oldest Writing in the New World." *Science*, vol. 313, issue 5793, 15 Sept. 2006, pp. 1610–14. https://doi.org/10.1126/science.1131492 .

McCulloch, Gretchen. *Because Internet: Understanding the New Rules of Language*. Riverhead Books, 2019.

———. "We Learned to Write the Way We Talk." *The New York Times*, 27 Dec. 2019, https://www.nytimes.com/interactive/2019/12/27/opinion/sunday/internet-writing-text-emotion.html.

McPhee, John. "Draft No. 4." *The New Yorker*, 29 Apr. 2013, https://www.newyorker.com/magazine/2013/04/29/draft-no-4.

Meeker, Mary. Internet Trends 2019. https://www.bondcap.com/report/itr19/.

Menoni, Burton. *Kings of Greek Mythology*. Lulu.com, 2016.

Metz, Cade. "Frances Allen: Who Helped Hardware Understand Software, Dies at 88." *The New York Times*, 8 Aug. 2020, https://www.nytimes.com/2020/08/08/technology/frances-allen-dead.html?searchResultPosition=2.

———. "Randy Suess, 74, Computer Bulletin Board Inventor." *The New York Times*, 20 Dec. 2019, updated 23 Dec. 2019, https://www.nytimes.com/2019/12/20/technology/randy-suess-dead.html.

———. "William English, Who Helped Build the Computer Mouse, Dies at 91." *The New York Times*, 31 Jul. 2020, updated 4 Aug. 2020, https://www.nytimes.com/2020/07/31/technology/william-english-who-helped-build-the-computer-mouse-dies-at-91.html.

Meyer, Richard E., editor. *Cemeteries & Gravemarkers Voices of American Culture*. Utah State UP, 1992, https://digitalcommons.usu.edu/usupress_pubs/179.

Micciche, Laura R. "Writers Have Always Loved Mobile Devices." *The Atlantic*, 18 Aug. 2018, https://www.theatlantic.com/technology/archive/2018/08/writers-have-always-loved-mobile-devices/567637/.

———. "Writing Material." *College English*, vol. 76, no. 6, Jul. 2014, pp. 488–505. http://www.ncte.org/library/NCTEFiles/Resources/Journals/CE/0766-july2014/CE0766Writing.pdf.

Millesgården Museum. "William Morris: More Than Floral Wallpaper." Exhibition, 15 Sep. 2018–3 Feb. 2019, https://www.millesgarden.se/exhibitions-2018.aspx.

Mirovalev, Mansure. "Kazakhstan's Troubles Switching from the Cyrillic to the Latin Alphabet." *TRT World*, 7 Feb. 2019. https://www.trtworld.com/magazine/kazakhstan-s-troubles-switching-from-the-cyrillic-to-the-latin-alphabet-23960.

Miss Cellania. "19 Authors and Their Typewriters." *Mental Floss*, 23 May 2016, https://www.mentalfloss.com/article/80104/19-authors-and-their-typewriters.

Molella, Arthur P., and Anna Karvellas, editors. *Places of Invention*. Smithsonian Institution Scholarly Press, 2015.

Monaghan, P. *Goddesses in World Culture, Volume I*. Praeger, 2010.

Moran, William L., editor and translator. *The Amarna Letters*. Johns Hopkins UP, 1992. [Originally published in French in 1987 as *Les Lettres de El-Amarna*.]

Morley, Madeleine. "The Women Redressing the Gender Imbalance in Typography." *Eye on Design*, 28 Sep. 2016., https://eyeondesign.aiga.org/the-women-readdressing-the-gender-imbalance-in-typography/.

Morris, W. *A Note by William Morris on His Aims in Founding the Kelmscott Press Together with a Short Description of the Press by S.C. Cockerell, & an Annotated List of the Books Printed Thereat*. Kelmscott Press, 1898.

Morton, Ella. "Letter-Writing Manuals Were the Self-Help Books of the 18th Century." *Atlas Obscura*, 2 Jun. 2016, https://www.atlasobscura.com/articles/letterwriting-manuals-were-the-selfhelp-books-of-the-18th-century.

Mossiker, Frances. *Life and Letters*. Columbia UP, 1985.

Moxon, Paul. "The Toy Press with a Journal That Means Business." American Printing History Association, 2 Sep. 2016, https://printinghistory.org/swiftset-journal/.

Mueller, Pam A., and Daniel M. Oppenheimer. "The Pen Is Mightier Than the Keyboard: Advantages of Longhand Over Laptop Note Taking." *Psychological Science*, vol. 25, no. 6, 23 Apr. 2014, pp. 1159–68.

Muffoletto, Mary-Ann Crow. Facebook post. 19 Jul. 2020. https://www.facebook.com/joyce.kinkead/.

Mullaney, Thomas S. *The Chinese Typewriter: A History*. MIT Press, 2017.

Murphy, Heather. "You Should Actually Send That Thank You Note You've Been Meaning to Write." *The New York Times*, 20 Jul. 2018, https://www.nytimes.com/2018/07/20/science/thank-you-notes.html.

Murphy, James J., editor. *A Short History of Writing Instruction: From Ancient Greece to Contemporary America*. 3rd ed., Routledge, 2012.

Musée Hèbre de St Clément. Rochefort, France. 24 Oct. 2018.

Museum of Far Eastern Antiquities. "China's History of Books." Stockholm, Sweden, https://www.ostasiatiskamuseet.se/en/exhibitions/chinas-history-of-books/.

Museum of Graffiti. 2020, https://museumofgraffiti.com/.

Museum of Printing, "QWERTY Festival: A Celebration of the Typewriter!" https://museumofprinting.org/news-and-events/celebration-of-the-typewriter/.

Nakanishi, Akira. *Writing Systems of the World*. Charles E. Tuttle, 1994.

National Commission on Writing for America's Families, Schools, and Colleges. *Writing: A Ticket to Work...Or a Ticket Out*. College Board, 2004, https://archive.nwp.org/cs/public/print/resource/2540.

National Commission on Writing in America's Schools and Colleges. *The Neglected "R": The Need for a Writing Revolution*. Apr. 2003. https://archive.nwp.org/cs/public/print/resource/2523.

National Council of Teachers of English. *CCCC Position Statement on Disability Studies in Composition: Position Statement on Policy and Best Practices*. Mar. 2020, https://cccc.ncte.org/cccc/resources/positions/disabilitypolicy.

National Geographic Society. "Christine de Pisan: France's First Lady of Letters." *National Geographic History*, vol. 6, no. 1, Mar./Apr. 2020, pp. 8–11.

National Park Service. William Holmes McGuffey and His Readers. *Museum Gazette*, Jefferson National Expansion Memorial. https://www.nps.gov/jeff/learn/historyculture/upload/mcguffey.pdf. Accessed 27 Jul. 2020.

National Park Service Whitman Mission National Historic Site. "The Mission Press." 1 Mar. 2015. https://www.nps.gov/whmi/learn/history-culture/the-mission-press.htm. Accessed 6 May 2019.

Newman, M. Sophia. "So, Gutenberg Didn't Actually Invent the Printing Press as We Know It: On the Unsung Chinese and Korean History of Movable Type." *Literary Hub*, 19 Jun. 2019, https://lithub.com/so-gutenberg-didnt-actually-invent-the-printing-press/.

Niffenegger, Audrey. "What Does It Mean to Make a Book?" Wasserman, pp. 12–13.

NordNordWest. Printing towns incunabula. https://commons.wikimedia. org/w/index.php?curid=16276810. Accessed 30 December 2017.

Norris, Mary. *Between You & Me: Confessions of a Comma Queen*. W.W. Norton, 2016.

———. *Greek to Me: Adventures of the Comma Queen*. W.W. Norton, 2019.

O'Connell, Mark. "Pencils and Nothingness." Review of *How to Sharpen Pencils*, by David Rees, *The New Yorker*, 11 May 2012, https://www. newyorker.com/books/page-turner/pencils-and-nothingness.

O'Connor, Patricia T. *Woe Is I: The Grammarphobe's Guide to Better English in Plain English*. Riverhead Books, 1996.

O'Connor, Sheila. *Until Tomorrow, Mr. Marsworth*. Deckle Edge, 2018.

Olson, David R. "History of Schools and Writing." In *Handbook of Research on Writing*, edited by Charles Bazerman, Lawrence Erlbaum Associates, 2008, pp. 283–92.

1000+ People of the Millennium and Beyond. https://web. archive.org/web/20120303082307/http://rhsweb.org/ library/1000PeopleMillennium.htm. Accessed 21 Aug. 2021.

Owens, Kim Hensley. "'Look Ma, No Hands!': Voice Recognition Software, Writing, and Ancient Rhetoric." *Enculturation: A Journal for Rhetoric, Writing, and Culture*, vol. 7, 2010. http://enculturation.net/ look-ma-no-hands.

Owens, Kim Hensley, and Derek Van Ittersum. "Writing With(out) Pain: Computing Injuries and the Role of the Body in Writing Activity." *Computers and Composition*, vol. 30, no. 2, 2013, pp. 87–100.

Oxford Dictionaries. "Why Is the Alphabet Arranged the Way It Is?" https://en.oxforddictionaries.com/explore/why-is-the-alphabet -arranged-the-way-it-is/.

Palumbo, Annalisa. "This Single Working Mom Was Europe's First Professional Woman Writer." *National Geographic History Magazine*, 12 Mar. 2020, https://www.nationalgeographic.com/history/history- magazine/article/ single-working-mom-europe-first-professional-woman-writer.

Paperchase. "It's Good to be Green." 22 Jun. 2020, https://www.paper- chase.com/the-journal/paperchase-progress-for-the-planet/.

———. "Journaling for Better Mental Health," 10 Oct. 2019, https://www. paperchase.com/the-journal/journaling-for-better-mental-health/.

Park, Joomi. "NaNoWriMo." Tombro, pp. 269–71.

Patchett, Ann. *This Is the Story of a Happy Marriage*. Harper, 2013.

Patrikarakos, David. *War in 140 Characters: How Social Media Is Reshaping Conflict in the Twenty-First Century*. Basic Books, 2017.

Periyakoil, VJ. "Writing a 'Last Letter' When You're Healthy." *The New*

York Times, 7 Sep. 2016, https://www.nytimes.com/2016/09/07/well/
family/writing-a-last-letter-before-you-get-sick.html.

Peterson, Jeremiah (anctxtmodtablet). Tweet, 5 Jul. 2021, https://twitter.
com/anctxtmodtablet/status/1412202311863123970.

Petrie, Nicholas. "Loud Noise from Impact: An Auto-Ethnographic
Exploration of the New York City Slam Poetry Community." Honors
Thesis, Wesleyan University, 2012, https://doi.org/10.14418/wes01.1.66.

Pirsig, Robert. *Zen and the Art of Motorcycle Maintenance*. HarperCollins, 1974.

"Playing Against Type: The Typewriter Orchestra." *Vimeo*, 2017. https://
vimeo.com/211731018. Accessed 4 May 2020.

Pleasant, Eric. "Literacy Sponsors and Learning: An Ethnography of Punk
Literacy in Mid 1980s Waco." *Young Scholars in Writing*, vol. 5, 2007,
pp. 137–45.

Polacco, Patricia. *G is for Goat*. Puffin, 2006.

PooPooPaper Company. https://www.poopoopaper.com/en/. Accessed 30
Sep. 2018.

Povolny, Bonnie. "Nabu Museum Opens in Lebanon." *Cultural
Property News*, 24 Oct. 2018, https://culturalpropertynews.org/
nabu-museum-opens-in-lebanon/.

Powers, Richard. "How to Speak a Book." *The New York Times*, 7
Jan. 2007, https://www.nytimes.com/2007/01/07/books/review/
Powers2.t.html?scp=4&sq=Richard%20Powers&st=cse&_r=0.

Public Broadcasting System (PBS). Sullivan Ballou Letter, 2015. https://
www.pbs.org/kenburns/civil-war/war/historical-documents/sullivan-
ballou-letter/. Accessed 11 January 2019.

Pyne, Lydia. *Bookshelf*. Bloomsbury, 2016.

Quintillian. *Quintillian on Education*. Translated by William M. Smail,
Teachers College Press, 1966.

Quito, Anne. "What Would Justus Do? The Graceful Restoration of a
200-Year-Old Serif Typeface Shows the Problem with Digital Fonts."
Quartz, 17 Jul. 2018, https://qz.com/quartzy/1310669/.

Rankin, Laura. *The Handmade Alphabet*. Puffin, 1996.

Rees, David. *How to Sharpen Pencils: A Practical and Theoretical Treatise
on the Artisanal Craft of Pencil Sharpening, for Writers, Artists, Contractors, Flange Turners, Anglesmiths, and Civil Servants, with Illustrations Showing Current Practice*. Melville Books, 2012.

Reuters. "Here's the Queen's Consent for Prince Harry's Wedding."
The New York Times, 13 May 2018, https://www.nytimes.com/2018/
05/13/world/europe/uk-queen-consent-wedding.html?smid=fb-nytimes
&smtyp=cur.

Reynolds, Simon. "Emma Thompson to Write 'My Fair Lady.'" *Digital Spy*, 17 Jul. 2008, https://www.digitalspy.com/movies/a112135/emma-thompson-to-write-my-fair-lady/

Rinker, Harry L. "Slatington Kept Schools in Slates." *The Morning Call*, 18 Apr. 1993, https://www.mcall.com/news/mc-xpm-1993-04-18-2922750-story.html.

Robb, Don. *Ox, House, Stick: The History of Our Alphabet*. Charlesbridge, 2007.

Robert C. Williams American Museum of Papermaking. *Teachers' Guide: Your Guide to the Science, History, Art and Technology of Papermaking*. Georgia Institute of Technology.

"Robert Frost." *The Writer's Almanac*, 7 Mar. 2017, https://www.writersalmanac.org/index.html%3Fp=209.html.

Roberts, William. *History of Letter-Writing*. 1843. HardPress, 2017.

Robinson, Andrew. *The Story of Writing: Alphabets, Hieroglyphs, and Pictograms*. 2nd ed., Thames and Hudson, 2007.

Rogers, Bruce, et al. *Bookmaking on the Distaff Side*. Marchbanks Press, 1937.

Romano, Frank. *The History of the Linotype Company*. RIT Press, 2014.

Rose, Deborah Lee. *Into the A, B, Sea*. Scholastic Press, 2000.

Sacks, David. *Letter Perfect: The Marvelous History of Our Alphabet from A to Z*. Broadway Books, 2004.

The Saint John's Bible. http://www.saintjohnsbible.org/. Accessed 12 May 2019.

Saintsbury, George. *A Letter Book: Selected with an Introduction on the History and Art of Letter-Writing*. London: G. Bell; New York: Harcourt, Brace, 1922.

Sales, Nancy Jo. *American Girls: Social Media and the Secret Lives of Teenagers*. Knopf, 2016.

Sand, Alexa. "Birds in Hand: Micro-books and the Devotional Experience." *Sensory Reflections: Traces of Experience in Medieval Artifacts*, edited by Fiona Griffiths and Kathryn Starkey Berlin, De Gruyter, 2018, pp. 181–202, https://doi.org/10.1515/9783110563443-009.

Sandomir, Richard. "Peter V. Tytell, a Typewriter Whisperer, Is Dead at 74." *The New York Times*, 18 Aug. 2020, https://www.nytimes.com/2020/08/18/us/peter-v-tytell-dead.html.

The Saturday Evening Post. Vol. 182, no. 3, pp. 37 and 48. https://www.google.com/books/edition/The_Saturday_Evening_Post/tV4wAQAAMAAJ?hl=en&gbpv=1&bsq=Bennett%20typewriter

Schmandt-Besserat, Denise. *How Writing Came About*. U of Texas P, 1997.

Schniedewind, William M., and Zipora Cochavi-Rainey. *The el-Amarna Correspondence*. Brill, 2014.

The School of Life. *Phone Detox*. https://www.theschooloflife.com/shop/us/phone-detox/.

Schultz, Lucille M. *The Young Composers: Composition's Beginnings in Nineteenth-Century Schools*. NCTE, 1999.

ScribeAmerica. https://www.scribeamerica.com/solutions-medical-scribes/. Accessed 14 Mar. 2020.

Scribes: The American Society of Legal Writers. https://www.scribes.org/. Accessed 14 Mar. 2020.

Scribner, Sylvia, and Michael Cole. *The Psychology of Literacy*. Harvard UP, 1981.

Seshat: Global History Databank. http://seshatdatabank.info/. Accessed 12 Aug. 2021.

Shain, Susan. "We Could All Use a Little Snail Mail Right Now." *The New York Times*, 8 Oct. 2018, https://www.nytimes.com/2018/10/08/smarter-living/we-could-all-use-a-little-snail-mail-right-now.html?smid=fb-nytimes&smtyp=cur.

Shepherd, Margaret. *The Art of the Handwritten Note*. Broadway Books, 2002.

———. *Learn Calligraphy: The Complete Book of Lettering and Design*. Watson-Guptill, 2013.

Shewan, Dan. "10 of the Most Innovative Chatbots on the Web." WordStream Blog, 26 Feb. 2020, https://www.wordstream.com/blog/ws/2017/10/04/chatbots.

Silva, Horacio. "Gloria in Extremis." *The New York Times*, 4 Dec. 2008, https://www.nytimes.com/2008/12/07/style/tmagazine/07gloria.html.

Silver, Margarita Gokun. "The City That Launched the Publishing Industry." BBC, 9 Jul. 2019, http://www.bbc.com/travel/story/20190708-the-city-that-launched-the-publishing-industry.

Simonds, Merilyn. *Gutenberg's Fingerprint: Paper Pixels, and the Lasting Impression of Books*. ECW Press, 2017.

Singer, P.W., and Emerson T. Brooking. *Like War: The Weaponization of Social Media*. Eamon Dolan/Houghton Mifflin Harcourt, 2018.

Smith, Keith A. *Non-Adhesive Binding: Books without Paste or Glue*. Rev. ed., Sigma Foundation, 1999.

———. *Non-Adhesive Bindings: Exposed Spine Sewings*. Keith A. Smith Books, 2011.

———. *Quick Leather Bindings*. Keith A. Smith Books, 2003.

———. *Structure of the Visual Book*. 4th ed., Keith A. Smith Books, 2003.

Smith, Keith A., and Fred Jordan. *Bookbinding for Book Artists*. Keith A. Smith Books, 1998.

Smithsonian National Postal Museum. *Mail Call*. Digital exhibition, 2011, https://postalmuseum.si.edu/mailcall/2b.html. Accessed 5 Dec. 2017.

Smithsonian National Postal Museum. *Missing You—Letters from Wartime*, 2011. https://www.youtube.com/watch?v=EtjYFhmEvkE. Accessed 5 Dec. 2017.

Society of Typographic Aficionados. https://www.typesociety.org. Accessed 12 Aug. 2021.

Spellerberg, Ian. *Reading & Writing Accessories: A Study of Paper-Knives, Paper Folders, Letter Openers and Mythical Page Turners*. Oak Knoll Press, 2016.

Spinney, Laura. "The Database That Is Rewriting History to Predict the Future." *New Scientist*, 12 Oct. 2016, https://www.newscientist.com/article/mg23230950-600-the-database-that-is-rewriting-history-to-predict-the-future/.

Spooner, Michael. "How Everything Happens: Notes on May Swenson's Theory of Writing." *Body My House: May Swenson's Work and Life*, edited by Paul Crumbley and Patricia M. Gantt, Utah State UP, 2006, pp. 167–80.

Springen, Karen. "Women Publishers of the Early American Era." *American Spirit: Daughters of the American Revolution Magazine*, Mar./Apr. 2019, pp. 36–38.

Stadler, Martin A. "Thoth." *UCLA Encyclopedia of Egyptology*, edited by Jacco Dieleman and Willeke Wendrich, UCLA Library, http://digital2.library.ucla.edu/viewItem.do?ark=21198/zz002c4k99. Accessed 14 Dec. 2019.

Standage, Tom. *The Victorian Internet*. Walker & Company, 1998.

———. 2013. *Writing on the Wall: Social Media—The First 2,000 Years*. Bloomsbury, 2013.

Steel, Danielle. "21st Century." Blog entry, 20 Jan. 2011, https://www.daniellesteel.net/21st-century/.

Stell, Marianna. "Female Printers in Sixteenth-Century Paris." Library of Congress, 20 Aug. 2018, https://blogs.loc.gov/law/2018/08/female-printers-in-sixteenth-century-paris/.

Stewart, Jessica. "Brilliant New Typeface Combines Touchable Braille with Visible Letters." *My Modern Met*, 3 Apr. 2018, https://mymodernmet.com/braille-neue-typeface-kosuke-takahashi/.

Strunk, William, Jr., and E.B. White. 1918. *The Elements of Style*. 4th ed., Pearson, 2019.

Tannen, Deborah. "How the Pandemic Has Changed the Way We Greet Each Other." *The Washington Post*, 21 Jun. 2020, https://www.washingtonpost.com/opinions/2020/06/21/how-pandemic-has-changed-way-we-greet-each-other/.

13 Moons Magical Supplies. Talisman for Poets & Writers. https://www.13moons.com/talisman-for-poets. Accessed 8 Mar. 2019.

This Day in History. July 6, http://www.history.com/this-day-in-history/mark-twain-begins-reporting-in-virginia-city.

"This Week in Court." Logan *Herald Journal.* 28 Mar. 2020, p. A3.

Thomas, Lewis. *The Medusa and the Snail: More Notes of a Biology Watcher.* Viking, 1979.

Tiffany, Kaitlyn. "This Font You Know from Old Pulp Novels Is All Over New Books." *Vox*, 17 Jan. 2019, https://www.vox.com/the-goods/2019/1/17/18185389/lydian-font-book-design-nancy-drew-against-everything.

Tilghman, Ben C. "The Shape of the Word: Extralinguistic Meaning in Insular Display Lettering." *Word & Image*, vol. 27, no. 3, 2011, pp. 292–308, https://doi.org/10.1080/02666286.2011.541129.

Tombro, Melissa. *Teaching Autoethnography: Personal Writing in the Classroom.* Open SUNY Textbooks, 2016.

Truss, Lynne. *Eats, Shoots & Leaves: The Zero Tolerance Approach to Punctuation.* Gotham Books, 2003.

———. *Eats, Shoots & Leaves: Why, Commas Really Do Make a Difference!* G.P. Putnam, 2006.

Tschudin, Peter. *A Short Illustrated History of Paper.* Gustav Gissler Printing, 1980.

"Type Couple." *Time*, vol. 22, no. 19, 6 Nov. 1933, p. 46.

"Typewriter Poetry." *Atlas Obscura.* https://www.atlasobscura.com/videos/poem-store-typewritten-poetry.

US Department of Education. Improving Basic Programs Offered by Local Educational Agencies, Title I, Part A. 2018, https://www2.ed.gov/programs/titleiparta/index.html.

US Department of Health and Human Services. Common Rule (45 CFR 46, Subpart A). https://www.hhs.gov/ohrp/regulations-and-policy/regulations/45-cfr-46/index.html.

Vaidhyanathan, Siva. *Anti-Social Media: How Facebook Disconnects Us and Underminds Democracy.* Oxford UP, 2018.

Veterans Writing Project. https://veteranswriting.org/. Accessed 12 Aug. 2021.

Voice of America. "US Secret Service Laboratory Studies Ink to Solve Crimes." *Learning English*, 21 Jul. 2019, https://learningenglish.voanews.com/a/us-secret-service-laboratory-studies-ink-to-solve-crimes/4997791.html.

Voon, Claire. "How Students Built a 16th-Century Engineer's Book-Reading Machine." *Atlas Obscura*, 1 Jul. 2020, https://www.atlasobscura.com/articles/behold-the-renaissance-bookwheel.

Vowell, Sarah. *Unfamiliar Fishes*. Riverhead Books, 2011.

Wagner, Josh, and Joel Stein. "Goldman Sachs Has Money. It Has Power. And Now It Has a Font." *The New York Times*, 21 Aug. 2020, updated 22 Oct. 2020, https://www.nytimes.com/2020/08/21/business/gold-man-sachs-font.html.

Waldman, Katy. "Are Tiny Books a Sign of the Twee-Identification of Literary Culture?" *The New Yorker*, 1 Dec. 2018, https://www.newyorker.com/books/page-turner/are-tiny-books-a-sign-of-the-twee-ification-of-literary-culture.

Wallace, Carey. *The Blind Contessa's New Machine*. Penguin, 2010.

Wallace, Lawrence. *George W. Jones: Printer Laureate*. The Plough Press/Mark Batty, 2004.

Walters, John. Personal communication, e-mail. 13 Mar. 2019.

Ward, Adrian F., et al. "Brain Drain: The Mere Presence of One's Own Smartphone Reduces Available Cognitive Capacity." *Journal of the Association for Consumer Research*, vol. 2, no. 2, 2017, pp. 140–54. https://doi.org/10.1086/691462.

Warde, Beatrice. "The Crystal Goblet, or Why Printing Should Be Invisible." 1930, Digital OneTwo, 11 Jan. 2019, https://medium.com/@digitalonetwo/the-crystal-goblet-or-why-printing-should-be-invisible-78ac2cb2503a.

Wardle, Elizabeth. "Identity, Authority, and Learning to Write in New Workplaces." *Enculturation*, vol. 5, no. 2, 2004, http://www.encultura-tion.net/5_2/wardle.html. Reprinted in Wardle and Downs, pp. 520–37.

Wardle, Elizabeth, and Douglas Downs. *Writing about Writing*. Bedford/St. Martin's, 2010.

Wasserman, Krystyna. *The Book as Art: Artists' Books from the National Museum of Women in the Arts*. 2nd ed., Princeton Architectural Press, 2011.

Watson, Cecelia. *Semicolon: The Past, Present, and Future of a Misunderstood Mark*. Ecco, 2019.

Weathers, Winston. "Teaching Style: A Possible Anatomy." *College Composition and Communication*, vol. 21, no. 2, May 1970, pp. 144–49.

Weaver, Caroline. *The Pencil Perfect: The Untold Story of a Cultural Icon*. Gestalten, 2017.

———. *Pencils You Should Know: A History of the Ultimate Writing Utensil in 75 Anecdotes*. Chronicle Books, 2020.

———. "Why the Pencil Is Perfect." TED Talk, Mar. 2018, https://www.ted.com/talks/caroline_weaver_why_the_pencil_is_perfect.

Weeks, Lyman Horace. *Paper Manufacturing in the United States*. Lockwood Trade Journal Company, 1916.

Weidmann, Jake. "Why Write? Penmanship for the 21st Century." TedxMileHigh, 14 Jul. 2014, https://www.youtube.com/watch?v=85bqT904VWA.

Weiss, Daniel. "The Emperor of Stones." *Archaeology*, Jul./Aug. 2020, pp. 9–10, https://www.archaeology.org/rok.

Wells-Barnett, Ida B. "To the Members of the Anti-Lynching Bureau." 1 Jan. 1902. Library of Congress, https://lccn.loc.gov/91898226.

Westover, Tara. *Educated*. Random House, 2018.

Wilcox, Ralph S. "Arkansas Listings in the National Register of Historic Places: Rosenwald Schools." *Arkansas Historical Quarterly*, vol. 78, no. 1, Spring 2019, pp. 84–93.

Winchester, Simon. *The Professor and the Madman*. HarperCollins, 1998.

Wisconsin Historical Society. "Invention of the Typewriter." https://www.wisconsinhistory.org/Records/Article/CS8998. Accessed 12 Aug. 2021.

Wong, Caleb. "The Saga of Writing in Space." Smithsonian National Air and Space Museum, 9 Jun. 2017, https://airandspace.si.edu/stories/editorial/saga-writing-space.

"Writers' Favorite Pens." *The Coil Magazine*, 10 Jun. 2017, https://medium.com/the-coil/writers-favorite-pens-291dfe5b677f.

Writing through the Lifespan Collaboration. https://www.lifespanwriting.org/. Accessed 12 Aug. 2021.

Wymer, Norman. *English Town Crafts: A Survey of Their Development from Early Times to the Present Day*. B.T. Batsford, 1949.

Zapf-von Hesse, Gudrun. *Bindings, Handwritten Books, Type Faces, Examples of Lettering and Drawing*. Mark Batty, 2012.

Zanerian College. IAMPETH. https://www.iampeth.com/zanerian-college. Accessed 12 Aug. 2021.

Zdenek, Sean. *Reading Sounds: Closed-Captioned Media and Popular Culture*. U of Chicago P, 2015.

———. "Transforming Access and Inclusion in Composition Studies and Technical Communication." *College English*, vol. 82, no. 5, May 2020, pp. 536–44.

Permissions Acknowledgments

Bartz, Andrea. "Social Media Fakeness Is Bad for Our Psyches...but Great for Crime Writers." *Crime Reads*, 24 Mar. 2020. Reproduced by permission of Andrea Bartz. https://crimereads.com/social-media-fakeness-crime-writers/.

Brady, Lois Smith. "Before Saying 'I Do,' Define Just What You Mean." *The New York Times*, 16 Aug. 2013. Copyright © 2013 The New York Times Company. All rights reserved. Used under license.

Christensen, John. "The Rag Man." Utah Stories from the Beehive Archive, 2017-02-03. Copyright © 2017 Utah Humanities. Reprinted by permission of Utah Humanities. http://www.utahhumanities.org/stories/items/show/307.

Daley, Jason. "Museum Offers $15,000 per Character to Decipher Oracle Bone Script." *Smithsonian Magazine*, 26 Jul. 2017. Copyright © 2017 Smithsonian Institution. Reprinted with permission from Smithsonian Enterprises. All rights reserved. Reproduction in any medium is strictly prohibited without permission from Smithsonian magazine.

DeGaine, Lauren Elle. "The 'eBay Archive': Recovering Early Women Type Designers." *Modernism/Modernity Print Plus* 4.2 (2019). Copyright © 2019 Johns Hopkins University Press. Reprinted with the permission of Johns Hopkins University Press.

Douglass, Frederick. "Letter to Thomas Auld (September 3, 1848)." In *Frederick Douglass: Selected Speeches and Writings*, ed. Philip Foner and Yuval Taylor. The Library of Black America series, Lawrence Hill Books, an imprint of Chicago Review Press, 1999. Copyright © 1999 Estate of Philip S. Foner and Yuval Taylor. Reproduced with the permission of Chicago Review Press Inc., conveyed through Copyright Clearance Center, Inc.

Hanks, Tom. "I Am TOM, I Like to TYPE, Hear That!" *The New York Times*, 3 Aug. 2013. Reproduced with the permission of ICM Partners.

Kennard, Jennifer. "Press Kit." *Letterology*, 3 Mar. 2014. Reproduced with permission. http://www.letterology.com/2014/03/press-kit.html?m=1.

Marantz, Andrew. "What the Coronavirus Crisis Has Changed about Social Media, and What It Hasn't Changed." *The New Yorker*, 26 Mar. 2020. Copyright © Condé Nast. Reprinted by permission of Condé Nast.

McCulloch, Gretchen. "We Learned to Write the Way We Talk." *The New York Times*, 27 Dec. 2019. Copyright © 2019 The New York Times Company. All rights reserved. Used under license.

National Commission on Writing for America's Families, Schools, and Colleges. From *Writing: A Ticket to Work ... or a Ticket Out*. Copyright © 2004 The College Board. www.collegeboard.org.

Patchett, Ann. From Chapter 2: "The Getaway Car." In *This Is the Story of a Happy Marriage* (pp. 51–60), HarperCollins Publishers. Copyright © 2013 Ann Patchett. Reprinted by permission of ICM Partners.

Quito, Anne. "What Would Justus Do? The Graceful Restoration of a 200-year-old Serif Typeface Shows the Problem with Digital Fonts." *Quartz*, 17 Jul. 2018. Copyright © 2018 Quartz Media, Inc. Reproduced with the permission of Wright's Media, LLC as agent for Quartz Media, Inc.

Thomas, Lewis. "Notes on Punctuation." In *The Medusa and the Snail: More Notes of a Biology Watcher*. The Viking Press, 1979; Penguin Books, 1995. Copyright © 1974, 1975, 1976, 1977, 1978, 1979 by Lewis Thomas. Used by permission of The Viking Press, an imprint and division of Penguin Random House LLC. All rights reserved.

Wong, Caleb. "The Saga of Writing in Space." 9 Jun. 2017. Archives Division, National Air and Space Museum, Smithsonian Institution, Washington, DC. https://airandspace.si.edu/stories/editorial/saga-writing-space.

Image Credits

Figure 1.1, p. 37: Graphs by Joyce Kinkead.

Figures 2.1 and 2.2, p. 47: Photographs by Joyce Kinkead.

Figure 2.3, p. 48: From the library of the Assyrian king Ashurbanipal II at Kouyunjik (Nineveh), Mesopotamia, Iraq. 7th century BCE. The British Museum, London. Uploaded by Osama Shukir Muhammed Amin, 7 Apr. 2016, licensed under CC BY-NC-SA 1.0; https://creativecommons.org/licenses/by-nc-sa/1.0/.

Figure 4.1, p. 88: Photograph by Joyce Kinkead.

Figure 4.2, p. 89: Museum for Communication, Nuremberg, Germany (photograph by Joyce Kinkead).

Figure 4.3, p. 90: Advertising poster for the green Castell 9000 pencil, by A.W. Faber, 1905. Reproduced with permission.

Figure 4.4, p. 91: Image courtesy of Thoreau Farm. https://thoreaufarm.org/2016/10/new-york-erases-concords-preeminent-pencil-past/.

Figure 4.5, p. 92: Rees, David. Cover image, *How to Sharpen Pencils*, published by Melville House, 2012. Reproduced with permission of Melville House Publishing. All rights reserved.

Figure 4.6, p. 93: National Archeological Museum of Naples. Photograph by Joyce Kinkead.

Figure 4.7, p. 96: Photograph by Joyce Kinkead.

Figure 4.8, p. 97: Dou, Gerrit. "Scholar Sharpening a Quill Pen," 1633. The Leiden Collection, New York.

Figure 4.9, p. 101: Goines, David Lance. India Ink Gallery poster (#43). Copyright © 1999 David Lance Goines. Reproduced by permission of David Lance Goines.

Figure 5.1, p. 116: Photograph by Joyce Kinkead.

Figure 5.2, p. 118: Photograph by Joyce Kinkead.

Figure 5.3, p. 118: Image of elephant dung stationery. Copyright © 2021 The POOPOOPAPER Online Store. Reproduced with permission. https://www.poopoopaper.com/.

Figure 5.4, p. 121: Photograph by Joyce Kinkead.

Figure 6.1, p. 130: Von Soest, Conrad. "Brillenapostel," 1403.

Figure 6.2, p. 132: Photograph by Joyce Kinkead.

Figure 6.3, p. 135: https://commons.wikimedia.org/wiki/File:Dwarsligger.PD_5363.jpg.

Figure 6.4, p. 137: Photograph by Joyce Kinkead.

Figure 6.5, p. 140: Photograph by Joyce Kinkead.

Figure 7.1, p. 149: Photograph by Joyce Kinkead.

Figure 7.2, p. 150: Photograph by Joyce Kinkead.

Figure 7.3, p. 154: From *La Grande Danse Macabre* (Lyon, France, 1499).

Figure 7.4, p. 155: Photograph by Joyce Kinkead.

Figure 7.5, p. 155: https://commons.wikimedia.org/wiki/File:Caxton_printers_mark.cropped.jpg.

Figure 7.6, p. 161: Photograph by Joyce Kinkead.

Figure 7.7, p. 163: https://williammorrissociety.org/event/online-launch-and-talk-the-kelmscott-press-books-in-a-19th-century-context/.

Figure 7.8, p. 164: Smy, Pam and Ness Wood. Poster. "Collections and Collaborations," 2019. Reproduced by permission of the St. Bride Foundation. https://stbridelibrary.bigcartel.com/.

Figure 9.1, p. 186: Image courtesy of Joyce Kinkead.

Figure 9.2, p. 187: From the *Nuremberg Chronicle* by Hartmann Schedel (1440–1514).

Figure 9.3, p. 189: Peterson, Jeremiah. Photos of Mesopotamian cuneiform clay tablet replicas by Jeremiah Peterson. Reproduced with permission. https://www.etsy.com/shop/AncientTextModTablet.

Figure 9.4, p. 190: Image by Jeff Dahl. Licensed under CC BY-SA 4.0; https://commons.wikimedia.org/wiki/File:Seshat.svg.

Figure 9.5, p. 193: Photograph by Joyce Kinkead.

Figure 10.1, p. 206: Image courtesy of the Library of Congress.

Figure 10.2, p. 208: https://img1.etsystatic.com/047/0/5398785/il_fullxfull.731170469_194u.jpg.

Figure 10.3, p. 209: *Linecasting Machine by Mergenthaler, c. 1890*, 2021, Museum of Applied Arts & Sciences, accessed 9 Dec. 2021, https://ma.as/207003.

Figure 10.4, p. 210: Photograph by Joyce Kinkead.

Figure 10.5, p. 210: Image courtesy of http://www.thinglink.com/scene/459839379272105986.

Figure 10.6, p. 211: https://www.shutterstock.com/image-photo/washington-dc-usa-may-1-2007-642541903.

Figure 10.7, p. 213: Image courtesy of the Virtual Typewriter Museum.

Figure 10.8, p. 214: Photograph by Joyce Kinkead.

Figure 10.9, p. 216: Photograph by Joyce Kinkead.

Figure 10.10, p. 219: Image courtesy of Utah State University Special Collections.

Figure 11.1, p. 237: Photograph by Joyce Kinkead.

Figure 11.2, p. 241: *Les Très Riches Heures de Duc du Berry*, 15th century.

Figure 11.3, p. 247: Braille Neue's alphabet. Copyright © 2018 Braille Neue. All rights reserved. Reprinted with permission. http://brailleneue.com/.

Figure 11.4, p. 248: Swenson, May. "How Everything Happens (Based on a Study of the Wave)." Copyright © 1970 May Swenson. Originally appeared in *Iconographs*, collected in *May Swenson: Collected Poems* (Library of America, 2013). Used with permission of the Literary Estate of May Swenson. All rights reserved.

Figure 11.5, p. 251: Used by permission of Kaitlin Johnson.

Figure 12.1, p. 266: Photograph by Joyce Kinkead.

Figure 12.2, p. 269: Photograph by Joyce Kinkead.

Figure 12.3, p. 281: Photograph by Joyce Kinkead.

Figure 12.4, p. 282: Photograph by Joyce Kinkead.

Figure 12.5, p. 285: https://www.shutterstock.com/image-vector/cute-kawaii-snail-mail-111978236.

Figure 13.1, p. 296: From the *Illustrated Catalogue of School Supplies* (1897–98).

Figure 13.2, p. 297: Photograph by Joyce Kinkead.

Figure 13.3, p. 301: Bibliothèque nationale de France.

Figure 15.1, p. 336: Paperchase, UK, 2020.

Figure 15.2, p. 337: Meeker, Mary. Digital media usage graph, "Daily Hours Spent with Digital Media per Adult User, USA." *Internet Trends 2019*, Bond. Reproduced with permission. https://www.bondcap.com/.

Figure 15.3, p. 341: Uploaded by Luis Rubio, 4 Sept. 2006, licensed under CC BY 2.0; https://commons.wikimedia.org/wiki/File:Kilroy_Was_Here__Washington_DC_WWII_Memorial.jpg.

Figure 16.1, p. 355: Image courtesy of Joyce Kinkead.

Index

ableism and ableist language, 308
accordion books, 137, 362–63
Adelman, Mary, 218, 225
Akhenaten (Egyptian monarch), 264
Alberic of Monte Cassino, 267
alphabets,
    Arabic, 73
    Braille, 74
    Cherokee, 68–70, 195
    Cyrillic, 72–73
    Deseret, 74
    Electronic, 75
    Greek, 49, 67, 68, 72, 75, 191, 369
    Hebrew, 73
    International Phonetic, 75–76
    Japanese, 70
    Phoenician, 64, 67, 73, 191, 298
    Roman, 64, 70, 72, 73, 75, 94, 157, 158, 252
    Runic, 70–72
    Viking, 70
Amarna, 264&n1
amate, 120
Americans with Disabilities Act (ADA), 205n1, 305
Anglo-Saxon, 63, 70, 286
Antiqua, 132, 152n3, 244, 245, 246, 254, 259, 260
apostrophe, 171, 173, 175, 176, 177, 180

app (application), 224, 332, 333, 334, 337, 342, 343, 344, 347
Apple, 218, 220, 306
Arabic, 56, 63, 64, 67, 73, 113, 114, 119, 129, 130, 195, 216, 236
Aristotle, 93, 129, 193, 300, 356
artifacts, 38, 43, 44, 49, 56, 61, 73, 107, 109, 137, 224, 258, 363, 370, 374
Arts and Crafts Movement, 134, 156, 162, 239, 258
asemic writing, 30, 250, 251, 369
Atlas Obscura, 60, 139
Atossa (Queen), 264
Austen, Jane, 133, 270
autobiography, 34, 41, 44, 181, 227, 309
autoethnography, 21, 34, 36, 38, 40, 41, 43–44, 106, 181, 227, 309, 362, 363
Aztecs, 194

Babylon, 49, 50, 374
bamboo, 120, 126, 127, 161, 236, 369
Bantock, Nick, 283
bark paper, 120, 369
Baskerville, John, 153&n6, 245, 248, 261
Bazerman, Charles, 21, 357
Berry, Wendell, 197
Bible, 72, 126, 127, 128, 132, 133, 142, 148, 149, 150, 151, 152, 153, 157, 158, 164, 264, 301

Baskerville Bible, 153&n6
Devil's Bible (or *Codex Gigas*), 149
Gutenberg Bible, 152, 153&n5, 161,
    243n5
St. John's Bible, 128n3, 242–43
Bich, Michel, 99
Bickham, George, 100, 110, 236
Bíró, László, 99
bíró pens, 99, 105, 107
black market, 19, 88, 115
Blickensderfer, George C., 209, 210, 215
blogs and bloggers, 40, 73, 141, 159,
    165, 166, 200, 213, 312, 333–34, 336,
    344, 345, 346, 355, 360, 365,
Bodoni, 133, 137, 245, 254, 259
Bonhomme, Yolande, 159
book arts, 134, 136–38, 139, 141, 258,
    369–70
book barrels, 153
Book of Kells, 240, 249
Book of Kildare, 186
Book of the Dead, 190, 297, 298, 370
book, parts of, 131
bookbinders, 126, 131, 158, 186, 187,
    246, 269
bookbinding, 136, 137, 139, 140, 141
    Coptic, 141
    Japanese Stab, 141
    Kettle stitch, 131
    Long stitch, 141
books,
    artists', 137, 138, 139, 369
    of curses, 139
    die-cut, 131, 137
    e-books, 126, 134&n4, 138
    handmade, 362, 363
    miniature, 135–36
    paperback, 134, 135
    sacred, 126–27, 128, 148, 161, 187,
        191, 236, 241, 268, 352
booksellers, 128, 132, 133, 186
bookwheel, 141
Boston Typewriter Orchestra (BTO),
    207

boustrophedon, 64
Bradbury, Ray, 207
Braille, 74, 205, 246, 247, 306, 370
Braille, Louis, 74, 205, 307
Bréjoux, Jacques, 15, 122
bronze, 46, 127, 153
Brown, Rollo Walter, 303
Buddhism, 102, 117, 126, 148, 373
bullet journal, 30, 39, 250, 356
Bullock, William, 147, 148
Burns, Ken, 271

Cadmus, 67, 69, 191
calligraphy, 30, 73, 96, 97, 99, 107, 126,
    128n3, 131, 162, 235–39, 240, 242,
    243, 249, 250, 257, 289, 316, 341,
    363, 370, 372
Calliope (Greek Muse), 192, 198
Cangjie, 193
Carolingian Minuscule, 151–52
Carolingian script, 187&n1, 244, 300
cartouche, 51&n3, 52, 58,
Carvalho, David, 102, 110, 235
Cascajal Block, 54–55
caster, 152
Catholic Church, 128, 153, 185, 268, 340
Caxton, William, 154–56
Celtic, 195, 252
Center for the Book, 141, 258
Cervantes, Miguel de, 139
chained books, 40, 150, 370
Champollion, Jean-François, 18,
    51–53, 376
Charlemagne, 151, 187n1, 244, 300–01,
    303
chatbot, 334
Cherokee, 68–70, 195, 231
China, 30, 46, 48, 58, 60, 66, 101, 102,
    112, 113&n1, 117&n5, 119, 120,
    126–27, 148, 153, 158, 193–94, 216–
    17, 236, 264, 269, 374, 375, 377
Christensen, Ward, 331
Cicero, 93, 129, 193, 267&n3, 268, 298,
    300

Civil War, 90, 105, 112, 116, 125, 271, 279, 280, 288, 303

clay tablets, 38, 46, 48, 56, 66, 94, 119, 126&n1, 188, 190, 265, 296–97, 370

COBOL, 219

Code of Hammurabi, 49–50, 51, 56, 189

codex and codices, 15, 54, 119, 120, 126, 137, 149, 370, 377

coffin, 157

colon, 171, 173, 174–75, 176, 178, 180, 181, 182

Colonial Era, USA, 112, 127n2, 159, 160, 373

colophon, 113, 155, 159, 162, 370, 407

Colwell, Elizabeth, 256–59

comma, 40, 171, 172, 173, 174, 176–77, 178, 179, 180, 181, 183, 271, 371, 375

compositor, 18, 65, 154, 220

computer age, 212, 306, 376, 377

computer mouse, 219–20

Computerized Bulletin Board System (CBBS), 331

computers, 20, 72, 94, 100, 103, 121, 152, 164, 213, 217–24, 225, 239, 244, 245, 260, 284, 314, 331, 332, 373, 374

Conté, Nicholas Jacques, 89, 91

correspondence, personal, 33, 136, 264, 265, 271, 283, 284, 288, 297, 319, 324, 355

crayon, 105, 143, 309

cuneiform, 20, 31, 45, 46, 48–51, 53, 54, 56, 57, 58, 66, 94, 102, 126n1, 188, 189, 190, 264n1, 296, 298, 370, 377

dauber, 370

Day, John, 156

de Pisan, Christine, 155, 241–42

de Sévigné, Madame, 18, 268, 269&n5, 270

de Worde, Wynkyn, 156

Defoe, Daniel, 139

demotic script, 51, 53, 54, 58, 85, 297, 370, 372

Denham, Henry, 178

Described and Captioned Media Program (DCMP), 306

desktop publishing, 164

dictionaries, 64, 270, 371

digital detox, 30, 335–38, 343&n4

digital devices, 19, 21, 36, 39, 44, 217, 220, 226–27, 335, 337, 342, 343

dip pen, 97, 98, 236, 371

diple, 173, 175

disabilities, 205n1, 224, 305–07, 308

divination, 46, 54, 194, 236, 290, 374

divorce decree, 358, 360

dot matrix printer, 164

Douglass, Frederick, 272–79

Dove Press, 254, 371

dragon bones, 46, 60

Dürer, Albrecht, 244

dwarsligger, 135, 138, 371

Ebert, Roger, 198

Ebla (Syria), 48, 66, 72

Edict of Nantes, 160

Edison, Thomas Alva, 215

eduba, 296

Egypt and Egyptians, 21, 46, 51–54, 56, 58, 66, 67, 73, 95, 102, 119, 127, 188, 189–91, 198, 216, 264, 296, 297–98, 358, 370, 372, 375, 377

em dash, 173, 176, 180, 371

email, 177, 214, 223, 226, 284, 288, 312, 313, 314, 315, 332, 337, 360

emoji, 178, 230, 346

en dash, 173, 176, 180, 371

Engelbart, Douglas, 219

engraving, 90, 100, 110, 117n5, 130, 236, 360

epistle and epistolary, 53, 78, 263–64, 267, 268, 270, 282, 291

epistolary novel, 221n4, 282–84, 288

epitaph, 235, 358–59, 362

eraser, 33, 87, 104, 211, 221, 252, 309, 371

Erasmus, Desiderius, 113, 159, 268&n4
ethical, 23, 24, 25, 41, 364
ethics, 40
exclamation point, 172, 173, 174, 177,
    178, 179, 180, 181, 182, 183, 228, 373

Faber-Castell, 87, 89–91, 105
Fabri, Anna, 159
Facebook, 42, 255, 312, 331, 332, 333,
    334, 336, 338, 339, 347, 348, 365
ferrule, 87, 104, 371
Fielding, Henry, 282–83
Fogarty, Mignon, 179
folding books, 371
folio, 143, 372
fonts, 131–32, 133, 152, 153, 158, 169,
    176, 215, 231, 243–46, 247–48, 253,
    256, 259–61, 372, 373, 377
Foudrinier brothers, 115, 116
France, 15, 22, 56, 95, 98, 113, 115, 122,
    136, 151, 154, 160, 161, 162, 187,
    192, 259, 269, 279, 283, 301, 302,
    303
    Ambert, 113, 404
    Angoulême, 15, 279
    Le Puy-en-Velay, 192
    Lyon, 151, 154
    Paris, 49, 50, 54, 56, 114n3, 129,
        132, 151, 159, 161, 269, 279,
        302n1, 303
Franklin, Ann, 160
Franklin, Benjamin, 111–12, 136–37,
    245, 267n3
frisket, 157
Froben, Johann, 113, 156
Frogmore Mill, 115
Frost, Robert, 197
furniture, 372, 376
Fust, Johannes, 153
Futhark (Viking alphabet), 70
Fuxi/Paoxi, 194

galley, 152, 372
Ganesha (Indian deity), 194

Garamond, 133, 245, 254
Garamond, Claude, 245, 261
genres, 25–29, 53, 106, 107, 166, 239,
    264, 312, 360
Germany, 112, 116, 117, 120, 137, 151,
    153, 159, 255, 259, 264, 280, 302,
    340
    Nuremberg, 87, 88, 89, 104, 216
Gilgamesh and *Epic of Gilgamesh*, 46,
    48, 49, 126n1, 190
Gill, Eric, 250, 254
Glidden, Carlos, 209
glyph, 20, 46, 54–55, 60, 66, 180, 243,
    372, 373
Goddard, Mary Katherine, 160
goddesses, 20, 49, 93n2, 119, 188–97,
    198
gods, 20, 51, 53, 54, 72, 126, 186, 188–
    97, 198, 199, 264, 290, 352
Goethe, Johann Wolfgang von, 259,
    263–64, 283
Gothic script/type, 132, 152&n3, 244,
    252, 372, 407
Goudy, 254
Goudy, Frederic W., 246&n6
Gourdie, Tom, 295
Graham, Bette Nesmith, 104
graffiti, 18, 340–41
grammar, 29, 49, 129, 157, 168, 171,
    173&n3, 174, 175, 177, 178, 179, 187,
    192, 193, 203, 268, 270, 299, 300,
    302, 311, 317, 326, 329, 377
Granjon, 156, 254
graphite, 19, 87–89, 90, 91, 92, 104, 372
Greece, 188, 267, 298, 341
Greek, 34, 48, 49, 51, 64, 67, 72, 75, 119,
    158, 159, 173, 179, 181, 191, 195,
    198, 235, 241, 264, 297, 298–99, 341,
    356, 369, 371, 372, 375, 376, 377
Green, Ann Catherine, 160
Grolier Club, 136
Guillard, Charlotte, 159
guillemets, 175
Gutenberg Bible, 153&n5, 164–65

Gutenberg, Johannes, 20, 102, 113, 117n5, 126, 127–28, 131, 160, 165, 244, 268, 373, 374
Gutenberg printing press, 113, 117n5, 127–28, 147, 148, 151–53, 156, 157, 164, 165, 187, 208, 224, 225, 302, 373
gutter, 372

handwriting, 95, 99–101, 110, 128, 131, 176, 189, 236, 237, 238, 249, 288, 295, 370, 372, 373, 374, 376, 377
    English Round Hand, 100, 236, 249
    physical posture, 36, 102
Hanks, Tom, 207, 217, 227, 230
Hanx Writer, 207
Harjo, Joy, 70
hashtag, 333, 340
Hawaii, 22, 147, 156–59, 352
Hebrew, 67, 73, 119, 158, 255
Helvetica, 133, 245, 254, 372
hermeneutic, 191
Hermes Trismegistus, 191
Hesiod, 192, 298
hieratic script, 53, 54, 58, 297, 370, 372, 376
hieroglyphs and hieroglyphics, 20, 31, 46, 51–54, 58, 66, 85, 190, 297, 298, 370, 372, 376, 377
Holmes, Kris, 246, 254
Homebrew Computer Club, 218, 219
Hopper, Grace, 218–19
Horie, Yukio, 99
hornbook, 372
Hubbard, Elbert, 162–63
humanism and humanists, 113, 129, 132, 223, 245, 254, 268&n4, 307
humanist script, 152&n3
Hunter, Dard, 103, 111, 115&n4, 116, 117

ideogram, 65, 86, 371, 372, 373, 375
illuminated manuscripts, 126, 128n3, 162, 186, 235, 240&n4, 241, 242, 251, 372, 373

incunabula, 153, 242, 373
India, 78, 100, 194, 239, 352
India ink, 101
ink, 39, 56, 94, 95, 96–99, 101–03, 105, 107, 108, 110, 119, 127, 143, 148, 150, 152, 157, 167, 190, 215, 232, 236, 238, 239, 240, 242, 244, 253, 297–98, 370, 371, 372, 373, 374, 375, 376, 377
ink ball, 152, 370
inkstone, 236
Instagram, 333, 336, 338, 344, 345, 347
insular script, 249, 377
International Business Machines (IBM), 207, 215, 219, 221, 222, 232, 254, 332
italics, 174, 175, 244, 309, 373, 377
Italy, 113, 115, 187, 208, 244, 259, 263, 302, 373
    Fabriano, 113, 115
    Pompeii, 92, 93, 95, 340
    Rome, 67, 92, 93, 120, 172, 188, 267, 298, 303, 377
    Venice, 174, 244
Itzamná (Mayan deity), 194

Japan, 22, 99, 113, 115n4, 117, 126, 133, 139, 140, 141, 194, 246, 315, 357, 377
Jefferson, Thomas, 127, 159
Jikji, 126, 161, 373
Jobs, Steve, 218, 220
The Jolly Postman, 283
Jones, George W., 156
journals, 30, 38, 39, 40, 44, 195, 250, 336, 354, 355, 356
Julian of Norwich, 128

Kanzi (Bonobo ape), 77–78
Kazakhstan, 73
Keller, Friedrich Gottlob, 116
Keller, Helen, 205, 207, 224
Kelmscott Chaucer, 156n7
Kelmscott Press, 134, 162, 163, 239
kerning, 244, 373

Ketubah, 357
keyboards, 22, 100, 104, 178, 201, 204,
    208, 209, 211, 212, 216, 217, 221,
    226, 229, 231, 232, 243, 373
King, Stephen, 105, 197
Kipling, Rudyard, 78, 79, 86
Knorozov, Yuri, 54
Korea, 20, 113, 117, 126, 133, 153, 160–
    62, 236n1, 279, 373, 374
    Cheongju, 161

Lancy, David, 21, 354
laptop, 94, 102, 109, 223, 231, 297, 337
Latin, 63, 95, 105, 119, 127, 128, 129,
    141, 143, 159, 172, 173, 193, 235,
    242, 247, 264, 299, 300, 301, 340,
    352, 371, 372, 374, 377
leaf, 112, 127, 143, 372, 373, 374
letter carriers, 279, 289
letterlocking, 18, 30, 265, 288
letterpress, 31, 136, 162, 166, 240, 255,
    258, 289, 370, 373, 376
letters (*see also* correspondence),
    dead letters, 286–87
    letter-writing manuals, 267–71, 282,
    287
    types of letters, 267
lexigrams, 77–78, 373
liberal arts, 129, 193, 244, 302, 377. *See
    also* trivium *and* quadrivium
libraries, 48, 53, 90, 119, 125, 129, 130,
    132, 136, 138, 139, 158, 190, 192,
    199, 242, 258, 260, 290, 370
    circulating, 133
Library of Congress, 69, 141, 159, 191
lifespan writing, 21, 35, 38, 44, 354,
    357–62
ligatures, 152, 373
Lindisfarne Gospels, 241, 249
linotype, 156, 163, 207, 374
Lipman, Hymen, 104
logic, 53, 63, 64, 129, 192, 193, 197, 300,
    302, 329, 377
logogram, 65, 66, 102, 374

logograph, 49, 374
Love Letters, A.R. Gurney, 283
lower case, 152, 187, 192, 260, 300, 373,
    374
Lucar, Elizabeth, 235, 239
Lun, Tsai (Cai), 112
Luther, Martin, 128, 131, 268, 340

madrassa, 129, 239
majuscule, 143, 374
Maldives, 63–64
Malo, David, 158, 352
Manutius, Aldus, 174, 176
Masters, Edgar Lee, 358
material culture, 19, 21, 33, 38, 44, 106,
    107, 123, 224, 259, 309, 336, 363,
    367, 374
matrices, 374
Mayan, 20, 54, 60, 66, 120, 194, 372
McCulloch, Gretchen, 178, 227, 230
McGuffey, William Holmes, 303
McPhee, John, 197
mechanical pencil, 39, 91, 108
mentor texts, 304–05
Mergenthaler, Ottmar, 163
Merovingian script, 244
Mesoamerica, 46, 194
Mesopotamia, 21, 48–49, 93, 190, 296,
    370, 374
Middle Ages, 40, 126, 129, 135, 141,
    142, 143, 148, 150, 155, 162, 173,
    187, 188, 193, 240, 242, 267, 268,
    302, 316, 370, 372, 373, 377
Miedinger, Max, 245, 372
minuscule, 143, 152, 244, 374
missionaries, 72, 133, 157–59, 352
mold, 112, 114, 133, 236
Moleskine notebooks, 30, 40, 290, 309
monks, 102, 148, 172, 173&n1, 241,
    242, 300, 316
monotype, 245, 246, 250, 259, 261
Morison, Stanley, 245
Morris, William, 117, 133–34, 136,
    156&n7, 162, 239, 240–41, 246n6, 257

Mount Helicon, 192
movable type, 46, 117n5, 126–27, 133,
    151, 153, 160, 161, 163, 164, 244,
    373, 374, 375
Murphy, James J., 267, 286, 296, 299
muses, 44, 186, 191&n2, 192, 196, 197,
    198, 199
Myspace, 332

Nabu (Mesopotamian deity), 189–90
Nairne, Edware, 104
Napoleon, 51&n3, 53, 104, 136, 259,
    376
NASA, 30, 107–08, 218, 247, 249
National Commission on Writing, 318
National Council of Teachers of Eng-
    lish (NCTE), 173n3, 222, 307
National Letter Writing Day, 289
National Letter Writing Week, 289
National Novel Writing Month, 42, 43
National Poetry Month, 289
National Punctuation Day, 171, 179,
    181
Nepal, 22, 117–18
Netherlands, The, 22, 135, 138, 160,
    371
newspapers, 70, 99, 103, 111, 116, 121,
    147–48, 156n8, 157, 160, 165, 167,
    198, 216, 220, 239, 245, 272, 291,
    354, 355, 361
Nez Percé, 158, 159
nib pen, 38, 371, 375
Nisaba (Sumerian deity), 49, 188–90
Nixon, Richard M., 266
Norris, Mary, 40, 179
Noyce, Robert, 220
nuns, 148, 316

Obookiah, Henry, 157
octothorpe (or hashtag), 180, 333, 374
Odin (Norse deity), 193
Ogma (Gaelic deity), 193
Olivetti (typewriter), 214, 215, 221, 231
Olmec, 54

Olympia (typewriter), 40, 213, 214, 232
Optima, 133, 246, 254
oracle bones, 19, 20, 30, 46, 47, 56, 58,
    60–61, 66, 194, 236, 374
orthography, 72, 74, 187, 374, 377
Oxford English Dictionary (OED), 193,
    371

page, 112, 119, 126, 130–31, 133, 134,
    135, 136, 137, 142, 143, 144, 147,
    148–49, 150, 152, 157, 211, 221–22,
    240, 315, 340, 369, 371, 372, 373,
    374, 376
paleography, 152n2, 374
palm leaves, 112, 127, 374
Palmer Method, 100&n3, 101
paper,
    bark, 120, 369
    handmade, 40, 117–19, 123, 162,
        290
    poo-poo, 40
    recycled, 40, 112, 117, 119, 122, 123,
        366
    rice, 120
paper mill, 15, 22, 112, 113–14, 115,
    123, 244, 279
paperchase, 118, 121, 336
papyrus, 31, 53, 54, 58, 94, 102, 112,
    119, 120, 127, 190, 254, 297, 240,
    374, 375, 376
parchment, 92, 97, 103, 112, 119, 127,
    142, 148, 151, 152, 153, 240, 316,
    370, 375, 376, 377
Patchett, Ann, 185, 197
patron saints, 20, 185–88, 197, 198
Peale, Charles Willson, 127&n2
pencil sharpener, 91, 106
pencils, 19, 20, 21, 33, 39, 40, 87–92,
    101, 104, 105–06, 107–10, 166, 252,
    287, 295, 309, 313, 371, 372
    Blackwing, 40
Penguin Books, 134, 135
penknife, 22
penmanship, 100, 232, 236, 238, 249, 270

penny dreadfuls, 134, 162
pens,
    ballpoint, 20, 38, 40, 91, 94, 98–99,
        100, 107, 108
    felt-tip, 39, 99, 108, 109
    Fude, 99
    fountain, 20, 39, 41, 97, 98, 99, 100,
        105, 106, 142, 290, 371, 372
    gel, 38, 99, 376
    quill, 18, 22, 30, 38, 94–97, 98, 105,
        143, 148, 242, 269, 375
    reed, 38, 48, 56, 93, 94, 96, 98, 102,
        105, 190, 377
    sign, 99
percontation point, 178, 180, 375
personal computer (PC), 20, 164, 215,
    218, 219, 220, 222, 223, 261
petroglyphs, 56, 375
Philyra (Greek deity), 191
Phoenicians, 64, 67, 73, 191, 298
pictograms, 49, 65, 78, 372, 373, 375
pictographs, 46, 48, 49, 59, 65, 77, 188
pictography, 65–66, 78, 86
Pinterest, 333, 336, 360
Plato, 41, 129, 268
Pocket Books, 134
poison pen, 266&n2
post office, 279, 286
postage stamp, 265, 279, 280, 286, 287,
    289
postal service, 231, 271, 279–81
    National Postal Museum, 279, 281,
        285, 286, 289, 290
postmark, 280–81
PostSecret, 285
Priestley, Joseph, 104&n5
Priscian, 193, 300
printing presses,
    British, 154–56. See also Caxton
    Gutenberg, 113, 117n5, 127, 128,
        147, 148, 151–53, 156, 157, 164,
        187, 208, 224, 225, 302, 373
    Hawaiian, 156–59
    Rotary, 147–48, 167–68

Project Gutenberg, 134&n4
psalter, 135, 139, 375
punch, 152, 374, 375
punctus, 173, 174, 175, 176, 375

quadrivium, 129, 192, 302, 377
question mark, 172, 173, 174, 177, 178,
    179, 180, 181, 183, 373, 375
Quetzalcoatl (Aztec deity), 194
Quintilian, 120, 298–99
quipu, 194&n5
quire, 114, 142, 143–44, 375, 376
quoin, 376
Quran, 126, 194, 236
QWERTY, 205, 206–07, 208, 209, 212,
    216, 217, 220, 221, 373

Rag Man, 122–23
rags, 19, 111–12, 113, 114, 115, 117, 123,
    153
ream, 40, 114, 207, 376
red-letter days, 135, 150
reed pen, 38, 94, 96, 105, 190, 377
Remington (typewriter), 206, 207, 208,
    211, 231
Renaissance, 98, 127n2, 153, 160, 162,
    165, 187, 245, 268, 303, 377
rhetoric, 21, 93, 129, 159, 187, 192, 193,
    224, 298–99, 300, 301, 302, 304,
    307, 317, 329, 377
rhetorical knowledge, 26–27
rhetorical question, 174, 176, 178, 375
Richardson, Samuel, 139, 270, 282
Rind, Clementina, 159
rites of passage, 21, 43, 351, 352, 353,
    363
Roman alphabet, 64, 70, 72, 73, 94,
    157, 158, 252
Rome, 67, 92, 93, 120, 172, 188, 267,
    298, 303, 377
Rosetta Stone, 51–53, 56, 73, 297, 376
Roycroft, 162–63,
rubric and rubrication, 150, 240
Ruffin, Josephine St. Pierre, 160

Rügerin, Anna, 159
Rural Free Delivery (RFD), 281
runes, 71–72, 376

Sagan, Carl, 125, 126, 138, 141
St. Anne, 185, 197
St. Augustine, 186
St. Bride Library, 156&n7, 164
St. Brigit, 186
St. Columba, 186
St. David of Wales, 186
St. Francis de Sales, 187, 197
St. Genesius, 186
St. John Bosco, 187
St. John of God, 186
St. Lucia, 187
Samarkand, 113
sans serif, 132, 244, 245, 246, 253, 372,
    376
Sarasvati (Indian deity), 194
scapulamancy, 46
Schmandt-Besserat, Denise, 21
Schoeffer, Peter, 132, 152&n4, 153, 244
Scholastica, 187
school writing, 35, 44, 286, 354, 357,
    362
schools, 100, 101, 120, 129, 156–57,
    187&n1, 188, 221, 238, 268n4, 286,
    295–305, 308, 329, 354–55
    Typing school, 212, 215
scribes, 49, 50, 51, 53, 95, 102, 119, 127,
    128, 132, 139, 148–49, 150, 151, 152,
    188–91, 194, 236, 241, 244, 249,
    264, 295, 296, 297–98, 300, 308,
    316, 340, 370, 376
script, 51, 53, 55, 60–61, 65, 67, 68,
    70, 72–73, 74, 100, 119, 132, 143,
    151–52, 187, 191, 216, 235, 239, 244,
    249, 297, 300, 351, 352, 370, 372,
    375, 376, 377
scroll, 54, 119, 126, 137, 190, 236, 297,
    369, 376
semicolon, 171, 173, 174, 176, 178, 180,
    181–83

Sequoyah, 68–70, 195
serif, 132, 244, 245, 246, 252, 253,
    259–61, 372, 376
Seshat (Egyptian deity), 119, 189–91,
    198
Shaw, George Bernard, 74, 177
Shepherd, Margaret, 239, 287
Shikibu, Murasaki, 139, 140
Sholes, Christopher L., 209, 217
signatures, 36, 43, 231
Sint-Holo (Indigenous deity), 195
Skype, 332
slow writing, 217, 290, 333
snail mail, 231, 284, 286, 288, 290
Snapchat, 37, 333, 338
social media, 18, 20, 36, 43, 44, 73, 171,
    178, 230, 284, 312, 315, 331, 332,
    333, 334, 335, 336, 337, 338–45, 347,
    348–49, 355, 358, 360, 361, 363
spectacles, 128
Sphinx, 51, 192
Stablio, 87
Staedtler, Friedrich, 87, 88–89, 91
Star Route (mail), 281
Steel, Danielle, 40, 213–15, 217, 225
stereotyping, 133
stylus, 20, 30, 38, 48, 56, 92, 93, 94,
    127, 143, 188, 296, 297, 298, 340,
    370, 377
Suess, Randy, 331
Sumer and Sumerians, 46, 48, 49, 119,
    188, 264, 296, 297, 358, 374
Swenson, May, 213n2, 248–49
Switzerland, 372
    Basel, 113, 156
syllabary, 57, 58, 67, 68–70, 77, 78

Tahmuras/Tahmurath (Persian ruler),
    191
The Tale of Genji, 139–40
talismans, 195–96, 197, 198, 365
Tenjin (Japanese deity), 194
Tesler, Lawrence, 220
text message, 37, 335, 362

Textura, 152

Thamyris, 192, 199

Thoreau, Henry David, 19, 91

Thoth (Egyptian deity), 190–91, 298

threshold concepts, 23, 24–26

threshold skill, 311, 314, 318, 320

Thurn-und-Taxis family, 280–81

TikTok, 333, 338

Times New Roman, 133, 245, 254

Timothy, Elizabeth, 160

Torah, 126

toys, writing, 148

trivium, 129, 192, 193, 300, 302, 377

Truss, Lynne, 174, 179

ttfn, 283, 333

Turing, Alan, 218, 332

Twain, Mark, 147, 165, 211, 267n3, 286

Twitter, 312, 331, 332, 333, 334, 335,
    339, 346, 347, 348, 349, 365

tympan, 157

typeface, 131, 137, 151, 152, 156, 158,
    166, 243–49, 253–61, 370, 371, 372,
    373, 375, 376, 377

Typewriter Rodeo, 225

typewriters,
    Arabic, 73, 216
    Braille, 205
    Chinese, 216–17
    IMB Selectric, 215, 221, 232
    Olympia, 40, 213, 214, 232
    Olivetti, 214, 215, 221, 231
    Remington, 206, 207, 208, 211, 231
    Royal, 207, 231

typing pool, 212

typographers, 159, 165, 176, 243, 245,
    246n6, 250, 255, 261, 377

typography, 132, 133, 137, 156n7, 162,
    235, 240, 243–49, 253, 373, 377

uncial script, 143, 249, 377

UNESCO, 133, 140

UNIX, 222, 223, 284

upper case, 152, 306

Uruk, 46

Vai script, 55–56

Van Vliet, Claire, 246

vellum, 95, 97, 103, 119, 127, 153, 162,
    238, 240, 242, 316, 373, 375, 377

Venerable Bede, 187

virgule, 173

voice recognition technology, 36, 226,
    306

volume, 377

Warde, Beatrice, 164, 165, 247, 250, 253

washi, 117, 194, 290, 357, 377

Watson, Hannah Bunch, 159–60

wax tablets, 30, 92–94, 120, 126, 193,
    298, 339–40, 376, 377

Wells-Barnett, Ida Bell, 291–92

Westover, Tara, 353–54

Women's Era, 160

women's history, 159, 257

woodblock, 126, 148, 374, 377

WordPress, 333–34

workplace writing, 311, 312–17, 318,
    321, 329

World War I, 105, 215, 279–80

World War II, 87, 91, 98, 103, 104, 107,
    115n4, 134, 215, 218, 220, 289, 332,
    340, 353

Wozniak, Steve, 218

writing as therapy, 356

writing, kinds of, 360–62

writing systems, 22, 45n1, 46, 48, 49,
    51, 54, 55, 56, 58, 60, 63, 64, 65, 67,
    74, 77, 78, 86, 217, 297, 316, 352,
    369, 370, 372, 377

WYSIWYG, 220, 222

Xerxes (Persian monarch), 264, 280

Young, Brigham, 74, 123

YouTube, 42, 166, 288

Zanerian College, 238

Zapf, Hermann, 246

Zapf-von Hesse, Gudrun, 246, 254, 255

Biography

Dr. Joyce Kinkead is Distinguished Professor of English at Utah State University. In 2012, she was named a Fellow of the Council on Undergraduate Research, an award that recognizes her national reputation for promoting undergraduate research, the first and only humanist to be so honored. The US Professors of the Year Program named her the Carnegie Professor for the State of Utah in 2013. USU designated her the 2018 D. Wynne Thorne Career Researcher, the highest honor awarded to a faculty researcher.

As Associate Vice President for Research overseeing undergraduate research, she instituted a number of programs: University Undergraduate Research Fellows; the Utah Conference on Undergraduate Research; and Research on Capitol Hill. In the role of Vice Provost, she oversaw undergraduate education as well as enrollment management. Previously, she directed writing programs and writing centers and created the Writing Fellows Program and the Undergraduate Teaching Fellows Program. Dr. Kinkead is a scholar of writing studies and undergraduate research, an advocate for hands-on learning and meaningful, authentic assignments.

She has authored or edited a number of books:

- *A Writing Studies Primer* (2022)
- *Researching Writing: An Introduction to Research Methods* (2016)
- *Undergraduate Research Offices & Programs* (2012)
- *Advancing Undergraduate Research: Marketing, Communications, and Fund-raising* (2011)
- *Undergraduate Research in English Studies*, with Laurie Grobman (2010)
- *Valuing and Supporting Undergraduate Research* (2003)
- *Farm: A Multimodal Reader* (2014, 2016, 2020)
- *The Center Will Hold*, with Michael Pemberton (2003)
- *A Schoolmarm All My Life: Personal Narratives from Early Utah* (1997)
- *Writing Centers in Context* (1993)

Colophon

This book was published in Peterborough, Ontario, Canada, by Broadview Press in Minion Pro and Trade Gothic. Minion is serif typeface created in 1990 for Adobe. The designer is Robert Slimbach. Inspired by late Renaissance type, Minion is intended for body text and particularly suited to textbooks. Unlike Minion, Trade Gothic is a sans-serif typeface, designed in 1948 by Jackson Burke, who refined the design over the years. Burke was director of type development for Linotype in the USA.

From the Publisher

A name never says it all, but the word "Broadview" expresses a good deal of the philosophy behind our company. We are open to a broad range of academic approaches and political viewpoints. We pay attention to the broad impact book publishing and book printing has in the wider world; for some years now we have used 100% recycled paper for most titles. Our publishing program is internationally oriented and broad-ranging. Our individual titles often appeal to a broad readership too; many are of interest as much to general readers as to academics and students.

Founded in 1985, Broadview remains a fully independent company owned by its shareholders—not an imprint or subsidiary of a larger multinational.

For the most accurate information on our books (including information on pricing, editions, and formats) please visit our website at www.broadviewpress.com. Our print books and ebooks are also available for sale on our site.

broadview press
www.broadviewpress.com